# THIRTEENTH CENTURY ENGLAND III

## PROCEEDINGS OF
## THE NEWCASTLE UPON TYNE CONFERENCE
### 1989

# THIRTEENTH CENTURY ENGLAND III

PROCEEDINGS OF
THE NEWCASTLE UPON TYNE CONFERENCE
1989

Edited by P. R. Coss and S. D. Lloyd

THE BOYDELL PRESS

First published 1991 by The Boydell Press, Woodbridge


The Boydell Press is an imprint of Boydell & Brewer Ltd
PO Box 9, Woodbridge, Suffolk IP12 3DF
and of Boydell & Brewer Inc.
PO Box 41026, Rochester, NY 14604, USA


ISBN  0 85115 548 0

ISSN  0269–6967


British Library Cataloguing in Publication Data
Thirteenth century England. — 3–
  1. England ; 1200–1300
  942.03'4
  ISBN  0–85115–548–0


This publication is printed on acid-free paper

Printed in Great Britain by
St Edmundsbury Press Ltd, Bury St Edmunds, Suffolk

# CONTENTS

# ILLUSTRATIONS

*The Early Thirteenth-Century Architecture of Beverley Minster*

(Plates 15-32 appear after page 196)

# PREFACE

The third biennial conference on thirteenth-century England met at Newcastle upon Tyne in early September 1989. The proceedings took place once again at the University's Henderson Hall of Residence and the Polytechnic's Coach Lane Campus, and to the staff of both we are deeply indebted for their now customary hard work and support on our behalf. Conference participants will be no less grateful to the University's Vice-Chancellor, Professor Laurence Martin, whose generosity made possible the opening reception, and to the Faculty of Arts and the Department of History, whose joint support ensured, among other things, that our dinners were liberally lubricated. To the Department of History and the Polytechnic's Department of Historical and Critical Studies go our thanks again for assistance with the burden of administration and for subsidy of certain conference items. We are also very grateful to Mr. Peter Ryder for acting as guide on the conference excursion to Aydon and Prudhoe castles and for sharing his expertise with us.

This third volume of *Proceedings* consists of thirteen of the sixteen papers that were delivered at the 1989 conference. Most of them appear below substantially as they were read, although a few have been modified or expanded since then. There is no single unifying theme or particular focus, for the invited papers given at the conference (as was the case with its predecessors) were precisely intended to cater for a range of historical interests and to attract conference participation by scholars from different specialized fields of study. The editors hope that, cumulatively over the years, it will have proved possible to print in the *Proceedings* contributions to the study of most aspects of thirteenth-century England – its society, economy, culture, politics, and external relations.

An index to the contents of this volume of the *Proceedings* will appear in the general index to volumes I–V, which will accompany volume V. The fourth conference is planned to take place in Newcastle between 2 and 5 September 1991.

Newcastle upon Tyne, March 1990　　　　　　　　　　　　Simon Lloyd
　　　　　　　　　　　　　　　　　　　　　　　　　　　　Peter Coss

# ABBREVIATIONS

| | |
|---|---|
| *Ann. Mon.* | *Annales Monastici*, ed. H. R. Luard (RS, 1864–9) |
| *BIHR* | *Bulletin of the Institute of Historical Research* |
| BL | British Library |
| BN | Bibliothèque Nationale |
| *CChR* | *Calendar of the Charter Rolls Preserved in the Public Record Office, 1226–1516* (London, 1903–27) |
| *CCR* | *Calendar of the Close Rolls Preserved in the Public Record Office, 1272–1307* (London, 1900–8) |
| *CDI* | *Calendar of Documents Relating to Ireland Preserved in Her Majesty's Record Office, 1171–1307*, ed. H. S. Sweetman and G. F. Handcock (London, 1877–86) |
| *CDS* | *Calendar of Documents Relating to Scotland Preserved in the Public Record Office*, ed. J. Bain (Edinburgh, 1881–8) |
| *CFR* | *Calendar of the Fine Rolls Preserved in the Public Record Office, 1272–1307* (London, 1911) |
| *CIMisc.* | *Calendar of Inquisitions Miscellaneous (Chancery) Preserved in the PRO, 1219–1349* (London, 1916) |
| *CIPM* | *Calendar of Inquisitions Post Mortem in the Public Record Office (Henry III – Edward II)* (London, 1904–10) |
| *CLR* | *Calendar of Liberate Rolls Preserved in the Public Record Office, 1226–1272* (London, 1917–64) |
| *CPR* | *Calendar of the Patent Rolls Preserved in the Public Record Office, 1232–1307* (London, 1898–1908) |
| *CR* | *Close Rolls of the Reign of Henry III Preserved in the Public Record Office, 1227–72* (London, 1902–38) |
| *CRR* | *Curia Regis Rolls Preserved in the Public Record Office, Richard I–*  (London, 1922–  , in progress ) |
| *DBM* | *Documents of the Baronial Movement of Reform and Rebellion, 1258–1267*, selected R. F. Treharne, ed. I. J. Sanders (Oxford, 1973) |
| *DNB* | *Dictionary of National Biography*, ed. L. Stephen and S. Lee (London, 1885–1900; repr. 1921–7) |
| *EHR* | *English Historical Review* |
| *Fees* | *Liber Feudorum: The Book of Fees Commonly Called Testa de Nevill, 1198–1293* (London, 1920–31) |
| *Foedera* | *Foedera, conventiones, litterae et cuiuscunque generis acta publica inter reges Angliae et alios quosvis imperatores, reges, pontifices, principes vel communitates, 1101–1654*, ed. T. Rymer; new edn., ed. A. Clarke *et al.* (London, 1816–69) |

| | |
|---|---|
| *GEC* | *The Complete Peerage of England, Scotland, Ireland, Great Britain and the United Kingdom by G.E.C.*, ed. V. Gibbs *et al.* (London, 1910–59) |
| HMC | Historical Manuscripts Commission |
| *Journ.* | *Journal* [*of the*] |
| Paris, *CM* | Matthew Paris, *Chronica majora*, ed. H. R. Luard (RS, 1872–83) |
| Powicke, *Henry III* | F. M. Powicke, *King Henry III and the Lord Edward: The Community of the Realm in the Thirteenth Century* (Oxford, 1947) |
| *PR* | *Patent Rolls of the Reign of Henry III Preserved in the Public Record Office, 1216–32* (London, 1901–3) |
| *Procs.* | *Proceedings* [*of the*] |
| PRO | Public Record Office |
| Rec. Comm. | Record Commission |
| Rec. ser. | Record series |
| Rec. soc. | Record society |
| *RF* | *Excerpta e Rotulis Finium in Turri Londinensi asservatis, 1216–72*, ed. C. Roberts (London, 1835–6) |
| *RH* | *Rotuli Hundredorum temp. Hen. III et Edw. I in turr. Lond. et in curia receptae scaccarii West. asservati* (London, 1812–18) |
| *RLC* | *Rotuli Litterarum Clausarum in Turri Londinensi asservati, 1204–27*, ed. T. D. Hardy (London, 1833–44) |
| *RLP* | *Rotuli Litterarum Patentium in Turri Londinensi asservati, 1201–16*, ed. T. D. Hardy (London, 1835) |
| *Rot. Parl.* | *Rotuli Parliamentorum* (London, 1783–1832) |
| *Royal Letters* | *Royal and Other Historical Letters Illustrative of the Reign of Henry III*, ed. W. W. Shirley (RS, 1862–6) |
| RS | (Rolls Series) *Rerum Brittanicarum Medii Aevi Scriptores* (London, 1858–96) |
| ser. | series |
| Soc. | Society |
| *Trans.* | *Transactions* [*of the*] |
| *TRHS* | *Transactions of the Royal Historical Society* |
| *VCH* | *Victoria History of the Counties of England*, ed. H. A. Doubleday *et al.* (London, 1900– , in progress ) |

# Lordship and Distraint in Thirteenth Century England

Paul Brand

On 25 August 1290 William de Vernun and Robert de Frechenvill seized three cows belonging to the abbot of Darley at a place called 'Collesley' in the Derbyshire village of Ripley.[1] They then drove the animals to Ralph de Frechenvill's manor of Crich, some four miles away, and placed them in a pound. The purpose of this distraint was to bring pressure on the abbot to perform the homage and fealty which, Ralph claimed, the abbot owed him, and to pay the £10 relief appropriate to a holding of two knights' fees. We may presume that the distraint had been preceded by some sort of request to the abbot to perform these services, but there is no evidence that there had been any formal legal proceedings about them, either in Ralph's court or elsewhere. The abbot did not perform the services. Instead, he secured the conditional release of his animals by initiating an action of replevin in the Derbyshire county court, challenging the lawfulness of this distraint.[2] Subsequently, the litigation was removed out of the county court and into the Bench at Westminster. What happened in court in Trinity term 1291 was recorded both on the plea roll of the court (in Latin) and in at least two different unofficial Year Book reports (in French). The abbot's count gave details of the distraint, and alleged both that the initial seizure had been unjustified and that the defendants had then committed a further wrong by refusing to release the distresses that they had taken when they were offered 'gage and pledges' (suitable sureties) for them. In reality, this 'offer' was almost certainly a legal fiction. All plaintiffs had, for historical reasons, to make the allegation of such an offer and refusal when bringing the action of replevin, but it did not matter in practice whether or not such an offer and

1  Details of this distraint and of subsequent proceedings in the Bench come from the plea roll enrolment of the case: PRO, CP 40/90, m. 50; reports of the case in Lincoln's Inn, MS Hale 188, f. 34v; BL, MSS Egerton 2811, fos. 94v–95r, and Add. 31826, f. 64v; Cambridge Univ. Library, MSS Ee.6.18, fos. 10r–11r, and Mm.1.30, fos. 8r–8v. All these reports, other than that in BL, MS Add. 31826, appear to derive from a single archetype. The abbot's count in the Bench alleges that it was not only William and Robert but also Ralph de Frechenvill who had taken and driven away the animals, but other evidence from replevin cases of the same period indicates that this should not necessarily be taken literally and that it was normal practice to include the lord in whose name (and on whose orders) a distraint was made among those who were alleged to have made the distraint, even though he was not personally present when it was made. (Unless otherwise noted, all further citations of unpublished plea rolls are from those in the PRO.)
2  The enrolment of the abbot's count in the Bench replevin case is one of a minority of such counts in Bench replevin cases in 1291 which do not specify whether release was obtained by royal order or simply by action of the king's bailiff(s). The former normally indicates litigation initiated by royal writ; the latter, litigation initiated by plaint. However, one of the reports of this case (BL, MS Add. 31826) shows that the case was initiated by plaint, since it refers to the removal of the case into the Bench by a writ of *recordari facias*.

refusal had actually taken place, and in a case like this it is extremely unlikely that they had.[3] The abbot concluded his count by claiming damages of 40 *s.* in respect of both these wrongs. Ralph answered for all those involved and 'avowed' the distraint that they had made as lawful and justified. He claimed that the abbot held the tenement where the distraint had been made, together with other tenements, by homage and the service of two knights' fees. He had distrained the abbot for homage, fealty and the relief due on the death of Abbot Henry, his immediate predecessor. By way of title to make the distraint, he asserted that he had been seised of the scutage appropriate to a holding of two knights' fees at Henry's hands. Almost certainly he also made a formal denial of the refusal to release the animals in return for the offer of 'gage and pledge', though neither reports nor enrolment record this, and the second allegation then played no further part in the case. The abbot (or rather the Bench serjeant, Nicholas of Warwick, who was speaking on his behalf) challenged Ralph's avowry. It was necessary when avowing a distraint, he said, to show that the lord who was distraining, or one of his ancestors, had been seised of the services for which the distraint had been made; but Ralph had failed to show that he or any of his ancestors had ever been seised of homage, fealty or relief for this holding from the abbot or any of his predecessors. Roger of Higham, another Bench serjeant, answered for Ralph de Frechenville. Homage, fealty and relief were, he claimed, merely 'accessories' (incidents of tenure). A lord who could show that he had been seised of scutage was *ipso facto* entitled to distrain for them as well. The chief justice showed himself sympathetic to Ralph's argument, but judgment was adjourned and no eventual resolution of the case is recorded, either on the plea roll or in the reports.

This case is of specific interest because it is the earliest replevin case to raise (but not resolve) the question of when, and under what circumstances, ecclesiastical tenants by knight service were liable to pay relief.[4] But its significance in the present context lies in the fact that it is a typical replevin case: just one of almost 1250 replevin cases heard in the Bench during the reign of Edward I in which a plaintiff challenged a distraint and the defendant avowed it as having been made for arrears of services owed him by a tenant (often but not necessarily the plaintiff).[5] These cases indicate that lords in later thirteenth-century England were making relatively frequent use of a procedure (distraint, or more precisely extrajudicial distraint) which appears to amount to no more than a relatively primitive kind of self-help. Lords were compelling tenants to perform services or incidents of tenure, not by bringing litigation against them, but simply by seizing property belonging to the tenant (or the tenant's sub-tenant) and retaining it until the tenant did or paid what the lord claimed that he owed. These very cases are, however, also evidence of the degree to which the lord's use of this powerful weapon was subject

---

3   Below, 9–10.
4   The general rule had been that such tenants were exempt, though it was accepted that they could specifically oblige themselves and their successors to pay relief by deed: H.E. Salter, 'Reliefs "per cartam" ', *EHR* xlv (1930), 281–5. In Edward I's later years a determined attempt seems to have been made to challenge and alter the general rule, and thus to make ecclesiastical tenants by knight service liable to pay relief. On the relationship between Darley abbey and the Freche(n)ville family, see *The Cartulary of Darley Abbey*, ed. R.R. Darlington (Kendal, 1945), i. xvi ff.; and ibid. 557 for a 1240 final concord between Ralph's grandfather and the abbot's predecessor about the services owed for these tenements.
5   In about 60% of these cases the plaintiff appears to have been the lord's tenant; in the remainder, he is normally a sub-tenant.

by this date to routine, external control. In each, the lord's exercise of his power has been challenged by his tenant or sub-tenant. The lord is being made to justify his distraint in the king's court, and to show that it conformed to the rules which the king's court laid down about the making of distraints. These cases may, moreover, form only the tip of a much larger iceberg, for many replevin cases involving services were probably heard and determined in county courts; and there, too, lords were compelled to justify their use of the weapon of distraint. Of course, not every distraint for services will have been challenged in this way, but the very existence of a ready mechanism for doing so is likely to have influenced the behaviour of both lords and tenants, and must have ensured that most unchallenged distraints went unchallenged precisely because they could readily have been justified in the courts.

My intention in this paper is to put these cases — and what they tell us about the use and control of extra-judicial distraint in later thirteenth-century England — in context by looking at the development of the law and practice relating to the enforcement of services and the use of extra-judicial distraint for this purpose during the century or so prior to 1300. In the first section of the paper I want to look at the origins of the use of extra-judicial distraint in the enforcement of services, and to suggest that these are much older than most scholars have supposed. In the second section I will look at the rules about the use of distraint being enforced through the action of replevin during the first half of the thirteenth century, and look for reasons why these may have meant that extra-judicial distraint was much less common as a method of enforcing services during this period than it later became. In the third section I look at extra-judicial distraint in the context of other competing remedies for the enforcement of services that existed during the same period (litigation in the lord's own court and litigation initiated by the royal writ of customs and services) and will suggest reasons why the latter may have been particularly important and popular during this period. The fourth section deals with the main statutory and non-statutory changes in the workings of the action of replevin during the second half of the thirteenth century; while in the fifth section I will be looking at the effects of these changes in converting lords to the virtues of the use of extra-judicial distraint for the enforcement of services. I will conclude by looking briefly at the effects of the changes I have been examining on the relative power of lords and tenants within the lord-tenant relationship.

I

Historians have expressed differing views about when, how and why lords in England gained the right to distrain their tenants to perform services without the need for any prior judicial authorization. Maitland believed that in the twelfth century lords had needed the permission of a court before they could distrain, and that they could only distrain tenants to appear in their courts to answer for the withholding of services, not to perform those services. By the time 'Bracton' was written, lords no longer needed such permission and were able to distrain tenants directly to perform services, though some lords still followed the older practice of distraining their tenants to answer in their courts for arrears of service instead. Maitland's explanation for the change is characteristically allusive. The lord's right to distrain his tenant to come to his court to answer for arrears of service was easily transformed under favourable circumstances into a right simply to distrain the tenant to do services, and such favourable circumstances were provided by the changes which allowed the law relating to distraint to be shaped by royal justices who 'had no love for feudal justice'.[6] Plucknett likewise believed that there had been no extra-judicial distraint in the twelfth century, and he pointed to 'Bracton''s treatise as the earliest evidence for the acceptance of its use. But he differed from Maitland in suggesting that in the twelfth century the only legitimate use of distraint had been to enforce the performance of services after proceedings in the lord's court to settle any differences as to the services due, and he did not adopt Maitland's explanation for the subsequent change or provide any alternative explanation of his own.[7] Professor Milsom shares Maitland's view that in 'feudal' twelfth-century England distraint had been proper only if used to secure the tenant's attendance at his lord's court to answer for the withholding of services, and that this was still the position when 'Glanvill' was written at the end of Henry II's reign. He also seems to share Maitland's belief that such distraints were then normally authorized by the court concerned, since he sees distraint by chattels as simply forming an intermediate stage in the process for enforcing attendance at the lord's court, coming after summons but before distraint by the tenant's holding.[8] Milsom, indeed, suggests that one of the main functions of the royal writ of customs and services which we find in 'Glanvill' was to provide a remedy for those exceptional petty 'lords' who did not possess a functioning court and so could not use the process of that court to secure their services from their tenants.[9] It is not altogether clear whether he believes that extra-judicial distraint had become licit by the time 'Bracton' was written. He says that the treatise 'almost consistently' assumes that the lord has a court and is working through it, but the 'almost' is an important qualification here, as is also the further prefatory phrase 'whatever the realities are in his day'.[10] We may conclude that Milsom believes that extra-judicial distraint had made an appearance by the time the treatise was written, and that it was recognized as licit then or soon afterwards. Milsom also provides an alternative explanation for the emergence of extra-judicial distraint and hints at yet another. There had been, he suggests, in the period between 'Glanvill' and 'Bracton', a substantial increase in the number of lords who did not possess their own courts. If all had needed to bring the action of customs and services each time their tenants were in arrears, this would have placed an intolerable burden on the county court, to which the *justicies* writ of customs and services brought most such litigation. The only solution was to allow lords to distrain for services without a prior judgment, but to make such distraints subject to review through the action of replevin.[11] The alternative explanation would relate the change to a second major development which, Milsom believes, occurred during the same period — that by which seignorial courts lost the power to hear cases about services, if the tenant denied holding of the lord or if he simply denied owing the services that the lord claimed.

6   F. Pollock and F.W. Maitland, *The History of English Law before the Time of Edward I* (2nd edn. Cambridge, 1898), i. 353–4; ii. 574–6.
7   T.F.T. Plucknett, *Legislation of Edward I* (2nd edn. Oxford, 1962), 56.
8   S.F.C. Milsom, *The Legal Framework of English Feudalism* (Cambridge, 1976), 10–11.
9   Milsom, *Legal Framework*, 33.
10  Milsom, *Legal Framework*, 31.
11  Milsom, *Legal Framework*, 33–4.

Once the lord's court had lost its competence to hear and determine a substantial proportion of all litigation about services, it must also have ceased to seem important whether or not a court had actually authorized the lord to make a distraint.[12] Richardson and Sayles, as so often, dissent. Extra-judicial distraint, they argue, had always existed in England, and such evidence as appeared to point to the contrary had been misunderstood and was susceptible of other and better explanations.[13] It is my belief that they are right.

Our starting-point must be the passage in the early twelfth-century *Leges Henrici Primi* which seems to suppose that prior judicial authorization is required for all distraint, and has generally been taken to prove that this was the position in early twelfth-century England. However, this passage is only repeating a rule of Anglo-Saxon law and, like much else in that treatise, cannot be accepted as a reliable guide to contemporary reality without supporting evidence.[14] There is certainly some contemporary evidence to the contrary in an early twelfth-century episode related in the chronicle of Abingdon abbey. A burgess of Oxford who held a wick by Oxford bridge of the abbot of Abingdon detained his rent for a year. It was then the abbot himself, and not his court, who gave orders for the seizure of all movables found on the land at harvest time and for some kind of formal seizure of the land itself. Only after the seizure had taken place did the matter become one for the abbot's court. The burgess sent two intermediaries to the abbot to procure the release of the chattels in return for sureties to appear in the court and answer for the service.[15] The evidence of a number of royal writs of the reigns of Henry I and Henry II has also to be taken into account. These envisage lords taking action to enforce their right to services through distraint without any kind of prior authorization from their own courts.[16] However, it is not clear how common such writs were. Nor, more significantly, is it possible to be certain whether what they are doing is spelling out and reinforcing existing customary procedures or consciously authorizing departures from them. It seems likely, however, that they did play some part in accustoming men to the idea of extra-judicial distraint for services.

Our main source for later twelfth-century law is 'Glanvill', and two passages in book IX of the treatise concern the use of distraint. In the first, which is concerned with services generally, although it is said that the distraint is to secure the tenant's appearance in the lord's court to answer for withholding all or part of his service, nothing is said of this distraint being made by the judgment of the court, and responsibility for making the distraint is ascribed solely to the lord.[17] The second passage concerns the use of distraint to enforce payment of 'reasonable' aids. Here, distraint by chattels (or, if necessary, distraint by the tenant's holding) is said to be made with judicial authorization ('per iudicium curie sue') as though this was a necessary requirement.[18] It is possible that the second passage simply makes explicit what was implicit in the first, but there are also good reasons for different

---

12 Milsom, *Legal Framework*, 30–1.
13 *Select Cases of Procedure without Writ under Henry III*, ed. H.G. Richardson and G.O. Sayles (Selden Soc. lx, 1941), xciii, n. 1.
14 *Leges Henrici Primi*, ed. L.J. Downer (Oxford, 1972), 166 (51, 3), 359–60.
15 *Chronicon Monasterii de Abingdon*, ed. J. Stevenson (RS, 1858), ii. 140–1.
16 E.g. *Regesta Regum Anglo-Normannorum, II*, ed. C. Johnson and H.A. Cronne (Oxford, 1956), nos. 1387 (1123?), 1860a (1100–33); *Reading Abbey Cartularies*, ed. B.R. Kemp (Camden Soc., 4th ser. xxxi, xxxiii, 1986–7), i. no. 24 (1155).
17 *Glanvill*, ed. G.D.G. Hall (London, 1965), 105.
18 *Glanvill*, 111–12.

rules being applied in the two different kinds of situation. Reasonable aids were different from other types of service or incidents of tenure. The amount of service owed by a tenant was something fixed in advance. The amount payable to a lord as aid was, however, subject to negotiation between a lord and his tenants on each occasion that an aid was paid, and it may already have been established by 'Glanvill''s time that this was done by the lord calling his tenants together to agree a standard rate for all the lord's tenants.[19] Distraint would only be proper if the individual tenant had failed to pay the appropriate amount after this. Such a collective grant might well have been described as a 'judgment' of the lord's court. If so, all this passage would mean is that a distraint for 'reasonable' aids, though not for other services, would need prior authorization through such a grant. An alternative explanation would focus on the fact that in this passage, though not in the earlier one, the author of 'Glanvill' mentions the possibility of distraint by the tenant's holding as well as by his chattels. Distraint of the former kind, involving the disseisin of the tenant, certainly did require the authorization of a court, and the author may mention court judgment in this passage precisely because he is thinking of the employment of this kind of distraint as well as distraint by chattels.

For the legal position with regard to extra-judicial distraint in the late twelfth and early thirteenth centuries we also have the evidence of the small number of replevin cases on the early plea rolls. During this period plaintiffs often added to the standard count (alleging unjust distraint and wrongful detention against gage and pledge) a number of further allegations of related wrongdoing. Yet in not one of these cases do we find a plaintiff alleging that a distraint had been wrongfully made because it had been made without the prior authorization of the defendant's court. A possible explanation is that in practice lords only distrained after obtaining such authorization. But if that had been the case, one might still have expected that tenants would sometimes allege a lack of authorization, and have the claim refuted. A more likely explanation is that authorization was not a requirement for a valid distraint.[20]

Seignorial courts certainly did on occasion, in the late twelfth and early thirteenth centuries, specifically authorize the use of distraint by chattels as well as distraint by the tenant's holding.[21] It may be that prior authorization had been a requirement of the custom of particular lordships. Perhaps weaker lords preferred to have the backing of their courts in making distraints because this strengthened their hands in dealing with potentially recalcitrant tenants. A third possibility is that

---

[19] Cf. F.M. Stenton, *The First Century of English Feudalism, 1066–1166* (2nd edn. Oxford, 1961), 173, 277: agreement of 1183–4 between William fitzRichard and the monks of St. Andrew's, Northampton about the services owed for land which the monks held of him, which mentions the specific occasions when the monks are to contribute aid like William's other free tenants, but does not go on to specify the amount payable, merely noting their liability to pay at the level fixed as appropriate by the tenants as a group. For 13th-c. evidence of meetings of a lord's knights and free tenants to fix the level of aid owed to a lord (whose collection has been specifically authorized by the king), subsequently followed by distraint to enforce their payment, see *Bracton's Note Book*, ed. F.W. Maitland (Cambridge, 1887), pl. 1146 (1235–6); and KB 26/149, m. 15d (1253).

[20] For early replevin cases which involve services and where there is no hint that the distraint was made with the authorization of the lord's court, see *Memoranda Roll 10 John*, ed. R.A. Brown (Pipe Roll Soc., new ser. xxxi, 1955), 96–7 (1198); *CRR* x. 297 (1222), and 306 (1222); *CRR* xii. no. 192 (1225); *CRR* xiv. no. 936 (1230); *CRR* xv. no. 7 (1233).

[21] For service cases in which it is alleged that a court has specifically authorized the use of distraint by chattels, see e.g. *CRR* iii. 98, 133–4, 207–8.

lords sought such authorization when they envisaged having to proceed to distrain the tenant by his holding. By the early thirteenth century, and probably for half a century prior to that, it was the rule that distraint 'by the fee' (by the tenant's holding) required judicial authorization; and late twelfth-century custom certainly insisted that before such a distraint could be authorized it was necessary to have gone through the prior stages of summoning and distraining the tenant by his chattels to answer for the service claimed. It is certainly the case that in a majority of the instances where we do know of court authorization being obtained for distraint by chattels, the lord and his court then went on to make a distraint 'by the fee' as well.[22]

Our evidence suggests that even when a tenant was distrained without judicial authorization, he could still choose to appear at the lord's court to contest the justice of the distraint, and was entitled to have the distresses released once he had found sureties to do this.[23] But this does not mean that extra-judicial distraint was seen simply as part of the process of securing the tenant's attendance at the lord's court. The earlier twelfth-century evidence already discussed indicates that extra-judicial distraint was then seen primarily as a way of compelling tenants to perform services, and that lords could distrain without any prior summons or other warning to the tenant.[24] This seems also to be the position in 'Glanvill', which says nothing to suggest that distraint by chattels is proper only if it is preceded by the summoning of the tenant to the lord's court.[25] There is also other evidence to disprove Milsom's thesis, which sees the origins of distraint for services in the mesne process of seignorial courts. That thesis requires that distraint should originally have been 'personal' in nature, legitimate only when used to seize the chattels of the tenant who was being pressured to make an appearance in his lord's court.[26] This was certainly not the position in the thirteenth century, when lords were entitled to seize any chattels found within their fee, whether or not they belonged to

---

22 Milsom, *Legal Framework*, 9. For evidence that may point to the imposition at some date prior to *c.* 1160–3 of a requirement that distraint by the fee be by judgment of the lord's court, see *Registrum Antiquissimum of the Cathedral Church of Lincoln*, ed. C.W. Foster and K. Major (Lincoln Rec. Soc. 1931–73), ii. 5 (no. 313).

23 Refusal to release distresses in return for 'gage and pledge' (the more serious of the two allegations made in the action of replevin) in the case of a distraint made for services, as in the case of distraints made for other reasons, seems originally to have meant a refusal by the lord to release distresses in return for sureties that the tenant would do this. 'Bracton' explains 'gage and pledge' in the case of distraint for all reasons other than for arrears of service as a surety to come to court and stand to right; but in the case of services (though only where the services have been acknowledged as due) it talks of the surety simply as surety to perform the service with arrears: *Bracton: On The Laws and Customs of England*, ed. G.E. Woodbine, revised and trans. S.E. Thorne (Cambridge, Mass. 1968–77), ii. 440. In this we see the distorting effect of the seignorial court's loss of jurisdiction in cases where the tenant denies owing the services claimed: below, 14–15. But a little later in the same passage we see what I take to be a survival from an older world, where an offer of 'gage and pledge' meant an offer of sureties for appearance in the lord's court even where the distraint was for services, for 'Bracton' tells us that where it has been found that the lord has wrongfully detained distresses against gage and pledge the sheriff will release the distresses on such terms that the distrainee will come to his lord's court to answer for the service he acknowledges, and the arrears. For 12th-c. evidence of a tenant who did precisely this when he was distrained by his lord, see above, 5.

24 Above, 5 and n. 16.

25 *Glanvill*, 105, 112.

26 By the later 13th c. it was clearly the case that any distraint intended to secure a defendant's appearance in court could only be made against his own chattels; and the rule has every appearance of being an old one.

their tenant. Milsom suggests that some customary rules and practices found in the early thirteenth century take us back into an earlier world where this had indeed been the position.[27] This evidence, however, is hardly conclusive, and there is other and stronger evidence to suggest that as early as the first half of the twelfth century it had been perfectly proper for a lord to distrain sub-tenants for services owed by his tenants. This takes the negative form of charters from lords to sub-tenants promising not to do this, for such charters contain no hint that what they are promising not to do would otherwise be wrong.[28] 'Glanvill', too, contains a writ which unmistakably assumes that distraint by the chief lord on a sub-tenant is only wrongful if the chief lord demands more than an appropriate amount of service from the sub-tenant.[29]

There was no major shift in the early or middle thirteenth century from a world where the only kind of distraint that was permissible was judicial to one where extra-judicial distraint for services became for the first time permissible; and there is thus no need to look for explanations as to why such a shift occurred. Extra-judicial distraint had long existed, but side by side with the judicial kind. However, as we will see, a related but distinct change probably did take place at about this time. Other legal developments made it increasingly uncommon in practice for lords to distrain with the prior authorization of their courts; and thus extra-judicial distraint became the main — indeed, in practice, virtually the only — kind of distraint commonly used by lords.


## II


The main legal mechanism for control of the lord's use of extra-judicial distraint during the first half of the thirteenth century was the action of replevin, an action which had to be initiated in the county court. The best-known account of the working of this action during this period is that provided by Plucknett. He suggested that the action did not, at this time, provide tenants with adequate protection against lords misusing their right of distraint to usurp services to which they were not entitled. The action was, indeed, comparatively simple and easy for a tenant to bring. All he had to do was to purchase the appropriate royal writ and he would have the distresses restored to him pending the outcome of the case, thus freeing him from the pressure of the lord's distraint until the case was decided.[30] But all the lord needed to do in order to make a successful avowry, and thus to secure a judgment for the return of the distresses, was to show that he possessed a 'short, recent seisin' of the services for which he had distrained.[31] Plucknett believed that the application of this standard was particularly likely to lead to injustice in the

---

[27] Milsom, *Legal Framework*, 113–14.
[28] *Early Yorkshire Charters*, ed. W. Farrer and C.T. Clay (Yorks. Arch. Soc., Rec. ser., Extra Ser. 1914–65), iii. 244–5 (no. 1567), 274–5 (no. 1608); iv. 26 (no. 24); *Documents Illustrative of the Social and Economic History of the Danelaw*, ed. F.M. Stenton (London, 1920), 151–2 (no. 219), 280 (no. 376); *Cartae Antiquae Rolls 11–20*, ed. J. Conway Davies (Pipe Roll Soc., new ser. xxxiii, 1957), 57.
[29] *Glanvill*, 143.
[30] Plucknett, *Legislation of Edward I*, 57.
[31] Plucknett, *Legislation of Edward I*, 57, 68.

aftermath of a period of civil war, when many lords were able to acquire seisin of services through the use of force. It was this, then, he suggested, that had brought distraint to the top of the legislators' agenda in 1267.[32] But the application of this standard was also problematic at other times, though perhaps less acutely so.[33] It was all too easy for lords to use distraint to gain seisin of services to which they were not entitled, and then subsequently to rely on this seisin as their title to the services when this was challenged by the tenant through an action of replevin.

More recently, Professor Milsom has emphasized that replevin was originally intended to provide a remedy not against unjust distraint as such, but against lords who refused to release distresses which they had taken in return for 'gage and pledge' (sureties for appearance in the lord's court) — in other words, against lords who were taking measures appropriate to making a claim against their tenants, but then refusing to allow that claim to be put to their own court. Although Milsom's chronology is not entirely clear, he seems to believe that replevin was still performing this function not just at the time 'Glanvill' was written (at the end of Henry II's reign), but also later, and that the question of whether or not a lord was entitled to the services for which he had distrained was then primarily a matter for the lord's own court.[34] By the time 'Bracton' was written the action of replevin had been transformed. It had now become an action which simply allowed a tenant to challenge the lord's distraint. To justify his distraint, a lord needed only to show a 'possessory' title to the services for which he had distrained (a recent seisin of them).[35]

It was certainly a distinctive characteristic of the action of replevin from at least the reign of Henry II onwards (and the action was probably created during Henry's reign) that in it the plaintiff alleged two separate but connected wrongs: that he had been unjustly distrained, and that the distresses so taken had then been detained 'against gage and pledge'.[36] 'Bracton' provides us with the first detailed account of the working of the action. This describes how the action worked in the county court (perhaps in one particular county court) probably at some date in the 1220s or 1230s.[37] It shows the plaintiff making (and probably having to make) both allegations in his initial count,[38] but being allowed to drop one of them once the defendant had made his avowry justifying the distraint, and had denied refusing to release the distresses after an offer of 'gage and pledge'.[39] Thus, in practice, it was possible

---

32 Plucknett, *Legislation of Edward I*, 54, 68, 71, 74.
33 Plucknett, *Legislation of Edward I*, 52.
34 Milsom, *Legal Framework*, 34.
35 Milsom, *Legal Framework*, 31.
36 It is impossible to prove this assertion for Henry II's reign in the absence of any general account of the action dating from that reign; but it is certainly consonant with such evidence as does survive and with the later evidence.
37 *Bracton*, ii. 439–49. Little in the account helps us to date it. I assume that its composition belongs to the same period as other, more readily datable parts of the treatise, though it is conceivable that it is older and once had an independent existence before being incorporated in the larger work.
38 One passage seems to envisage the possibility that the plaintiff might choose to sue for only one of these two wrongs (*Bracton*, ii. 441) but this probably refers to a later stage in pleading, after the defendant has made his avowry, making it clear that at this stage the plaintiff can, if he wishes, continue to maintain both allegations.
39 That the plaintiff could choose to counterplead the avowry alone seems clear from some answers to avowries that 'Bracton' mentions, which, in effect, amount to claims that the plaintiff was entitled to the unconditional release of the distresses, and that this was refused but which effectively concede that 'gage and pledge' was never offered since such an offer was inappropri-

for plaintiffs to bring the action of replevin (alleging both unjust distraint and detention against gage and pledge) but then to opt to continue only with the allegation of unjust distraint, and thereby (where the distraint was by a lord and for services) to test through this action whether or not the lord's distraint for services had been justified. This is not likely to have been a recent development, as Milsom suggests, for the author seems to go out of his way to make it clear that a plaintiff can, if he so wishes, maintain his allegation of both wrongs, as though this was already uncommon or becoming so.[40] We can see the same thing in replevin actions in the Bench. By 1201 it was possible for a plaintiff here to take issue simply on the justice of a distraint, without also having to take issue on whether or not distresses had been detained against gage and pledge.[41] It is, indeed, possible that this particular characteristic of the action of replevin is a very old one. An allegation of unjust distraint was something, as 'Bracton' tells us, which could be redressed by 'neighbours', and here he may well be thinking of seignorial and hundred courts as well as more informal procedures;[42] and other evidence from the thirteenth century shows us the lords of seignorial and hundred courts claiming to exercise a jurisdiction in such cases without any special authorization and, apparently, merely by virtue of their possession of such courts.[43] If a tenant or other distrainee made a complaint of this kind in the county court, his lord could probably claim the case for hearing in his own court. It was the allegation of detention against gage and pledge which made the plea one which only the sheriff and the county court (and earlier the king and his justices) were competent to hear.[44] Thus, if a tenant or other distrainee wanted to ensure that his complaint of unjust distraint was heard and determined in the county court, it was essential for him to make both allegations. If the king and his advisers had wanted to encourage such cases to come to the county court (or earlier, to the king's courts) they may well have been willing, from a fairly early stage, to allow litigants to give colour to their jurisdiction by making both allegations initially, but then to allow them to continue with one allegation alone. The suggestion is not provable, but the main point remains. There are good reasons for supposing that allowing a tenant or other distrainee to use the action of replevin simply to contest the justice of a distraint was not something new when 'Bracton' wrote, and the practice may well be much older.

'Bracton''s account must also be the starting-point for a discussion of how the question of whether or not a distraint for services was justified was decided during the second quarter of the thirteenth century. As we have already seen, Plucknett's view appears to have been that then, as earlier and later, this was done by reference to whether or not the lord could show a 'short, recent seisin' of the services for

---

ate, e.g. where the lord has distrained for services by judgment of court and the tenant has refused to answer without the king's writ: *Bracton*, ii. 444; where the defendant claims distresses were taken in his several: ibid. ii. 445. That the plaintiff could choose to counterplead the detention against gage and pledge alone is clear from the discussion of damage feasant: ibid. ii. 445; as also elsewhere, when the author takes care to refute the view that the defendant could only be made to answer for detention against gage and pledge when the taking was found to be unjust: ibid. ii. 447.
[40] Above, n. 38. 'Bracton' also explains in a cautionary passage why it might be unwise to do so: *Bracton*, ii. 441.
[41] *CRR* i. 408. For another early example (1206), see *CRR* iv. 266–7.
[42] *Bracton*, ii. 446.
[43] KB 26/143, m. 9; JUST 1/912A, m. 40; CP 40/23, m. 13; CP 40/55, m. 52; *Placita de Quo Warranto*, ed. W. Illingworth and J. Caley (London, 1818), 739, 751.
[44] Above, n. 42.

which he had distrained; and Milsom, too, cites 'Bracton''s account to support his contention that by 'Bracton''s time the question of entitlement was being decided in replevin on a possessory basis. But 'Bracton''s account shows something rather different. The author discusses two different kinds of situation: where there had been no prior litigation between the parties in the lord's own court, and where such litigation had taken place. He considers the first type of situation in two separate passages, and lays down somewhat different rules in each. In the first, he suggests that all a tenant has to do in the county court is to produce 'suit' (witnesses) that distresses had been taken for a service which he does not acknowledge owing. The lord's distraint will then be adjudged wrongful, whether or not he has been in seisin of the services for which he has distrained. A tenant cannot be made to answer for the services without the appropriate royal writ, the writ of 'customs and services'.[45] In the second passage, he suggests that the lord will be allowed to make his avowry for the services for which he has distrained, but that the tenant can make the distraint wrongful simply by responding that he does not owe the services and has never done them. Since this assertion cannot be tested by the county court because it is outside its jurisdiction, it must give judgment for the tenant.[46] His discussion of the second type of situation reveals that a similar rule applies in the lord's court. If the lord has distrained his tenant for a service which he does not acknowledge owing, and the tenant secures the release of his distresses for sureties to appear in the lord's court, he can appear there and simply deny owing the service and refuse to answer for it without a royal writ. If he does this, the litigation should be at an end. The lord's court is only entitled to adjudge the service to the lord if the tenant admits owing it. If it acts without this acknowledgement, then it has exceeded its jurisdiction.[47] It is clear that for 'Bracton' a possessory title to services was not in itself enough. A tenant had also to acknowledge that he owed the service, or be willing to answer for it without the king's writ. 'Bracton''s account suggests that, in his day, the action of replevin was heavily weighted in favour not of lords, as Plucknett suggested, but of their tenants. A similar conclusion is suggested by a passage in 'Bracton' which deals with the situation where a tenant acknowledges a service for which the lord has avowed a distraint, but denies that it is in arrears. Here, the author suggests that if the tenant simply produces sufficient 'suit' (enough witnesses) that the service is not in arrears, the lord will not be allowed to deny this by waging his law, and thus the distraint will be adjudged wrongful.[48]

'Bracton''s account does not stand alone. There is other evidence for the rule that distraint is wrongful if the tenant does not acknowledge owing the service concerned. Although, as we have seen, 'Glanvill' (in book IX) specifically says that the lord may distrain his tenant to answer in his court for the withholding of all or part of his services, elsewhere (in book XII) we find a special form of replevin writ, where the plaintiff's complaint is said to be that: 'R. has taken and detained [his animals] unjustly for customs which he demands from him which he does not acknowledge that he owes.'[49] It is possible that this envisages litigation about these customs, though if so, the use of the phrase 'does not acknowledge that he owes', rather than just 'does not owe', seems strange. It is possible that the 'customs'

---

[45] *Bracton*, ii. 439–41.
[46] *Bracton*, ii. 444–5.
[47] *Bracton*, ii. 443–4.
[48] *Bracton*, ii. 446 (in an *addicio* wrongly inserted into a passage on distraint damage feasant).
[49] *Glanvill*, 142.

being demanded are non-tenurial dues of some kind, but it is at least equally possible that this writ was intended to enforce the principle found in 'Bracton'. The two parts of 'Glanvill' could have been compiled at different dates, and thus embody different principles. Perhaps, at this stage, the tenant could only claim the protection of the rule by specifically purchasing the king's writ. We can also see the principle being invoked in litigation in the court *coram rege* in 1201 between the earls of Clare and Chester. The earl of Clare sued the earl of Chester for taking animals from his fee 'for customs and services which he demands from that fee which he does not acknowledge owing'.[50] In 1232 we find Hugh of Clive bringing litigation against William le Normaunt for distraining him to do suit of court and attend view of frankpledge. In answer, William claimed that Hugh did owe him suit and that he was in seisin of it. The jury was asked to give its verdict as to which animals he had taken, and as to whether he had detained them for 'suit and services which the same Hugh does not acknowledge'.[51] In fact, in this case, Hugh did not merely deny owing the services; he also denied holding of William. But the principle applied seems to be simply that distraint is wrongful if made for services which the distrainee does not acknowledge owing.

In a fairly small number of replevin cases heard in the Bench during the period prior to 1249 we can see parties to replevin cases taking issue on whether or not the lord was entitled to the services for which he had distrained.[52] In these cases the tenant seems, in effect, to have waived his right to have the issue of entitlement to services determined through a different form of action, and agreed to have it settled in replevin instead: they do not show that a lord could force his tenant to do this. The rule seems to have changed *c*.1250. The Bench plea rolls from 1250 onwards contain significantly larger numbers of replevin cases in which lords avow distraints as made for arrears of service and, in a number of these, issue is taken on whether or not the tenants owe the service concerned.[53] But even when the action of replevin came to function in this way, decisions as to whether or not a lord was entitled to the services for which he had distrained were not, initially at least, always reached simply on the basis of whether or not the lord could show a 'short, recent seisin' of the services for which he had distrained. Thus, in a case of 1260, in which the prior of Harmondsworth avowed a distraint against Robert de Perers for refusing to perform the service of accompanying him throughout England on horseback at the prior's cost, Robert did not deny owing the services but asserted that he and his ancestors had customarily appointed substitutes to perform this service for them, and that he had acted for his father in just this way. But the court would not allow this even to be submitted to a jury. The form of the feoffment was decisive and subsequent seisin, even recent seisin, was judged of no relevance.[54] In a case of 1254 the prioress of Grace Dieu avowed a distraint as made for homage, suit of court and rent, but the tenant, John d'Oyly, claimed that his wife's lord, Rose de

---

[50] *Pleas before the King or his Justices, 1198–1202, I*, ed. D.M. Stenton (Selden Soc. lxvii, 1953), no. 3296; *CRR* i. 383, 425; *CRR* ii. 44.

[51] *Bracton's Note Book*, pl. 677.

[52] E.g. *CRR* vii. 104; *CRR* x. 297 (but the parties do not join issue on the services); *CRR* xv. no. 697.

[53] For such cases from the period prior to 1267, see e.g. KB 26/138. m. 14 (and for related litigation, see KB 26/135, m. 11d); KB 26/148, m. 8; KB 26/154, m. 16; KB 26/165, mm. 8d, 11; KB 26/169, mm. 36d, 56; KB 26/171, m. 62; KB 26/172, m. 5; KB 26/173, m. 1d; KB 26/210, m. 17.

[54] KB 26/165, m. 8d.

Verdun, had only assigned rent from the tenement to the prioress and not granted her the seignory. When the prioress claimed to have been granted the whole of the seignory and to have been seised of the suit till two years previously, she was instructed to bring the charter of grant to court, and not simply allowed to join issue on this seisin.[55] But other cases did concentrate on recent seisin. Thus, in a case of 1260, the prior of Monk's Horton avowed a distraint against Simon of Holt because he had refused to come to his court to make a judgment there (as one of its suitors). Simon denied that he ought to come to the court for this purpose or was accustomed to doing so. The issue actually put to the jury was whether Simon had customarily performed the suit until one year previously.[56] Most replevin cases about services, of the period 1260–7, do, however, seem to be concerned only with fairly recent seisin.[57] The action of replevin seems only just to have been becoming an action in which entitlement to services was decided on a possessory basis on the eve of the enactment of the Statute of Marlborough (1267): it was not, as Plucknett suggested, a long-established characteristic of the action.

## III

Extra-judicial distraint was one of three mechanisms that lords employed during the first half of the thirteenth century to secure the performance of services. As Plucknett noted, the oldest of these in origin was proceedings brought in the lord's own court.[58] He believed that such proceedings were still being brought as late as the middle of the thirteenth century, but that they had largely, if not entirely, fallen into disuse by the reign of Edward I.[59] The second was litigation initiated by the lord through the royal writ of 'customs and services'. Plucknett thought that this action was comparatively little used. His characterization of the action suggested good reasons. It was a 'solemn' action, and in it trial was by battle or the grand assize. Thus it was both slow and inconvenient.[60] He also thought that it set a fairly difficult standard of proof for the lord. In order to succeed in this action, it was necessary for him to be able to prove a long-continued seisin of the services claimed.[61] It was extra-judicial distraint that Plucknett seems to have considered as being the most common way for lords to enforce what they considered to be their rights.[62] There is an ambiguity about what Plucknett has to say here: in some passages he seems to assume that distraint was already the most common way of enforcing services at the beginning of the thirteenth century;[63] but in others he

---

55  KB 26/154, m. 16.
56  KB 26/169, m. 36d.
57  E.g. KB 26/169, m. 56; KB 26/171, m. 62; KB 26/210, m. 17. But for exceptions, see KB 26/173, m. 1d and KB 26/172, m. 5.
58  Plucknett, *Legislation of Edward I*, 56.
59  Plucknett, *Legislation of Edward I*, 55.
60  Plucknett, *Legislation of Edward I*, 56, 68.
61  Plucknett, *Legislation of Edward I*, 52.
62  Plucknett, *Legislation of Edward I*, 55, 56–7.
63  Thus a passage which describes the action of replevin as 'by far the most frequent method of litigating these questions' (and implies the frequent use of distraint) follows straight on from the passage describing the actions of 'customs and services' and *ne vexes*, and appears, like them, to

seems to imply that this only came to be true during the period now under consideration, perhaps as a result of the decline of the jurisdiction of seignorial courts.[64]

For Professor Milsom, as we have seen, extra-judicial distraint was the direct successor, rather than the successful competitor, of proceedings in the lord's court, though his account does perhaps allow for a period of overlap when both existed side by side. He also suggests that there were significant developments in the action of customs and services in the early thirteenth century. In 'Glanvill''s day, it was the remedy of the exceptional lord who was unable to compel his tenant to attend his court and answer for the withholding of services; by 'Bracton''s day, it had become the 'proprietary' remedy for all lords, something like the remedy Plucknett describes.[65]

The decline in the enforcement of services through the lord's own court certainly took place, but rather earlier than Plucknett suggested. His only reason for placing this as late as he did was his belief that 'in the middle of the century Bracton had frequently considered the case of the lord who distrained his tenant by judgment of his court'.[66] We now know, however, that much of the treatise ascribed to Bracton (almost certainly the part including the section on replevin) belongs not to the middle of the thirteenth century but to the late 1220s or early 1230s;[67] and if we can deduce anything at all about the frequency of proceedings about services in lords' courts from what is said in 'Bracton', the treatise suggests that the jurisdiction was already in decline by the time this part of 'Bracton' was written. Other evidence supports an earlier date for the decline of this jurisdiction. The latest in the series of early thirteenth-century cases which refer to distraint by the fee as part of the process intended to secure the tenant's appearance to answer in his lord's court for arrears of service belongs to 1228.[68] Rare are subsequent references to distraint by chattels for arrears of service as having been made by the judgment of a court, and therefore, perhaps, as forming part of the process for securing the appearance of a tenant to answer for services in the court.[69] The explanation for the decline of this jurisdiction is clear. Even in 'Glanvill''s day, it was beginning to look anomalous that the lord might make a tenant answer for services in his court without needing a royal writ, especially since, at this time at least, such proceedings might lead to the tenant losing his tenement.[70] By 1230 at the latest, to judge from the gloss we find on the same passage of 'Glanvill' in the text of the so-called 'Glanvill Revised', it had apparently become the rule that a tenant could refuse to answer in such litigation by claiming the protection of the 'free tenement' rule. He could say that he was not obliged to answer for his free tenement, or anything which 'touched' his free tenement, without the king's writ. The effect of this, as the

be talking about the position from the late 12th c. onwards: Plucknett, *Legislation of Edward I*, 56–7.
[64]  Plucknett, *Legislation of Edward I*, 52, 55.
[65]  Milsom, *Legal Framework*, 31–4.
[66]  Plucknett, *Legislation of Edward I*, 55.
[67]  S.E. Thorne, 'Translator's Introduction', in id. *Bracton*, iii. pp. xiii–xxxiii.
[68]  *Bracton's Note Book*, pl. 270.
[69]  The only Bench replevin cases of Henry III's reign in which the lord specifically avows a distraint as made by the judgment of his court both involve suit of court. In one, the distraint was for an amercement adjudged for defaults at the lord's court: KB 26/169, m. 7d; in the other, simply for defaults at the court (though this possibly means the same): KB 26/200A, m. 14. Neither implies the existence of litigation about the suit.
[70]  *Glanvill*, 105.

author of the gloss himself suggests, is to prevent lords actually bringing such litigation in their own courts.[71] 'Bracton', too, tells us of the extension of the 'free tenement' rule to cover services owed by the tenant for his tenement. As we have seen, when a tenant was summoned to his lord's court to answer for services or customs, he could deny that he owed the service specified, and he could claim the protection of the rule since the demand was one which 'touched' his free tenement. This would then bring proceedings to a halt.[72] This does not mean that lords' courts ceased to be competent to hear litigation about services initiated by lords. They were still able to do this if the tenant did not invoke the protection of the rule (and not all tenants may have done so); and if all that was in dispute was whether or not particular services were in arrears, then the rule could not be invoked. It was appropriate only where the dispute was about the quantum of services owed. But the overall effect, particularly as the lord could not necessarily know in advance whether or not his tenant would deny liability and invoke the rule, was probably to discourage litigation over service in lords' courts; and this explains the virtual disappearance of references to such litigation after 1230.

The action of customs and services was much easier for a lord to use than Plucknett's account of the action would suggest. One important factor here was the kind of title which the lord needed to make, if he were to succeed in the action. The earliest actions of customs and services enrolled on the Bench plea-rolls do not specify any kind of seisin as the plaintiff's title to the services he claimed; and while this may be the result of drastic abbreviation on the part of the enrolling clerks, this seems unlikely.[73] Once it does become the norm for lords to make a title to the services they are claiming, we do indeed find a few cases in which lords seem to be alleging a long-established seisin of the services they claim, though even in these it often turns out to be a specific, and sometimes quite recent, seisin that they actually rely on subsequently to establish their right.[74] There are also a few cases where lords seem to be relying on a comparatively ancient, though not necessarily long-continued, seisin.[75] But at least as common, indeed probably more common, is reliance on what was clearly a recent, and sometimes a very recent, seisin of the services claimed.[76] It was not, in practice, very difficult to establish or prove a title to services which was adequate for the purposes of bringing this action.

Also important were the methods of proof thought appropriate in this action.

---

71  F.W. Maitland, 'Glanvill revised', in *The Collected Papers of Frederic William Maitland*, ed. H.L. Fisher (Cambridge, 1911), ii. 282. On the date of 'Glanvill Revised', see G.D.G. Hall's note in *Glanvill*, 195–8.

72  *Bracton*, ii. 444.

73  There are only three cases prior to 1220 in which the seisin of the plaintiff or his ancestors is mentioned: *CRR* iv. 292; *CRR* vi. 135; *CRR* vii. 314. Thereafter it becomes much more common and the last case enrolled without such a title (where the case is not settled by agreement or in some way which makes an enrolled title irrelevant) seems to be one of 1242: KB 26/124, m. 30d.

74  See e.g. *CRR* iv. 292; *CRR* vi. 135; *CRR* xii. no. 1453; *CRR* xii. no. 2043; *CRR* xiv. no. 2386; *CRR* xviii. no. 345; KB 26/145, m. 12.

75  See e.g. *CRR* ix. 228; *CRR* x. 30; KB 26/129, m. 13 (1243 case in which, for some of the services claimed, Gilbert de Gaunt relies on the seisin of his ancestor Gilbert, earl of Lincoln (d. 1156). See also *CRR* xiii, no. 1425.

76  For cases where the plaintiff not only claims on his own seisin but also asserts that the defendant has only ceased to perform the services owed at some date in the recent past, see e.g. *CRR* xii. no. 524; KB 26/162, m. 36 (cesser one year ago); *CRR* xv. no. 1570 (cesser one and a half years ago). Seisin by the ward's ancestor at the time of his death (and possibly by the guardian since then) was the only title which a guardian could make and this was necessarily a recent seisin: see e.g. *CRR* ix. no. 25; *CRR* xvi. no. 2347; KB 26/166, m. 20d.

Although battle was sometimes formally offered by plaintiffs at the end of their counts,[77] this does not seem to have been a technical requirement of the action; and there is not a single case in which battle was actually fought.[78] Thus, although battle was probably a theoretical possibility, it was not something that a lord would need to take into account when deciding whether or not to use this action. The grand assize was commonly used to decide the outcome of such cases. It is not at all clear that lords would have seen the finality of the grand assize as any kind of drawback. In fact, if anything, it may have been seen by some as an advantage. Its disadvantage was probably the slowness with which it worked: it required the summoning of electors to elect the grand assize jury prior to the summoning of the grand assize jurors themselves, and with the knights often proving reluctant to appear. But by no means all cases of customs and services were so determined. Trial by an ordinary jury (and perhaps, in theory, at a less decisive level) was also used in many such cases, in all cases involving guardians,[79] in most cases where the plaintiff was claiming villein services,[80] where the seignory had only recently passed to the plaintiff, or there was some other recent transaction relevant to his title to the services,[81] and simply where the plaintiff alleged a recent seisin of the services.[82] In this latter case it seems that the plaintiff could actually insist on jury trial and prevent the defendant getting to a grand assize, though on what seem to be similar facts, plaintiffs did sometimes agree to trial by the grand assize.[83] In other words, lords themselves did at least to some extent determine how their litigation would be determined, and could choose the form of trial that they themselves wanted.

By the end of the reign of Edward I, as we will see, the action of customs and services had become comparatively rare, certainly in the Bench; and most litigation about services took place through the action of replevin. This was certainly not the case in the period that we are now considering. During the whole of the period 1200–67 there is a total of just under fifty replevin cases in the Bench in which we find the defendant avowing as a lord for arrears of service, or in which it is known from other information that this was the purpose of the distraint; and of these, no

---

[77] For cases where battle was offered, see *CRR* ii. 242 (and *CRR* iii. 36); *CRR* iv. 292; *CRR* vi. 135; *CRR* vii. 314; *CRR* x. 30; *CRR* xi. nos. 308, 1706, 2045, 2441; *CRR* xii. nos. 584, 1453; *CRR* xiv. no. 1898; *CRR* xv. no. 1818; *CRR* xviii. no. 350; KB 26/142, m. 29d; KB 26/162, mm. 26d, 36; KB 26/164, mm. 1d, 14d; KB 26/169, mm. 56, 59d; KB 26/171, m. 18.

[78] For cases in which one or both of the parties showed signs of wanting to go ahead with battle but in which the court successfully deflected this, see *CRR* xi. nos. 1532, 1706, 2045; *CRR* xii. no. 1453.

[79] See cases cited above, n. 76.

[80] *CRR* xi. no. 2045 (though not apparently for this reason); *CRR* xii. no. 2043 (but also because of the plaintiff's recent seisin); KB 26/124, m. 30d; *CRR* xviii. nos. 1382, 1547. But for a grand assize on such a claim, see KB 26/143, m. 15d.

[81] *CRR* xii. no. 1466 (sale to predecessor); *CRR* xiv. no. 1101 (d); *CRR* xv. no. 1959; *CRR* xvi. no. 991; KB 26/129, m. 19; *CRR* xviii. no. 1466.

[82] *CRR* xii. nos. 2043 (but also because villein services are claimed), 2420; *CRR* xiv. no. 2386; *CRR* xviii. no. 350; KB 26/143, m. 24; KB 26/169, m. 2; cf. *CRR* xi. no. 2045 (where one of the arguments advanced by the plaintiff for seeking jury trial rather than joining battle with the defendant is that the defendant ought not to deny his right when he had such recent seisin, up to three years previously).

[83] For cases where the plaintiff may have insisted on jury trial when the defendant wanted trial by the grand assize, see *CRR* xii. nos. 2043, 2420 (despite the defendant producing a charter of the plaintiff's grandfather specifying lesser services); KB 26/169, m. 2 (grand assize rejected because seeks on such recent seisin and is own seisin at hands of defendant). For an apparently similar case where trial was by the grand assize, see KB 26/162, m. 36 (own seisin at defendant's hands till one year previously).

fewer than thirty fall during the period after 1250. By contrast, during the same period there are around 175 cases brought by the writ of customs and services in the Bench. This does not, of course, prove anything about the relative frequency of the two actions in the county court, where most such litigation clearly took place. Still less does it establish that the action of customs and services was more commonly used as a method of enforcing the performance of services during this period than distraint, for not every distraint will have been challenged through an action of replevin. But the relative frequency with which the action of customs and services was brought is, at least, suggestive; and it seems to indicate that in this period distraint may have been less common as a method of enforcing the performance of services than it was later to become. The explanation for this seems to be a two-fold one. As we have already seen, prior to *c.*1250 lords may have been under a considerable disadvantage in using the weapon of distraint;[84] and during the first half of the thirteenth century lords possessed a comparatively simple and handy remedy in the action of customs and services when their tenants failed to perform the services owed.

## IV

During the second half of the thirteenth century the action of replevin continued to function as the main legal mechanism for controlling the lord's use of extra-judicial distraint, but the way in which the action worked was affected by a series of changes, some statutory and some non-statutory.

Clause 17 of the Provisions of Westminster (1259), re-enacted in 1267 as Statute of Marlborough, c.21, provided that:

> if anyone's animals are taken and unjustly detained the sheriff can release them without the obstruction or contradiction of the person who took them, once a plaint is made to him about this, if they were taken outside franchises; and if such animals are taken within franchises and the bailiffs of the franchises refuse to release them then the sheriff is to have them released by reason of the default of the said bailiffs.[85]

This clause provided statutory authority for the initiation of actions of replevin through the convenient local mechanism of a verbal complaint to the sheriff of the appropriate county, but there is good evidence that this mechanism had, in fact, long existed without such authority side by side with the procedure for initiating such pleas through a royal writ purchased in chancery. Despite first appearances, then, the legislation did not mark the introduction of a new and more convenient procedure for the initiation of such pleas.[86] It is, indeed, far from clear why this legislation was thought to be necessary at all. Possibly, some doubt had arisen as to

---

84 Above, 10–12.
85 *CR 1259–61*, 149; *Statutes of the Realm*, ed. A. Luders *et al.* (London, 1810–28), i. 24.
86 P.A. Brand, 'The Contribution of the Period of Baronial Reform (1258–67) to the Development of the Common Law in England' (Oxford Univ. D. Phil. thesis, 1974), 165–9.

whether it was proper to initiate replevin litigation by plaint. In at least two eyres of the 1250s juries had made presentments against local sheriffs for holding pleas of replevin 'without warrant', although the article of the eyre under which these presentments were made had simply sought information about sheriffs and others who allowed trial by jury to be used to determine replevin and other litigation initiated without writ. (The rule apparently was that jury trial could only be used in litigation initiated by writ.)[87] Possibly, some actual change had been intended but dropped during drafting, leaving us with a clause which did no more than reaffirm the *status quo*.

Real changes were, however, made by the Statute of Westminster II (1285), c.2. Three sub-sections of this chapter each purport to be directed against different kinds of abuse of the action of replevin by tenants (and other plaintiffs): in other words, they were concerned with tilting the balance of advantage in this action away from the tenant and in favour of his lord. One sub-section dealt with a loophole which had allowed a tenant (or other plaintiff), once he had secured the release of his animals as a preliminary to bringing the action, to sell them or take them outside the jurisdiction before the case was determined and thus, if judgment was given in favour of the lord, prevent the return to him of the distresses that he had originally taken. The remedy provided was to require the plaintiff at the outset of the litigation to find sureties not just to prosecute his case, but also for the return of the distresses if return was adjudged, and to make the bailiff, who had made the release, himself responsible for the value of the distresses if he had failed to secure adequate sureties before making the release.[88] It is unlikely that this had been a major problem prior to 1285. Even if they succeeded in taking the original distresses outside the county, or in selling them once they were replevied, few plaintiffs will have removed or sold all their animals or chattels at the same time, and any that remained were vulnerable to further distraints by their lords. County courts under such circumstances were, moreover, also probably willing and competent to authorize the use of 'withernam' or counter-distraint to force plaintiffs to return the distresses originally taken. The legislators may have overreacted to a comparatively infrequent problem, perhaps in response to a single recent case.

A second sub-section dealt with another such loophole. When a tenant or other plaintiff failed to prosecute his plea, and the lord (or other defendant) obtained a judgment for the return of the distresses by reason of this want of prosecution, it was open to the tenant to replevy the same distresses a second time and bring a second action of replevin (and in theory to continue being non-suited and then replevying in this way indefinitely). The remedy provided was to ensure that when judgment was awarded in the lord's favour in such circumstances, the lord was to get a writ to the sheriff directing him to return the distresses to the lord, a writ which specifically instructed him not to release the distresses a second time without a special judicial writ authorized by the court to this effect. The plaintiff was still to be allowed a second suit initiated by the special judicial writ, but if he again failed to prosecute, or otherwise had judgment given against him, the court was now to adjudge their return to the lord who had made the distraint without possibility of release ('irreplevisable').[89] Again, it is not clear that this was a major problem prior

[87] PRO, JUST 1/564, m. 8; JUST 1/233, m. 50; *Statutes of the Realm*, i. 23.
[88] *Statutes of the Realm*, i. 73.
[89] *Statutes of the Realm*, i. 73.

to 1285, though we certainly can see the legislation in action after 1285. A number of replevin pleas are specifically enrolled on the Bench plea rolls as having been initiated by 'judicial writ', and there are also a number of judgments for 'return irreplevisable' recorded there.[90] What is ironic, however, is that although the problem, insofar as it existed, was a problem as much for the county court as for the Bench and other royal courts, the legislation did not apply to these courts, and in a case of 1298 we find one of the justices of the Bench disallowing a plea based on a purported judgment for 'return irreplevisable' made by the Yorkshire county court.[91] This case indicates, however, that at least one county court did attempt to adopt the provisions of the legislation, and there is evidence of a similar move in 1307 on the part of the mayor and aldermen of London.[92]

A third sub-section purported to be concerned with a problem which arose only when tenants brought their action of replevin in the county court or other lower court. In such courts, it was said, when lords avowed a distraint for arrears of service, the tenant was able to disavow holding of the lord and thus have his lord amerced for an unjust distraint (for such a disavowal brought the litigation to an end without more ado). But because the disavowal had been made in a court which did not bear record, the tenant escaped the consequences which such a disavowal would have had in a court which bore record (one of the king's courts), since the lord could not bring an action of right to recover the tenement held by the tenant on the basis of this disclaimer. The remedy given by the statute was to allow all lords intending to avow for arrears of service in lower courts to have the replevin litigation removed into the Bench or Eyre, where any disclaimer would be of record. As I have argued elsewhere, however, there are good reasons for doubting whether it was the practice in all, or even most, local courts prior to 1285 to accept such disavowals as terminating replevin litigation; and there are even better reasons for supposing that the possibility of disavowals not of record occurring in local courts was no more than an excuse proffered by the legislators for allowing lords, as of right, to have replevin litigation removed out of local courts into the Bench, and the Eyre.[93] It is more difficult to discover precisely why lords wished to have the right to secure the removal of replevin litigation of this kind into the Bench. Access to trial by jury for those lords whose opponents had initiated the litigation by plaint rather than writ is one possible explanation, for jury trial was available once the litigation reached the Bench whatever the procedure used for initiating the plea. And with access to jury trial, lords probably also gained access to the possibility of joining issue with their tenants on the quantum of services which those tenants owed, for the position on the eve of the statute seems to have been that, since the county court was not competent to decide litigation about the quantum of services owed in litigation initiated by plaint, the county would give judgment for the tenant if he denied owing the services for which the lord had avowed.[94] Lords

90  Not all such actions were, however, recorded as such. The maximum number of recorded cases in any one year is the 11 cases of 1293.
91  BL, MS Add. 5925, f. 42r; and Lincoln's Inn, MS Hale 188, f. 38r (reports of case enrolled as *Stelingflet v. Coygners et al.* on CP 40/122, m. 114d).
92  City of London Record Office, Common Pleas Roll 32, m. 15.
93  P.A. Brand, 'Legal Change in the Later Thirteenth Century: Statutory and Judicial Remodelling of the Action of Replevin', *American Journ. of Legal History*, xxxi (1987), 44–7.
94  That the county court was not competent to determine such litigation is clear from the *causa* clause given for a *recordari* writ in a case of Easter term 1285, enrolled on CP 40/58, m. 20d.

may also have wanted to have the plea and its outcome a matter of record in the king's court. A third possibility is that some lords may have wished to raise the stakes in litigation by transferring the case to a court where litigation was perhaps more expensive in the hope of deterring their tenants from pursuing their cases against them.

A fourth sub-section of c.2 is phrased in much more neutral language, citing as its purpose nothing more than a wish that the justices should be 'certain' as to what kind of recent seisin would support an avowry in the action of replevin. It established that a distraint by a lord against his tenant for services could be avowed as reasonable (or just) if it was supported by seisin on the part of the lord's ancestors or predecessors after the limitation date for the assize of novel disseisin (currently 1242).[95] Elsewhere, I have shown that this sub-section was, in fact, much more significant than it appears, for the rule normally observed in replevin cases during the fifteen years or so prior to the statute, and spelled out in a case of 1282, was that a lord could only justify his distraint in the action of replevin if he could show that he himself had been seised of the service he claimed, or that his immediate precedessor in title (normally his immediate ancestor) had died in seisin of it. Thus the statute legitimized the use of distraint in a significantly wider range of situations than had been the case prior to 1285. In a majority of replevin cases of the period 1285–1307 where avowries for services are recorded, lords avowed on their own seisin. This was true in around 57% of the just under 700 cases. But in the remainder they generally relied on the seisin of a predecessor in title. While some of these might have qualified under the old rules, many would not.[96]

The major non-statutory change in the action of replevin during the second half of the thirteenth century was in the form and substance of the lord's avowry. By the 1290s, as we have seen, the lord's avowry was a complex and detailed entity, comprising a number of separate elements: an assertion that the plaintiff or some third party held a specified tenement in a particular village or villages of the defendant by certain specified services (given in full); a statement of the defendant's title to those services (usually, but not invariably, that he or a predecessor in title had been seised of them at the hands of the tenant named, or of his predecessor in title); an assertion that the distraint had been made because certain of the services mentioned were in arrears; and, though this is not found in all enrolments, an assertion that the distraint was made within the lord's fee. This 'standard' avowry was, however, a recent creation and some of its elements were only just then becoming standard. The older practice had been to specify only those services which were in arrears. A full list of all services owed for the tenement, whether or not the services concerned were in arrears, is found occasionally in Bench replevin avowries as early as 1260, but it did not become common until the later 1280s, and did not become the norm until the mid-1290s.[97] This change is probably to be associated with the growth of a belief among the serjeants of the Bench that a lord who failed to list all the services owed to him in an avowry would find himself excluded on a future occasion from claiming or distraining for any of the services omitted. Such a doctrine is found in at least two separate Year Book notes, which

---

95  *Statutes of the Realm*, i. 72–3.
96  Brand, 'Legal Change', 48–50.
97  For one clear example from as early as 1260, see KB 26/165, m. 11.
98  *Year Book 21 & 22 Edward I*, ed. A.J. Horwood (RS, 1873), 361; Lincoln's Inn, MS Misc. 738, f. 99v.

may well be derived from lessons given by law teachers to Bench apprentices. There seem to be no traces of it in decided cases, or even in reports of pleading in such cases.[98] It was an important change, for it allowed plaintiffs (though only if they were the tenants named in the avowry) to take issue with the lord, not just on his right to the services for which he had distrained, but also on any other services which the lord claimed and the tenant denied owing. In this way, replevin became a much more flexible instrument for resolving disputes, and potential disputes, between lords and tenants about services. A second element in the full standard avowry, which likewise is to be found on occasion as early as 1260,[99] but which is only to be found sporadically until the late 1280s and only became standard after 1293, is the statement of title to the services mentioned in the avowry.[100] This was, however, a less significant development, since even prior to this a lord could apparently be forced through pleading to make out a title to the services that he claimed, even if he had not done so in his original avowry.

V

Although proceedings in the lord's court remained a theoretical possibility — and in a small number of replevin cases of Edward I's reign, we do indeed read that a distraint has been made by judgment of the lord's court — the limitations on the jurisdiction of such courts (already discussed) seem to have meant that by Edward I's reign, for almost all practical purposes, the only real alternatives for a lord wanting to enforce his right to services were distraint or the action of customs and services.[101] In the early years of Edward I's reign the action of customs and services was still in common use. Thus, in 1279, we find pleadings in no less than fourteen such cases in the Bench,[102] as compared with just five replevin cases where the distraint is avowed as made for arrears of service.[103] This is, of course, not a reliable

---

99 The earliest case in which it is to be found is on KB 26/165, m. 8d.

100 But note that it was being asserted as early as 1270 that such a statement was a necessary part of every avowry for services: Cambridge Univ. Library, MS Dd. 7. 14, fos. 387r–v (report of *Wateley v. St. Martin*: KB 26/200C, m. 40d). The court did not agree, though this may have been because the plaintiff was not the tenant named in the avowry (and could therefore not counterplead the lord's title to the services he claimed).

101 The theoretical possibility of proceedings in the lord's court may be reflected in a Year Book note of the late 13th or early 14th c. (probably giving the doctrine of an anonymous teacher): 'Nota quod dominus non potest advocare justam districcionem super tenentem nisi in duabus causis. Ou par agarde de sa court ou pur services qe sount dues des tenemens . . .': Lincoln's Inn, MS Misc. 738, f. 99v (but he may be thinking of litigation in the court which is not concerned with services). There are many replevin avowries which state that the distraint was made by the judgment of the lord's court, but in all except two cases (CP 40/9, m. 42; CP 40/29, m. 13d) the distraint was for suit of court and awarded by the court after a default there, and the avowry does not seem to presuppose any kind of litigation between lord and tenant over the suit. But for evidence that as late as 1326 such a distraint for suit might lead to litigation about suit in the lord's court determining whether or not the suit was owed, see *Luffield Priory Charters, I*, ed. G.R. Elvey (Bucks. and Northants. Rec. Socs. 1968), 159–60.

102 CP 40/28, mm. 7, 10d; CP 40/29, mm. 49, 54d, 46d, 22d; CP 40/30, mm. 45, 83, 74d, 10d, 3d; CP 40/31, mm. 85d, 63d, 2d. Of these cases, no less than 5 ended with the defendant disavowing tenure of the plaintiff (CP 40/29, mm. 49, 46d; CP 40/30, mm. 45, 10d; CP 40/31, m. 85d) and a 6th case with the defendant simply agreeing to perform the services demanded: CP 40/31, m. 2d.

103 CP 40/29, mm. 13d, 75; CP 40/30, mm. 84d, 24d; CP 40/31, m. 43d.

guide to the relative frequency of distraint and litigation by the writ of customs and services, for much distraint may simply have succeeded in its object of compelling the tenant to perform the services he owed without litigation. Nor, as I have previously acknowledged, is it even necessarily a reliable guide to the relative frequency of contested distraints and litigation by customs and services, for much of this went on in county courts and may not have been in the same proportions there as it was in the Bench. But what does seem to be clear is that there was a steep decline during Edward I's reign in the use of the action of customs and services, both in relative and in absolute terms. Again, our only information is from the Bench, but here it is very noticeable that by 1299 there is only a single such case during the whole year,[104] as compared with some forty-one replevin cases where the avowries are for service arrears.[105] Nor is this relative decline difficult to explain. As we have already seen, two of the changes made by the Statute of Westminster II (1285), c.2 — that allowing lords to remove replevin litigation where they were intending to avow for services into the Bench, and that which allowed them to avow distraints, if they could show any seisin subsequent to 1242 — had the consequence of allowing lords to use distraint in a wider range of circumstances than had hitherto been the case, and with less risk that the distraint would subsequently be challenged and found wrongful; and non-statutory changes in the action of replevin had turned it into a flexible instrument for resolving potential, as well as actual, disputes between lords and tenants over services.[106] We also know, moreover, that lords or their future legal advisers were now being counselled, or taught, to use distraint in preference to litigation. Thus, in the *Modus Componendi Brevia* (*c.* 1278–85, but revised soon after 1285) the lord is told to bring the action of customs and services only if he were unable to distrain his tenant; and in the *Natura Brevium* (*c.* 1290) the advice given is that, 'if the lord is wise he will try to recover withdrawn services by distraint . . . before he brings this writ [of customs and services] which is of such a high nature and so perilous in itself' (because of the possibility of the case going to battle or the grand assize).[107] By the later years of Edward I's reign this advice was being followed, and distraint had become the normal remedy for lords whose tenants were withholding their services.

However, there is also some evidence to suggest that, by the latter part of the reign of Edward I, the ready availability of the action of replevin may have been beginning to have the effect of transforming distraint from a weapon for the enforcement of services into a mere preliminary to litigation about title to services, with the consequent growth of legal fictions relating to the distraints mentioned in replevin counts. Thus, we learn from an early fourteenth-century action of mesne that one possible action open to a mesne lord, when his sub-tenant was distrained for services that he himself owed, was to substitute his animals for those taken from

---

104 CP 40/127, m. 148d: this litigation may well have been collusive, for the parties came to an agreement without any recorded pleading.
105 CP 40/126, mm. 13, 75, 105, 137, 139, 146, 105d; CP 40/127, mm. 48, 67, 110, 164d, 55d; CP 40/129, mm. 1, 27, 31, 56, 138, 149d, 129d, 118d, 97d, 27d, 20d (*bis*); CP 40/130, mm. 17 (*bis*), 61, 73, 163, 181, 204, 241, 314, 293d, 268d, 259d, 258d, 249d, 125d, 119d, 46d.
106 Above, 19–21. The elimination of loopholes in replevin procedure which favoured tenants were probably less important here: above, 18–19.
107 *Four Thirteenth Century Law Tracts*, ed. G.E. Woodbine (New Haven, 1910), 156–7; Harvard Law Library, MS Dunn 162, f. 163v.

the sub-tenant.[108] The mesne lord would then presumably bring his own action of replevin to challenge the distraint. But if this did happen, it is not reflected in recorded replevin counts. Without exception, these talk only of the plaintiff himself being distrained, never of a sub-tenant being initially distrained, and the tenant then substituting his animals for those of the sub-tenant.[109] Other evidence suggests that we should even be cautious about supposing that every distraint was really quite the forcible seizure which it appears to be. In a case heard in 1302, Richard of Marton alleged among other things that the prior of Guisborough and his men had taken a horse from his stable at Marton. The prior said that he had not taken the horse, but that he had demanded certain services from John and they had agreed to a love-day. They had failed to reach agreement at the love-day, and the prior had said he would now distrain him. Richard had then himself delivered the horse up to the prior without waiting to be distrained. Richard denied this, but the truth of the prior's story was confirmed by a jury.[110] By choosing to deny Richard's claim that he had been distrained, the prior had lost the chance to have the underlying matter in dispute between them discussed, which may indeed have been a dispute about entitlement to services since there is a further replevin plea between them in 1309 which did raise precisely this issue.[111] Other lords in similar circumstances may well have chosen differently, and thus passed over the chance to object that they had in reality not distrained the tenant at all. What one of the Bench serjeants says in this case also suggests that Richard's behaviour was not simple eccentricity on his part, but an accepted part of social norms, for some tenants at least. Serjeant Tothby, apparently acting for the prior, says that 'we are alleging "curtesy" [i.e. on Richard's behalf] and you "villainy" '.[112] Replevin had become a means of litigating about title to services, the preliminary distraint merely the trigger to set off this litigation. The 'courteous' tenant might even save his lord the bother of having to make a distraint by doing this himself. But just how common this practice was it is impossible to estimate; most lords would probably have chosen to ignore the fictitious nature of the distraint and to raise the real issue instead, the dispute between the parties over services.

Extra-judicial distraint was already well established as a mechanism for the enforcement of services by 1200, but its use was effectively restricted by rules enforced through the action of replevin. The great increase in its use during the second half of the thirteenth century — and there probably was such an increase, even if not every 'distraint' of which we read in the plea-rolls was quite what it seems — resulted both from changes in the rules enforced by the courts and practices followed there, and from statutory modifications of the action of replevin. There is no reason to think that its increased use either reflects, or contributed to, any significant increase in seignorial power: for the changes took place, and are understandable only, in the context of the continuing effective control and monitor-

---

108 *Malm'*: 'Coment voet il dire qe nous avoms gre fet: qe quant ses bestes furent prises qe nous feimes la deliverance ou meimes les noz pur les voz ou qe nous avom fet la suite pur H?': BL, MS Add. 35116, f. 189v.
109 But for a case in which the defendant claimed that the plaintiff had forced his way into a pound to substitute a horse for the sheep which the defendant had originally taken in distraint (though both horse and sheep were the property of the plaintiff), see *Neweman v. Pannecak*: CP 40/95, m. 6 (1292).
110 CP 40/144, m. 244d: reported in BL, MS Add. 31826, f. 175r.
111 *Year Books 2 & 3 Edward II*, ed. F.W. Maitland (Selden Soc. xix, 1904), 21–30.
112 'Nus allegoms cortesie e vus vileynie . . .': BL, MS Add. 31826, f. 175r.

ing of the use of distraint through the action of replevin. Extra-judicial distraint remained acceptable and became much more common during the course of the thirteenth century only because it was not what it seemed. It was not a crude form of self-help, wide open to seignorial exploitation at the hands of lords able to use it to accroach additional services from their tenants. It was a convenient procedure for enforcing the payment of arrears where lord and tenant had no disagreement about what was owed, and a satisfactory mechanism for initiating litigation about services in the county court, or in the king's court, where lord and tenant disagreed about what was owed.

# Requests for Prayers and Royal Propaganda under Edward I

### D.W. Burton

During the reign of Edward I an unprecedented series of demands was made upon his English subjects in order to fight his wars against Wales, France and Scotland. For these wars, especially in the 1290s, he drew heavily upon the military and financial resources of the realm in a way which Henry III had never done, and which did much to bring about the political crisis of 1297. It is therefore not really surprising that Edward's reign should have seen the rapid growth of royal propaganda, as the government sought to secure the co-operation of the king's subjects in the war effort in various ways. The most evident are the written methods, the issuing of proclamations and the inclusion of explanatory material in such writs as those for military service or taxation. Equally important, but leaving fewer traces in the records, were the arguments rehearsed by royal officials in parliament before the assembled magnates and knights, or in the shires. The church, too, had a role to play, with its issue of excommunications and the parading of holy banners before the king's armies.[1] But here it is proposed to examine just one aspect of Edward's propaganda, his requests to the church that they pray for the success of his military campaigns.

The holding of special services and the saying of prayers to support the king and his causes were, of course, not new at the end of the thirteenth century. It was a duty which can be traced back to the early Anglo-Saxon church, while contemporary service books, which contain not only votive masses for the king but also masses in time of war, against invaders, against the enemy, and in pursuit of peace, show that such prayers were a standard part of the church liturgy.[2] It is, however, difficult to establish the precise role that prayers had to play during the thirteenth century before the evidence becomes clearer during Edward I's reign. Occasional references show that the clergy believed that they had a duty to offer spiritual support to the king. Matthew Paris mentions two occasions, in 1242 and 1256, when a Cistercian assembly refused to give financial aid but offered prayers in-

---

1   For Edward's I's reign, see M.C. Prestwich, *Edward I* (London, 1988); for political propaganda, see D.W. Burton, 'Politics, Propaganda and Public Opinion in the Reigns of Henry III and Edward I' (Oxford Univ. D.Phil. thesis, 1985).

2   For some early examples of prayers, see *The Laws of the Earliest English Kings*, ed. F.L. Attenborough (Cambridge, 1922), 24; *Councils and Ecclesiastical Documents relating to Great Britain and Ireland*, ed. A.W. Haddan and W. Stubbs (Oxford, 1869–78), iii.375; *Councils and Synods with Other Documents relating to the English Church: I*, ed. D. Whitelock, M. Brett and C.N.L. Brooke (Oxford, 1981), 54, 206; S. Keynes, *The Diplomas of King Aethelred 'The Unready'* (Cambridge, 1980), 217–19. For service books, see e.g. *The Sarum Missal*, ed. J. Wickham Legg (Oxford, 1916), 395–8, 408, 411–12; *Missale ad Usum Insignis Ecclesiae Eboracensis*, ed. W.G. Henderson (Surtees Soc. lx, 1872), ii.169–70, 174, 177–8.

stead. On the second occasion, the assembled abbots protested that it was more fitting for a king to seek their prayers than their money, and the abbot of Buildwas claimed that they would not be able to pray at all if Henry took all their money.[3] This duty to perform spiritual service is also implied in a plea involving the abbey of St. Werburgh's, Chester, whose abbot in 1292 successfully claimed that the abbey held its property by the service of prayers alone.[4] Such claims were, of course, special pleading, but they are supported by other, more objective evidence. In 1282, for example, Archbishop Pecham wrote to the chancellor, Bishop Burnell, referring to the custom of his predecessors to give spiritual aid to the king when he was on an expedition, while in 1286 Archbishop Romeyn of York similarly pointed out in a letter to his official that it was the practice of the church to pray for all the faithful, especially for the king and for princes.[5]

Not only was it the practice of the church to pray for the king, but we can also find occasions when Henry III sought such prayers. At different times he requested prayers for the welfare of himself and his family, for the souls of his relations, and for the success of his expeditions overseas.[6] Yet the evidence, fragmentary as it is, does not allow us to argue that such spiritual support was regularly sought when the king went overseas or on campaign, or that it was organized in any systematic way. That, it seems, was a development of the latter part of Edward I's reign.

The first years of Edward's reign probably saw little change in the informal nature of the church's spiritual support for royal undertakings. The only surviving evidence of such support for his first Welsh expedition of 1277 is a letter sent to Edward by the abbot of Bury St. Edmunds. Therein, the abbot observes that he understands that it has pleased the king that spiritual support has been provided for him, his wife and children, his *familia* and especially those who were fighting in Wales; and he writes to inform the king of the precise arrangements made by the abbey. He then outlines a programme of 3000 masses and 800 psalters, and other prayers and devotions, to be said every year all the while the army was in Wales. The tone of the letter suggests that this spiritual support was unsolicited, and its preservation in Liber A of the exchequer may well point to its exceptional nature.[7]

The evidence for the church's support of Edward's second Welsh campaign of 1282–3 is equally slim, but it does confirm the impression that such support was still organized on an informal basis. The war began at the end of March 1282. The archbishop of Dublin may well have ordered all the bishops and clergy of his province to pray for peace as early as April, but it was not until late July that Archbishop Pecham wrote to the king's chancellor, Bishop Burnell, saying that he had been told that it was the custom of his predecessors to give spiritual support to

3   Paris, *CM* iv. 234–5; v. 553–4.
4   J.H. Tillotson, 'Pensions, Corrodies and Religious Houses: An Aspect of the Relations of Crown and Church in Early Fourteenth Century England', *Journ. Religious History*, viii (1974–5), 129.
5   *Registrum Epistolarum Fratris Johannis Peckham Archiepiscopi Cantuariensis (1279–92)*, ed. C.T. Martin (RS, 1882–5), i.389; *The Register of John le Romeyn, Lord Archbishop of York, 1286–96*, ed. W. Brown (Surtees Soc. cxxiii, cxxviii, 1913–16), i.16.
6   *CR 1234–7*, 339; *Foedera*, I. i.246; *Ecclesiastical Letter-Books of the Thirteenth Century*, ed. R.M.T. Hill (privately printed, no date), 74–5; Paris, *CM* iv.639; PRO, SC1/2/168; *Flores Historiarum*, ed. H.R. Luard (RS, 1890), iii.22.
7   *Foedera*, I.ii.604. Rymer assigns this undated letter from 'S. minister' to 1282, but in 1277 the abbot was Simon de Luton, and 1282 John de Northwold: *VCH Suffolk*, ii.72.

royal expeditions, and asking what should be done on this occasion.[8] His apparent ignorance of this custom, even when allowances are made for his long absence from England (and, presumably, the inability of his own clerks to give him detailed advice), suggests that the practice was not yet as well established as it was to become. The date of the letter, too (several months after the war had begun), suggests that the initiative lay with the archbishop, and that in his ignorance of the custom nothing had been done. It is certainly a contrast to the way in which Edward, later in his reign, regularly ordered prayers at the very start of his campaigns.

The apparent uncertainty of 1282 may have prompted a more organized response by the church to Edward's absence in Gascony between 1286 and 1289. Prayers and spiritual devotions were ordered in at least two dioceses, Worcester and York, although the wide discrepancy in the dates (December 1285 in Worcester, and May 1286 in York) may still point to local initiative.[9] But some degree of organization is suggested by the ecclesiastical council of October 1286, which discussed whether such special prayers should be continued or not.[10] The answer was perhaps in the affirmative, for there is a memorandum in the archbishop of York's register that his prayer letter was reissued on 25 November, although the accuracy of this memorandum is doubtful.[11]

So far, the rather fragmentary evidence does not lead us to argue that the king was playing a leading part in the organization of these spiritual devotions. But from 1294 there is a very noticeable change, for on virtually every occasion when Edward went overseas or to Scotland he issued orders at the start of the campaign for prayers to be said throughout the country on his behalf. So strong is the pattern that the few exceptions probably reflect no more than the failure of the evidence to survive.[12] This apparent change in 1294 cannot really be explained by the better survival of the evidence, for it is the long-established close rolls which record many of the king's writs, while sufficient bishops' registers survive from the early 1280s for evidence of the practice to be apparent there, had it existed. Rather, it may have been the vacancy at Canterbury in 1294 which prompted Edward to take the initiative in this matter, as he prepared to go overseas to meet Philip IV early in the

---

8   *Liber Epistolaris of Richard de Bury*, ed. N. Denholm-Young (Roxburghe Club, 1950), no. 522; *Reg. Peckham*, i.389. The letter of the archbishop of Dublin is undated, but since it also orders the excommunication of disturbers of the peace, which Edward had requested the archbishop to do on 28 Mar. (*Foedera*, I.ii.603), it was probably issued in Apr. There is no suggestion in either of the letters that the king has requested the prayers.

9   *Register of Bishop Godfrey Giffard, 1268–1301*, ed. J.W. Willis-Bund (Worcestershire History Soc. 1898–1902), ii.276; *Reg. Romeyn*, i.16. There is also an undated order for prayers in the register of the bishop of Exeter in the middle of entries for 1285: *Registers of Walter Bronescombe (1257–1280) and Peter Quivil (1280–1291), Bishops of Exeter*, ed. F.C. Hingeston-Randolph (London, 1889), 326. This may relate to Edward's journey overseas in 1286, or possibly to his cancelled journey in 1285, for which see Prestwich, *Edward I*, 321–2. An undated order for prayers issued by Bishop Bek of St. Davids, probably in 1287, may have more to do with the Welsh war than Edward's journey overseas: Bodleian Library, Oxford, MS Auct.F.5.25, f. 154v.

10   *Councils and Synods with Other Documents relating to the English Church, II: 1205–1313*, ed. F.M. Powicke and C.R. Cheney (Oxford, 1964), ii.977, cal. in *Reg. Giffard*, ii. 298.

11   *Reg. Romeyn*, i.16 n. 17. However, 25 Nov. 1286 may be a scribal error for 25 Nov. 1288 when, according to another memorandum, the letter was again issued: *Reg. Romeyn*, i.16 n. 2. Both issues were apparently dated at Cawood, and whereas the archbishop was definitely there in 1288, he is perhaps more likely to have been at Bishop Wilton in 1286: see his itinerary in *Reg. Romeyn*, ii.192, 194.

12   See app. below, 33–5 for a full list of Edward's requests for prayers.

year, just as he later took the initiative in summoning the ecclesiastical council in September of that year. Presumably pleased with the result, and Canterbury still being vacant, Edward repeated his request in June 1294 in preparation for his proposed Gascon expedition; thereafter, it became the customary practice. The church, well used to praying for the king, and to receiving occasional requests for such prayers, probably found little unusual or objectionable in that.

Although Edward was quick to realize the propaganda value of such requests for prayers, it would be wrong to suppose that he had no concern for the spiritual benefits which they brought him. His first request for prayers in February 1294, as he went overseas to meet Philip IV, contains little that could be regarded strictly as propaganda.[13] A few months later, in June 1294, as he prepared for his first expedition to Gascony, he requested that people pray for him since the weakness of man made God's assistance necessary, while in August 1297 he wrote that he put more trust in the prayers of the faithful than in his own military power.[14] Such statements are, of course, not entirely unexpected in requests to the church for its spiritual support. Yet, they were probably more than pious platitudes, for the number of private offerings which Edward made to the church, on receipt of good news about the progress of the war, indicates that he felt God as much as man to be responsible.[15]

Yet whatever the spiritual value of the church's prayers, Edward was quick to appreciate that they were also an opportunity for propaganda, for the writs requesting them could contain a detailed explanation of the king's policies. The writs which sought prayers on behalf of his Gascon expeditions put forward the argument that the war had been caused by the injustice of Philip IV's confiscation of Gascony, and that Edward was acting in the interests of peace and of the realm. His writ of June 1294, for example, the first issued in connection with a military expedition, accused the king of France of having been prompted by the Devil into confiscating Gascony, after an unjust trial and at the very moment when lengthy discussions had seemed to be on the point of achieving the peace which Edward desired. He now had to go overseas to recover his inheritance and his hereditary rights, and he asked all to pray that God would defend his just cause and bring honour and benefit to the kingdom.[16] A prayer letter in August 1297 complained in similar terms that the king of France had fraudulently deceived him of Gascony and had refused to consider the peace proposals put forward. Edward was undertaking his expedition unwillingly, but with the help of his allies and the prayers of the church he hoped to recover his hereditary rights, to the glory and honour of the kingdom, and so that Christian peace might arise.[17]

Few of Edward's requests for prayers relating to his Scottish expeditions survive, but it is possible to see him treating the Scots in contemptuous manner, justifying his expeditions as necessary for the welfare of the realm. In October 1299 he explained that he was exposing himself to danger in order to repress the im-

---

13  *Foedera,* I.ii.796.
14  *Foedera,* I.ii.802, 872.
15  Many examples can be found in the wardrobe accounts, e.g. *Liber Quotidianus Contrarotulatoris Garderobiae, 1299–1300,* ed. J. Topham (London, 1787), 28, 31, 36, 42, 43. For Edward's piety in general, see M.C. Prestwich, 'The Piety of Edward I', in *England in the Thirteenth Century: Procs. 1984 Harlaxton Symposium,* ed. W.M. Ormrod (Harlaxton, 1985), 120–8.
16  *Foedera,* I.ii.802.
17  *Foedera,* I.ii.872.

pudence and malice of the Scots who had invaded the kingdom, so that the kingdom might have peace and tranquillity.[18] A letter of the bishop of Worcester in July 1303, which was probably based on a royal writ, put this in even stronger terms. The bishop said that the Scots, forgetful of their fealty, had seditiously invaded England on many occasions, spilling the blood of innocent people, burning and plundering the churches, monasteries and other holy places, and that Edward needed prayers as he went to suppress the Scots, exposing himself to great danger for the public benefit.[19] Such sentiments were, of course, not unique to Edward's prayer letters, and they reflect the views which he was seeking to put across elsewhere. Yet, repeated by the church, they would gain additional credence, and help to foster the impression which Edward encouraged, that his undertakings in Gascony and Scotland were holy missions approved by God, requiring the support of the people, not only as the king's subjects, but also as members of the Christian church.[20]

The success of such propaganda inevitably depended on the letters' becoming known as widely as possible, and the machinery for the circulation of such material within the dioceses already existed. Occasional glimpses of this machinery in operation can be seen before the 1290s. In 1252, for example, when Henry III was seeking to build up support for his proposed crusade, the royal chancery issued the tenor of papal crusading bulls to the archbishops and bishops for publication throughout their dioceses.[21] An example of the machinery's operation within the dioceses comes from a letter sent by the bishop of Salisbury to the religious of his diocese, enclosing a letter of Henry III requesting prayers for his daughter, Margaret of Scotland, who was with child, and for the soul of Aymer, bishop of Winchester.[22] Later, in 1291–2, the diocesan chanceries were used in a similar manner to distribute copies of Pope Nicholas IV's crusading bulls throughout the dioceses.[23]

In the 1290s Edward I used this existing diocesan machinery to disseminate his prayer letters, and there is good reason to believe that they were widely circulated. Generally, the king's request was sent to all the bishops, although sometimes other prelates were involved as well. In June 1294, for example, the prior provincial of the Dominicans and all Dominican houses, the minister general of the Franciscans, and the chancellor of Oxford university all received writs; and in 1296, seventeen abbots, the master of the order of Sempringham, the Dominican prior provincial, and the Franciscan minister general also received a copy of the request for prayers issued for the Gascon expedition of that year.[24] Generally, however, the king's request was sent to the bishops, who on receipt of the king's writ would send his

18 *Foedera*, I.ii.914.

19 *Register of Bishop William Ginsborough, 1303–7*, ed. J.W. Willis-Bund (Worcestershire History Soc. xix, 1907), 45–6. The royal writ does not survive, but the bishop's letter was perhaps based on it, for it repeats several phrases used in an earlier royal letter of 1297: *Foedera*, I.ii.872.

20 Cf. the arguments of these prayer letters with e.g. those in the military summonses, in *Parliamentary Writs and Writs of Military Summons, Edw. I–Edw. II*, ed. F. Palgrave (London, 1827–34), i. For the argument that the Scottish war was a holy undertaking, see Burton, 'Politics, Propaganda', 340–4.

21 *CR 1251–3*, 437–8; S. Lloyd, *English Society and the Crusade 1216–1307* (Oxford, 1988), 44.

22 *Ecclesiastical Letter-Books*, 74–5. The letter cannot be dated precisely: Aymer died on 4 Dec. 1260, and Margaret gave birth to a daughter, Margaret, on 28 Feb. 1261.

23 Lloyd, *English Society and the Crusade*, 42–3.

24 *Foedera*, I.ii.802; *CCR 1288–96*, 506–7. Presumably the Franciscan houses should also have been included in the chancery's list of recipients in 1294.

request to each of their archdeacons — sometimes enclosing the writ, sometimes merely paraphrasing it — ordering them to have it observed in all the churches of their archdeaconries. The archdeacons, in turn, would have passed the request on to the parish clergy. In 1295 Archbishop Winchelsey ordered the details of his own prayers for the Holy Land to be passed on to the local clergy in writing, but it is possible that at other times they preferred to make known the king's request through deanery meetings.[25]

Sometimes, individual bishops prescribed the form of prayers to be used in their dioceses. Usually, they followed the same pattern, this apparent standardization suggesting that such services were not new in the 1290s, but the varying details, and indeed the need to outline the services at all, perhaps indicate that they had not yet become routine. The brief order of prayer was usually to be inserted into the mass between the peace and the *Agnus Dei* and was to be said daily. It would begin with some psalms and continue with the *Kyrie*, the Lord's Prayer and several versicles and responses, ending with one or more collects. For the bishops, the purpose of this short order of service was not primarily political (to praise and glorify the king) but penitential (to commit the king and kingdom to God's mercy and protection). Archbishop Corbridge of York wrote in 1301, and again in 1303, that the king's affairs would have a more prosperous outcome when they were entrusted to God. Similarly, in 1303, Bishop Gainsborough of Worcester repeated Edward's earlier assertion that he had more need of the prayers of the faithful than ranks of soldiers, and of divine assistance than his own power.[26] Such concerns are apparent in the psalms and prayers they selected. Psalm 121, for example, which was chosen by the bishop of Salisbury in 1298 and 1306, looks to God for aid and protection against evil. Psalm 67, which he also used in 1298, asks God to be gracious to his people and give them guidance, and praises Him for the benefits of His government on earth. In 1301 the bishop of Lincoln prescribed this psalm together with Psalms 79 and 123. Psalm 79 is a plea for the mercy of God, seeking deliverance from His anger, while Psalm 123 is similarly a psalm of repentance. The bishops' purpose was to encourage penitence as a means to deliverance from the evils of the Scots. Only Psalm 21, which was selected by the bishop of Lincoln in 1294, and perhaps again in 1296 and 1297, represented a different mood, in rejoicing that God has given strength and glory to the king and will destroy all his enemies.[27] The penitential mood would have been continued in the *Kyrie* pres-

[25] *Registrum Roberti de Winchelsey, Archiepiscopi Cantuariensis, 1294–1313*, ed. R. Graham (Canterbury and York Soc. li, lii, 1952–6), i.27–8. Deanery meetings to pass on information (though not prayer letters) are mentioned in Cambridge Univ. Library, MS Ee.v.31, f. 63 (meeting of the deanery of Shoreham to hear a report of the convocation of Sept. 1294); Canterbury, Dean and Chapter Archives, Chartae Antiquae A 20a (a meeting of the deaneries of Sandwich, Dover and Elmham, in Nov. 1294); and Sede Vacante Scrap Book 1, p. 105 (a meeting of the deanery of Bergavenny in the diocese of Llandaff, July 1293).
[26] *The Register of Thomas Corbridge, Lord Archbishop of York, 1300–4*, ed. W. Brown and A.H. Thompson (Surtees Soc. cxxxviii, cxli, 1925–8), i.6; *Memorials of Beverley Minster: The Chapter Act Book*, ed. A.F. Leach (Surtees Soc. xcviii, cviii, 1898–1903), i.10, cal. in *Reg. Corbridge*, i.15; *Reg. Ginsborough*, 45, perhaps reflecting the lost royal writ, for Edward used a similar phrase in 1297; *Foedera*, I.ii.872.
[27] *Registrum Simonis de Gandavo Diocesis Saresbiriensis, 1297–1315*, ed. C.T. Flower and M.C.B. Dawes (Canterbury and York Soc. xl, 1934), 10, 177; Lincoln Record Office, Register of Bishop Dalderby (III), f. 32v; *The Rolls and Register of Bishop Oliver Sutton, 1280–99*, ed. R.M.T. Hill (Lincoln Rec. Soc. xxxix, xliii, xlviii, lii, lx, lxiv, lxix, 1948–86), iv.175; v.14, 125; vi.22. See also the similar form of service drawn up by the bishop of Exeter in 1285: *Reg. Bronescombe and Quivil*, 326.

cribed in all the orders of service. The collects which concluded this brief order of prayer often included that from the mass for the king, which asked God to strengthen the king with virtue so that he might avoid evil and overcome his enemies, although others, such as the collect for peace, could be prescribed.

Some bishops required, in addition, that processions should be held, usually on Wednesdays and Saturdays, with the intention of further encouraging penitence.[28] The pattern of such processions was probably similar to that in the Sarum processional to petition for peace, which was itself based closely on the penitential processions made on Lenten weekdays. Choir and clergy would process either to another altar within the same church or to another church within the city or even in the suburbs. Various penitential responses to seek God's mercy were prescribed for their use as they went, as well as the seven penitential psalms, the litany and various collects for peace.[29] Edward's bishops certainly intended that their processions should likewise be penitential in tone, for they often specifically prescribed the seven penitential psalms and the litany.[30] The only exception to the penitential tone of these services and processions was the thanksgiving service of 1298, following the Falkirk campaign. On this occasion the bishop of Lincoln ordered that in all churches throughout his diocese thanks and praise should be given to God during mass every Sunday and feast day, with prayers of devotion and hymns of praise.[31]

Although it has been possible to outline the spiritual arrangements made by the bishops, it is much harder to assess how well they were carried out. Much, of course, would depend on the vigour with which the bishops urged these devotions upon their clergy, and the surviving evidence suggests that they did take their duties seriously. The wording of their writs indicates that on the whole they accepted the arguments and explanations which Edward had put forward, and passed them on, often verbatim, to their archdeacons. They were also anxious that as many people as possible should take part in these spiritual devotions. In June 1294, for example, Bishop Sutton of Lincoln not only laid down the form of prayer to be used, but also ordered that on Sundays, feast days and other suitable occasions the clergy and laity should be urged to pray as God inspired them.[32] Several bishops also asked their archdeacons to urge the prayers even upon those monasteries which were exempt from their jurisdiction. In 1301 Bishop Dalderby of Lincoln justified this by saying that the danger from Scotland affected the exempt monasteries as much as those which were not exempt.[33] Other bishops on occasion encouraged

---

28 *Rolls Sutton*, v.14; *Reg. Gandavo*, i.9; Reg. Dalderby, f. 32v; *Reg. Corbridge*, i.6; *Memorials of Beverley*, i.11.
29 *Processionale ad Usum Insignis ac Praeclarae Ecclesiae Sarum*, ed. W.G. Henderson (Leeds, 1882), 164–6, 32–4, 103–4.
30 The penitential psalms are Psalms 6, 32, 38, 51, 102, 130 and 143. In 1301 the bishop of Lincoln also prescribed the 15 psalms of ascents (Psalms 120–134), which look to God as the source of mercy, protection and peace: Reg. Dalderby, f. 32v.
31 *Rolls Sutton*, vi.108. *The Chronicle of Pierre de Langtoft*, ed. T. Wright (RS, 1866–8), ii.272, says that in Nov. 1296 the clergy agreed to give thanks to God after the Dunbar campaign, but no trace of this survives in the bishops' registers. Two undated royal writs to the provincial chapters of the Dominicans and Franciscans, asking that they give thanks for the suppression of a rebellious people and their prince, may date from about the same time: *Liber Epistolaris*, nos. 109–10.
32 *Rolls Sutton*, v.14.
33 *Rolls Sutton*, vi.108; *Memorials of Beverley*, i.11; *Reg. Ginsborough*, 45; Reg. Dalderby, f. 32v.

participation by offering an indulgence of forty days to those who took part in such supplications.[34]

However, it is not at all easy to see what the response was in the parishes to the urgings of the bishops. Some bishops asked for reports on what had been done (another indication of the seriousness with which they took their task) but only one such report has survived, that from Bishop Sutton of Lincoln to the archbishop of Canterbury, which merely said that the prayers had been ordered in his diocese as requested.[35] Since Sutton's register suggests that he took such prayers seriously, his rather bland report may perhaps indicate that all had gone smoothly. On several other occasions Sutton's writs also required that the prayers already ordered should be continued, but only once did he feel it necessary to add that where they had ceased they should be resumed.[36] Interestingly, this was in August 1297, at the height of the political crisis.

Even if the clergy were, on the whole, willingly involved in praying for Edward's success, the impact of such services on the laity is much harder to assess. It can only be assumed that the clergy, wanting to secure the laity's participation, would have expounded to them the need for their prayers. In 1282 the archbishop of Dublin certainly ordered sermons to be preached, to make the processions for peace which he had prescribed more effective.[37] The services themselves, conducted in Latin, would have made full involvement for most rather difficult. Yet, with vernacular sermons and explanations from the clergy, the laity cannot have been totally unaware of what was happening, especially when the prayers were accompanied by processions. It would have been difficult, otherwise, for Rishanger to remark that when the king's request had been made known in 1299, all the people willingly and joyfully prayed for the king.[38] This is certainly what the king wanted, not so much because such prayers glorified his person or gave him added political support, but because he believed that it was important to gain God's approval and aid for his undertakings. Yet he cannot have been unaware of the political advantages to be gained from having his needs publicized throughout the parishes with the apparent approval of the clergy, and his expeditions set in a religious context. During the 1290s, it was this as much as anything else which led Edward to develop the practice of seeking the prayers of the church in support of his undertakings.

[34] *Reg. Winchelsey*, i.66; *Memorials of Beverley*, i.11; *Reg. Ginsborough*, 46; *Liber Albus of the Priory of Worcester*, ed. J.M. Wilson (Worcestershire History Soc. xxxiii, 1919), 11; *Registrum Radulphi Baldock, Gilberti Segrave, Ricardi Newport et Stephani Gravesend, Episcoporum Londoniensium, 1304–1338*, ed. R.C. Fowler (Canterbury and York Soc. vii, 1911), 10–11.
[35] *Rolls Sutton*, iv. 174–5; *Reg. Winchelsey*, i.272; *Reg. Corbridge*, i.6; *Memorials of Beverley*, i.11–12; *Reg. Gandavo*, 9, 177. The report is in *Rolls Sutton*, vi. 187–8.
[36] *Rolls Sutton*, v.14, 174; vi.22.
[37] *Liber Epistolaris*, no. 522.
[38] William Rishanger, *Chronica et Annales*, ed. H.T. Riley (RS, 1865), 194.

## Appendix

## Edward I's Requests for Prayers, 1294–1307[39]

1. *14 Feb. 1294*. Edward's request to all the bishops that prayers be said for him as he went to negotiate with Philip IV: *Foedera*, I.ii.796. French and Latin drafts survive: PRO, SC1/37/169. A copy is entered without comment in *Registrum Johannis de Pontissara Episcopi Wintoniensis, 1282–1304*, ed. C. Deedes (Canterbury and York Soc. xix, xxx, 1915–24), ii.490–1. Evidence for the implementation of the request: *Reg. Romeyn*, i.40; ii.124, letters (undated) of Archbishop Romeyn of York to his archdeacons, the bishop of Carlisle and the official of the bishop of Whithorn (1 Mar.) ordering prayers for the king; *Concilia Magnae Britanniae et Hiberniae*, ed. D. Wilkins (London, 1737), ii.197, a letter (2 Mar.) of the prior of Canterbury, acting *sede vacante*, to the archdeacon of Canterbury, passing on the king's writ; *Rolls Sutton*, iv.175, 176, letters (11 Mar.) of Bishop Sutton of Lincoln to the dean and chapter and the archdeacons specifying the prayers to be used.

2. *18 June 1294*. Edward's request to all the bishops, the prior provincial of the Dominicans and all Dominican houses, the minister general of the Franciscans, and Roger de Martival, chancellor of Oxford University, for prayers for his French expedition: *Foedera*, I.ii.802. Copies (all dated 16 June) are entered without comment in *Registrum Ricardi de Swinfield Episcopi Herefordensis, 1283–1317*, ed. W.W. Capes (Canterbury and York Soc. vi, 1909), 310 (wrongly dated 1293); *Reg. Giffard*, ii.443; *Register of John de Halton, Bishop of Carlisle, 1292–1324*, ed. W.N. Thompson (Canterbury and York Soc. xii, 1913), i.15. The Worcester chronicle also notes the request, reflecting the words of the writ itself: *Ann. Mon.* iv.516. Further evidence of the implementation of the writ: *Rolls Sutton*, v.14, instructions (30 June) of Bishop Sutton of Lincoln to his archdeacons concerning the arrangements to be made.

3. *Jan. 1296*. Edward's request to the bishops (1 Jan.) and to 17 abbots, the master of the order of Sempringham, the Dominican prior provincial and the Franciscan minister general (12 Jan.) for prayers to be said to support the military expedition to France: *CCR 1288–96*, 506–7; *Foedera*, I.ii.834. A copy is entered without comment in *Reg. Halton*, i.70. Evidence for the implementation of this request: *Reg. Winchelsey*, i.65–6, letter (undated) from Archbishop Winchelsey to his commissary passing on the request; *Rolls Sutton*, v.123–5, letters (27 Jan.) of Bishop Sutton of Lincoln to his archdeacons, and the dean and chapter, ordering prayers as previously arranged.

4. *Nov. 1296*. At Edward's request, Archbishop Winchelsey agreed to order prayers to be said for the king, and to give thanks to God for what had been done: *Chron. Langtoft*, ii.272. Two royal writs (undated) to the provincial chapters of the

---

39 Omitted are Edward's requests for masses to be said for the souls of his relations, and those letters which he seems to have routinely sent to chapters of the Franciscans, Dominicans and other orders seeking their prayers. For examples of such requests, see J.R. Wright, *The Church and the English Crown, 1305–1334* (Toronto, 1980), 348.

Dominicans and Franciscans, asking that they give thanks for the suppression of a rebellious people and their prince, may date from about the same time: *Liber Epistolaris*, nos. 109–10.

5.  *7 Aug. 1297.* Edward's request to the archbishop of Canterbury (and presumably to the other bishops as well) ordering prayers for his expedition overseas: *Foedera*, I.ii.872. A similar request was also sent to Westminster Abbey: Westminster Abbey Muniments, MS 12201. Evidence for the implementation of this request: *Rolls Sutton*, vi.21–3, a letter (21 Aug.) of Bishop Sutton of Lincoln to his archdeacons ordering prayers as previously arranged.

6.  *June 1298.* Edward's request to convocation that they pray for him and his Scottish expedition: *Reg. Winchelsey*, i.261. Evidence for the implementation of this request: ibid. i.271, a letter (15 July) of Archbishop Winchelsey to the bishop of London ordering prayers to be offered; *Concilia*, ed. Wilkins, ii.240–2, a letter (25 July) of Bishop Gravesend of London to the dean and chapter of St. Paul's passing on the request; *Reg. Gandavo*, i.9–10, letter (undated) of Bishop Ghent of Salisbury to his archdeacons, ordering prayers to be said in response to the archbishop's letter, which is also entered, i.17–21; *Rolls Sutton*, vi.187–8, a letter (30 June 1299) of Bishop Sutton of Lincoln to Archbishop Winchelsey, confirming that the latter's request had been carried out.

7.  *23 Aug. 1298.* A letter of Archbishop Winchelsey to his suffragans, in response to Edward's request, ordering them to give thanks for the success of the king's expedition to Scotland: *Reg. Winchelsey*, i.278–80. The letter is also entered without comment in *Reg. Giffard*, ii.493. Further evidence of the implementation of this request: *Rolls Sutton*, vi.107–9, letters (4 Sept.) of Bishop Sutton of Lincoln to his archdeacons and the dean and chapter passing on the request.

8.  *Oct. 1299.* (i) Edward's request (undated) to the archbishop of Canterbury that he assemble the bishops and abbots and ask them to pray for his Scottish expedition: Rishanger, *Chron.* 193–4, 399 (2 copies).
     (ii) Edward's letter (22 Oct.) to the prior provincial of the Dominicans and the minister general of the Franciscans asking for prayers for the same: *Foedera*, I.ii.914.

9.  *7 June 1301.* A warrant for a mandate to men of religion to pray for the king and his son and those going to Scotland: *Calendar of Chancery Warrants, 1244–1326* (London, 1927), 127. Evidence for the implementation of this request: *Reg. Corbridge*, i.6, letters (6 June) of Archbishop Corbridge of York to his official and to the dean and chapter passing on the request; Reg. Dalderby, f. 32v, letters (16 June) of Bishop Dalderby of Lincoln to his archdeacons and the dean and chapter prescribing the form of prayer to be used.

10.  *1303.* (i) A letter (13 Apr.) of Archbishop Corbridge of York to the dean and chapter of Beverley requesting prayers for Edward's Scottish expedition: *Reg.*

*Corbridge*, i.15.[40] There is no evidence that this was at Edward's request. The writ (5 Apr.) is entered in the Beverley chapter act book without comment: *Memorials of Beverley*, i.10–12.

(ii) Letters (4 July) of Bishop Gainsborough of Worcester to the archdeacons of Worcester and Gloucester ordering specified prayers to be offered for the king and his Scottish expedition: *Reg. Ginsborough*, 45–6, perhaps in response to a royal request, for the bishop's letter repeated several phrases used in the royal request of 1297.

11.   *c. June 1306.*   A letter (undated) of Bishop Ghent of Salisbury to his archdeacons requesting specified prayers for the king and his Scottish expedition: *Reg. Gandavo*, i.176–7. No royal mandate survives for this, or for the indulgence of 40 days issued by Bishop Baldock of London about the same time for those who prayed for the prince of Wales and the peace of the church and kingdom: *Reg. Baldock*, 10–11.

---

[40] On p. xi are also letters (undated) to the dean and chapter of Beverley and the archdeacon of the E. Riding. Since they ask for prayers on the octave of Easter, they probably relate to the 1301 campaign — the campaigns of 1300, 1301, and 1306, the only other possibilities, taking place rather later in the year.

# Leperhouses and Borough Status in the Thirteenth Century*

## P.H. Cullum

This paper examines the links between the presence of leperhouses and the existence of boroughs, the use that can be made of this by the historian, and the implications for our understanding of the medieval attitude to leprosaria. The area covered is that of Yorkshire and the period is the 'long' thirteenth century, of *c.* 1120–1320.

Leprosaria comprised the single largest group of hospitals founded for a particular named purpose during the Middle Ages and all or most were established before 1300. About one-quarter of all Yorkshire hospitals known to have been in existence before 1300 were founded for the care and protection of lepers.[1] As such, leper hospitals were clearly a very important aspect of hospital provision, yet as a group they are poorly documented. The reasons for this are various: most leprosaria are fairly early foundations, probably of the twelfth and early thirteenth century mostly; indeed, there are no known post-1300 foundations in Yorkshire, though a number are first recorded after this date. Thus most leprosaria were founded when there was least chance of relevant documents surviving. Moreover, the disappearance of leprosy by the later fifteenth or sixteenth century meant that a number of these houses were already defunct by the Dissolution.[2] Thus the survival of any documents that once existed is less likely for these hospitals.

Other problems derive from changes in use from the mid-fourteenth century onwards, when leprosy began to decline. Thereafter, houses making provision for the poor and sick may disguise an original function intended for lepers. Indeed, though charters of foundation or endowment survive for a number of leprosaria, for example, St. Leonard's, Lowcross, for many others, such as the York city hospitals (with the exception of St. Nicholas), there is no evidence for the origin of the foundation, either in date or in patronage. How these institutions came into existence we cannot know: whether they were the creations of individuals, lay or clerical; or of groups of burgesses; or whether, as elsewhere, they came into existence casually — by the congregation of lepers at a site convenient for the begging of alms from passers by on a thoroughfare close to, but beyond, the town

---

* This paper is taken from my 'Hospitals and Charitable Provision in Medieval Yorkshire, 936–1547' (York Univ. D.Phil. thesis, 1989).
1    About fourteen out of fifty-nine hospitals known to have been founded before 1300 were leprosaria, although the total number of leper hospitals known by the end of the Middle Ages was higher than this.
2    P. Richards, *The Medieval Leper* (Cambridge, 1977), 11; R.M. Clay, *Medieval Hospitals of England* (London, 1909), 36; e.g. St. James, Doncaster: *Yorkshire Chantry Survey II*, ed. W. Page (Surtees Soc. xcii, 1893), 393.

boundary, close by a supposedly healing spring or pond, or on land left unclaimed by others which, by the use of custom, had become the established site of a leperhouse where the inhabitants had their own buildings, cemetery and, perhaps, gardens.[3] It seems likely that most of these houses must have survived largely on the alms begged or given at the gates, or from bequests in wills. Indeed, royal licences to beg, or archiepiscopal indulgences to those giving alms, are often the first, sometimes the only, indication of the existence of a leper hospital.[4] As such, leper hospitals often appear much more recent in foundation than they actually were. Almsgiving, whether in money or kind, leaves little trace in the records of even the greatest and most bureaucratically developed of medieval institutions, and none at all in such small institutions where internal documents are quite non-existent.

Any attempt to produce a chronology showing the rate of foundations in York-shire is therefore bedevilled by the sort of problems of documentation considered above, which have a tendency to bias towards a rather later date of origin than is likely to have reflected the true pattern. In the case of some fourteen leper hospitals which are known to have been founded before 1300 they show the pattern of foundations as follows:[5]

**Distribution of pre-1300 leprosaria by foundation or first occurrence**

| pre-1100 | –  | 1201–25   | 3 |
|----------|----|-----------|---|
| 1101–25  | 2  | 1226–50   | 1 |
| 1126–50  | 2  | 1251–75   | – |
| 1151–75  | 1  | 1276–1300 | 2 |
| 1176–1200| 3  | post-1300 | – |

This shows the emphasis of foundation in the twelfth and early thirteenth centuries, with a concentration in the half-century around 1200. Remembering that the evidence is likely to show a bias towards a later period, it would appear that the foundation of leper hospitals was very much a twelfth-century phenomenon. It is impossible to be certain whether this was in response to a real problem of wide-spread leprosy, necessitating provision for the sufferers, or to a fashion for pious care of the leper developed from the imitation of St. Margaret of Scotland and her daughter (Edith) Matilda, queen of Henry I, who had an ostentatious personal

---

[3]   A grant to St. Nicholas, York (dated 1161x84) includes a vegetable garden: *Early Yorkshire Charters*, ed. W. Farrer (Yorks. Arch. Soc., Rec. ser., Extra ser. 1914–16), i. 251 (no. 329 n.).
[4]   E.g. St. Katherine's, York: *CPR 1330–4*, 452; *Register of John le Romeyn, Lord Archbishop of York, 1286–96*, ed. W. Brown (Surtees Soc. cxxiii, cxxviii, 1913–16), i. 14–15, on behalf of St. Mary Magdalene, Pontefract.
[5]   Bordelbi; St. James, Doncaster; St. Michael, Foulsnape; St. Mary Magdalene, Newton Garth, Hedon; St. Sepulchre, Hedon; St. Leonard, Lowcross; St. Mary Magdalene, Pontefract; St. Mary Magdalene, Ripon; St. Leonard, Sheffield; Tadcaster; Tickhill; St. Lawrence, Upsall-in-Cleveland; St. Michael, Whitby; St. Nicholas, York. To these may be added St. Mary Magdalene, Malton, known to have been in existence by 1154 but nowhere explicitly described as a leperhouse. The dedication, and a bequest of 1497 to the leperhouse of Malton, suggest that St. Mary Magdalene should be identified as a leperhouse: Borthwick Institute of Historical Research, York, Arch-bishops' Registers, Vol. 23 (Rotherham), fos. 362–3 (will of John Somerby of Bridlington). For the Sutton leperhouse, see below, n. 27.

devotion to lepers (itself an aspect of developments in twelfth-century piety towards a view of a more human Christ), or whether it was based on a greater fear of, and desire to isolate, this particularly disfiguring disease.[6] It is likely that elements of all of these were involved.

The extent to which the problem of leprosy was a genuine one is hard to define. How widespread was leprosy in the population in the twelfth century? How accurate were people at identifying it correctly, bearing in mind that diagnosis was probably performed by the local priest (later, at least in London, by the barbers)? Only in the fifteenth century was the diagnosis of leprosy medicalized.[7] Moreover, at what stage was the sufferer regarded as requiring isolation? Clearly, if segregation was only considered necessary when the disease was well advanced, and the characteristic disfigurements of hands, feet and face obvious, the chances of an accurate diagnosis were far better than if it was hurried through on appearance of persistent skin disfigurement which might be the symptom of many other diseases. Guy de Chauliac, the mid-fourteenth-century medical writer, emphasized the importance of being cautious over pronouncing an individual to be a leper because of the dreadful consequences of such a decision.[8] However, few of those called upon to make such a decision can have read the *Lilium*, the *Chirurgie*, or any of their antecedents. Nevertheless, the evidence of excavations at the leper graveyard at Naestved (Denmark) does indicate considerable accuracy in the diagnosis of the disease. In this excavation over 200 skeletons were examined and 77% were found showing signs of leprous change.[9] While this alone is impressive evidence of the accuracy of diagnosis, it is made more so by the fact that bone does not exhibit leprous change in all those who are today diagnosed as suffering from Hansen's Disease. Such change only occurs in some 50% of the skeletons of those who die of the disease today.[10] This may be because the modern population has a higher resistance to the disease than the medieval one (which would partly explain the prevalence of the disease in earlier centuries), and thus less frequently exhibits the most severe form of leprosy. It is, nevertheless, a reminder that true leprosy does not, and presumably did not, invariably cause skeletal change. Under these circumstances, a higher than 77% accuracy rate for diagnosis must be regarded as indicative of a clear understanding of the symptoms of the disease. Naestved was a relatively substantial hospital; it is another matter whether those priests and laymen called upon to judge the issue in more isolated communities where the local leper hospital was very small could have had the experience to make such accurate diagnoses. The partial excavation of the cemetery of the rather obscure leperhouse of South Acre (Norf.) would suggest that here, too, diagnosis was highly accurate:

6   See R.I. Moore, *The Formation of a Persecuting Society* (Oxford, 1987), 45–65.
7   According to Bishop Bronescombe of Exeter (1258–80), 'It belongs to the office of a priest to distinguish between one form of leprosy and another.' See F.F. Cartwright, *A Social History of Medicine* (London, 1977), 23–4, 28; Richards, *Medieval Leper*, 40–1.
8   Quoted in Clay, *Medieval Hospitals*, 61: 'In the examination and judgement of lepers, there must be great circumspection, because the injury is very great, whether we thus submit to confinement those that ought not to be confined, or allow lepers to mix with the people, seeing the disease is contagious and infectious.' And see L. Demaitre, 'The Description and Diagnosis of Leprosy by Fourteenth Century Physicians', *Bulletin of the Institute of the History of Medecine*, lix (1985), 341.
9   Richards, *Medieval Leper*, 118.
10  Keith Manchester, in an unpublished paper delivered to the Medieval Hospitals Conference, Oxford, 1984.

of twelve skeletons excavated, four were too fragmentary for analysis; but of the rest, seven showed some signs of leprous change.[11] If diagnosis was delayed until the symptoms were very obvious, as seems to have been the case in the seventeenth century in Denmark, it would be possible for diagnosis to be reasonably good, at the expense of the risk of an infectious person remaining in the community.[12]

As records are extremely poor, it is often difficult to know by whom leper hospitals were founded, and evidence is more likely to survive for noble and ecclesiastical founders than for any other group. Archiepiscopal interest in the foundation of leper hospitals appears to have been limited to Thurstan (1114–40), who was probably responsible for foundations at Ripon and his manor of Otley.[13] Nor are there signs of other secular ecclesiastics in Yorkshire being concerned with this disease. Monastic foundations of leperhouses, however, form a significant group, including St. Nicholas, York, founded by Stephen or Savary, abbots of St. Mary's, York,[14] Bordelby, by Richmond priory, St. Michael, Whitby, by the abbey there, and St. Michael, Foulsnape (near Pontefract) by Burton Lazars, the only English house of the Order of Lazarus. Monastic interest in the movement appears to have been largely self-interested, concerned with making provision for leprous monks of the larger Benedictine houses, as at Bordelby and Whitby. Other houses and orders, less wealthy, or less concerned about the isolation of leprous members of their community, made no such provision. Indeed, Nostell priory was so unconcerned by this need that it was willing to accept a leper as a full brother ('in plenarium fratrem') for a consideration.[15] A number of monastic houses also had direction of leper hospitals founded by others, particularly members of the nobility. These included Tadcaster, granted to Sawley abbey by Henry de Percy, being of the foundation of Matilda de Percy after 1186,[16] and Lowcross, given to Guisborough priory by 1275.[17] Monastic supervision of these, as other early hospitals, was based on trust in the reliability of the monasteries as perpetual corporations, as well as being particularly suitable for those who were 'dead to the world but alive again unto God'.[18] However, monastically supervised leper houses were only a minority of leper houses. Finance may also have been an issue for leper hospitals with only a minimal endowment. Henry de Percy claimed, perhaps disingenuously, that he was giving Tadcaster to Sawley because it was too poor to support itself.

As an identifiable group, the noble foundations are the most important and range from houses created by major figures like William le Gros, count of Aumâle, at Newton Garth, Hedon, to substantial local families like the Huttons at Lowcross.[19] Links between these families can rarely be drawn, though Alan fitzHubert

11  C. Wells, 'A Leper Cemetery at South Acre, Norfolk', *Medieval Archaeology*, xi (1967), 242–8.
12  Richards, *Medieval Leper*, 64.
13  *Memorials of the Church of SS. Peter and Wilfrid, Ripon*, ed. J.T. Fowler (Surtees Soc. lxxiv, lxxviii, lxxxi, cxv, 1882–1908), i. 228; Clay, *Medieval Hospitals*, 344.
14  See Cullum, 'Hospitals and Charitable Provision', 37–8 for further discussion.
15  *Early Yorkshire Charters*, iii. 275–6 (no. 1610).
16  *The Chartulary of the Cistercian Abbey of St. Mary of Sallay*, ed. J. McNulty (Yorks. Arch. Soc., Rec. ser. lxxxvii, xc, 1933–4), ii. 130 (no. 616).
17  *Cartularium prioratus de Gyseburne*, ed. W. Brown (Surtees Soc. lxxxvi, lxxxix, 1889–94), i. 190 (no. 383).
18  From the office at the seclusion of a leper, from the Use of Sarum: printed in Clay, *Medieval Hospitals*, 273–6, and Richards, *Medieval Leper*, 123–4.
19  B. English, *The Lords of Holderness, 1086–1260* (Oxford, 1979), 26; D. Nicholl, *Thurstan, Archbishop of York (1114–40)* (York, 1964), 145; *Cartularium Gyseburne, passim*.

Yorkshire Leperhouses

founded a leper hospital close to that of his lord, William le Gros, at Hedon,[20] and two branches of the Percy family patronized houses at Tadcaster and Upsall-in-Cleveland. William, influenced by the events of the anarchy of Stephen's reign, and perhaps by Archbishop Thurstan, was a notable founder of monastic houses. His interest in leper hospitals was limited to Hedon, but this fits within the pattern of his other donations.

There is also evidence, both direct and circumstantial, for collective action lying behind the establishment of a number of leperhouses. Though the early endowment of St. Lawrence, Upsall-in-Cleveland seems to have been a piecemeal affair, during the priorate of Michael of Guisborough (1218–34) the eleven descendants of the first benefactors gave these benefactions to the neighbouring leperhouse of St. Leonard, Lowcross.[21] The reason for the transfer is not made clear, but it is most likely that there were by this date not enough lepers to fill both houses, as they were only two miles apart. Moreover, St. Leonard was closer to the town of Guisborough and therefore better placed for the solicitation of alms. Nevertheless, the closure of one leperhouse, and the re-endowing of the other, required a collective action of the local community (or its more important members) and a concerted policy, suggesting that such houses could be the object, or vehicle, of local

20  J.R. Boyle, *The Early History of Hedon* (Hull, 1895), 165; English, *Lords of Holderness*, 174.
21  *Cartularium Gyseburne*, i. 190 (no. 382).

communal action. A similar situation existed at Scarborough, where there were two hospitals in existence by 1297–8.[22] It is not clear from the relevant document that either was a leper hospital, but the combination of a dedication to St. Nicholas (as at York and at Harbledown, near Canterbury) and a fourteenth-century royal letter close seeking entry for a leprous clerk is suggestive, and later Scarborough wills confirm that St. Nicholas was a leper hospital.[23] Both the Scarborough hospitals claimed to have been founded by the burgesses, an indication that possibly as early as the end of the twelfth century borough communities were taking responsibility for this kind of provision.[24] Certainly, by the later thirteenth century, the mayor and commonalty of York were electing the nominee for the mastership of St. Nicholas.[25]

Comparison of leper hospitals with borough foundations shows that there is a very good correlation between the presence of a leperhouse and a substantial community at an early date, that is by 1200. Of twenty boroughs founded before 1200, nine acquired leper hospitals and two had hospitals which probably catered for lepers. Thus at least 50% of boroughs established before 1200 had leper hospitals. If to these are added Ripon (which was an early and important centre of population, larger than many boroughs, even if it did not acquire its charter of incorporation until 1316) and Otley, another archbishop's manor which also acquired its charter late, the correlation is much improved. Not every town was a borough when it acquired a leperhouse (as, for example, Ripon) but all the leper-houses were in communities which eventually became boroughs. This emphasizes the link between civic status and the provision of a leper hospital, and also suggests that a certain level of population and of economic activity was necessary for both to be established. Such a correlation cannot be drawn so explicitly for other kinds of hospital. Thus the noting of the existence of leper hospitals can be a useful tool for indicating substantial communities in the twelfth and early thirteenth centuries where other material is missing, in the same way that the presence of friaries does for a slightly later period.[26] Boroughs which were not major centres of population before the later thirteenth century never acquired leper hospitals. Hull, which did not become a borough until 1299, and was little more than a trans-shipment point before that date, never had a leper hospital (although there is some evidence for one in a nearby community at a later date) despite the fact that in the fourteenth century it rapidly became the third town of Yorkshire.[27] By 1300, leprosy was in decline and there was accordingly no need for further foundations, even if the lack of foundations immediately after 1300 may also reflect famine, war and acute land-hunger in the first two decades of the fourteenth century.

Hedon, five miles to the east of Hull, and the original port for much of the

[22] *Yorkshire Inquisitions (1241–1316)*, ed. W. Brown (Yorks. Arch. Soc., Rec. ser. xii, xxiii, xxxi, xxxvii, 1892–1906), iii. 88–90.
[23] *CCR 1341–3*, 650; Borthwick Institute of Historical Research, York, Probate Register 1, f. 83v (Crosse).
[24] *Yorkshire Inquisitions*, iii. 88–90.
[25] As one hospital is dedicated to St. Thomas of Canterbury, it at least must be post-1173, and a dispute over the hospital suggests it must date to the late twelfth or early thirteenth century: *Yorkshire Inquisitions*, iii. 88–90.
[26] S.J. Reynolds, *Introduction to the History of Medieval Towns* (Oxford, 1977), 51; R.B. Dobson, 'Yorkshire Towns in the Late Fourteenth Century', *Procs. Thoresby Soc.* lix (1983), 6–7.
[27] Borthwick Institute of Historical Research, York, Probate Register 2, f. 110: Edmund Wynter of Drypool (d. 1445), buried in Sutton in Holderness, left 6s. 8d. to the 'hospitali domus lazarorum sive leprosis'. This is not located, but the next bequest is to the poor of Sutton, Stoneferry and Drypool, all of which lie to the east of Hull on the other side of the R. Hull.

hinterland, had two leprosaria, reflecting its greater age and prosperous state in the twelfth and thirteenth centuries, before the creation of Hull, and the silting up of Hedon's harbour, turned it first into a backwater and then into an inland town. However, Hedon had been an important town from *c.* 1140, perhaps earlier, receiving its borough charter in 1167x70, and it had one leper hospital from 1155x62, the other by 1205.[28] The first of these hospitals therefore dates from before the formal chartering of the town, but at a date when it was clearly already flourishing. Other boroughs which were of some substance at an early date are Pontefract, Ripon and Tickhill, all of which had leperhouses, whereas those which came to prominence in the fifteenth and sixteenth centuries, such as Wakefield, Leeds and Bradford, did not. Moreover, the presence, and occasional plurality, of leperhouses, is clearly related to a town's prosperity and population. York's four or five far outstrips any other community in the county and compares with London's six and Norwich's five, while Hedon and Pontefract each supported two, as did Beverley.[29]

The degree to which the borough community took a collective responsibility for the provision of support for the leperhouse is, however, unclear, and probably varied from one community to another. Nevertheless, leperhouses were to some extent the responsibility of the community. That this might comprise both a charitable function and a regulatory one is to be expected. It is best exemplified at Lowcross, to which a group of benefactors transferred their grants from another house at Upsall, provided that the lepers did not build on the ground granted, nor make a dwelling in the field of Upsall.[30] This ensured that all the lepers would be settled at Lowcross and away from Upsall, but it also meant that the enlarged hospital was on a site closer to Guisborough, and so more accessible to alms. Although most alms were probably individual, there are instances of communal provision of alms to lepers. At Guisborough, the only record of these comes when they ceased to be applied to their proper end. In 1275 it was complained that whereas formerly the brewers and bakers used to give alms of bread and ale at their will, now the prior levied ½*d.* each week upon them whenever they baked or brewed, and farmed out the alms.[31] So that whereas the alms had been voluntary, now they were compulsory, and not all the money went to the lepers. At York, too, the civic ordinances of 1301 stated that if any butcher was convicted of breaking the Statutes 'any measly meat shall go to the lepers'.[32] This was a situation which also pertained in Scotland, where it also included wild beasts found dead, or wounded or rotten salmon.[33] The citizens of York clearly took a major interest in provision for its lepers; at St. Leonard's Hospital, the great York hospital, there existed a regular 'Opus Leprosorum', providing 'v lagenis cervisia' each day and 'viij ferculis carnis pro eisdem leprosis qualibet die dominica';[34] and by 1364 it was supplying bread, ale and food to the leperhouses of York. Furthermore, the estab-

---

[28] T.R. Slater, 'A Medieval Town and Port: A Plan Analysis of Hedon, E.Yorks.', *Yorkshire Archaeological Journ.* lvii (1985), 26–7.

[29] N.P. Tanner, *The Church in Late Medieval Norwich, 1370–1532* (Toronto, 1984), xii; C.N.L. Brooke and G. Keir, *London 800–1216: The Shaping of a City* (London, 1975), 106–7.

[30] *Cartularium Gyseburne*, i. 190 (no. 382).

[31] *RH* i. 129.

[32] M. Prestwich, *York Civic Ordinances, 1301* (Borthwick Papers, xlix, 1976), 13. Mesel is another word for leper, so that measly meat is particularly appropriate for lepers. Mesel and measly presumably both refer to the spotted appearance of the leper.

[33] Richards, *Medieval Leper*, 35.

[34] Lichfield Joint Record Office, Lichfield, MS QQ2.

lishment of the city's maisondieu on Ousebridge in 1302 was claimed to be the refoundation of an old civic hospital, which catered for lepers among others. This claim must be treated with some suspicion because it formed part of the justification for the establishment of a guild then under royal investigation, but it is worth emphasizing that at this date it was clearly considered that it was part of the city's function to provide a hospital for lepers and others.

Moreover, this was not the first time that the civic government had been involved in the administration of a leperhouse. The oldest of York's leperhouses, St. Nicholas, had been founded by one of the abbots of St. Mary's by the middle of the twelfth century, possibly with royal assistance. Nevertheless, by 1291 the city had acquired the patronage of the hospital, and was appointing masters and performing visitations there. As this example shows, the fact that the city or borough was not the founder of a leperhouse does not necessarily indicate that it did not subsequently take an interest in the hospital, possibly a close one. It is clear that elsewhere civic government could take a keen interest in the control of leperhouses, although this might also be a duty foisted upon them by a patron. At Berwick-upon-Tweed, lepers might not enter the town upon pain of their clothes being removed and burnt, and their being ejected naked, 'for we have already taken care that a proper place shall be kept up outside the town, and that alms shall be there given to them'.[35] As at Lowcross, the leper hospital of Carlisle was granted each Sunday a pottle of ale from every brewhouse and a farthing loaf from every baker selling on a Saturday. At Shrewsbury, King John gave the lepers in 1204 the right to take a handful of corn or flour from each sack open for sale in the market. At Chester, the earl had granted the right to a toll on grain, malt, fish, fruit, vegetables and salt, as well as a cheese or salmon from every load of these going into the market. At Chester, the lepers must have eaten well, at least on market days, but the other grants also show a concern that the lepers should receive a steady supply of basic foodstuffs. As well as taking a toll in kind on markets, leperhouses might also be given markets as a source of revenue. The only leperhouse in Yorkshire to have this right was St. Mary Magdalene, Newton Garth, Hedon, given by Henry II in the years 1155–62, but it was common elsewhere, as at Maiden Bradley (Wilts.) and St. Mary Magdalene, Stourbridge, near Cambridge.[36]

Civic provision of this kind had a two-fold effect. On the one hand, as is clear at Berwick, the establishment of a leperhouse enabled the civic authorities to designate where the lepers might live (and thus where not), and so to exclude them from the town, placing them 'in a habitation outside the camp' according to Levitical instruction.[37] Although segregation, due to fear of contagion, might be expected to lie behind these regulations — and by the fourteenth century clearly did, as the London rules show — yet the examples of Chester, Shrewsbury and, above all, Exeter demonstrate that this was not the case at an earlier date.[38] By providing housing, basic sustenance and a customary place for others to give alms, the civic authorities established their control over the lepers, who were in most senses no longer under temporal authority: being dead to the world they no longer had legal status, having no, or few, legal rights.

---

35 Clay, *Medieval Hospitals*, 54.
36 Ibid. 184; Richards, *Medieval Leper*, 35; Boyle, *Early History of Hedon*, app. EE, pp. clxxxvii–cxc.
37 Leviticus 13:46.
38 Clay, *Medieval Hospitals*, 53, 55.

Another reason for civic provision for lepers lies in the medieval understanding, or rather misunderstanding, of the various Biblical figures called Lazarus. Thus, the Lazarus full of sores identified with Pauper at the gates of Dives is confused with Lazarus, the brother of Martha and Mary, identified with Mary Magdalene. Accordingly, the leper was identified as an outcast who nevertheless received the personal attention of Christ, and at the last was received into the bosom of Abraham. That this conflation was well known from an early date is reflected in the large number of leperhouses dedicated to St. Mary Magdalene.[39] To avoid the fate of Dives, the Christian community is obliged to accept the duty of providing for the lepers at its gate. Religious duty, spiritual self-interest and political pragmatism were all therefore intertwined in the medieval civic treatment of lepers.

Although the foundation of leperhouses clearly indicates a desire to provide housing for lepers, and thus to segregate them from the rest of the community, it can only have been in some houses that there was an expectation that, once admitted, the leper would remain for the rest of his or her life. This assumption can only be found, perforce, where some form of constitution or rule survives, and these were the houses which were supervised by, or established on the pattern of, a monastery. These were, like St. Nicholas, York, and St. Leonard, Lowcross, among the best endowed of the leprosaria; they had an endowment, and could give regular doles of food and clothing, as well as housing, to a (usually) regulated number of inhabitants. But most leperhouses were not so well endowed and could not have aspired to such a status. It is only the over-represented survival of documents relating to the wealthier and more securely established houses that has led commentators to assume that these were the norm. They were not; they were the grand hotels of their day, and it is no wonder that even the non-leprous occasionally sought entry to them. Most leperhouses were very small, very poor, and barely, if at all, endowed. They depended on casual alms, the sense of responsibility of the local community, and what they might grow on their own land. In times of hardship the hospital might not be able to support all its inhabitants, forcing some or all to disperse, as nearly happened at Harbledown (Kent) in 1276.[40]

Despite the numbers of such hospitals, there was no guarantee that if an individual was declared leprous there would be a leperhouse nearby to receive him or her. St. Mary Magdalene, Ripon received 'omnes leprosos in Ripschire procreatos et genitos', and both Sherburn (Co. Durham) and Harbledown took lepers from the whole of their respective counties. The Office for the Seclusion of a Leper does not assume entry into a leper hospital, but that a secluded house must be prepared for the leper.[41] With an inadequate supply of places within hospitals, and the fact that at times these hospitals could not always support all their inhabitants, it is not surprising that the medieval image of the leper is less that of an inhabitant of an institution than of a wandering beggar. The very threat of expulsion from the leper hospital shows that residence within a hospital was regarded as a privilege which might be withdrawn. As wandering beggars, unenclosed lepers might be eligible for doles, particularly at leprosaria. At St. Mary Magdalene, Ripon, food and clothing were provided for those within the hospital, and possibly also for any simply coming (or in this case not) to the house for food 'quia nulli venerunt, nec venient

---

39 Richards, *Medieval Leper*, 8.
40 Clay, *Medieval Hospitals*, 40.
41 Ibid. 273–6.

ibidem'.[42] It is not clear whether these lepers came to enter the hospital or simply to receive food; both are possible. The Empress Matilda also allegedly endowed a feast on the obit of her father, Henry I, for lepers in the area of York.[43] Together with the reference to St. Leonard's 'opus (rather than 'domus') leprosorum', this might suggest a lack of general concern about the segregation of lepers until the late thirteenth or fourteenth century.

In conclusion, the leperhouses comprised a significant proportion of all hospitals established before 1300, and especially in the twelfth century, even if this dating may often be obscured by the paucity of documentation, which tends to suggest a later date than was probably the case. The founders of leperhouses number few secular ecclesiastics among their company, but besides several monastic houses, mostly for religious, there are also large numbers of lay people, both noble and non-noble. Where founders are not noble they can often be found acting in groups, usually as representatives of their town communities. There appears to be a close correlation between communities which were of considerable importance before 1200 and the presence of a leper hospital. This correlation shows that (with a few explicable exceptions) only communities big enough to have acquired borough status by 1300 ever had leper hospitals. Not all boroughs had leper hospitals, so that the presence of one or more is an indicator of a particularly prosperous borough at an early date. Borough governments took a great interest in the administration of their leperhouses as an expression of their status, their ability to regulate the community, and as fulfilling a communal Christian duty.

42   *Memorials of Ripon*, i. 225.
43   *CCR 1272–9*, 280.

# The Political Role of the Archbishops of York during the Reign of Edward I

R.B. Dobson

It would be hard for any medievalist to deny that the episcopal bench of Henry III and Edward I was responsible for the last genuinely fundamental transformation of the administrative structures of the English church before the Reformation. On the other hand, and by a curious irony, the motives of the pontiffs who presided over the ecclesiastical changes of thirteenth-century England can be more difficult to fathom than in any other period of post-Conquest history. Not that the medieval church historian can complain either of a scarcity of interesting original sources or of a lack of talented secondary historians in the case of a century adorned by scholars of the calibre of the late Professors Maurice Powicke and Christopher Cheney. However, even the latter was compelled to acknowledge the 'cold light' often thrown by surviving records on the methods used by the hierarchy and its ecclesiastical lawyers; and accordingly the thirteenth century was for him a period in which, perhaps more than usually, the surviving documents 'represent unattained ideals'.[1] As for Professor Powicke, one hardly needs to urge the familiar point that his last and most ambitious book, *The Thirteenth Century*, illustrates to perfection what one takes to be that century's greatest problem for the historian: despite the comparative abundance of the evidence, and Powicke's own strenuous attempts to identify with its protagonists, it can be quite extraordinarily difficult to uncover the mainsprings of political or ecclesiastical action.[2] Not surprisingly, such problems of interpretation have recently re-emerged very clearly, as the author is at pains to point out, in Professor Michael Prestwich's authoritative study of the best-documented and most influential thirteenth-century Englishman of them all.[3] May it be too facile to suggest that the historian of thirteenth-century England is confronted with an extreme example of a well-known paradox? There are few periods in English history during which rhetoric lies so close to public action as in the years between Magna Carta and the death of Edward I, but again and again we

---

1   C.R. Cheney, 'Statute-Making in the English Church in the Thirteenth Century', *Proc. Second International Congress of Medieval Canon Law, Boston College, 1963*, ed. S. Kuttner and J.J. Ryan (Monumenta Iuris Canonici, Series C: Subsidia I; Vatican, 1965), repr. in C.R. Cheney, *Medieval Texts and Studies* (Oxford, 1973), 155–7; cf. J.R.H. Moorman, *Church Life in England in the Thirteenth Century* (Cambridge, 1955), 238: 'we can only feel disappointed that so little progress was made'.
2   See e.g. F.M. Powicke, *The Thirteenth Century, 1216–1307* (Oxford, 2nd edn. 1962), 227–30.
3   M. Prestwich, *Edward I* (London, 1988), 108–22, 558–67; cf. id., 'The Piety of Edward I', in *England in the Thirteenth Century*, ed. W.M. Ormrod (Harlaxton, 1985), 120–8.

are left peculiarly uncertain as to whether the chief actors on the political and ecclesiastical stage actually believed their own rhetoric.

Such general and no doubt very hypothetical considerations, if valid at all, seem to apply especially forcibly to any attempts to understand the role and status of the six different ecclesiastics who sat on the metropolitan throne of St. Peter of York during the thirty-five years of King Edward I's reign. Although a very great deal can be known and surmised about how these six men administered their diocese and province, on two absolutely central issues — their own order of spiritual and temporal priorities, and their conception of their role as primates within the English realm — they can only be seen through a glass very darkly indeed. Such opacity is all the more regrettable because it might well be argued that the reign of Edward I was one of the few genuinely critical epochs for the transformation of ecclesiastical authority within the 1750 years of the history of the see of York. The nature of that transformation has been recently emphasized by Mr. Peter Heath, who rightly stresses the significance of some alarming developments perhaps unduly neglected by Professor Powicke, Dr. W.A. Pantin and even Professor Alexander Hamilton Thompson. In Mr. Peter Heath's words,

> Not always through royal initiative, and certainly not by a deliberate policy, Edward I's reign witnessed some major developments to the long-term disadvantage of the English church. Some serious steps had been taken towards that outburst of anticlericalism and, in particular, antipapalism which marked the later fourteenth century . . . resentment against the papacy — by the clergy as well as the laity — was growing . . . parliament was providing an assembly where hostility could be orchestrated, diffused and preserved. What an irony that a king renowned for his piety, who prefaced some of his legislation by alluding to his duty to defend the church, and who sought a quick end to his wars in order to pursue the crusade, should preside over these changes![4]

Ironical indeed; and against the background of Mr. Heath's not unpersuasive diagnosis, how far are we to see Edward's six archbishops of York as the accomplices or the victims, or both, of changes so important to the *ecclesia Anglicana* in the north? There is no easy answer to that question, as already seen; but at least it is important to be reminded at the outset that to be an archbishop of York in the years around 1300 was not a responsibility to be taken lightly. Of Edward I's six northern metropolitans, one died as a frustrated expatriate at Pontigny in Burgundy, one was publicly humiliated and narrowly escaped imprisonment at the hands of his royal master, a third was so nervous of his suffragan bishop of Durham that he preferred not to take any prominent initiative against him at all, and yet a fourth was supposedly harassed by Edward I into a nervous breakdown so severe that it led to his premature death.[5]

---

[4]  P. Heath, *Church and Realm, 1272–1461: Conflict and Collaboration in an Age of Crises* (London, 1988), 63; cf. Powicke, *Thirteenth Century*, 445–509; W.A. Pantin, *The English Church in the Fourteenth Century* (Cambridge, 1955), 47–81; A.H. Thompson, *The English Clergy and their Organization in the Later Middle Ages* (Oxford, 1947), 10–11, 30–1.
[5]  *Ann. Mon.* iv. 491 (Worcester annals); *The Chronicle of Walter of Guisborough*, ed. H. Rothwell (Camden Soc., 3rd ser. lxxxix, 1957), 250, 351, 358–9; Prestwich, *Edward I*, 547.

Such difficulties and such tensions are all the more ironic, more poignant indeed, when one considers that they figure so very fleetingly in the administrative
records that make these six metropolitans among the best-documented figures of
the English episcopal bench in the entire middle ages. After the precocious experi-
ment between 1225 and 1255 (during the pontificate of Walter de Gray) of preserv-
ing copies of administrative documents in roll form, the celebrated and
uninterrupted series of York archiepiscopal registers proper begins to survive when
Archbishop Giffard's clerks decided to adopt book form shortly after their master's
translation to the north from the see of Bath and Wells in December 1266.[6] Perhaps
the first scholar to appreciate fully the way in which these early registers could put
the study of ecclesiastical history in the north on a new footing was James Raine
the younger. By means of his enlarged edition of W.H. Dixon's *Fasti Eboracenses*
as early as 1863, by his several contributions to the Rolls Series, and by his
sponsorship of editions of these registers under the auspices of the Surtees Society,
Raine proved himself the most effective posthumous advocate of Edward I's six
archbishops of York there had ever been.[7] More significantly still, by the time that
the Surtees Society had at last (as late as 1940) completed the lengthy task of
publishing editions of all the York registers to 1315, Hamilton Thompson had
emerged as their supreme analyst and commentator.[8]

To the extent that the most magisterial and influential of all historians of the
medieval English church knew the registers of Archbishops Giffard to Greenfield
more intimately than any others in the country, it is hardly an exaggeration to state
that Hamilton Thompson's scrutiny of those registers lies at the centre of how the
operations of the late medieval English church are still viewed today. On the whole,
and all the more interestingly when one remembers the severity that he could
display towards many members of the fifteenth-century episcopate ('not a strong
body of men'), Hamilton Thompson was very impressed.[9] In the first place, his
admiration for the the system of registration at York, possibly influenced during
these years by the Nassington family, officials-principal at York under five successive archbishops, was itself considerable; and as the gradual improvement in the
format and organization of the York registers attained its greatest heights of sophistication under William de Greenfield and William Melton ('the finest volumes in
the entire series'), Hamilton Thompson came equally to admire what he took to be
the efficiency of the metropolitans for whom those volumes were compiled.[10] More
specifically still, Hamilton Thompson came to be much impressed by the evidence
that their registers seemed to provide of the capacity of Edward I's archbishops for

6   *The Register or Rolls of Walter Gray, Lord Archbishop of York*, ed. J. Raine (Surtees Soc. lvi,
1872), pp. vii–xiii; A.H. Thompson, 'The Registers of the Archbishops of York', *Yorkshire Arch.
Journ.* xxxii (1936), 245–54; D.M. Smith, *Guide to Bishops' Registers of England and Wales*
(London, 1981), 232–4.
7   W.H. Dixon, *Fasti Eboracenses: 'Lives' of the Archbishops of York, I*, ed. J. Raine (London,
1863); *Historical Papers and Letters from the Northern Registers*, ed. J. Raine (RS, 1873);
*Historians of the Church of York and its Archbishops*, ed. J. Raine (RS, 1879–94).
8   See the Introductions to *The Register of William Greenfield, Lord Archbishop of York, 1306–15*,
ed. W. Brown and A.H. Thompson (Surtees Soc. cxlv, cxlix, cli–cliii, 1931–40); and cf. *An
Address Presented to Alexander Hamilton Thompson with a Bibliography of his Writings* (privately
printed, Oxford, 1948), *passim*.
9   Thompson, *English Clergy*, 45; cf. *The Church, Politics and Patronage in the Fifteenth Century*, ed. R.B. Dobson (Gloucester, 1984), 16, 22.
10  Thompson, 'Registers of the Archbishops of York', 245–63; id. *English Clergy*, 1–9; cf. *VCH
Yorkshire*, iii. 28–36.

very laborious administrative and judicial work indeed. The most frequently cited of Hamilton Thompson's commendations in this sphere is all the more ironical because this was praise for an archbishop (Thomas de Corbridge) who eventually had his temporalities seized by a considerably less appreciative Edward I. For Hamilton Thompson, however,

> there are few examples of consistent diligence in the episcopal office more conspicuous than that which is disclosed to us by the itinerary of Corbridge; and it is doubtful whether any other English prelate in the middle ages managed, in the short space of 4½ years, to come within measurable distance of completing two visitations, and those exceptionally thorough, of his diocese.[11]

Such praise for such reasons exposes especially clearly its author's very influential tendency to assess the worth of a medieval bishop by the assiduity with which he made formal visitations of the churches, and especially the religious houses, of his diocese. As Hamilton Thompson saw it, and taught his readers to see it, the registers of Edward I's six archbishops of York tell a story of considerable and perhaps even remarkable success. In the first place, here is the archdiocese of York revealed, for the very first time, as a huge and complex organization subjected nevertheless to the most detailed and vigilant bureaucratic control. Secondly, those registers seem equally to reveal archbishops who were personally intent on maintaining and indeed enhancing the spiritual standards of their flock, and above all of their clerical flock. From this point of view, the early registers of the church of York are the critical documents for the case that the most important achievement of the archbishops was to bring ecclesiastical order to a north which had never fully experienced such order before. To put that success in the way it was formulated over fifty years ago by Marion Gibbs and Jane Lang, these were the archbishops who pursued a deliberate programme of implementing the decrees of the Fourth Lateran Council (1215) and thereby finally 'fulfilled the promise of 1215' north of the Humber.[12]

So favourable an interpretation of the ecclesiastical objectives of Edward I's six archbishops of York — one which for obvious reasons would presumably have met with their own approval — cannot be easily discounted and could indeed be elaborated; but the purpose of this paper, as already implied, is to explore some of the factors which so often vitiated and even negated the initiatives of these would-be reforming pontiffs. How far were their failures to attain their aims the result of personal weaknesses in their own temperaments, experience and administrative skills? As ever in the case of late medieval English bishops, no confident answer to that question can be offered, regrettably.[13] However, and having made all allowan-

---

[11] *The Register of Thomas of Corbridge, Lord Archbishop of York, 1300–1304,* ed. W. Brown (Surtees Soc. cxxxviii, cxli, 1925–8), ii. p. xx.
[12] M. Gibbs and J. Lang, *Bishops and Reform, 1215–1272, with Special Reference to the Lateran Council of 1215* (Oxford, 1934), 11–24, 131–79, which concludes with the observation, certainly relevant to York, that 'always the bishops were too much occupied' to carry out the Lateran decrees in full.
[13] See e.g. R.G. Davies, 'The Episcopate', in *Profession, Vocation and Culture in Later Medieval England,* ed. C.H. Clough (Liverpool, 1982), 51–90; Moorman, *Church Life,* 169–96; K. Edwards,

ces for the near impossibility of categorizing the members of the late medieval episcopal bench with any precision, the most important conclusion must be that Edward I's six archbishops fell into two very different groups. Much the most experienced and most nationally influential figures of the sextet were the two archbishops of York who respectively saw Edward I onto his throne and into his grave. Archbishop Walter Giffard (1266–79) was the son of Hugh Giffard of Boyton (Wilts.) and hence a member of a powerful clerical dynasty. This, together with his great administrative ability, led him to the chancellorship of England in 1265–6.[14] As the senior ecclesiastic in the country when the Lord Edward left Dover for the Holy Land in August 1270, Giffard was not only the first English prelate to swear an oath of allegiance to the absent Edward over Henry III's dead body in 1272 but probably did more than anyone — even more than Robert Burnell — to ensure an untroubled accession for the new king.[15] More than a generation later, it was similarly to be William de Greenfield, archbishop of York (1304–15) and also an ex-chancellor (1302–4) of the king, who acted as Edward's senior churchman at the parliament of Carlisle, only a few months before the monarch's death at Burgh-upon-the-Sands, not far away.[16] Immediately thereafter, like Giffard thirty-five years earlier, Greenfield found himself serving as one of the joint regents of the realm. In their not at all dissimilar ways — and after all, Greenfield was almost certainly a junior kinsman of Archbishop Giffard, who had supported him as an Oxford student as early as 1269 — these two archbishops might well serve as classic exemplars of what an English king might hope for from his archbishops of York, especially at times when his archbishops of Canterbury were proving exceptionally non-cooperative and intransigent.[17] To state the obvious, the prestige and influence of the *primates Angliae* were never likely to be higher than when the *primates totius Angliae* were suffering from the slings and arrows of royal displeasure, as so often occurred during the reign of Edward I.

Not, in fact, that this was an asset from which Edward I's other four archbishops of York proved capable of making as much capital as one might have expected. The most important common denominator shared by Archbishops William Wickwane (1279–85), John le Romeyn (1285–96), Henry de Newark (1296–99) and Thomas de Corbridge (1299–1304) was less their remarkably poor life-expectancy as metropolitans than the fact that, before their elevation, all four were very distin-

'The Social Origins and the Provenance of the English Bishops during the Reign of Edward II', *TRHS* 5th ser. ix (1959), 51–79; R.B. Dobson, 'The Bishops of Late Medieval England as Intermediaries between Church and State', in *Etat et Eglise dans La Genese de l'Etat Moderne*, ed. J-P. Genet and B. Vincent (Madrid, 1986), 227–38.

14 *The Register of Walter Giffard, Lord Archbishop of York, 1266–1279*, ed. W. Brown (Surtees Soc. cix, 1904), pp. i–iv; A.B. Emden, *A Biographical Register of the University of Oxford to 1540* (Oxford, 1957–74) ii. 762–3. [Hereafter, *BRUO*]

15 *Ann. Mon.* iv. 462; Powicke, *Henry III*, ii. 532, 581–7, 593, 595; Prestwich, *Edward I*, 73, 90. Archbishop Giffard, Roger Mortimer and Robert Burnell were Edward I's three regents between the king's accession (20 Nov. 1272) and his return to England (2 Aug. 1274): *Handbook of British Chronology*, ed. E.B. Fryde *et al.* (3rd edn. London, 1986), 38.

16 *Chronicon de Lanercost, 1201–1346*, ed. J. Stevenson (Edinburgh, 1839), 206; *Fasti Eboracenses*, 367; cf. H. Johnstone, *Edward of Carnarvon, 1284–1307* (Manchester, 1946), 119 n. 5.

17 *Reg. Giffard*, 121, 123; *Fasti Eboracenses*, 313. Cf. D.L. Douie, *Archbishop Pecham* (Oxford, 1952); J.H. Denton, *Robert Winchelsey and the Crown, 1294–1313* (Cambridge, 1980). As Heath, *Church and Realm*, 31 has recently observed, much of the antagonism between Edward I and these two archbishops of Canterbury centred, as in the church of York, upon the king's need to exploit ecclesiastical patronage on behalf of his own clerks.

guished within the York cathedral chapter but comparatively unknown outside it. Thus Wickwane, whose geographical origins remain extremely uncertain, had been chancellor of York Minster for fifteen years before his election as archbishop;[18] Romeyn was almost certainly the bastard son (possibly by a waiting woman) of that Croesus of early thirteenth-century canons of York, John le Romeyn;[19] Newark had found his way to the archdeaconry of Richmond, and eventually to the deanery of York, almost twenty years before his election as archbishop in 1296;[20] while Thomas de Corbridge, chancellor of the Minster in the 1280s, holds something of a record for apparently never having held any significant benefice outside York cathedral at all.[21] Not only, therefore, was the metropolitan see of St. Peter still completely immune from the slightest sign of what one might term aristocratic invasion: if anything, it tended to be the prize awarded to the long-standing canon of York most esteemed by his own fellows in the York Minster chapter. To that generalisation admittedly one needs to add the all-important qualification that the canon in question was by now required to have some genuine claims to university learning. Of these six archbishops, John le Romeyn (an outstanding scholar according to Rishanger, and 'theologus magnus' according to Walter of Guisborough) was at some time a graduate and lecturer at Paris as well as Oxford; while Greenfield (a doctor in both canon and civil law) seems similarly to have taught at both those universities early in his career.[22] Thomas de Corbridge, another doctor of theology, almost certainly emerged from the Oxford schools; Wickwane and Newark definitely did so; and to Walter Giffard fell the unusual distinction of being the only Cambridge graduate, although he also studied at Oxford, to become archbishop of York before Henry Bowet inaugurated a more regular succession of Cambridge metropolitans in the north after 1407.[23]

Whatever the precise significance of their university training for the careers of Edward I's six archbishops of York — and the choice of a canon lawyer rather than the traditional theologian in 1304 did in fact prove a portent of things to come — its general import needs no particular urging. By the second half of the thirteenth century it was already more or less inconceivable to imagine an archbishop of York who was not a university graduate: within fifty years of the mysterious genesis of the University of Oxford it had become imperative that the metropolitan could be plausibly presented to the wider world as 'profunde ad plenum litteratus', to use William Rishanger's words about Thomas de Corbridge.[24] More surprising perhaps, and more fundamental to their future relationships with their monarch, is Edward

---

18 *The Register of William Wickwane, Lord Archbishop of York, 1279–85*, ed. W. Brown (Surtees Soc. cxiv, 1907), pp. iii–v; R. Brentano, *York Metropolitan Jurisdiction and Papal Judges Delegate (1279–1296)* (Berkeley, 1959), 42–51; cf. C.R. Cheney, 'Letters of William Wickwane, Chancellor of York, 1266–68', *EHR* xlvii (1932), 626–42.
19 Guisborough, *Chron.* 260; *The Register of John le Romeyn, Lord Archbishop of York, 1286–1294*, ed. W. Brown (Surtees Soc. cxxiii, cxxviii, 1913–17), pp. iii–x; *BRUO* ii. 1134–5.
20 Guisborough, *Chron.* 260; *York Minster Fasti*, ed. C.T. Clay (Yorkshire Arch. Soc., Rec. ser. cxxiii, cxxiv, 1958–9), i. 48–9; *BRUO* iii. 2200.
21 *Reg. Corbridge*, ii. pp. xiii–xiv; *BRUO* i. 485. Thomas de Corbridge did however visit the Roman Curia as Archbishop Wickwane's proctor in 1281: *Reg. Wickwane*, 6, 203–6, 276, 321.
22 William Rishanger, *Chronica et Annales*, ed. H.T. Riley (RS, 1865), 111; Guisborough, *Chron.* 260; *BRUO* ii. 820–1; iii. 1134–5.
23 *Historians of the Church of York*, ii. 411–12; *Letters from Northern Registers*, 4; *Reg. Giffard*, 201; A.B. Emden, *A Biographical Dictionary of the University of Cambridge to 1500* (Cambridge, 1963), 83–4, 257.
24 Rishanger, *Chron.* 477; cf. Gibbs and Lang, *Bishops and Reform*, 25–50.

I's apparent willingness to allow the election to the northern metropolitan see of so many clerks who had devoted their scholarly talents so exclusively to the concerns of the York cathedral chapter and to nowhere else. Can it be that the strongest of strong kings in the history of the medieval English monarchy generally allowed the canons of York more liberty in electing their own archbishop from their own number than had ever been the case before or was ever to be the case again? On the balance of the evidence available to us, the answer to that question almost certainly has to be in the affirmative. Although the formal *decreta* of English episcopal elections notoriously often conceal the personal pressures which were brought to bear on these momentous occasions, there survive what seem to be reliable accounts of the elections of Archbishops William Wickwane and John le Romeyn as they were reported to the Roman Curia in 1279 and 1286 respectively. On both occasions the successful candidate won quite decisively (with eighteen votes out of twenty-one in the case of Wickwane, and fourteen votes from a larger gathering in the case of le Romeyn) at the close of what were undoubtedly genuinely competitive capitular elections, showing no traces of royal intervention.[25] Similarly, Thomas de Corbridge was to emerge as the unanimously favoured new archbishop of York in the chapter's election meeting of 12 November 1299.[26] Nor is there much reason to suppose that the York canons did anything but welcome the prospect of electing Edward I's chancellor, William de Greenfield, as their archbishop in December 1304, which they did: within a few weeks of that election indeed, their own dean, William de Hambleton, had actually replaced Greenfield as royal chancellor — a particularly instructive instance of that interchange between high office at York and high office under the king to which this paper must eventually return.[27]

Meanwhile, it might not be at all misleading to suggest that the only occasion in the second half of the thirteenth century when the canons of York failed to secure the appointment as their archbishop of the clerk they personally most favoured was in 1266, when Walter Giffard, who had never held a Minster prebend, was translated to York from Bath and Wells. Even in Giffard's case, however, it seems clear enough that it was neither the king nor the Lord Edward who blocked the chapter's original election of their own dean, William Langton. The latter's otherwise excellent prospects of promotion were dashed by none other than Pope Clement IV himself, who intervened in the vain hope that he might persuade St. Bonaventure to accept the pallium rather than remain, as he still does, the most distinguished archbishop of York there never was.[28] In any case, the main conclusion seems incontrovertible: the majority of Edward I's archbishops of York were not among the king's own most-trusted and favoured clerks. This apparently curious phenomenon has, of course, its parallels elsewhere in the thirteenth-century English church, most obviously perhaps in Edward's remarkable failure to provide his most favoured clerk of all, Robert Burnell, with a bishop's throne more impressive than

---

25 *Reg. Wickwane*, 305–8; *Reg. Romeyn*, ii. pp. x–xiii. The complex procedures followed in the case of both these archiepiscopal elections are described in Brentano, *York Metropolitan Jurisdiction*, 46–7, 52–3.
26 *Historians of the Church of York*, ii. 411; Le Neve, *Fasti Ecclesiae Anglicanae, 1300–1541*, ed. B. Jones *et al.* (London, 1962–7), vi (*Northern Province*), 3.
27 *Historians of the Church of York*, ii. 413; Le Neve, *Fasti*, ed. Jones, vi. 3, 6; *BRUO* ii. 820–1; *Handbook of Chronology*, 85.
28 *Historians of the Church of York*, ii. 406; Guisborough, *Chron.* 203; Gibbs and Lang, *Bishops and Reform*, 73–4.

that of Bath and Wells.[29] The electoral experience of the late thirteenth-century church of York, therefore, more than confirms the unduly cautious judgement that in the thirteenth century 'the best ordered [secular] chapters were more than once able to press home the claims of the worthiest of their members'.[30] Such successes were alas to become more or less completely unattainable in secular as in monastic cathedrals during the fourteenth and fifteenth centuries. Accordingly, the choice of archbishops of York during the reign of Edward I illustrates remarkably clearly not only the short-term victory for the post-1215 principle of free capitular election, but also the genuine sensitivity on this issue of a king in whom sensitivity was hardly a characteristic trait. On the other hand, a harsh price was often exacted by the king from those who attained the archbishop's throne after so comparatively 'free' an election. Edward I's readiness to accept comparatively unknown canons of the Minster as his archbishops of York made it only too likely that his rapport with those metropolitans might deteriorate and even disintegrate during the strains of a strenuous reign.

Moreover, there are good grounds for believing that the king's relationship with his northern metropolitans became progressively more and more important to Edward I as the church of York itself gradually acquired greater political significance in his own eyes. The main reason for this development was undoubtedly the extremely unsatisfactory behaviour, from Edward's point of view, of John Pecham and Robert Winchelsey, his primates of Canterbury between 1279 and the end of his reign; but then it is equally obvious that the rapid escalation of the king's involvement in Scottish affairs after Alexander III's death in 1286 was bound to give the city and church of York, as well as its archbishops, an enhanced importance for the English sovereign.[31] It had indeed been in York Minster that Alexander III had married Edward's own sister, Margaret, on the day after Christmas 1251; and even then York was already well established as the most obvious *mise en scène* for political treaties as well as marriage alliances between the kings of Scotland and England.[32] Although Edward himself seems to have only made five brief visits to York before 1290, he could never have been in any doubt of the cathedral city's role as the central agency of his authority in the north. One of the more macabre of many possible examples was the king's decision to have Rhys ap Maredudd hung, drawn and quartered at York after that unfortunate Welsh rebel was finally captured in 1292.[33] More striking still, and now well documented by Dr. Simon Lloyd, is the way in which Edward I (like contemporary popes) gave to his archbishops of York, even more than to his archbishops of Canterbury perhaps, extensive responsibility for promoting the crusade. The most notable of several instances of the archbishops

[29] When in Jan. 1279 Burnell's election as archbishop of Canterbury was quashed by Nicholas III in favour of the Franciscan John Pecham, Edward I raised no objections and immediately admitted the latter to his council: Powicke, *Thirteenth Century*, 469–70.
[30] Gibbs and Lang, *Bishops and Reform*, 93; cf. C.H. Lawrence, 'The Thirteenth Century', in *The English Church and the Papacy in the Middle Ages*, ed. C.H. Lawrence (London, 1965), 146–7.
[31] E. Miller, 'Medieval York', in *VCH Yorkshire, City of York*, 28–9, 54–6; cf. D.M. Broome, 'Exchequer Migrations to York in the Thirteenth and Fourteenth Centuries', in *Essays in Medieval History presented to T.F. Tout*, ed. A.G. Little and F.M. Powicke (Manchester, 1925), 291–300.
[32] Guisborough, *Chron.* 183, 232; *VCH City of York*, 28; and for the Treaty of York negotiated between the English and Scottish kings by the papal legate Otto in 1237, see A.A.M. Duncan, *Scotland: The Making of a Kingdom* (Edinburgh, 1975), 533.
[33] Rishanger, *Chron.* 129; Guisborough, *Chron.* 224; R.A. Griffiths, 'The Revolt of Rhys ap Maredudd', *Welsh History Review*, iii (1967), 121–43; *VCH City of York*, 28–9.

of York taking this responsibility very seriously indeed is the highly-organized series of mendicant sermons throughout his diocese orchestrated by John le Romeyn on 14 September 1291, presumably just after the news of the loss of Acre had reached the north of England. The most important sermon of all was to be delivered by Romeyn himself in York Minster on the same day. Preaching is unfortunately one of the more evanescent of human activities, and it may therefore be too easy to forget that oratorical gifts were among the most desirable qualities of a thirteenth-century archbishop.[34]

Not long after the *débâcle* at Acre, however, Edward I found it even more urgent to rely upon the prayers and sermons of his archbishops of York when in military confrontation with an enemy very much nearer York Minster than the eastern Mediterranean. He was not to be disappointed; and in June 1301, for example, the comparatively new Archbishop Corbridge, who had recently baptized Edward's first son by his second marriage, not only led his church in its devotions and processions but also offered a forty-day indulgence to those who prayed for the king's success in his impending expedition to Scotland.[35] During the previous summer, by yet another example of what Dr. Lloyd, Dr. Christopher Tyerman and other historians might interpret as a potentially improper extension of a crusading practice outside the crusading arena, the same archbishop had empowered two Franciscan friars to hear the confessions of those inhabitants of the province of York who planned to follow Henry de Lacy, earl of Lincoln, into the hazards which awaited them north of the Border.[36] In recent years, Dr. Alison McHardy has properly drawn attention to the much-valued services of the English prelates of a slightly later period in providing prayers and propaganda for the English royal cause during the Hundred Years War.[37] It seems equally worthy of emphasis that such services were deliberately called for, and quite as highly valued if not more so, by Edward I when he was confronted by the Scots a generation earlier.

Of all the prayers to be said on the king's behalf in the province of York, no doubt the ones Edward himself thought most efficacious were those uttered in the cathedral itself. Edward I self-evidently knew York Minster well, not least because during his increasingly frequent visits to the city after 1290 he was as likely to stay in the adjacent archiepiscopal palace as in his own castle, overcrowded as the latter was between 1298 and 1304 with the personnel and paraphernalia of the exchequer, king's bench and other governmental offices.[38] During those turbulent

---

34 *Letters from Northern Registers*, 93–6; *Reg. Romeyn*, i. 113; ii. 8–9; S. Lloyd, *English Society and the Crusade, 1216–1307* (Oxford, 1988), 42, 53, 55–6. For Thomas de Corbridge's sermon on the occasion of the election of an abbot of St. Mary's, York in 1298, the year before Corbridge was promoted to the archiepiscopate, see *The Chronicle of St. Mary's Abbey, York*, ed. H.H.E. Craster (Surtees Soc. cxlviii, 1934), 27.

35 *Letters from Northern Registers*, 149–50; *Chron. St. Mary's*, 30.

36 *Letters from Northern Registers*, 143. For Edward I's use of Dominicans and Franciscans to preach the crusade, see Lloyd, *English Society and the Crusade*, 51–6, 63–4; and for the possibility that the king adopted a crusading banner in his Scottish campaign of 1300, see C. Tyerman, *England and the Crusades, 1095–1588* (Chicago, 1988), 330–1.

37 A. McHardy, 'The English Clergy and the Hundred Years War', *Studies in Church History*, xx (1983), 171–8; id., 'Religious Ritual and Political Persuasion: the Case of England in the Hundred Years War', *International Journ. of Moral and Social Studies*, iii (1988), 41–57.

38 *Select Cases in the Court of King's Bench under Edward I*, ed. G.O. Sayles, iv (Selden Soc. lxxiv, 1957), pp. xcix–cv; Broome, 'Exchequer Migrations', 291–3; *VCH City of York*, 54–5, 340–1, 522. Like his son, Edward I may well have found that the most secluded accommodation available in York was within the Franciscan convent adjacent to his castle: see C. Bullock-Davies, *Register of Royal and Baronial Domestic Minstrels, 1272–1327* (Woodbridge, 1986), 32, 143.

years, moreover, Edward must have observed at first hand the early stages of the building of the new Minster nave, started as it was on 6 April 1291. Recently, Mr. David O'Connor has gone so far as to suggest (not at all implausibly perhaps) that it was the king himself who 'may have found the eleventh-century nave gloomy and old-fashioned, and put pressure on the authorities to hasten the construction of a new nave'.[39] On that possibility, however, judgement must remain suspended. Despite the characteristically strenuous efforts of Dr. John Harvey, no one has yet been able to prove who exactly was the architect responsible for the revolutionary Decorated design of the new York Minster nave. Whether he was at all associated with the royal masons who worked for Edward I in and around Westminster seems likely, but it is by no means certain.[40] In fact, and quite appropriately, the only indisputable memorial to Edward still surviving in York Minster is not in stone but in stained glass. Within the so-called Heraldic Window, on the north aisle of the nave and immediately opposite what seems to be a memorial window to Archbishop Greenfield, a set of eight shields, together with an accompanying series of royal figures, proclaims the arms of England and its king's relationships with the other monarchies of Christendom. It is no surprise to discover that the window in question was given by a prominent canon of York, Dr. Peter de Dene, who typifies the residentiary element within the York chapter particularly well in serving his two very different masters with apparent ease — his archbishop as a vicar general, and his king as a confidential envoy and councillor during the 1290s and 1300s.[41]

Of all Edward I's associations with York Minster, however, none was more carefully remembered by the cathedral clergy there than his presence for that auspicious occasion, on 9 January 1284, when the bones of their patron and recently-canonized saint were elevated 'ad altiorem locum' behind the High Altar, transferred, that is, from their previous resting place in a tomb towards the east end of the Minster nave.[42] The Translation of St. William of York, which made possible the construction of the new nave a few years later, must be seen, to adapt a phrase of Dr. Anne Duggan, as one of the grand 'state occasions' of thirteenth-century England, only comparable perhaps to the translation of St. Thomas Becket's relics at Christ Church, Canterbury, in 1220, and of St. Edward the Confessor's remains at Westminster in 1269.[43] The York ceremony of January 1284 itself was attended by both King Edward and Queen Eleanor as well as at least ten bishops and numerous magnates. The king himself not only helped to carry the chest containing St. William's bones to its new place of veneration, but also paid for the feeding of 200 poor: as Dr. Christopher Wilson has recently pointed out, he continued to make

[39] T. French and D. O'Connor, *York Minster: A Catalogue of Medieval Stained Glass*, fasc. 1: *The West Windows of the Nave* (Oxford, 1987), 3.
[40] J. Harvey, 'Architectural History from 1291 to 1558', in *A History of York Minster*, ed. G.E. Aylmer and R. Cant (Oxford, 1977), 149–60, 190; N. Coldstream, 'York Minster and the Decorated Style in Yorkshire', *Yorkshire Arch. Journ.* lii (1980), 93–5; J. Bony, *The English Decorated Style: Gothic Architecture Transformed, 1250–1350* (Oxford, 1979), 7–8.
[41] F. Harrison, *The Painted Glass of York* (London, 1927), 43–4; D.E. O'Connor, 'The Stained and Painted Glass', in *History of York Minster*, 349–50; *BRUO* iii. 2168–9.
[42] *Historians of the Church of York*, ii. 544–50; C. Wilson, *The Shrines of St. William of York* (York, 1977), 8–9.
[43] A.J. Duggan, 'The Cult of Saint Thomas Becket in the Thirteenth Century', in *St. Thomas Cantilupe, Bishop of Hereford: Essays in his Honour*, ed. M. Jancey (Hereford, 1982), 38–9; J.G.O. Neilly and L.E. Tanner, 'The Shrine of St. Edward the Confessor', *Archaeologia*, c (1966), 129–54.

gifts to the two shrines of the saint into the early years of the fourteenth century.[44] For the archbishop and chapter it was more gratifying still that St. William managed to perform a miracle for the occasion, even if a somewhat unusual and unexpected one. According to later York tradition, on the very morning of St. William's translation a certain Roger de Rypon, one of the servants of the Minster canons, was unwise enough to rest his head, presumably because of either exhaustion or boredom, on the base of the lectern from which the lessons for matins were actually being recited at the time. However, when a weighty stone crashed down on his skull from above, to everyone's astonishment, including his own, Roger shook his head to find that it was completely intact.[45] Not perhaps a very extraordinary nor prestigious miracle, but then it is usually agreed by hagiographers that St. William of York was a somewhat prosaic saint. Although it is not at all surprising that the late thirteenth-century canons of York were eager to make as much as they could of the supposed sanctity of the most obscure of their twelfth-century archbishops, it has alas to be conceded that the translation of his earthly remains in the 1280s failed in its primary purpose of transforming St. William into one of the more powerful of the great galaxy of northern saints.[46]

In a quite different way the events surrounding the Translation of St. William of York on 9 January 1284 exposed some of the political weaknesses of his archiepiscopal successors during the reign of Edward I. In the eyes of many contemporary chroniclers the most important event to occur in the Minster that day was not the translation of a dead archbishop but the consecration of a new bishop, none other than Antony Bek of Durham, at the hands of William Wickwane.[47] For the next twenty-seven years, until well after Edward I's own death, the archbishops of York were to be made acutely aware that their flamboyant suffragan was to be everything they could not be. Their sense of inferiority to that suffragan was indeed made evident at the very outset, for it was the new bishop-elect of Durham, and not Archbishop Wickwane, who actually undertook the expenses of St. William's translation.[48] More revealing still is the story, surely true in spirit if not necessarily to the letter, told by the Durham chronicler, Robert Graystanes, of an angry exchange between Wickwane and his new suffragan on the day after the ceremonies at York Minster. When the archbishop commanded Bek, by virtue of his new oath of canonical obedience to York, to excommunicate the prior and convent of Durham, the bishop allegedly rejoined with a forthright refusal: 'Yesterday, I was consecrated their bishop; and shall I excommunicate them today? No obedience will induce me to it.'[49] It has been correctly pointed out that the shadow of the recent humiliating conflict between Wickwane and the intransigent monks of St. Cuthbert over the former's right to visit the Durham chapter must have lain heavily over the

---

44 *Historians of the Church of York*, ii. 544–5; Wilson, *Shrines*, 8–9, 24.

45 *Historians of the Church of York*, ii. 545–6, 549.

46 However, Margery Kempe was only one of the many late medieval visitors to York who 'come on pilgrimage to offyr her at Seynt Wiliam': *The Book of Margery Kempe* (Early English Text Soc., Old ser. ccxii, 1940), 122. Cf. R.B. Dobson, 'The Later Middle Ages', in *History of York Minster*, 85–6.

47 *Records of Antony Bek, Bishop and Patriarch, 1283–1311*, ed. C.M. Fraser (Surtees Soc. clxii, 1953), 1–2; C.M. Fraser, *A History of Antony Bek, Bishop of Durham, 1283–1311* (Oxford, 1957), 37–8.

48 *Historians of the Church of York*, ii. 407–8. More remarkably still, Bek took part in the task of translating St. William's body to its new shrine in York Minster: Fraser, *Antony Bek*, 37.

49 *Historiae Dunelmensis Scriptores Tres*, ed. J. Raine (Surtees Soc. ix, 1839), 64.

proceedings at York in January 1284; but then that shadow was never really to lift for the rest of the reign, despite the temporary relief from violent conflict afforded by Wickwane's death at Pontigny in the following year.[50] Bishop Bek was to have his own even more spectacular collisions with the community of St. Cuthbert during the years ahead, but at no point did those collisions enable the archbishop of York to intervene in the diocese of Durham as *tertium gaudens*. Indeed, we are informed by the chroniclers in so many words that John le Romeyn allowed York's conflict with the Durham monks to go to sleep because he lacked the resources to do otherwise, that Henry de Newark was unwilling to re-open past issues because he was a subservient *familiarius* of Bek, and that Thomas de Corbridge similarly made no attempt to visit Durham 'eo quod timuit regem et vexacionem'.[51] Only after Bek had reached the end of his turbulent career, and Archbishop Greenfield was able to come to Durham cathedral to preside over his suffragan's interment ceremonies on 3 May 1311, did a viable *modus operandi* — and one highly favourable to the church of Durham at that — at last return to the northern province.[52]

So bald a summary naturally pays inadequate justice to the quite extraordinary, and quite extraordinarily well-documented, conjuncture of complex and insoluble disputes which makes the province of York during the reign of Edward I the *locus classicus* of jurisdictional confrontation within the late thirteenth-century English church. Needless to say, this cannot be the occasion to venture into territory so well traversed a generation ago, although perhaps not absolutely exhaustively, by Professor Robert Brentano and Dr. Constance Fraser.[53] However, it seems undeniable that what the obsessive York *versus* Durham disputes of the late thirteenth century reveal most of all, and more transparently that at any other time in the middle ages, are what might be termed the inherent structural weaknesses which underlay the metropolitical authority of the archbishops of York. What those weaknesses were is obvious enough; and all ultimately stemmed from the failure of the medieval north ever to achieve that metropolitan province with twelve subordinate bishops so over-optimistically envisaged by Pope Gregory I, when he ordered St. Augustine to re-found the Roman see of Eboracum in 601.[54] The problem facing Edward I's archbishops was not just that their province was so small, although it was indeed one of the smallest in Christendom; it was not just that their province suffered, in Brentano's phrase, from a 'lack of coherence', although it was indeed honeycombed by what Hamilton Thompson called 'spiritual republics' to a quite exceptional extent; and it was not just that the archbishops often suffered from irresponsive or even disobedient suffragans, although it was indeed an exceptional

50 Fraser, *Antony Bek*, 35–9; *Ann. Mon.* iv. 491. A reasonably successful compromise on the contentious issue of the archbishop of York's right to visit the church of Durham in vacancies of that see was achieved in Nov. 1286; but in effect it gave future bishops of Durham freedom from York metropolitan jurisdiction *sede plena*: Brentano, *York Metropolitan Jurisdiction*, 142–7.
51 Guisborough, *Chron.* 260, 351; cf. Brentano, *York Metropolitan Jurisdiction*, 165–74. After Romeyn's attempts to enforce his spiritual lordship over Bek were crushed in the parliament of Apr. 1293, 'no future archbishop of York meddled with his suffragan of Durham unless first sure of royal support': Fraser, *Antony Bek*, 114.
52 *Scriptores Tres*, 91; Guisborough, *Chron.* 391; Fraser, *Antony Bek*, 226–9.
53 Brentano, *York Metropolitan Jurisdiction, passim*; Fraser, *Antony Bek*, 100–75.
54 *Bede's Ecclesiastical History of the English People*, ed. B. Colgrave and R.A.B. Mynors (Oxford, 1969), 105–6.

misfortune to have Antony Bek as one's greatest subject.[55] Perhaps a more crippling weakness than any of these, as Professor Archie Duncan suggested some years ago, was quite simply that the metropolitan of York lacked enough suffragans.[56] Despite occasional attempts to lure the bishops of Whithorn, and occasionally even those of Orkney and the Isles, into his jurisdiction, as the archbishop of York gazed sadly at his overmighty subject of Durham and undermighty subject of Carlisle, he must always have been aware that he was forever denied the essential political function of a metropolitan — to promote episcopal harmony and common intent within his province or, if that failed, at least to play one bishop against another. To this extent at least, the archbishops of York during the reign of Edward I were nearly always like generals without an army.

Some such considerations may help to explain two of the more important and, at first sight, surprising features, one positive and one negative, of York metropolitical policy during the reign of Edward I. In the first place, no one examining contemporary comments upon Edward I's six archbishops of York can fail to be struck by the notorious readiness of them all to risk ridicule and personal humiliation, not to say the irritation and downright hostility of the king himself, in the cause of carrying their primatial cross erect within the province of Canterbury as well as that of York. Although the full story of this more or less interminable and very well-documented *casus belli* has never been told at length, it seems clear enough that it was in Edward I's reign that, to use Hamilton Thompson's phrase, 'the perennial squabble became a public nuisance'.[57] So much was this the case that an archbishop of York's abortive attempts to process through southern England with his cross erect before him was often the only activity of a northern metropolitan that the Edwardian chroniclers actually bothered to mention at all. In an age when chroniclers like Thomas Wykes thought the archbishops' behaviour 'frivolam' and even 'pompatice', and when this issue might lead to so distinguished a prelate as Greenfield being sent packing from a meeting of parliament, why did the Edwardian archbishops of York persist for so long in doing the pointless and even dangerous?[58] No doubt one must never underestimate the alarm felt by any medieval prelate at the prospect that he might appear before his church's patron saint on Judgement Day to answer the charge that he had alienated even an iota of that church's traditional liberties, but in the case of Edward I's archbishops of York one might be tempted to go even further. The tenacity and passion with which they fought to retain the privilege of making ceremonial progresses in the southern province *cruce elevate* presumably had its roots in the belief that this was both the single most concrete and potent symbol of an otherwise excessively feeble metropolitan position, and also the most flamboyant means possible of trying to redeem an otherwise acute inferiority of status.[59]

55 Brentano, *York Metropolitan Jurisdiction*, 23–41; *Reg. Romeyn*, ii. pp. xxv–xxxi; Thompson, *English Clergy*, 1–2.
56 Duncan, *Scotland*, 258–9, 275–80.
57 A.H. Thompson, 'The Dispute with Canterbury', in *York Minster Historical Tracts*, ed. A.H. Thompson (York, 1927), 14. Instances of the carrying of the archiepiscopal cross in the southern province were naturally the source of particular indignation within the community of Christ Church, Canterbury: see Gervase of Canterbury, *The Historical Works of Gervase of Canterbury*, ed. W. Stubbs (RS, 1879–80), ii. 247–8, 313, 322–3.
58 *Ann. Mon.* iv. 260, 281; Rishanger, *Chron.* 477; Gervase of Canterbury, *Hist. Works*, 322–3; *Johannis de Trokelowe et Henrici de Blaneforde, Chronica et Annales* (RS, 1866), 142–3.
59 The archbishop's right to have his cross carried before him anywhere in England had been long

Such status inferiority, to use an anachronistic phrase, also seems the most likely explanation for the failure of the archbishops of York to pursue their ambitions in a very different metropolitical sphere. On all the evidence at present available, they made no serious attempt to exploit the political and ideological conflict which arose between Edward I and the Scots in the early 1290s to revivify the traditional claim of their own metropolitan supremacy over the whole of Scotland. Such a claim one might certainly have expected, for the church of York's title to metropolitan authority throughout northern *Britannia*, also based on Gregory I's letter to St. Augustine in 601, had of course been stridently urged by twelfth-century archbishops, at least until the nine Scottish sees were made directly subject to the papacy itself by Celestine III's *Cum Universi* in 1192.[60] Nor is there any doubt that thereafter, and indeed to the very end of the middle ages, various archbishops and even more canons of York still toyed, if not usually very seriously, with the idea of reclaiming so prestigious a northern ecclesiastical empire. Shortly before he usurped the throne in 1483, Richard of Gloucester seems to have encouraged his partisans within the York cathedral chapter to re-open the case for English spiritual overlordship in Scotland; and it is even more remarkable that one of Henry VIII's most immediate responses to the news of Lord Thomas Howard's crushing victory at Flodden was to declare his intention of restoring York's metropolitan authority north of the Border.[61] By contrast, the Scottish ambitions of the northern metropolitans during the reign of Edward I seem much more muted. The Scottish clergy themselves, until and beyond the Agreement of Perth in 1335, were apparently highly apprehensive that an Edwardian political overlordship might carry in its wake a York ecclesiastical overlordship of their country: here was one of the most obvious reasons why the bishops of Scotland proved to be such staunch and influential supporters of Robert Bruce and his successors.[62] However, during Scotland's twenty years of trial at the hands of Edward I, and despite his archbishops of York's close and personal involvement in Scottish diplomacy from at least 1291, when le Romeyn, Newark and Greenfield all played a role in helping to administer the Great Cause at Norham together, there seems little evidence that they ever

established as the clearest possible expression of the traditional York view that 'there is nothing wonderful in there being two metropolitans in one kingdom, one of whom is not subject to the other': Hugh the Chantor, *History of the Church of York, 1069–1127*, ed. C. Johnson (London, 1961), 105, and cf. 129. In the event, the compromise finally reached on the issues at stake by Archbishops Islip and Thoresby in 1353 allowed each primate the liberty to have his cross born upright in the other's province: A.H. Thompson, 'Dispute with Canterbury', 14–15.

60  Hugh the Chantor, *Hist.* 126, 129; Duncan, *Scotland*, 274–8; J. Green, 'Anglo-Scottish Relations, 1066–1174', in *England and her Neighbours, 1066–1453: Essays in Honour of Pierre Chaplais*, ed. M. Jones and M. Vale (London, 1989), 62–3.

61  R.B. Dobson, 'Richard III and the Church of York', in *Kings and Nobles in the Later Middle Ages: A Tribute to Charles Ross*, ed. R.A. Griffiths and J. Sherborne (Gloucester, 1986), 146, 153–4; *Letters and Papers, Foreign and Domestic, of the Reign of Henry VIII*, ed. J.S. Brewer *et al.* (2nd edn. London, 1920) i. 1047–8; R.B. Dobson, 'The Last English Monks on Scottish Soil', *Scottish Historical Review*, xlvi (1967), 25.

62  The Anglo-Scottish agreement concluded at Perth on 18 Aug. 1335 specifically safeguarded the liberties of the holy church in Scotland and was therefore presumably designed to 'prevent the resurrection of metropolitan claims by Canterbury or York': R.S. Nicholson, *Edward III and the Scots* (Oxford, 1965), 215. Cf. A. Grant, *Independence and Nationhood: Scotland, 1306–1469* (London, 1984), 91; R.S. Nicholson, *Scotland: The Later Middle Ages* (Edinburgh, 1974), 52–3, 70–2; and for Edward I's own remarkably savage treatment of the bishops of St. Andrews and Glasgow after their capture in 1306, see M. Prestwich, 'England and Scotland during the Wars of Independence', in *England and her Neighbours*, 193–5.

claimed to exercise metropolitical authority north of the Tweed.[63] For whatever reason, perhaps because they were obstructed by Antony Bek or by Edward I himself, here again the archbishops of York seemed incapable of seizing one of their major opportunities.

One major reason for that incapacity, and for the weakness of the archbishops of York when confronted by their rivals, is almost certainly those archbishops' lack of material resources. By an unfortunate irony, most of the administrative activities centred around the medieval metropolitans of York are particularly well documented with the notable exception of the sources and extent of their revenues. However, and even though this is a hazardous field, there seems every reason to believe that most and perhaps all of Edward I's six archbishops of York suffered from intermittent financial emergencies and not infrequently genuine financial crises. The keepers' accounts (now preserved among the Ministers' Accounts in the Public Record Office) of the York temporalities during the period (1304–6), after Edward had confiscated the latter from Archbishop Thomas de Corbridge, are by no means easy to interpret, but they do seem to suggest the fundamental weakness that, by comparison with their fellow bishops, the archbishops of York were comparatively under-endowed with landed estates.[64] More certain still, because Edward's archbishops complained about these burdens bitterly and incessantly, were the baneful effects of papal *servitia* and other exactions at the time they received the pallium. Perhaps the most eloquent example of these lamentations is the letter sent by Archbishop Giffard to the Curia in 1270, which complains that: 'I am worn out with work, continually weary and obliged to consume the whole of my substance, both spiritual and temporal.'[65] To judge from their own surviving letters, debt was the spectre most dreaded by the York archbishops just as, according to the chroniclers, prudence, circumspection and even avarice had to be their most common characteristics.[66] As early as 1267 Archbishop Giffard had been in debt to two merchants of Lucca for no less than 1000 marks, and for the next twenty years his successors were more or less continuously involved in dealings with the Riccardi, who took the highly unusual step of opening a resident branch in the city of York at this very period. It is now well known that there existed a highly active credit network in late thirteenth-century, post-1290 Yorkshire; but all the evidence there is suggests that the archbishops of York were more likely to be the debtors than the creditors of that network.[67]

63 Rishanger, *Chron.* 240; *BRUO* iii. 2200; *Edward I and the Throne of Scotland, 1290–1296*, ed. E.L.G. Stones and G.G. Simpson (Oxford, 1978), ii. 22, 80.
64 PRO, SC 6/ 1,144 (1). Despite the survival of the occasional cartulary, *valor* (as in 1482–3) and other documents, the sources for the history of the pre-Reformation archbishops of York's estates are 'sparse in the extreme': see *British Library Harleian Manuscript 433*, ed. R. Horrox (Gloucester, 1979–83), iii. 217–32; C. Cross, 'The Economic Problems of the See of York: Decline and Recovery in the Sixteenth Century', *Agricultural History Review*, xviii (1970), 64–6.
65 *Letters from Northern Registers*, 35–7, 44–5; *Historians of the Church of York*, iii. 205; *VCH Yorkshire*, iii. 28; *Reg. Giffard*, 245; *Reg. Wickwane*, 288.
66 For the alleged 'avaricia maxima' of le Romeyn, see Guisborough, *Chron.* 260; and for Corbridge's qualities of prudence and circumspection, see Rishanger, *Chron.* 477.
67 *Reg. Giffard*, 153; and cf. 106, 115, 153, 254, 274; *Records of the Wardrobe and Household, 1286–1289*, ed. B.F. Byerly and C.R. Byerly (London, 1986), 235, 238; R.W. Kaeuper, *Bankers to the Crown: The Riccardi of Lucca and Edward I* (Princeton, 1973), 30–1, 61. For the most notorious case of an archbishop of York (le Romeyn) denounced in parliament for his illegal dealings with a Jewish financier (Bonamy of York), see R.B. Dobson, 'The Decline and Expulsion of the Medieval Jews of York', *Trans. Jewish Historical Society of England*, xxvi (1979), 45–6.

If Edward's six archbishops of York had little to offer in the way of capital, they did, however, have at their disposal something even more valuable to a needy king than money, namely ecclesiastical benefices. Whatever the deficiencies and limitations of the authority of an archbishop of York, he did control (at least in theory) perhaps the most extensive range of ecclesiastical patronage in Edward I's England. Such patronage was, moreover, all the more desirable because so many of its fruits, at Beverley, at Ripon, at Southwell and above all in his own cathedral church, could be enjoyed by clerks who had no intention of ever coming to reside in northern England at all.[68] It would therefore seem that for late thirteenth-century archbishops of York, as for fifteenth-century monks of Durham, such valuable patronage might justify Benjamin Disraeli's definition: 'Patronage is the visible and outward sign of an inward and spiritual grace, and that is Power.'[69] Alas, the archbishops of York in the years around 1300 probably saw their control over appointments in a very different light. So harried were the northern metropolitans of Edward's reign by the voracious appetites of pope, king and their own canons that in many ways this period in the history of the church of York provides the best-documented case in medieval England of what might happen when an extensive ecclesiastical patronage system could no longer be controlled by its overlord. It was precisely because York cathedral prebends like those of Masham, South Cave, Driffield, Langtoft and Wetwang were among the very wealthiest in the kingdom that 'canonries at York always led to dispute', a remark that seems even more applicable to the pontificate of Boniface VIII (1294–1303) than to those immediately before and afterwards.[70]

Accordingly, during the reign of Edward I, the archbishops of York usually found that their nominal control over the richest ecclesiastical benefices in the north brought them more pain than profit. In the eloquent words of Archbishop Wickwane to the notorious absentee treasurer of his cathedral, Bogo de Clare, there seemed a grave danger that greed for its milk and wool might lead to the death of the ecclesiastical sheep. If anything, Edward I's archbishops of York progressively found it more and more difficult to resist external presures to divert the wealth of York Minster's prebends to either papal or (much more often) royal administrators. Perhaps the most instructive example is provided by the 'golden prebend' of Masham itself, with revenues valued at £166 13s. 4d. in the *Taxatio Vetus* of 1291 and thus the richest single cathedral prebend in medieval England.[71] During the thirty years (1265–94) when the notorious Bogo de Clare ('multarum rector ecclesiarum vel potius incubator') held the prebend *in absentia*, he was more or less continuously resistant to any mandate issued by successive archbishops of York; and his successor as prebendary of Masham, John de Droxford (1296–1309), was not only one of Edward I's most distinguished clerical administrators, and keeper of his wardrobe, but also capable of an attempt to wrench the treasurership of York

---

The credit transactions of Edward I's archbishops of York would repay much greater attention than they have received here.

[68] *History of York Minster*, 52–75; K. Edwards, *The English Secular Cathedrals in the Middle Ages* (2nd edn. Manchester, 1967), 83–96.

[69] W.F. Monypenny and G.E. Buckle, *The Life of Benjamin Disraeli* (London, 1910–20), iv. 174; cited in R.B.Dobson, *Durham Priory, 1400–1450* (Cambridge, 1973), 144.

[70] T.S.R. Boase, *Boniface VIII* (London, 1933), 310; cf. *History of York Minster*, 55–6.

[71] *Reg. Wickwane*, 286; *Taxatio Ecclesiastica Angliae et Walliae Auctoritate P. Nicholai IV* (London, 1802), 297–8.

Minster from another royal clerk, Walter Bedwin.[72] In what Professor Prestwich has called the competition for rich livings among Edward I's clerks, the competition for dignities and prebends at the cathedral of York was the keenest of all.[73] No wonder that in the late 1280s and 1290s Archbishops John le Romeyn and Henry de Newark believed that the only solution to such scandals might be to divide outstandingly wealthy York cathedral prebends like Masham into three or five portions.[74] However, despite such intense competition and despite the ensuing legal disputes of almost unfathomable complexity — for many years during the reign of Edward I no one could be quite sure who the rightful dean or treasurer of York Minster actually was — the voracious appetite for these York dignities and prebends on the part of royal and papal *curiales* had its occasional compensations for Edward's archbishops.[75] The ferocity of the competition for their patronage may have put the latter under intolerable pressure, as indeed they often complained, but at least it ensured that they were never ignored. More interestingly still, it was the large number of prebends at the archbishops' disposal which provided the economic basis for that famous connection between the royal chancery and those south Yorkshire and northern Lincolnshire clergy who operated much of the engine of the English state for at least the next two generations. According to John Grassi, it was the first of Edward I's archbishops, Walter Giffard, who originally forged this connection; and there can in any case be no doubt that this clerical affinity was the most influential legacy of the thirteenth-century church of York to the England of Edward II and III.[76]

However, as Edward I's archbishops struggled to preserve their patronage from what they saw as the predators in high places around them, they were unlikely and unable to take so sanguine and long-term a view. When, to take the most striking case of all, Archbishop Thomas de Corbridge tried to retain control over his own favourite, and extremely lucrative, benefice at York Minster (the sacristship of St. Sepulchre's Chapel) he illustrated to perfection the dangers of resistance to the royal will in the matter of ecclesiastical patronage. Corbridge himself had been sacrist of this chapel, alternatively known as the chapel of St. Mary and the Holy Angels, for a decade before his election to the archbishopric in November 1299; and while at the Curia to receive consecration at the hands of Boniface VIII in February 1300, he had taken steps to secure for himself the future nomination to

72 *Flores Historiarum*, ed. H.R. Luard (RS, 1890), iii. 93; Le Neve, *Fasti*, ed. Jones, vi. 66; *CCR 1296–1302*, 223, 301; M. Prestwich, *War, Politics and Finance under Edward I* (London, 1972), 154.
73 Prestwich, *Edward I*, 546–7; A. Deeley, 'Papal Provision and Royal Rights of Patronage in the Early Fourteenth Century', *EHR* xliii (1928), 497–527.
74 *Reg. Gray*, 216–17; *Reg. Romeyn*, ii. 25, 306; *Calendar of Entries in the Papal Registers relating to Great Britain and Ireland: Papal Letters I (1198–1304)*, ed. W.H. Bliss (London, 1893), 496; Le Neve, *Fasti*, ed. Jones, vi. 66.
75 External pressures to control the choice of dean and treasurer of York Minster were never more intense than during the last decade of Edward I's reign, not least because of the ambitions of Francis Gaetani senior and junior, Boniface VIII's kinsmen: see *Reg. Romeyn*, ii. 302; *Reg. Greenfield*, i. 10–11, 12; *Cal. Papal Regs.* i. 580, 586, 611; ii. 28; *Select Cases before the King's Council, 1243–1482*, ed. I.S. Leadam and J.F. Baldwin (Selden Soc. xxxv, 1918), 18–27; Le Neve, *Fasti*, ed. Jones, vi. 6, 12–13; A.H. Thompson, 'The Treasurership of York and the Prebend of Wilton', in *Reg. Greenfield*, i. 299–305.
76 J.L. Grassi, 'Royal Clerks from the Diocese of York in the Fourteenth Century', *Northern History*, v (1970), 15–18; cf. *Reg. Corbridge*, ii. p. xxvii.

the sacristship.[77] Archbishop Corbridge's explicit refusal to confirm the appointment to the sacristship of Edward I's nominee, his notary, Master John Bush, was therefore understandable, but it led to an impasse which exposed the vulnerability of the archbishop of York more starkly than any other incident in the reign. When no lawyer could be found to speak on his behalf, the unfortunate Corbridge was sentenced to lose the York temporalities, provoking not only his own early demise but, according to Walter of Guisborough, Edward I's famous and mordant comment that 'Our father the archbishop has a lion's heart: soon he will have a sheep's tail.'[78] Whether or not that remark provides an insight into the personality of an often enigmatic monarch, it certainly illustrates only too well the dangers in store for an archbishop of York who dared to resist the royal will on any grounds whatsoever.

Nearly thirty years ago the late Dom David Knowles ended a lecture on the medieval archbishops of York in a somewhat disenchanted manner: 'We could not have expected the northern province to have rivalled Canterbury with its galaxy of great men, but if bishops are to be marked, like Tripos candidates, with Alpha and Beta, it is probable that Durham, Winchester and Lincoln, and perhaps other sees also, would be able to show more of the First Class than York.'[79] If so, and a considered judgement of the medieval metropolitans in the north as a whole is by no means easy to make, then it is not hard to diagnose some of the external pressures and internal weaknesses which prevented the late thirteenth-century archbishops of York from attaining that much desired First Class mark.

[77] A.H. Thompson, 'The Chapel of St. Mary and the Holy Angels, otherwise known as St. Sepulchre's Chapel, at York', *York Arch. Soc.* xxxvi (1945), Part II, 216–17; *Reg. Corbridge*, ii. pp. xiii–xiv; *Reg. Romeyn*, i. 134, 301, 385–9.

[78] As soon as Archbishop Corbridge had died (on 22 Sept. 1304), the dean and chapter of York admitted John Bush to the sacristship of St. Sepulchre's at Edward's request: see Borthwick Institute of Historical Research, York, Reg. 5A (Sede Vacante), f. 645; *Reg. Corbridge*, i. 31–2; Guisborough, *Chron.* 358–9; *Historians of the Church of York*, ii. 411–12; Dixon, *Fasti Eboracenses*, 356; Prestwich, *Edward I*, 547.

[79] M.D. Knowles, *The Medieval Archbishops of York* (Oliver Sheldon Memorial Lecture, York, 1961), 15–16. I am most grateful to Dr. David Smith for his comments upon an earlier version of this paper.

# The Ecclesiastical Patronage of the Earls during the Reign of Edward I

Elizabeth Gemmill

In some ways, ecclesiastical patronage rights may be thought to have declined in importance by the thirteenth century. The rights of most lay patrons were, qualitatively, a mere remnant of what they had once been for, by the late twelfth century, canon law had forbidden lay appointments to ecclesiastical benefices, and had suppressed the lay claim to possess and dispose of tithes or to grant out churches.[1] Yet decline was by no means the salient feature of patronage in the thirteenth century. The rights of patrons were, if circumscribed, firmly established as a form of property. They were protected by both canon and secular law, and they were eagerly exercised and defended. In at least one quarter, moreover, patronage rights were thriving, for the late thirteenth and the early fourteenth centuries saw an important increase in the quantity of royal presentations to benefices. Some of this growth can be explained in terms of the use of new rights acquired by the annexation to the Crown of several comital baronies; and there was, in addition, greater exploitation of wardship patronage and of patronage in the king's control by reason of episcopal and monastic vacancies.[2]

The subject of this paper is the ecclesiastical patronage of the twelve earls contemporary with Edward I. Their rights command special attention because of their sheer extent; together with other great lay landowners, the earls controlled an important proportion of the ecclesiastical patronage rights within the kingdom as a whole. However, while a study of their rights may shed light on the position of all lay patrons, the earls cannot be thought of as in any sense typical. There was no such person as a typical lay patron, because patronage was a right which could be enjoyed by men of widely different social, economic and political standing. The earls had little in common with the patron at the other end of the scale — the

---

1 For the development of canon law on the subject of patronage, see *Decretum*, II. C. 16, q.7 *passim*; and *Extra*, III. tit. 38 *passim*, in *Corpus Iuris Canonici*, ed. E. Friedberg (Leipzig, 1879–81). For the 11th-c. councils in England promulgating canonist doctrine, see *Concilia Magnae Britanniae et Hiberniae*, ed. D. Wilkins (London, 1737), i. 408, 410, 412–13, 415, 417. For a history of the development of patronage rights, see P. Thomas, *Le Droit de Propriété des Laïques sur les Eglises et le Patronage Laïque au Moyen Age* (Paris, 1906). A study of vital importance, esp. on the cognizance of advowson cases, is J.W. Gray, 'The *Ius Praesentandi* in England from the Constitutions of Clarendon to Bracton', *EHR* lxvii (1952), 481–509; see also C.R. Cheney, *From Becket to Langton: English Church Government 1170–1213* (Manchester, 1956), 109–17.
2 A. Deeley, 'Papal Provision and Royal Rights of Patronage in the Fourteenth Century', *EHR* xliii (1928), 497–527; P.C. Saunders, 'Royal Ecclesiastical Patronage in England, 1199–1351' (Oxford Univ. D.Phil. thesis, 1978), esp. 251–328.

humble knight, lord of perhaps only one manor, who presented to the church within it. The earls had rights in a number of churches and in several monasteries, and these rights were part and parcel of the landed inheritance which made them pre-eminent.

The nature of patronage rights depended on the type of ecclesiastical establishment in which they were exercised. Patronage rights were exercised in chapels and churches, monasteries and colleges, and episcopal sees, but in different ways. First, there was the patronage of chapels and churches, more usually known as the right of presentation or advowson. In common law, as a right which could be inherited or granted out, the advowson of a church was the ability to choose a clerk to be the next incumbent of that church when the last one had died or resigned, or had been removed for canonical reasons. When the patron had made his choice, he presented his man, usually by means of a formal letter, to the bishop of the diocese in which the benefice was situated. The bishop would then instigate enquiries to make sure the benefice was actually vacant, that the person presenting was the true patron, and that the candidate was qualified and suitable to minister to the needs of the people in the parish. If everything was in order, he then instituted him.

The patronage of religious houses was quite different from the advowson of churches, and it was much more heterogeneous. There were many ways in which the patron of a monastery might be recognized, depending on custom and according to the rule followed by the different religious orders. The commonest rights were licence and assent in elections, and custody during vacancies. Licence to elect was given by the patron when the old head of house had ceased to preside and a new head was needed. The patron would signify his willingness for the election to go ahead, and when it was over he would assent to the choice made. It is possible, indeed highly likely, that some patrons in practice exercised some influence in the choice of the new head, but there was no formal recognition in canon law of their right to do so. The right of custody was, at its fullest, the patron's enjoyment of the temporal income of the house, and of the advowson of churches in its gift falling vacant during the vacancy of the house itself.

These rights obtaining in vacancies and in the electoral process were those by which the patron was generally identifiable, even if he did not exercise all of them, because they were exclusive to him. Monasteries might recognize and honour their patron in a variety of other ways: by performing spiritual services, by showing him hospitality, by giving him (or those connected with him) pensions or corrodies, or even merely by maintaining close links with him and his family. This last was frequently true of Cistercian houses, which did not, on the other hand, allow their patrons the formal and traditional rights in vacancies and elections.[3] But although services such as these could certainly imply recognition of a patron, a house might well favour others than its legal patron in these ways, especially when it had received endowments from others than its original founder and his descendants.[4]

Most of the earls' patronage rights were in chapels, churches, monasteries and colleges, but there were other kinds of patronage too. Certain Marcher lords had rights of custody of the temporalities of Welsh episcopal sees during vacancies. Of

---

[3]   S. Wood, *The English Monasteries and their Patrons in the Thirteenth Century* (Oxford, 1955), esp. 3–4.
[4]   On patronage rights in English monasteries, see esp. H.M. Colvin, *The White Canons in England* (Oxford, 1951), 291–306; and Wood, *English Monasteries*.

these, the rights of Gilbert de Clare, earl of Gloucester, in the see of Llandaff were the most important. As well as enjoying the custody of the temporalities of the see within his lordship of Glamorgan, he had the right to collate prebends in the bishop's gift *sede plena*.[5] The king, however, was patron of most English bishoprics, and it was partly this, together with the rights enjoyed by the Crown in certain exempt royal chapels, which made the king a uniquely important patron.[6]

Patronage rights belonged to lands, and were inherited or transferred with them. They were accorded to the founder of a church or monastery as a way of acknowledging his gifts, and after his death they passed to his heir, or the new owner of his lands who became his representative. Lordship of a manor did not necessarily imply ownership of the advowson of the church within it, however, because the advowson might have been granted out to a monastery or episcopal see. Conversely, the manor itself might have been granted out or subinfeudated, and the advowson retained by the grantor. Manors and parishes were by no means always co-terminous, of course, but patronage rights were intimately bound up with land ownership and descent, and, more specifically, with the lordship of manors, baronies and honours.

The importance of the patron's rights to him depended very much on how he used them. The advowson of churches, first, could be a useful means of providing for clerks connected with him. An examination of the names of men whom the earls presented to benefices reveals some clear and not unexpected patterns.[7] Some of those presented were the earls' own relatives, the members of the family whom the laws of primogeniture did not favour. It was accepted by the church, and expected in the higher ranks of lay society, that younger sons and brothers would enter the church to secure an income in the form of an ecclesiastical benefice — or several. When Edward I wrote to Pope Martin IV on 24 May 1282, asking him to grant the (unspecified) request of Aymer, then the youngest son of William de Valence, earl of Pembroke, he pointed out that it was usual for the younger sons of magnates to hold a plurality of benefices.[8] There was, indeed, a precedent in canon law for special treatment of noble clerks: the decree of the Fourth Lateran Council of 1215, *De multa providentia*, while it forbade clerks to hold more than one benefice with cure of souls at the same time, admitted that 'noble and lettered' clerks deserved larger benefices, and it reserved the right of granting dispensations to such men under reasonable circumstances.[9] While the church's rules about pluralism, nonresidence and lack of age or orders tended to operate with a degree of flexibility in respect of noble clerks, the church by no means approved flagrant abuses such as those of the notorious occupier of benefices, Bogo de Clare, brother of Gilbert de Clare, earl of Gloucester.[10] While we can point to the excesses of Bogo de Clare

5 See esp. the explanation of these rights given by Gilbert Marshal, earl of Pembroke, in 1241: *Cartae et alia Munimenta quae ad Dominium de Glamorgancia Pertinent*, ed. G.T. Clark (2nd edn. Cardiff, 1910), ii. 518–19.
6 See M. Howell, *Regalian Right in Medieval England* (London, 1962); J.H. Denton, *The English Royal Free Chapels 1100–1300: A Constitutional Study* (Manchester, 1970).
7 For a list of the earls' presentations, see E.A. Gemmill, 'The Ecclesiastical Patronage of the English Earls during the Reign of Edward I' (Manchester Univ. Ph.D. thesis, 1988), 501–32.
8 *CCR 1279–88*, 188.
9 *Extra*, III. tit. 5, C. 28.
10 For Bogo de Clare's career, see A.H. Thompson, 'Pluralism in the Mediaeval Church', *Associated Architectural Societies' Reports and Papers*, xxxiii (1915–16), 53–7; M. Altschul, *A Baronial Family in Medieval England: The Clares, 1217–1314* (Baltimore, Md. 1965), 176–87, 306–8.

and others like him, for example, John le Bigod, brother of Roger le Bigod, earl of Norfolk, by no means all noble clerks were as greedy for benefices as they were.[11]

Provision for his clerical relatives was by no means the only consideration for an earl when he presented to a benefice. A larger number of the earls' presentations were of clerks engaged in their service. An examination of their ministers' accounts, of the witnesses to their charters, and of the numerous references to their clerks in royal records show that clerks were employed by earls in a variety of capacities. Typically, we find clerks working for the earls as local and household receivers, auditors, treasurers, secretaries, attorneys and executors. Many of these men would be presented by their masters to benefices.

The amount of annual income a clerk would get from his benefice obviously depended on the value of the church itself, which could vary from as little as, say, £5 per annum to as much as £100. The benefice might make up the clerk's entire salary or be only supplementary to it, but the important thing was that by using the churches in their gift to remunerate their clerical staff, the earls were able to save a good deal of their own money. Again, the church seems to have accepted this as a fact of life. Several bishops, for example, gave clerks of their dioceses leave of absence from their churches to serve their comital masters for given periods of time,[12] and some earls were able to secure from the papacy grants of leave of absence for longer periods for their clerks.[13]

These two groups (the earls' relatives and their servants) are perhaps the most important to notice among the men they presented, but a couple of other types are distinguishable as well. First, the earls sponsored scholars by presenting them to churches to provide them with an income while they pursued their studies.[14] Of course, a presentation was not the only way of giving support. Henry de Lacy, earl of Lincoln gave allowances in money to several scholars: in 1295–6, William of Fockerby and William of Litton were being given 73s. 4d. and 33s. 4d. respectively from the earl's manor of Bicester (Oxon.), though another scholar, Robert of Twyneham, fared less well; he had been paid 16s. 8d., but the payments were ordered to cease, 'quia male recessit de scolis'.[15] In 1304–5 Thomas of Litton, a scholar of Oxford, was being paid 33s. 4d. from Bicester, while John Mey, a poor scholar, was getting 41s. 4d. from Holborn, London, for his sustenance and cloth-

[11] In 1306 John le Bigod was given a papal dispensation to keep four churches so long as he resigned the other three he held: *Calendar of Entries in the Papal Registers relating to Great Britain and Ireland: Papal Letters 1305–1342*, ed. W.H. Bliss (London, 1895), 13.

[12] E.g. *The Rolls and Register of Bishop Oliver Sutton, 1280–1299*, ed. R.M.T. Hill (Lincoln Rec. Soc. xxxix, xliii, xlviii, lii, lx, lxiv, lxix, 1948–86), ii. 27; *The Register of Thomas of Corbridge, Lord Archbishop of York, 1300–1304*, ed. W. Brown and A.H. Thompson (Surtees Soc. cxxxviii, cxli, 1925–8), i. 72, 78; *The Register of William Greenfield, Lord Archbishop of York, 1306–1315*, ed. W. Brown and A.H. Thompson (Surtees Soc. cxlv, cxlix, cli–cliii, 1931–40), ii. 3 n. 2.

[13] E.g. *Reg. Sutton*, iii. 190–1: papal indulgence to John, duke of Brittany and earl of Richmond allowing six of his clerks to enjoy the fruits of their benefices without the obligation to reside in them; and *Cal. Papal Regs.* 7: papal indult to Henry de Lacy, earl of Lincoln allowing six clerks in his service to hold one benefice apiece, and two, already beneficed, to be non-resident for five years.

[14] Henry de Lacy and his mother assisted several clerks by presenting them to churches and then petitioning the diocesan on their behalf for leave of absence to attend the schools: see *The Registers of John le Romeyn, 1286–96, and of Henry of Newark, 1296–9*, ed. W. Brown (Surtees Soc. cxxiii, cxxviii, 1913–17), i. 69, 91, 137, 155; *Reg. Corbridge*, i. 78, 206; *Reg. Greenfield*, ii. 3 and n. 2.

[15] PRO, DL 29/1/1, m. 16r.

ing.[16] William of Fockerby was presented by the earl to a moiety of Kirkby la Thorpe (Lincs.) in 1296, while Thomas of Litton was presented to Winterbourne Earl's (Wilts.) in 1309.[17] This kind of support may have arisen out of a disinterested desire to promote learning, but it seems likely too that it was a form of investment. It is not unlikely that earls sponsored the education of clerks with a view to employing them as their own administrators.

Finally, the earls presented a number of royal clerks to the churches in their gift. That they should have done so is not in itself surprising, and sometimes the circumstances in which individual presentations were made suggest a reason for the choice. Edmund, earl of Cornwall presented Ralph of Hengham to Lanteglos-by-Camelford (Cornwall) in 1275 and to Middleton (W. Yorks.) in 1287.[18] Edmund owed his right to present to the latter church to the fact that the advowson belonged to the lands of Baldwin Wake, of which the king had given Edmund custody in 1282.[19] (Perhaps his choice of the prominent royal justice was an acknowledgement of the royal grant.) Sometimes the presentation of a royal clerk seems to have been the result of the king's interest in the benefice itself. In 1290 John of Brittany, earl of Richmond presented Walter Langton, then a clerk in the royal wardrobe, to West Thurrock (Essex).[20] His choice of Langton may have been influenced by the fact that the church was a prebend of St. Mary's, Hastings, which was one of the special royal free chapels mentioned above. And finally, the presentation of a royal clerk could be a way of appeasing the king when he had lost the right to an advowson: in 1293 Edmund, earl of Lancaster presented the royal clerk Adam of Osgodby to Gargrave (W. Yorks.) after recovering the advowson from Edward I in a suit of darrein presentment.[21]

In order to appreciate fully the importance of the earls' advowson rights — both to themselves as a sort of financial asset, and to the clerks for whom they were able to provide — it is worth pointing out the actual scale of their presentations. It is not possible to compile a list as full as that which can be made of royal presentations in this period because there survive very few of the earls' letters patent, in which their presentations would have been made. Nearly all the evidence comes from entries in episcopal registers, recording the institution of clerks to benefices and giving the name of the patron. Although we have excellent records for some dioceses in the latter part of the thirteenth century, for others (most especially the Welsh dioceses) there is very little.[22] Thus, we know a good deal about presentations made by the earls of Cornwall and Lincoln, whose ecclesiastical interests were, for the most part, located in dioceses for which the records are good (Lincoln, Exeter and York). On the other hand, we know proportionately little about the earl of Gloucester's presentations, since so many of the churches in his gift were in the diocese of Llandaff, for which we have but few institution records in this period. And there are many other gaps. Having said all this, the twelve earls contemporary with Edward I were responsible collectively for 225 successful presentations, most of which were

16 PRO, DL 29/1/2, m. 15d.
17 *Reg. Sutton*, i. 211; *Registrum Simonis de Gandavo, Diocesis Saresbiriensis, A.D. 1297–1315,* ed. C.T. Flower and M.C.B. Dawes (Canterbury and York Soc. xl, xli, 1934), ii. 717.
18 *Episcopal Registers of the Diocese of Exeter*, ed. F.C. Hingeston-Randolph (London, Exeter, 1889), i. 149; *Reg. Romeyn*, i. 167–72.
19 *CPR 1281–92*, 35.
20 *CPR 1281–92*, 362.
21 *Reg. Romeyn*, i. 134; PRO, KB 27/138, m. 58r.
22 See D.M. Smith, *Guide to Bishops' Registers of England and Wales* (London, 1981).

made between the late 1260s and the early 1300s.[23] The real total is probably a great deal higher. This does not, perhaps, compare very favourably with the number of royal presentations in this period (nearly 1000 presentations were made by Edward I) but it is, nevertheless, a sizeable total.[24]

Monastic patronage, like the advowson of churches, had a real financial value to the patron. First, the right of custody in vacancies was a direct source of profit. The issues of a monastery's lay fees could be put in the patron's own pocket for his use once necessary expenses had been met. How much profit a patron made during a period of custody would obviously depend on the length of the vacancy and the wealth of the house, but we know sadly little about custodies enjoyed by others than the king. Custody was not supervised by bishops, and consequently there is very little evidence about it in episcopal registers. There are, however, some very interesting accounts of the earl of Cornwall's custody of the priory of Eye (Suffolk) with its manors in the years 1296–8.[25] These show that he got income not only from purely temporal things, mostly rents and corn sales, but also, surprisingly, from tithes, which were, strictly speaking, spiritualities. His net profit, after outgoings, for the periods covered by the accounts was just over £111. This custody was, admittedly, an unusually long one: Eye priory was alien; and the vacancy was probably protracted by the Anglo-French war. Custodies often only lasted for a matter of weeks, but the profits made by the earl do go some way towards explaining why custodies were considered such an important right.

It is difficult to assess the evidence about presentations during vacancies to benefices in the gift of the house concerned. On the one hand, not one of the 225 presentations made by the earls seems to have been by reason of a monastic custody; on the other hand, there were complaints to the pope about papal reservations, which prevented patrons from exercising the right of presentation to churches in the gift of monasteries.[26] Furthermore, when the earl of Lincoln actually gave up his right of custody in the priory of Spalding (Lincs.) in 1309, he reserved his right to present to the benefices in its gift during vacancies, and to put a porter at the gate at such times.[27] What is plain is that monasteries would often present livings in their gift to clerks of their patron's affiliation, a case in point being the Cluniac priory of Lewes (W. Sussex), which presented clerks connected with its patron, John de Warenne, earl of Surrey, to churches in its gift on several occasions.[28] Many of the churches belonging to the prior had, in fact, been given to it by the earl's ancestors.[29] Monasteries would, in addition, sometimes provide their patron's clerks with pensions or corrodies. An interesting arrangement was made by the earl of Lincoln at the priory of Bradenstoke (Wilts.). The earl asked the prior

---

23 Gemmill, 'Ecclesiastical Patronage', 501–32.

24 See R.A.R. Hartridge, 'Edward I's Exercise of the Right of Presentation to Benefices as shown by the Patent Rolls', *Cambridge Historical Journ.* ii (1927), 171–7.

25 *Ministers' Accounts of the Earldom of Cornwall, 1296–1297*, ed. L.M. Midgley (Camden Soc., 3rd ser. lxvi, lxvii, 1942–5), ii. 156–7 (1 Aug. 1296 – 1 Aug. 1297); and PRO, SC 6/996/12, mm. 4–5 (21 Nov. 1297 – 21 Apr. 1298).

26 See e.g. the draft proposals for discussion in the king's council in March 1274 prior to the Council of Lyons II (1274): *Councils and Synods, with other Documents Relating to the English Church, II: 1205–1313*, ed. F.M. Powicke and C.R. Cheney (Oxford, 1964), ii. 811.

27 PRO, DL 36/2/132. Copies of this charter are in DL 42/2, f. 271v, and BL Add. MS 35296, fos. 73v, 108, 143v–144r.

28 Gemmill, 'Ecclesiastical Patronage', 168–9.

29 See esp. *The Chartulary of the Priory of St. Pancras of Lewes* (Sussex Portion), ed. L.F. Salzman (Sussex Rec. Soc. xxxviii, xl, 1933–5), i. 10–23.

to give a clerk, Gilbert de Rolling, an annual pension until he, the earl, should provide him with a benefice to the value of 40 marks. Not wishing, apparently, that the priory itself should be solely responsible for the payment, the earl arranged for the sum of 66s. 8d. to be paid to the prior annually from his own estates.[30]

This kind of co-operation must have depended on the amount of goodwill which existed between a house and its patron — it was not a formally constituted right. Returning to the more traditional patronage rights, licence and assent were of symbolic importance as representing the patron's interest in elections. Although patrons had no right to intervene in the elections themselves, their right to know what was going on, and to give their consent to it, was often jealously guarded. If the patron was not consulted, or if he failed to execute his rights in accordance with canon law, the appointment of the new head of house could be seriously delayed.

The importance of patronage rights is perhaps most clearly revealed in royal attempts to acquire them. Part of the increase in royal ecclesiastical patronage at the end of the thirteenth century, and at the beginning of the fourteenth, was at the expense of the earls. This can be accounted for largely by the fact that the earldoms of Cornwall and Norfolk, with their appurtenant patronage rights, came into the hands of the Crown by inheritance and forfeiture respectively. Also important was Edward I's acquisition of estates belonging to the earldoms of Albemarle and Devon.[31] In addition, in the early 1290s, Edward managed to annex to the Crown the patronage rights in Welsh bishoprics traditionally associated with a number of Marcher lordships, on the basis that they were usurped *regalia* and ought rightfully to belong to the Crown.[32] Rather less successful, at least in relation to the earls, were the king's attempts to wrest patronage rights by a new interpretation of royal charters, and by the assertion that they did not really belong to land held by the other party, but to the Crown.

Sometimes royal claims had a firm basis, although there was room for dispute. In 1282 the abbey of Tewkesbury (Gloucs.) fell vacant. It was in the patronage of Gilbert de Clare, and there was no question about that; but there was a difficulty with the abbey's dependent house, St. James, Bristol. The earl claimed custody of the priory because of the vacancy at Tewkesbury which was of his patronage.[33] The constable of Bristol castle, however, was certain that the custody should belong to the king because the priory was appurtenant to the castle.[34] The crux of the problem was that Tewkesbury belonged to the honour of Gloucester, held by the earl, and St. James belonged to the *caput* of the honour, Bristol. When the Clares acquired the honour through marriage in 1217, the town and castle of Bristol were retained by the Crown.[35] Another case involved the advowson of the church of Rockingham (Northants). In a suit of darrein presentment brought by the Crown against the earl of Cornwall in 1295, one of the royal arguments was that the king held the castle of

---

30 PRO, DL 29/1/1, mm. 12d, 14r; DL 29/1/2, m. 18d.
31 K.B. McFarlane, 'Had Edward I a "Policy" towards the Earls?', *History*, l (1965), 145–59; repr. in id. *The Nobility of Later Medieval England* (Oxford, 1973), 248–67.
32 *Rot. Parl.* i. 42–3, 93–4, 97–8. See esp. for discussion of royal rights in Welsh bishoprics, M. Howell, 'Regalian Right in Wales and the March: The Relation of Theory to Practice', *Welsh History Review*, vii (1975), 269–88.
33 PRO, SC 1/10/17.
34 PRO, SC 1/2/186.
35 Altschul, *A Baronial Family*, 25–8. For the foundation of the priory, see W. Dugdale, *Monasticon anglicanum* (new edn. ed. J. Caley, H. Ellis and B. Bandinel, London, 1817–30; repr. 1846), ii. 61; iv. 333–5; *VCH Gloucestershire*, ii. 74.

Rockingham and the lands and demesnes which constituted the chief part of the manor or town. In fact, the earl owned the manor of Rockingham, but the royal attorney preferred to refer to his possessions as 'other lands and tenements', which were merely 'other members' of the manor held by the king to which the advowson ought to belong. In the end, the earl granted his right to the king.[36]

A corollary of royal acquisitiveness of patronage rights was the practice of reserving them in grants of lands. The 'statute' *Prerogativa Regis*, which probably dates from the early years of Edward I's reign, made this quite clear:

> When the lord king gives or grants any manor or land with appurtenan-
> ces, unless he makes in his charter or writing express mention of the
> knights' fees, advowsons of churches and dowers, when they fall in,
> belonging to the aforesaid manor or land, then nowadays, the king
> reserves to himself the same fees and advowsons, with the dowers;
> although among other persons it has been observed otherwise.[37]

The 'statute' had a retrospective as well as a future application. It was used as a basis of royal arguments in lawsuits, including the Rockingham case already referred to. Particularly thought-provoking is the last statement in the 'statute' about other people's practices in their charters. Advowsons are frequently mentioned in the earls' charters, when they were granting them out as appurtenances of manors; also noteworthy are the occasions on which the earls, and others too, made it quite clear that they did not wish to part with their patronage rights. The earl of Cornwall had a policy of reserving advowsons, wardships, marriages, escheats and entry fines when he farmed out manors;[38] and when he and his wife were legally separated in 1294, he made a settlement on her of estates to the value of £800, but kept for himself the knights' fees, advowson of priories and churches and escheats.[39] There are several examples of earls subinfeudating manors and reserving the advowsons for themselves;[40] and we have already seen how the earl of Lincoln kept the advowsons when he gave up his custody right in Spalding priory.[41] The earls did, however, continue to give advowsons to the church.[42]

By reserving their patronage rights in the grants they made, the earls were, in effect, doing the same as the king. To what extent they were consciously learning from royal policies it is difficult to say, but they were certainly in a position to know of, and to be influenced by, royal thinking and practices. That the king took the lead

---

36 PRO, KB 27/144, m. 35d; see also *Reg. Sutton*, ii. 144–5.

37 *Statutes of the Realm*, ed. A. Luders *et al.* (London, 1810), ii. 227. For the dating of the 'statute', see F.W. Maitland, 'The "Prerogativa Regis"', *EHR* vi (1891), 367–72; repr. in id. *Collected Papers*, ed. H.A.L. Fisher (Cambridge, 1911), ii. 182–9.

38 The manors of Chesterton (Oxon.), Hambleden (Bucks.) and Remenham (Berks.) were farmed out in 1285–6 with these exceptions, as were Harwell (Oxon.) in 1290–1, and Hambleden in 1297–8: PRO, SC 6/1095/12–14.

39 *CPR 1292–1301*, 63–5. For the dispute between the earl and his wife, see *Registrum Epistolarum Fratris Johannis Peckham, Archiepiscopi Cantuariensis*, ed. C.T. Martin (RS, 1882–5), iii. 982, 995–6; *The Register of John Pecham, Archbishop of Canterbury, 1279–1292*, ed. F.N. Davis *et al.* (Canterbury and York Soc. lxiv, lxv, 1908–69), ii. 246; *Reg. Sutton*, iii. 33–7.

40 Gemmill, 'Ecclesiastical Patronage', 277–9, 281–6.

41 Above, 70.

42 Gemmill, 'Ecclesiastical Patronage', esp. 366–83.

in this matter, and that the earls followed his policy, is just one aspect of the way in which Edward I strengthened the Crown's role as the interpreter, controller and protector of lay patronage rights, and as the leader of all lay patrons in the kingdom. For example, on several occasions in his reign there were complaints voiced by the laity about papal provisions to English benefices and about financial exactions, not only by the papacy but by foreign mother houses as well.[43] A recurrent theme in these complaints was the impoverishment of the English church, which had been endowed by the king and the lay magnates. All such grievances were expressed under royal auspices, were subjects for discussion in the king's council, were written at the king's behest, or were presented in the king's parliament. Often, the interests represented were mainly those of the Crown, and those of the magnates and other patrons were only indirectly concerned; but there is no real need to doubt the involvement of the magnates — themselves, in a sense, the representatives of all lay patrons — in the drafting of these complaints.

Royal legislation, too, served to control and to interpret the right of patronage and all that went with it. The Statute of Westminster I (1275) confirmed the right of free election and protected monasteries from having to offer hospitality to all and sundry.[44] The Statute of Mortmain (1279) initiated what became a licencing system for endowments.[45] The Statute of Westminster II (1285) forbade alienation by religious of their endowments, and provided means of recovery of endowments when the services for which they had been given were not performed.[46]

In the light of all this, what happened in 1297 is most interesting. Edward I, as we know, outlawed the clergy and seized their lay fees because they would not grant him a subsidy.[47] The reaction of the earls and barons — the very patrons who had founded and endowed the church, whose possessions had now been seized in such high-handed manner — does not seem to have been one of outrage. They seem *not* to have remonstrated with the king, nor to have pleaded on behalf of the clergy; it seems likely that we would know about it had they done so, just as we know about the petitions on behalf of alien religious, whose goods the king had seized in 1295.[48] On the contrary, it appears as if the lay magnates actually supported the king's action. According to the Evesham chronicler, it was the barons and knights who determined the date of Easter 1297 as the term for the final forfeiture of clerical goods.[49] And the earl of Cornwall, who had custody of the priory of Eye at this time, made sure that the fine for redemption of its lay fees was paid to the king.[50] Moreover, while the magnates supported the king's actions, the king, for his part, respected the rights of patrons. When clerical goods were to be finally forfeited, they were, ultimately, to revert to the original patrons.[51] And the

---

43 The texts of these grievances are in *Councils and Synods, II*, ii. 811–14, 1232–6; *CCR 1288–96*, 134–5; *Memoranda de Parliamento, 1305: Records of the Parliament at Westminster in 1305*, ed. F.W. Maitland (RS, 1893), 313–14; and see *Rot. Parl.* i. 207–8, 220–1.
44 *Statutes of the Realm, I*, ii. 26–7.
45 *Councils and Synods, II*, ii. 864–5. For the history of the statute and its effects, see S. Raban, *Mortmain Legislation and the English Church 1279–1500* (Cambridge, 1982).
46 *Statutes of the Realm, I*, ii. 91–2; and see Wood, *English Monasteries*, 36–7.
47 On the crisis faced by the clergy in 1297, see J.H. Denton, *Robert Winchelsey and the Crown 1294–1313* (Cambridge, 1980), esp. 100–35.
48 Gemmill, 'Ecclesiastical Patronage', 335–41.
49 J.H. Denton, 'The Crisis of 1297 from the Evesham Chronicle', *EHR* xciii (1978), 570.
50 *Ministers' Accounts of the Earldom of Cornwall*, ii. 156–7.
51 Denton, 'The Crisis of 1297', 570; M.N. Blount, 'A Critical Edition of the Annals of Hailes

royal threat made at the ecclesiastical council in January 1297, attempting to induce the clergy to pay up, was that the king, earls and barons would dispose of clerical goods according to their own wishes, if they did not.[52]

I have laid considerable emphasis in this paper on the practical and financial value of patronage. No less important, but altogether more immeasurable, was the social influence and the prestige which patronage could bring. All these survived the limitations which the church had imposed on the rights of patrons; and the notion on which patronage rights was based — that the clergy were bound to give the laity some kind of return for their endowments — was in some ways gaining ground, in terms of its broader implications. Not only were individuals concerned with their rights in individual churches and monasteries; the laity saw themselves collectively as endowers of the church as a whole, and expected to have a say in how its endowments were used. The church's possessions, in short, were held in trust, and the conditions of their tenure were being forcefully laid down.

(MS Cotton Cleopatra D iii, fos. 33–59v) with an Examination of their Sources' (Manchester Univ. MA thesis, 1974), 107.
52 *Bartholomaei de Cotton Monachi Norwicensis Historia Anglicana*, ed. H.R. Luard (RS, 1859), 317–18.

# The Public and The Private:
## Women in the Pre-Plague Economy

### P.J.P. Goldberg

The historian of women below the level of the aristocracy is not overburdened with sources for the thirteenth century. Two sources of especial value, viz. court rolls and coroners' rolls, do, however, survive in some quantity from at least the latter part of that century. This essay will, by way of reviewing some recent work that makes use of these two sources, explore aspects of the lives of women, with particular reference to their economic function and the independence of action that may or may not have followed from this. Two related issues are directly addressed. How far were women's lives bounded by the private realm of the home as opposed to the public realm of the community? And how far were women's identities submerged within a patriarchal family structure?

Perhaps because of the comparative paucity of sources, or the greater attractiveness of urban records, the study of women in English rural society before the Plague is still in its infancy. None of the earlier writers (Power, Dale, Abrams) attempted to reconstruct manorial court rolls or coroners' inquests. Other more accessible sources (wills, or records of indictments under the Statute of Labourers) are too late to be of use. The few writings on the subject consequently command attention and, in the case of the three recent works considered here, deservedly so, for each has an important contribution to make derived from painstaking and highly imaginative analysis of primary source materials.[1] Pioneering research is no easy matter, and this present essay is not intended to negate these pioneering efforts. Indeed, each of the works explored here has raised important questions and served to open up new areas of research. Scholarly endeavour can, however, only be furthered by constructive debate. This paper is concerned to show that some of the patterns initially suggested, though attractive, may be optical illusions. In so doing, it offers in the context of social change in the decades before the Black Death some alternative hypotheses, but no dogmatic solutions. In this respect it is designed to open doors, not to slam them shut.

The use of coroners' rolls as a major source for the social historian of the later Middle Ages has been pioneered by Hanawalt. This may not at first sight appear an

---

1   I am grateful to participants at the Newcastle conference for their questions and observations, and to Peter Biller for commenting on an earlier draft. The recent works considered here are B.A. Hanawalt, *The Ties that Bound: Peasant Families in Medieval England* (New York, 1986); J.M. Bennett, *Women in the Medieval English Countryside: Gender and Household in Brigstock Before the Plague* (New York, 1987); R.H. Hilton, 'Lords, Burgesses and Hucksters', *Past and Present*, xcvii (1982), 3–15; repr. in id. *Class Conflict and the Crisis of Feudalism* (London, 1985), 194–204.

obvious source, but its advantage is that it throws a rare light on the everyday activities even of the poor, the young, and the old of either sex, groups usually lacking from other sources, including court rolls. In her recent major study of peasant society, Hanawalt has used evidence relating to death by misadventure to explore the lives of peasant women and men. She argues that this is a source 'free of many of the recording biases of manorial, ecclesiastical, or royal courts', because individuals are recorded 'on an involuntary basis'.[2] From a sample of coroners' rolls drawn from six counties and ranging in date from the second half of the thirteenth to the early fifteenth centuries, she reconstructs a familial economy based on complementary, but separate, gender-specific spheres of activity. By employing data relating to place of death, she attempts to show 'women's chief sphere of work as the home and men's as the fields and the forests'.[3] This version of the public-private dichotomy may appear superficially attractive, but it is the contention here that as a conceptual framework it neither reflects contemporary circumstances nor accords with the evidence presented. To consider Hanawalt's thesis further it is necessary to reconstruct these circumstances from her own data.

Hanawalt divides the particular circumstances of the individual at the time of death under eight broad heads, viz. agricultural work, construction, crafts, supplementary economic activities, housework, travel, playing, and personal. Note that she classifies housework apart from supplementary economic activities, surely an unreal distinction. The numbers of adults and of children of either sex falling under each of these heads, as shown in tables 2, 6, and 7, unfortunately do not tally precisely with those presented in the aggregative table 8. The differences are, however, comparatively minor in all but three instances.[4] Under travel, the aggre-

---

2   B.A. Hanawalt, 'Seeking the Flesh and Blood of Manorial Families', *Journ. Medieval History*, xiv (1988), 35. The coroners' rolls are a more problematic source than Hanawalt's observations indicate. It has been shown elsewhere that much material has been lost and that more was never recorded. The reporting of suspicious and accidental deaths seems to have been directly related to accessibility to the coroner. The distance the community was from the main road or from the coroner's place of abode, the state of the roads according to the time of the year, and the length of time to the next 'return day', were all related to the chance of a death being investigated and recorded. There is little here to suggest that the cases that were reported were not broadly representative of all cases 'at risk' to be reported. Further difficulties arise, however, with the way circumstances of any given case are reported by the jurors. Many accidental deaths were unwitnessed, and the jurors thus obliged to reconstruct the causes from circumstantial evidence. As shall be argued below, some deaths may have been homicides or suicides, but were presented by the jurors as 'accidents', either through genuine error or uncertainty, or in response to wider communal interests. For a discussion of these problems, see R.F. Hunnisett, 'The Reliability of Inquisitions as Historical Evidence', in *The Study of Medieval Records*, ed. D.A. Bullough and R.L. Storey (Oxford, 1971), 206–35; S.J. Stevenson, 'The Rise of Suicide Verdicts in South-East England, 1530–1590: the Legal Process', *Continuity and Change*, ii (1989), 37–75; J.B. Post, 'Crime in Later Medieval England: Some Historiographical Limitations', *Continuity and Change*, ii (1989), 219–21; S.J. Stevenson, 'Social and Economic Contributions to the Pattern of "Suicide" in South-East England, 1530–1590', *Continuity and Change*, ii (1989), 225–62.
3   Hanawalt, *Ties that Bound*, 145. Much the same assertion is made by Given in his study of homicide from the observation that women were more likely than men to be killed at home: J.B. Given, *Society and Homicide in Thirteenth-Century England* (Stanford, 1977), 117, 141–2, 147–8, 180. Such a spatial division is very much a male ideal, most clearly articulated in instructional treatises and at times when the economic status of women was particularly depressed, as in the 16th and 19th c.: Stevenson, 'Social and Economic Contributions', 227–8 citing Dod and Cleaver; P.J.P. Goldberg, 'Women in Fifteenth-Centuiy Town Life', in *Towns and Townspeople in the Fifteenth Century*, ed. J.A.F. Thomson (Gloucester, 1988), 109.
4   The totals given in tables 2, 6, and 7 combined are as follows (the equivalent total in table 8 is shown in parentheses): agricultural work 224 (227); construction 119 (104); crafts 46 (47); sup-

gative table is short by sixty-eight. Likewise under construction, a smaller category, it is short by fifteen, but under personal it includes twenty-one additional individuals. The breakdown of the broad heads into specific activities, for example 'cutting timber' or 'going to the mill', is only presented in the aggregative table 8. It thus follows that the attempt to reconstruct gender-specific patterns of activity associated with accidental death is hazardous on two counts: on the one hand, tables 2, 6, and 7 record only the broad heads; and on the other, table 8, which does provide greater detail, is not absolutely compatible with the earlier gender-specific tables. There must, therefore, be an element of guess-work in attempting to reconstruct gender-specific patterns from Hanawalt's incomplete data in order to test Hanawalt's own conclusions.

It must immediately be regretted that Hanawalt attempts to distinguish neither chronological trends nor contrasting regional patterns, though much of her material is drawn from the East Midlands and predates the Peasants' Revolt, and her most detailed sources are the published Bedfordshire rolls for the years 1265–76 and 1300–17.[5] The basic premise on which Hanawalt's interpretation rests, namely that the circumstances surrounding accidental death reflect everyday reality, is, moreover, of itself questionable. It fails to pursue questions relating to the regularity with which death by misadventure was duly reported and recorded (an issue to which this essay will return) and relative risk attached to specific activities. If all activities were equally hazardous, her premise might have some merit, but patently this is not the case. Some tasks are, and were, inherently far more risky than others. The coroners' evidence demonstrates this. The corollary is that certain other tasks were comparatively risk-free. The circumstances surrounding accidental deaths thus do not reflect everyday reality, but merely activities that were inherently risky. Table 8 shows, for example, that working with carts, horses or carriages accounted for 380 incidents, or rather more than one-fifth of all the accidental deaths in the sample. Carting itself accounted for well over half of all the incidents classified under agricultural work. In contrast, fieldwork, herding, and milking collectively accounted for less than one-quarter of the incidents so classified. Indeed, only one accidental death is recorded within the sample associated with milking, a traditional female employment to which some time must have been devoted twice daily for lengthy periods of the year. Under the heading housework, drawing water was far and away the most dangerous activity, accounting for 92 of the 162 recorded incidents.

To sum up briefly, a high proportion of deaths in the fields was associated with carting and a high proportion of deaths around the home was associated with fetching water. If these twin observations are set against what is known of the sexual division of labour in medieval society (i.e. carting was men's work, fetching water was women's work — the coroners' rolls confirm this) then the foundations for Hanawalt's observations regarding separate spheres of activity begin to appear flimsy. Men more often suffered death by misadventure in the fields because some of the work they did there was much more dangerous than most of the work performed by women, for example, weeding crops, milking, shearing, reaping, and

plementary economic activities 112 (119); housework 168 (162); travel 620 (552); playing 299 (304); personal 223 (244).
5    Hanawalt, *Ties that Bound*, 269–70; *Bedfordshire Coroners' Rolls*, ed. R.F. Hunnisett (Bedfordshire Historical Rec. soc. xli, 1961).

binding.[6] Women more often suffered death by misadventure around the home because some women's work, notably fetching water, but to a lesser degree cooking over an open fire, was considerably more hazardous than most male household activities. However, this is not the same as saying that 'women's chief sphere of work' was the home, and men's was 'the fields and the forests'.

The point is further illustrated from Hanawalt's analysis of the seasonality of accidents. Seasonality is determined by three factors, viz. the greater administrative enthusiasm of some coroners around 'return days', notably in February, April, July, and October, seasonal factors influencing ease of communications, and the underlying incidence of accidental deaths. Hanawalt considers only the last, but administrative factors do not in this case appear to detract unduly from her conclusions. She finds that there was a peak in accidental deaths around June and August, which she attributes to exhaustion over the long harvest season, but she is puzzled by the peak in female deaths during May.[7] The answer probably lies in a similar pattern of exhaustion associated with the seasonal concentration of work associated with lambing, calving, haymaking, weeding, and dairying, all tasks that drew disproportionately on female labour. The absence of reference within the coroners' rolls to women being savaged by rabid sheep, or smothered by stacks of hay, probably explains Hanawalt's own assertion that women's work 'does not seem to be particularly seasonal'.[8]

Some other disturbing observations follow from the data presented in the tables previously noted. Hanawalt argues that there is comparatively little evidence that infanticide was practised in medieval England. She has noted only three cases from a sample of over 4000 homicides recorded in coroners' rolls and gaol delivery rolls.[9] Infanticide is, of course, a secret crime, and is by its nature unlikely to be recorded as such in official sources, but she further claims that the coroners' rolls provide no evidence that infanticides were disguised as accidental deaths, since the majority of infants below one year 'died in fires in their cradle or in their house, thus indicating that they were cared for'.[10] The dubious quality of this care is

---

6  Ironically, the one death associated with milking a cow was that of a man: *Beds. Coroners' Rolls*, 15–16. For a brief discussion of women's work in the countryside, see Bennett, *Women in the Med. English Countryside*, 115–20.
7  Hanawalt, *Ties that Bound*, 146. It may be that the seasonal pattern only reflects the types of work undertaken, e.g. carting grain was specifically a harvest-time task. For a fuller discussion of seasonality, see Post, 'Crime in Later Medieval England', 219 and n. 33; Stevenson, 'Rise of Suicide', 44–5, 48–50.
8  Hanawalt, *Ties that Bound*, 146. For women's seasonal tasks, see K.D.M. Snell, *Annals of the Labouring Poor: Social Change and Agrarian England 1660–1900* (Cambridge, 1985), 19, 53–5, 393; G.E. and K.R. Fussell, *The English Countrywoman* (London, 1953), 35–42.
9  Hanawalt, *Ties that Bound*, 102.
10  Ibid. 102. It is striking that the destruction of infants either by burning or by drowning are the most common means of actual infanticide recorded in ecclesiastical courts during the 15th c. In one atypical case a boy of nearly seven was drowned: R.H.Helmholz, 'Infanticide in the Province of Canterbury during the Fifteenth Century', in id. *Canon Law and the Law of England* (London, 1987), 158–9, 164. Hanawalt has previously suggested that 'it seems plausible that at least some of the accidental drownings and burnings of children might have been concealed infanticides', but she ultimately concluded that there was 'little evidence of infanticide', on the apparent grounds that the level of accidental deaths associated with female infants was not disproportionately large: B.A. Hanawalt, *Crime and Conflict in English Communities 1300–1348* (Cambridge, Mass. 1979), 156, 182. Schmitt has noted that infanticide commonly took the form of 'simulated accidents': J-C. Schmitt, *The Holy Greyhound: Guinefort, Healer of Children since the Thirteenth Century*, trans. M. Thom (Cambridge, 1983), 35.

illustrated in a case cited by Hanawalt of a one-year-old boy left in the charge of his five-year-old brother. 'Because the older boy was such a poor custodian ... the cradle caught fire.'[11] Hanawalt further reasons that 'one would expect that a higher proportion of female infants would be killed compared to male infants, but the sex ratios are quite close'.[12] This last observation is not supported by the evidence. Tables 4–7 show that thirty-seven female infants died at home, mostly whilst engaged in 'personal' activities, which invariably means sleeping in a cradle, as against only fifteen male infants in equivalent circumstances. For children of one year, there is indeed a more equitable balance in the numbers of either sex dying at home or under 'personal'; but for older children, many more boys than girls are recorded as suffering death by misadventure at home, for the most part in play-related accidents.

Hanawalt comments on the lack of adequate supervision that often lies behind these accidents, but the observation noted in 1267 in respect of a Bedfordshire house fire in which two little girls of two and five years died — that both the father *and* the mother were working in the fields — is significant.[13] Child-rearing did not necessarily confine married women to the home. It is unclear from Hanawalt's analysis of childhood accidents why boys aged between two and twelve should have been so much more susceptible to accidents at home than their sisters, but the finding only makes the comparatively large number of deaths of female babies in the privacy of the family home all the more suspicious. One is tempted to suggest that the ostentatious staging of an accident that was duly reported to the appropriate authorities is, like the bride burnings of contemporary India, the most logical intepretation of the evidence. Far from showing that infanticide, and specifically female infanticide, was not practised, the coroners' rolls may, in fact, lend weight to the suspicion that it was.

A related observation concerns the number of adult males (N = 79) as opposed to adult females (N = 16), a ratio of 5:1, recorded as dying as a consequence of 'personal' activities.[14] The imbalance between the sexes is just as marked, sometimes more so, under the heads of agricultural work, construction, crafts, supplementary economic activities, travel, and play; but in these cases some imbalance is to be expected, since adult males were more likely to engage in dangerous activities contained within these categories. Only under household–related activities did the number of recorded deaths of women outnumber those of men. As previously seen, most of these deaths were associated with fetching water, and thus took place not in the privacy of the house at all but outside, albeit within close proximity of the house. The pattern of 'personal' accidents is, however, more puzzling. These, according to table 8, happened for the most part whilst the victim was sleeping, sitting and, to a lesser degree, bathing. Comparison between tables 1 and 2 further suggests that a proportion of the deaths of males, presumably whilst sitting or sleeping, must have happened at home. It is again difficult to see how men

---

11 Hanawalt, *Ties that Bound*, 158.
12 Ibid. 102.
13 Ibid. 176–8; *Beds. Coroners' Rolls*, 5. The frequency with which children were left unattended is independently suggested by the activities of one Agnes Kaynel on the manor of Wakefield, who was said to deceive the neighbours' children into giving her bread, barley, and oats: *Court Rolls of the Manor of Wakefield, 1274–1297, I*, ed. W.P. Baildon (Yorkshire Arch. Soc., Rec. ser. xxix, 1901), 127.
14 Hanawalt, *Ties that Bound*, table 2, 271.

were so much more vulnerable than women to death by misadventure under these circumstances, particularly as Hanawalt notes that many night-time accidents were associated with fires and collapse of buildings.[15]

The lack of a more detailed breakdown of the evidence must make this present analysis hazardous. One worrying possibility, however, is that accidents relating to women in the actual privacy of the home were not as regularly recorded as similar accidents involving men. The same may also be true of accidents within the home involving small girls. Perhaps the clue lies in Hanawalt's own account of how information came to the coroner. She describes that 'when villagers saw someone die or found a body that showed evidence of unnatural death, they notified one of the coroners'.[16] However, what if 'the villagers' did not witness the accident or find the body, but only the immediate family within the confines of the family home? There would not have been the same need for witnesses to have their names publicly cleared of possible complicity in the death of a neighbour or even a stranger by the inquest jurors, and the loss of the deodand (the profit that accrued to the king at the expense of the misfortunes of others) may have been resented. Whereas the death of an adult male, often a householder and tenant, would need to be made public, for example in the manorial court, the death by misadventure of a woman, not herself the head of a household or a tenant, would not demand the same publicity. The family, and the community, would have little cause to involve the coroner so long as there was no suspicion that the death was other than an accident.

Let us turn again to Hanawalt's basic thesis regarding the gender-specific division of labour into spatially distinct spheres of activity. The statistical basis for her analysis of place of accident is set out in table 1, but certain problems of interpretation arise. Hanawalt has chosen to round the sample sizes at her disposal. In the case of adult males, the sample is rounded down from the 1058 noted in table 2 to 1000. The difference is thus comparatively slight and should have little impact on the numbers recorded under each of five heads, viz. home, private property, public areas, work areas, and bodies of water. The number of adult women in the sample, however, is rounded up without explanation from 237 to 300, an increase of nearly 27% per cent. Perhaps a number of women were identified by location, but not by activity, within the rolls, but the way the extra sixty-three individuals are distributed could have a statistically significant effect on the proportion under each head. Hanawalt compares the proportions of women dying by misadventure according to location with the equivalent proportion of males whose deaths are similarly located. Table 1 shows, for example, that whereas 29.5% of women died at home, the same was true of only 11.8% of men. Similarly, 37.7% of men died in work areas, including fields, but only 17.5% of women. These figures may be broken down further: 5.9% of women died in a public well as against only 1.6% of men; 5.8% of women died in a neighbour's home or close, but the same was true of only 3.8% of men. These figures demonstrate, so Hanawalt claims, that '*when women did venture from their home* [my emphasis], it was often in connection with their domestic duties', and that women 'spent more time than men visiting and working with their neighbors'.[17]

15 Ibid. 146.
16 Ibid. 12.
17 Ibid. 145.

These are spurious conclusions based on a flawed methodology. This present analysis has suggested that many facets of women's work are under-reported because they are not intrinsically dangerous. A further problem has been suggested, namely, that female deaths by misadventure within the family home may also be under-reported. Gender-specific patterns of where accidents occur will thus only reflect patterns of where most *risky* gender-specific activities occur and are reported. It is thus rather more significant that only eighty-seven female deaths are recorded in the home, as against 118 male deaths, than that the proportion of female deaths is greater than the equivalent proportion of male deaths. Since Hanawalt almost certainly includes the close under 'home', the point is all the more significant given the evidence that two domestic activities specific to women, viz. cooking and fetching water, are known to have been unusually hazardous, and that the latter activity, at least, was sufficiently public that accidents were likely to be recorded.[18] If the two more detailed statistics cited by Hanawalt are converted from percentages to absolute numbers, then a different picture emerges. Falling down a public well, surely equally risky for males and females, in fact accounts for almost as many male deaths (N = 16) as female (N = 18). Visiting neighbours seems, despite Hanawalt's remarks, which are no doubt influenced by contemporary literature, to have been much more of a male activity, or at least more hazardous for men. Thirty-eight men met accidental deaths whilst on their neighbours' property, but less than half that number (N = 17) of women.[19]

As Bennett has observed, 'medieval peasants lived in a very public world', and

---

18  The number of women included under 'home' in table 1 exactly equals the number of women included under 'household related', which specifically includes fetching water (table 8) in table 2: Hanawalt: ibid. 271, 274. Not all accidents involving falling down wells can have been witnessed. This raises the possibility that some such 'accidents' were in fact suicides or even homicides. Hanawalt does not consider suicides in her study despite acknowledging that they were part of the coroner's business. This must be because suicides are not so recorded in the medieval rolls. Stevenson has argued that the 'accidental' drownings of female servants in wells may often disguise suicides. The 13th-c. Beds. coroners' rolls contain an instance of a female servant so drowning, but also of a male servant. That another male servant discovered a body when he went to fetch water from a well suggests that fetching water from wells was a task assigned to servants regardless of gender. The same rolls record the death from falling down a well of a man who had been ill for several days. The circumstances, though not the verdict, suggest suicide. To be thrown down a well appears also as a recognized mode of homicide. In a telling incident recorded in a York case of 1362, a father threatened to throw his daughter down the well if she would not agree to marry the man he had chosen to be her husband. In 1269 the jurors reported that one Ivetta, sempster was murdered and her body thrown down a well by her husband. This may suggest a more common pattern not reported in the coroners' rolls; in parts of contemporary India wives are sometimes murdered by being pushed down wells. (I am grateful to Jean Charsley for this observation.) Hanawalt, *Ties that Bound*, 11, 13; Stevenson, 'Rise of Suicide', 64–5; id., 'Social and Economic Contributions', 227–8; Borthwick Institute of Historical Research, York, CP.E.85; *Beds. Coroners' Rolls*, 11, 42, 52, 63, 86.

19  It was not always the case, as Hanawalt implies, that people fell down public wells whilst fetching water. She cites the case of an old woman who fell down a public well allegedly trying to retrieve a straw when drunk: Hanawalt, *Ties that Bound*, 236. This last raises the question of how the jurors were in a position to know. Where accidents were unwitnessed, and this may often be inferred from the record, the jurors must often have relied on circumstantial evidence. Their verdicts may often thus border on fiction. Jurors may, moreover, sometimes have had vested social and communal interests in concealing suspected suicides and even homicides as accidental deaths: Stevenson, 'Social and Economic Contributions', 227–41. For male prejudice against women going outside the home to visit neighbours, see n. 3 above.

peasant women were drawn into that public world as a matter of course throughout their lives.[20] Even married women with young families *did* venture from their homes; only part of the married woman's day was spent preparing food, lighting fires, fetching water, cooking, washing, cleaning, making beds or in other domestic tasks. Older daughters and, in some more substantial households, female servants must often have assisted with at least some of these tasks.[21] Spinning, exclusively a female prerogative and a useful supplement to the household economy, was not specifically an indoor activity. Rather more time must have been spent in a range of activities associated with agriculture. The nature of these tasks would have varied according to the time of year, the type of agriculture practised, the status of the woman, and the amount of land being worked. It has already been suggested that spring was an exceptionally busy time for women, though this would have been most true of pastoral regions. Harvest, likewise, may have placed particular demands upon women as reapers and binders. Women were generally responsible for dairying activities, milking both cows and ewes, and manufacturing butter and cheese. They also cared for any poultry, geese and chickens alike, and collected the eggs. The garden or croft was probably also the woman's domain, by nature of the range of plants regularly found growing there. These included herbs, used both for cooking and medicinally, various vegetables and pulses that could either be for domestic consumption or for sale and, according to the *Inquisitiones Nonarum* of 1341, apples, hemp, and flax, these last being industrial crops regularly worked by women.[22] It was women also who sold some of the surplus produce that fell within their domain in the local market or neighbouring town.[23] The cash return that resulted from the sale of spun yarn, eggs, butter, cheese, poultry, flax, bread, ale and even woven cloth may have afforded women some independence of action, and a very real degree of economic clout within the familial economy.[24]

This last observation serves to question Bennett's assertion, in her recent study of women in English manorial society of the later thirteenth and early fourteenth centuries, that women were then, as at other periods, subordinate to men, and that this subordination 'was rooted in neither government nor economy, but rather in the household'.[25] Her analysis transforms the public-private definition of gender from the broad spatial dimension, adopted by Hanawalt, to the cultural dimension and the dynamics of the 'small, conjugal household'. Whereas 'public men' (hus-

---

20 Hanawalt, *Ties that Bound*, 6.
21 In 1274 a female servant rising at dawn to fetch water was accidentally drowned: *Beds. Coroners' Rolls*, 63; Hanawalt, *Ties that Bound*, 159–62, 183–4.
22 Bennett, *Women in the Med. English Countryside*, 117; C.Dyer, paper given to York Univ. Medieval Society, May 1989; 'Ballad of a Tyrannical Husband', in *Reliquiae Antiquae*, ed. T. Wright and J.O. Halliwell (London, 1843), ii. 196–9; R.H. Hilton, 'Small Town Society in England Before the Black Death', *Past and Present*, cv (1984), 62; A. Clark, *Working Life of Women in the Seventeenth Century* (London, 1919), 47–9.
23 Bennett, *Women in the Med. English Countryside*, 119; Hanawalt, *Ties that Bound*, 116; Clark, *Working Life of Women*, 49, 51.
24 This observation is hard to document, but women did have access to money in rural society. Hilton comments on the part played by women as money-lenders. Margery Kempe, to cite urban evidence from a later date, had use of the profits of her brewing business: R.H. Hilton, *The English Peasantry in the Later Middle Ages* (Oxford, 1975), 103–4; *The Book of Margery Kempe*, ed. S.B. Meech and H.E. Allen (Early English Text Soc. cxii, 1940), 9; Clark, *Working Life of Women*, 28–9, 49.
25 Bennett, *Women in the Med. English Countryside*, 198.

bands) spent much of their lives as independent householders, 'private women' (wives), and to a lesser degree daughters, passed their lives as dependants.[26] Leaving aside the probability that not all who achieved adulthood married, and so acquired status as householders or dependants, this view is perhaps unduly influenced by the source material from which it is derived.[27] Manor court rolls are a legal record. As such, they were compiled according to legal conventions and relate solely to business conducted within the customary court according to customary law. Customary law afforded single women, including widows, different legal rights and standing from married women. The latter were liable to be represented in court by their husbands, who were legally responsible for any debts that they might incur, whereas single women, if tenants of the lord, personally owed suit of court and, as was apparently true of some Brigstock widows, might occasionally act as pledges in their own right. This legal discrimination against women, and especially married women, clearly supports Bennett's wider thesis, but the court's need to identify and record the marital and household status of the women who were from time to time the subject of its deliberations may tend to accentuate the significance of these distinctions in the mind of the historian. As Eileen Power long ago observed, legal demands do not always correspond to wider social realities.[28] The way peasant women and men appear, or fail to appear, within the court rolls may be an imperfect, or even misleading, guide to how they were perceived outside the court.[29]

The economy, as much as the nuclear family, served to shape women's lives. For those in peasant society with insufficient land and no craft, the period was characterized by growing hardship as demographic pressure intensified through the later thirteenth century and culminated in the famine years of the early fourteenth century. Increasingly, smallholders must have been forced to surrender their holdings to their more substantial neighbours, or enter into maintenance agreements with younger folk not their heirs, in the face of mounting debt and price inflation. The parallel growth in the numbers of the landless served only to depress wages and intensify competition for work.[30] The consequence of these processes was an increase in poverty. The point may be illustrated on both the manorial and the individual level. In 1326 the bishop of Ely's court at Littleport registered disquiet at

---

[26] This position is qualified: ibid. 7–8.
[27] The current trend is to emphasize the opportunities open to non-inheriting sons to acquire land and to marry, but this is to underestimate the probability that in some arable regions at this period widows with land found marriage partners at the expense of landless daughters, that many smallholdings ceased to be economically viable, and that the numbers of the landless and the poor increased: L.R. Poos and R.M. Smith, ' "Legal Windows Onto Historical Populations"? Recent Research on Demography and the Manor Court in Medieval England', *Law and History Review*, ii (1984), 143–4; R. M. Smith, 'Hypothèses sur la Nuptialité en Angleterre aux xiiie–xive Siècles', *Annales: Economies Sociétés, Civilisations*, xxxviii (1983), 124–7; id., 'Some Thoughts on "Hereditary" and "Proprietary" Rights in Land under Customary Law in Thirteenth and Early Fourteenth Century England', *Law and History Review*, i (1983), 115–26.
[28] E. Power, *Medieval Women* (Cambridge, 1975), 34; Goldberg, 'Women in Fifteenth-Century Town Life', 107.
[29] Adult male customary tenants are most frequently recorded. Women, on the other hand, are not particularly well represented in manor court rolls; and the young, the old, and the landless of either sex are only noted by chance.
[30] C. Dyer, *Standards of Living in the Later Middle Ages: Social Change in England c. 1200–1520* (Cambridge, 1989), 124–5, 133, 218.

the influx of landless migrants onto the manor to take advantage of common land of the fen. The court ruled that they were to perform the same services demanded of any resident 'anelepyman' or 'anelepywymman'.[31] Two examples from the Bedfordshire coroners' rolls demonstrate something of the plight of individuals. In 1273 Joan Fine came from Milton Bryant to Houghton Regis, carrying her two-year-old son, and begged shelter. Three years earlier, Lucy Pofot, a widow whose enhanced legal status helped to alleviate her impoverished circumstances not one jot, apparently made at least part of her living by prostitution. But Joan and Lucy are known to us only because their poverty led to tragedy.[32] How typical were they? In the face of greater competition in the labour market, a possible decline in numbers of family holdings, and an intensification of arable agriculture at the expense of pastoral (with its superior work opportunities for female labour) was there then a feminization of poverty such as was to occur again in the south-east during the eighteenth century?[33] To this question there are no easy answers, but some fragmentary pieces of evidence demand consideration.

The dire poverty that was the lot of both women and men on the margins of society is well illustrated from coroners' evidence. The late thirteenth-century coroners' rolls for Bedfordshire reveal a number of cases of poor folk, mostly women, dying of exposure or of misadventure whilst begging from door to door of their neighbours. In 1267, for example, Sabinia, an old woman, drowned in a stream when out begging bread and in 1273 Beatrice Bone collapsed and died whilst begging from door to door.[34] The Spalding serf lists, dating to the second half of the thirteenth century, likewise record numbers of 'vagabond' offspring, both female and male.[35] The problem was perhaps most acute in the towns, a constant magnet for the poor and dispossessed, as can be most graphically illustrated from London sources. Trokelowe described seeing the poor and needy starving in the streets in 1316, the corpses of those who had already succumbed lying in the lanes.[36] In 1315 a crush for alms ended in the deaths of five men and four women. Similarly, in 1322, twenty-six women were among the fifty-five poor folk who were crushed to death awaiting a distribution of alms outside the gates of the house of the Dominicans.[37] One unfortunate woman, Lucy Faukes, was murdered the same year, as she returned to her lodging house, by a couple who wanted to steal her clothes.[38] Ironically, it may in part have been the greater welfare provision of urban society, and the greater efforts made to ensure food supplies, that attracted

31 *The Court Baron*, ed. F.W. Maitland and W.P. Baildon (Selden Soc. iv, 1891), 146.

32 *Beds. Coroners' Rolls*, 42, 66. The widow Wymark was held in prison for three weeks charged with taking a hare found in her yard; she was released because she had no goods: *Court Rolls Manor of Wakefield, I*, 141.

33 Snell, *Annals of the Labouring Poor*, 50, 56–8, 65, 309, 348–50.

34 *Beds. Coroners' Rolls*, 4, 87. For an example of an old man dying in similar circumstances, see ibid. 89.

35 BL, Add. MS 35,296, fos. 209–11v, 221v.

36 H.S. Lucas, 'The Great European Famine of 1315, 1316, and 1317', in *Essays in Economic History*, ed. E.M. Carus-Wilson (London, 1962), ii. 58.

37 E. Rickert, *Chaucer's World*, ed. C.C. Olson and M.M. Crow (New York, 1948), 349–50; *Calendar of Coroners' Rolls of the City of London 1300–1378*, ed. R.R. Sharpe (London, 1913), 61. These represent sex ratios of 125 and 111.5 respectively. Little weight can be placed on two small, chance samples but they accord with the view that women did not outnumber men in town society before the Plague: see below 85–7.

38 *Cal. Coroners' Rolls of the City of London*, 68.

some rural migrants. The question arises: if rural society did witness a feminization of poverty, did more women than men migrate into towns as a consequence?

Hilton has argued that female migrants were especially prominent among the 'flood of recruits' into town society prior to the Black Death, and he has claimed that, in the case of Halesowen, women constituted 'perhaps three-quarters of the total between 1272 and 1350'.[39] This is a remarkable assertion, but the court roll evidence upon which it is apparently based is probably spurious. Certainly women feature prominently in the borough court rolls, and may even outnumber men in the frequency of their appearance, but this is only a reflection of the gender-specific incidence of the sorts of transgression of borough custom most likely to feature in the court rolls. These mostly concern trading offences, such as forestalling and regrating, for which women were frequently presented. The earliest surviving Norwich leet rolls (dated 1287–1313), for example, record considerable numbers of women presented for forestalling grain and fish, or regrating cheese.[40] Large numbers of York women were similarly presented in 1304 for regrating in breach of the city's ordinances of 1301.[41] One Alice Bompe is noted in the first surviving Colchester court roll (dated 1310–11), indicted for forestalling grain, poultry, butter, cheese, and eggs.[42] Other presentments concern slander, in which women again feature prominently — as at Hull in 1308–9, when Emma de Karlel called Joan de Wilflet a common whore and priest's whore, thus losing her credit in the eyes of another woman trader with whom Joan was hoping to do business — and assault, the victims of which were often women.[43]

This high profile within the borough court would only serve to strengthen the prejudice that the 'ungoverned' woman was a trouble-maker. Two examples from the earliest Colchester court roll illustrate the point and help explain why, in the much smaller borough of Halesowen, there was particular need for women seeking lodging within the community to find pledges to guarantee their good conduct. Alice la Spellere was indicted as a receiver of stolen wool and poultry, for breaking her neighbour's fences, and for receiving thieves. Agnes de Ardleye was similarly indicted for selling ale after hours to foreigners 'that by their drunkenness and noise the neighbours are frightened'.[44] It is apparently this high incidence of pledging that Hilton has identified as evidence of a very high rate of female migration into the town of Halesowen from the surrounding countryside, such that women greatly outnumbered men. This may in fact be an optical illusion.[45] What the evidence actually reflects is the marginal economic status of women in towns before the Plague, a status that forced many the wrong side of the law simply to survive, rather that any underlying preponderance of females.[46]

The early fourteenth-century pentice rolls for Chester list numbers of women

39 Hilton, *Class Conflict*, 200.
40 Norfolk Record Office, Norwich, NCR Case 5 Shelf b, leet rolls 3, 5–8, 19; *Leet Jurisdiction in the City of Norwich during the XIIIth and XIVth Centuries*, ed. W. Hudson (Selden Soc. v, 1892).
41 M. Prestwich, *York Civic Ordinances, 1301* (Borthwick Papers, xlix, 1976), 27–8.
42 *Court Rolls of the Borough of Colchester*, trans. I.H. Jeayes, ed. W.G. Benham (Colchester, 1921), i. 2.
43 Hilton, 'Small Town Society', 71; PRO, SC 2/211/11, m. 10; *Court Rolls Borough of Colchester*, 2, 7, 11, 16 etc.
44 *Court Rolls Borough of Colchester*, 19, 45.
45 Hilton, *Class Conflict*, 200, 212; id., 'Small Town Society', 65.
46 See n. 37 above.

seeking legal restitution of goods pawned, often for small cash sums.[47] A more distressing circumstance is suggested by the evidence for particular civic concern with prostitution at this period; the beadle of one London ward was even running a protection racket for prostitutes in 1344.[48] Such concern was not voiced again until the depression of the later fifteenth century and surely reflects the scale of the problem.[49] Urban sources thus paint a very negative picture of opportunities for women, something that may well have discouraged potential migrants. Nor does analogy with post-Plague evidence, or an assertion that low sex ratios are characteristic of medieval urban society, stand up to critical scrutiny. The low sex ratios found for a number of north European towns of the late fourteenth and fifteenth centuries apply specifically to the post-Plague economy and are not, for example, applicable to the towns of Tuscany, with their preference for male labour, over the same period, or even to London in the sixteenth century where a similar pattern of demographic expansion at a time of economic stagnation worked to the disadvantage of women.[50]

If towns did indeed fail to attract women migrants on the same scale as men, then is there evidence to suggest that opportunities for women in the countryside were rather greater than the evidence for a deteriorating economic climate (for those with little or no land and widespread poverty) would suggest? Bennett suggests, from an analysis of the incidence of fines paid by women for breach of the Assizes of Bread and Ale on three Midland manors, that this may indeed have been true in respect of brewing and baking, craft activities that she argues were increasingly feminized in the face of 'the economic problems of the decades that preceded the plague'.[51] This hypothesis does not address the problem of poorer women and unmarried women who would not have had access to such crafts, but it also raises a number of problems of interpretation.[52] Bennett's explanation depends on the sort of public-private spatial analysis pursued by Hanawalt. She argues that 'because brewing was an almost universal female skill that confined workers to the

---

47  *Selected Rolls of the Chester City Courts*, ed. A. Hopkins (Chetham Soc., 3rd ser. ii, 1950), 54, 68, 94–5: *Court Rolls Manor of Wakefield, I*, 274–5.

48  *Calendar of Plea and Memoranda Rolls of the City of London 1323–1364*, ed. A.H. Thomas (Cambridge, 1926), 212.

49  Ibid. 109, 125, 173, 188, 212; *The Making of King's Lynn*, ed. D.M. Owen (London, 1984), 249, 268, 419; PRO, SC 2/211/11, m. 5v; Goldberg, 'Women in Fifteenth-Century Town Life', 118–21; R.M. Karras, 'The Regulation of Brothels in Later Medieval England', *Signs*, xiv (1989), 399–433.

50  P.J.P. Goldberg, 'Women and Work in Two English Medieval Towns: A Study in Social Topography', in *Regional and Spatial Patterns in Past Populations*, ed. R.M. Smith (forthcoming). Herlihy has argued that the high sex ratio found in post-Plague Florence is a phenomenon of the large industrial city, and that rather lower sex ratios are to be associated with smaller towns; e.g. in Bologna in 1395 males slightly outnumbered by females. It may be, however, that north Italian towns became more masculinized between the late 14th and early 15th c.: D. Herlihy, 'The Tuscan Town in the Quattrocento: A Demographic Profile', *Medievalia et Humanistica*, new ser. i (1970), 99–101.

51  Bennett, *Women in the Med. English Countryside*, 126.

52  McIntosh has argued that at Havering in the later medieval period 'the great majority of . . . tradeswomen and craftswomen were married, usually to men of middling economic level': M.J. McIntosh, *Autonomy and Community: The Royal Manor of Havering, 1200–1500* (Cambridge, 1986), 173. See also Goldberg, 'Women in Fifteenth-Century Town Life', 116. Bennett's assertion that 'probably all women on the manor were knowledgeable about producing ale' seems to be unfounded: Bennett, *Women in the Med. English Countryside*, 121.

household area, families faced with economic hardship could most easily relegate commercial brewing to its female members and, hence, release males to seek economic relief in other sectors'.[53] Although it has been suggested that women may have faced increasing competition for paid employment, and their role may thus have been increasingly marginalized, it is nevertheless almost certain that the unpaid labour potential of married women would still have been retained to help work the family land. The same may well have been true of daughters in the absence of substantial opportunities outside the home.[54]

Bennett's analysis rests upon the understanding that those recorded as paying fines for breach of the Assizes are those who, by their activities, were responsible for the transgressions against the Assize, in effect all who brewed and all who baked. The Brigstock court rolls are thus unusual in suggesting that brewing was there an almost exclusively female activity, and one dominated by married women.[55] In law, however, a married woman was not personally responsible for her debts, which fell instead to her husband.[56] Insofar as brewing or baking were undertaken by married women, therefore, the clerk of the court could choose to enter either the name of the person whose activities incurred the fine, or the name of the person legally responsible for that fine. The former was apparently the case at Brigstock, but the latter may have been the case at Iver, where relatively few female names were recorded. Changing patterns may thus reflect changes in record-keeping, but also the numbers of widows engaged in brewing.[57] Graham has suggested a third possibility, namely that the clerk could record the name of the person who actually paid the fine.[58] In the case of the wives of tenants of the lord this would be the husband since he would owe suit of court, but in the case of poorer couples who may not otherwise have been present in the court, the fine was paid by the wife. Such a pattern would accord with Bennett's observation that women from the lower ranks of peasant society are proportionately better reported in the court rolls than their more prosperous sisters.[59]

The picture that emerges is thus not one that readily satisfies any of the public-private models that have been explored here. Indeed, the process of model-building serves only to obscure the very considerable problems of interpretation inherent in the source material. Certainly, Hanawalt has shown considerable imagination in demonstrating the very real value of coroners' rolls, but they demand a more rigorous analysis for their full potential to be realized. The problems associated with court rolls have been debated at length, but no consensus has been reached,

---

53 Bennett, *Women in the Med. English Countryside*, 126.
54 R. Wall, 'Leaving Home and the Process of Household Formation in pre-Industrial England', *Continuity and Change*, ii (1987), 92–5.
55 Bennett, *Women in the Med. English Countryside*, 123, 125.
56 F. Pollock and F.W. Maitland, *The History of English Law* (2nd edn. Cambridge, 1968), ii. 399–436.
57 The number of widows remaining single may have increased in the decades before the Black Death due to an observed lower level of widow remarriage. A higher proportion of widows might also be expected in the decades immediately following the agrarian crisis of 1315–17: Smith, 'Hypothèses sur la Nuptialité', 124–7.
58 H. Graham, 'A Woman's Work . . .: Labour and Gender in the Late Medieval Countryside', in *Woman is a Worthy Wight*, ed. P.J.P. Goldberg (forthcoming).
59 Conversely, higher status males were more likely to be recorded as paying brewing fines than was true of lower status men, status being defined in relation to office-holding: Bennett, *Women in the Med. English Countryside*, 128, 183, 212–15.

beyond the realization that they are more limited and more enigmatic than once thought.[60]

One further source, viz. litigation in the church courts, is no less problematical, but it is nevertheless valuable to the historian of women. It deserves to be better known. Records of matrimonial and related litigation contained in Act books and cause papers can throw much light on marriage practices and incidental light on aspects of economic life and social structure.[61] More mundane sources will take us only so far. The Spalding serf lists, for example, indicate that in the villages of south Lincolnshire, unlike Montaillou at the same date, marriage was exogamous. They may even suggest, again unlike Montaillou with its distinctive Mediterranean marriage regime, that marriage was comparatively late for both sexes.[62] Manor court rolls indicate that widow remarriage was common, especially in the early decades of the fourteenth century.[63] They tell us that women often paid their own marriage fines, or merchets, but that, perhaps uniquely at this period, lords sometimes tried to pressure their tenants to enter into marriages not of their own making.[64] We thus learn something about social structure and the demography of marriage, but almost nothing about individuals, or the implications in terms of choice and constraint of this structure.

Only church records will tell us anything about the degree to which parents arranged the marriages of their children, specifically those of their daughters, and conversely the freedom allowed to women to make their own marriage choices. They thus serve to lend life to the dry bones exhumed from more anonymous records. Some material survives particularly from Canterbury, but also from Rochester and York, for the decades before the Black Death, but no comprehensive analysis has yet been attempted.[65] An examination of some of the York evidence does, however, suggest a high level of parental control, either in terms of making marriages or breaking unions of which they disapproved.[66] In the context of limited economic opportunity for women outside the home, and hence greater dependence

[60] See e.g. Poos and Smith, ' "Legal Windows Onto Historical Populations"? ', 128–152; n. 29 above.

[61] The most useful introduction to this class of document is R.H. Helmholz, *Marriage Litigation in Medieval England* (Cambridge, 1974).

[62] Smith, 'Hypothèses sur la Nuptialité', 120–4, 128; E. Le Roy Ladurie, *Montaillou*, trans. B. Bray (Harmondsworth, 1980), 182–3, 190–1.

[63] This again differs from the pattern of Montaillou where the remarriage of widows, though not unknown, was regarded as somewhat shameful: Le Roy Ladurie, *Montaillou*, trans. Bray, 200–1.

[64] J.M. Bennett, 'Medieval Peasant Marriage: an Examination of Marriage License Fines in *Liber Gersumarum*', in *Pathways to Medieval Peasants*, ed. J.A. Raftis (Toronto, 1981), 193–246; *Court Rolls Manor of Wakefield, I*, 298.

[65] The Canterbury and York material is briefly listed in Helmholz, *Marriage Litigation*, 233–4. The Rochester Act Book is published as *Registrum Hamonis Hethe*, ed. C. Johnson (Canterbury and York Soc. xlviii, xlix, 1914–48). Some Canterbury evidence is published in *Select Cases from the Ecclesiastical Courts of the Province of Canterbury, c. 1200–1301*, ed. N. Adams and C. Donahue (Selden Soc. xcv, 1981).

[66] Based on an analysis of Borthwick Institute of Historical Research, York, CP.E.1, 18, 23, 25, 26, 28, 33, 36, 37, 40, 241B, 248, 257. These include one allegation of forced marriage, one of under-age marriage, and two of affinity. A similar pattern has been described in respect of the Anglo-Irish population of Armagh dioc. for the post-Plague period. This is clearly associated with a high level of parental control of marriage: A. Cosgrove, 'Marriage in medieval Ireland', in *Marriage in Ireland*, ed. A. Cosgrove (Dublin, 1985), 44, 47. The Rochester evidence is analysed by A.J. Finch, 'Crime and Marriage in Three Late Medieval Ecclesiastical Jurisdictions: Cerisy, Rochester and Hereford' (York Univ. D.Phil. thesis, 1988), 44–53, 266, 270–1.

upon parents, such a pattern would not appear surprising. At the risk of stating the obvious, it only serves to emphasize how different the century that preceded the Plague was from that which followed; for the earlier period, women may after all have stayed at home.[67]

---

[67] For a brief statement of the case that opportunities for women expanded as a consequence of the Plague, see P.J.P. Goldberg, 'Mortality and Economic Change in the Diocese of York, 1390–1514', *Northern History*, xxiv (1988), 49–52. Direct comparison between the two periods is hampered by the lack of common sources.

# John de Northwold, Abbot of Bury St. Edmunds (1279–1301) and his Defence of its Liberties*

Antonia Gransden

John de Northwold had no Jocelin of Brakelond to write his biography. I have found only one contemporary impression of him, and this is in a highly-coloured story.[1] It says that in about 1291, Edward I, moved by the need for money to pay for his wars, took private franchises, especially ecclesiastical ones, into his hands. Every prelate laboured for the restoration of his church's liberty. Among them John, abbot of St. Edmunds, toiled at great expense and without intermission. But cupidity grew and the counsel of the wicked ruled, so that, regardless of God and the saints, fiscal considerations prevailed. Abbot John, observing this, and realizing that hitherto his efforts were in vain, produced St. Edmund's royal charters of privilege in parliament at Westminster, accusing the king of wilfully revoking what his predecessors had granted. He concluded: 'I am broken by age and exhausted by my labours to recover these [privileges]; I can do no more, but commit the case between the martyred Edmund and his church, and you, my Lord King, to the Supreme Judge.' John took his leave and sadly went home. That night, when he

* I am deeply indebted especially to Dr. Paul Brand, and also to Dr. David Crook, for kindly reading this article in typescript and making invaluable comments. Any errors remaining are my own. The following abbreviations of manuscript registers from the abbey of Bury St. Edmunds are used in the notes below:

British Library MSS

Add. 14847   Additional 14847, White Register, late 13th–14th c. (R.M. Thomson, *The Archives of the Abbey of Bury St. Edmunds* (Suffolk Rec. Soc. xxi, 1980), no. 1278.)

Harl. 230   Harleian 230, Register of Abbot Thomas de Tottington and Abbot Richard de Draughton etc., late 13th–early 14th c. (Thomson, *Archives*, 132–3, no. 1286.)

Harl. 638   Harleian 638, 'Werketone' register, 13th–15th c. (Thomson, *Archives*, 126–7, no. 1281.)

Harl. 645   Harleian 645, 'Kempe' register, 14th–15th c. (Thomson, *Archives*, 127–9, no. 1282.)

Harl. 743   Harleian 743, 'Lakenheath' register, 14th c. (Thomson, *Archives*, 129–30, no. 1283.)

Harl. 1005   Harleian 1005, White Book, 13th–14th c. (Thomson, *Archives*, 142–5, no. 1293)

Cambridge Univ. Library MSS

Ff.ii.29   Red Vestry Register, pt. I, early 15th c. (Thomson, *Archives*, 130–1, no. 1284.)

Ff. ii. 33   Sacrist's register, late 13th–14th c. (Thomson, *Archives*, 148–9, no. 1296.)

Ff. iv. 35   Red Vestry Register, pt. II, 15th c. (Thomson, *Archives*, 131–2, no. 1285.)

Mm. iv. 19   Black Register (of the vestry), early 13th–14th c. (Thomson, *Archives*, 119–21, no. 1277.)

[1] This story is in the late 14th-c. Bury version of the *Historia Aurea*: Bodleian Library, Oxford, MS Bodley 240; printed in *Memorials of St. Edmund's Abbey*, ed. T. Arnold (RS, 1890–6), ii. 365.

went to bed, Edward was suddenly struck with terror, leapt to his feet and called his household. He said that he had had a vision: St. Edmund would punish him as a second King Swein, whom the saint had killed at Gainsborough. Immediately afterwards Edward had it pronounced that whoever claimed a liberty should come to court without delay; St. Edmund, he said, had raised his banner for them all.

This story, first known from a late fourteenth-century text in the Bury version of the *Historia Aurea*, occurs also in one of the fifteenth-century registers[2] as the preliminary to an account of the *Quo Warranto* proceedings of 1290, insofar as they related to Bury, and of the abbey's subsequent defence of its liberties until Edward III's confirmation of 1346. The *Quo Warranto* proceedings of 1290 marked the culmination of Abbot John's struggle to protect the Liberty. His rule is of particular importance because it coincided with the period of Edward I's greatest reforming and legislative activity. Before discussing the *Quo Warranto* proceedings it is necessary to describe briefly St. Edmund's Liberty itself, the progressive definition of its privileges, and Abbot John's previous struggles to defend them.

Edward the Confessor had granted the abbey its Liberty of Eight and a Half Hundreds, a jurisdictional area covering West Suffolk.[3] Here the abbot had regalian rights, powers which the sheriff of a county normally exercised. He had the return of writs; the steward of the Liberty, on the abbot's behalf, received writs through the sheriff, and executed and returned them as the sheriff himself would have done. He also held a court equivalent to a county court. Meanwhile, this wide Liberty contained within itself one much smaller but more highly privileged, the Liberty of the *banleuca*, the area inside the four crosses of Bury St. Edmunds.[4] There no secular person and no minister of the king could enter and exercise power; the abbot was second only to the king himself. His court heard and determined pleas over property in the town and felonies and crimes committed there, and over the townsmen. In addition, by grant of Edward the Confessor, the abbot had a mint in the vill.[5] Besides these secular privileges, the abbot, by Alexander II's bull of 1071, had spiritual jurisdiction within the *banleuca*;[6] the abbey was directly subject to the pope, and exempt from any other ecclesiastical authority except, later, a papal legate *a latere*.

This, in brief, was St. Edmund's Liberty, already well established before the Norman Conquest. After the Conquest, it could not retain its Anglo-Saxon simplicity. In the twelfth and thirteenth centuries, and indeed later, it was subject to frequent definition and elaboration in order to accommodate new developments in royal government. For instance, there was the problem of that characteristic feature of the judicial system of the late twelfth and thirteenth centuries, the general eyre. How could the abbot's claim to jurisdiction in the Liberty be reconciled with the visits of itinerant justices? Because of the privilege that no minister of the king could exercise authority within the *banleuca*, the abbot could exclude them from Bury itself; there he appointed his own justices in eyre. But he could not exclude them from the Liberty of the Eight and a Half Hundreds. For that, the royal justices

---

2  Ff. iv. 35, f. 3.
3  For St. Edmund's Liberty, see F.E. Harmer, *Anglo-Saxon Writs* (Manchester, 1952; repr. Stamford, Lincs., 1989), 138–48.
4  See M.D. Lobel, *The Borough of Bury St. Edmunds* (Oxford, 1935), 2–7.
5  Harmer, *Writs*, 150–1 and n. 2, 165 (no. 25); R.J. Eaglen, 'The Mint of Bury St. Edmunds to 1279' (London Univ. Ph.D. thesis, 1989), *passim*.
6  *Pinchbeck Register*, ed. F. Hervey (Brighton, 1925), i. 3–4.

held special sessions at Cattishall, near Bury. A point of contention between abbot and king was which of them should have the amercements accruing from those sessions. There was also the question of some profits of justice from the king's courts, such as the chattels of felons and fugitives, which normally belonged to the king but which the abbot claimed as part of the regalian rights of the Liberty of the Eight and a Half Hundreds.

That Henry III recognized the importance of the abbot's court, and also wanted to define its relationship with the jurisdiction of the general eyre, appears in a grant of 4 May 1231. To bring its procedures up to date he conceded the abbot the right to use a petty jury.[7] All pleas of the Crown involving life and limb brought in the abbot's court by the appeal of an individual accuser and customarily tried by fire and water, 'which has no place nowadays' ('quod modo locum non habet'), might henceforth be determined by an inquisition of legal men of the Liberty. But pleas of the Crown where there is no such accuser, but the king brings the suit by means of a jury of presentment, should not be determined in that court but before the king's itinerant justices.

The general eyres themselves made an important contribution to clarifying the abbot's jurisdictional rights, particularly important because the justices' rolls included written record of them and relevant extracts were copied into the Bury registers. In this way the abbot accumulated a body of precedents. The rolls of the eyre of Martin de Pattishall and his fellows in the autumn of 1228 provide an example. On 23 October, when sitting at Cattishall, the justices conceded that rules relating to essoin and distraint in land pleas should be the same in the court of St. Edmund's as in a county court. However, unlike a county court, it should sit every three weeks, and the portmanmoot be held in the customary way; for this concession the abbot gave the king a palfrey.[8] A jury was also asked how writs of novel disseisin and other pleas of the Crown should be determined in the *banleuca*. The jurors said that the abbot should settle them; on the coming of the king's justices he should receive the writs and hold the pleas and assizes in the vill.[9] The same thing was done ('similiter actus fuit') before Robert de Lexington and his fellows in their eyre of Norfolk and Suffolk in 1234, on 22 November at Cattishall.[10] Both judgements were enrolled.

Another example of such codification of rights is supplied by the general eyre of William of York in the spring of 1240.[11] At the session at Ipswich the jurors of Babergh hundred testified on 29 April that Englishry for any dead man is presented in the court of St. Edmund's Liberty in the same way as in a county court, and that murder fines fall on the Liberty as elsewhere. If anyone accuse another for a breach of the king's peace in the court of the Liberty, and both the accuser and the accused

---

7 Ff. ii. 33, f. 31v; Harl. 230, f. 60; and Harl. 743, fos. 63v–4; *CChR 1226–57*, 131–2. I speak below of Henry III and Edward I as if they were *personally* responsible for *all* acts of government. This was not, of course, the case. By this date much governmental activity was in the hands of royal administrators.

8 Harl. 645, fos. 81v, 137v. The concession is recorded in the mutilated civil plea roll of the Cattishall session of Martin de Pattishall's Suffolk eyre, 20–9 Oct. 1228: PRO, JUST. 1/819, rot. 22d. I owe this reference to Dr. Paul Brand. Cf. *The Letter-Book of William of Hoo, Sacrist of Bury St. Edmunds 1280–1294*, ed. A. Gransden (Suffolk Rec. Soc. v, 1963), 61 n. 1. For this eyre, see also D. Crook, *Records of the General Eyre* (PRO Handbooks, no. 20, 1982), 83.

9 *Letter-Book of Hoo*, 60–1 and n. 1.

10 Ibid. 61. For this eyre, see Crook, *Records*, 90, who dates the session 24 Nov.–14 Dec.

11 Crook, *Records*, 101.

are of the Liberty, the plea ought to be determined there by duel or in another way. But if the accused cannot be found, then the court should tell the accuser to go to the county court and sue him there, until he is summoned or outlawed.[12]

This was John de Northwold's inheritance. His predecessor, Abbot Simon de Luton, died on 9 April 1279, and John was elected on 5 May 1279.[13] He went straight to Rome for papal confirmation, which Nicholas III issued on 18 September.[14] The royal mandate for the restoration of temporalities is dated 5 November,[15] and John was received at Bury on 28 December.[16] While in Rome he had obtained Nicholas III's confirmation of all the 'liberties and immunities' granted to the abbey by previous popes. The bull is dated 20 September.[17] On 22 September Nicholas also granted that any 'privileges and indulgences' which the abbot and convent had not used should nevertheless remain in force,[18] and he issued two other bulls strengthening the authority of the abbot and convent to enforce their rights against those who usurped or opposed them.[19]

Like his predecessors, John de Northwold obtained royal confirmation of St. Edmund's liberties early in his abbatiate. Edward confirmed them on 16 November 1281.[20] It should be noted that on the same day, at the instance of the prior and convent, he confirmed the division of their property from the abbot's barony.[21] They had sought written confirmation because, during the vacancy preceding John's succession, the king had taken the monks' portion into his hands as well as the barony; 'neither prayer nor price,' the chronicler indignantly writes, 'it could wring it from his grasp'.[22] The royal official, John de Berwick, had everything at his disposal, allowing the monks only enough for their subsistence.[23] This, the chronicler exclaims, 'was a thing unheard of'. The case vividly illustrates the need for written definition, accompanied by royal confirmation, of the abbey's rights. Only thus could the abbey successfully resist encroachments on its privileges.

Edward's aggressive policy towards private franchises was, as is well known, caused by the need for money and the desire for reform. It brought him into conflict with St. Edmunds, as it did with many other liberty holders. Whether he was ignorant of the exact nature of St. Edmund's Liberty, or was just high-handed, is hard to say; probably he was a bit of both. Certainly, trouble began before John de Northwold's succession, in the last years of Simon de Luton. One early reason for conflict was Edward's reform of the coinage. Reform was begun as a result of

---

12  Ff. iv. 35, f. 1.
13  *The Chronicle of Bury St. Edmunds 1212–1301*, ed. A. Gransden (London, 1964), 68.
14  *Les Registres de Nicholas III (1277–1280)*, ed. J. Gay (Bibliothèque des Écoles Françaises d'Athènes et de Rome, 1898–1938), no. 562.
15  *CPR 1272–81*, 331.
16  *Chron. Bury*, 70.
17  Mm. iv. 19, f. 78; *Pinchbeck Reg.* i. 39–40. This confirmation of St. Edmund's 'liberties and immunities' is not in Pope Nicholas's register.
18  Mm. iv. 19, f. 78v; *Pinchbeck Reg.* i. 40.
19  Mm. iv. 19, fos. 78v–9v; *Pinchbeck Reg.* i. 40–1.
20  *CChR 1257–1300*, 258.
21  Ibid. 259. The text of the division itself is printed in W. Dugdale, *Monasticon Anglicanum*, ed. J. Caley, H. Ellis and B. Bandinel (London, 1817–30), iii. 156.
22  *Chron. Bury*, 68.
23  For the commission, dated 21 April 1279, appointing de Berwick keeper of the abbey during the vacancy, see *CFR 1272–1307*, 110.

discussion in the parliament at Gloucester in July and August 1278.[24] There had been no change in the currency for more than thirty years and the coinage had become debased, not surprisingly. A preliminary to the issue of a new coinage was the recall of the old, and preliminary to that was an inquiry into the clipping of coin, followed by the arrest and trial of suspect goldsmiths and keepers of mints.[25] That winter, five goldsmiths and three others were taken from Bury to London, according to the chronicler.[26] He also says that, although this was done by a town bailiff and not by a royal official, many regarded it as an infringement of St. Edmund's Liberty. When the king realized this, he sent the prisoners back for trial in Bury. However, the trial itself gave grave offence, for it was conducted by two royal justices, John de Cobham and Walter de Helion. They held a court in the town guildhall and assigned the amercements to the royal treasury — even the sacrist had to pay 100 marks *ad redempcionem*. Their holding of the court was itself contrary to the privilege that no royal 'minister' could exercise office within the *banleuca*; and the abbot, not the king, should at least have had the amercements. Thus, writes the chronicler, 'they flouted the liberties of St. Edmund's church in an unheard-of way, without regard for either papal or royal privileges'.[27]

Nor did Abbot John's trouble over the new currency end here. Edward issued a mandate for the delivery of a new die to him on 8 November 1279.[28] But he did not send a 'standard' (the measure for the legal rate of the intrinsic value of coins) or an assay (a piece of test silver). This was odd, because Henry III had sent them to one of John's predecessors, Henry de Rushbrook, in 1247, together with a die for the new long-cross coinage.[29] John asked for them, basing his claim on prescriptive right. But since, apparently, neither the above precedent nor any other could be found in the rolls, the most Edward would concede, after long discussion with his council, was that the abbot should have the information by word of mouth.[30]

An important motive for Edward's reform of the currency was to promote trade, a lucrative source of Crown revenue. Equally important for that end was that weights and measures should be standard throughout England.[31] The standard was enforced by the king's marshal or the marshal's clerk of the market, who held the view of weights and measures in the marshalsea court within the verge. A session of the clerk of the market in Bury provoked the abbey's second major confrontation with Edward over its Liberty. Edward, when he came to Bury in April 1275, had confirmed the convent's right to hold the view in the town without the presence of his official.[32] (The concession was to the convent rather than to the abbot because

[24] *The Chronicle of Walter of Guisborough*, ed. H. Rothwell (Camden Soc., 3rd ser. lxxxix, 1957), 216. Cf. F.M. Powicke, *The Thirteenth Century 1216–1307* (2nd edn. Oxford, 1962), 632, 633 and nn. 1, 2; H.B. Earle Fox and J.S. Shirley-Fox, 'Numismatic History of the Reigns of Edward I., II., and III.', *British Numismatic Journ. and Procs. of the British Numismatic Soc. 1910*, vii (1911), 97–9.
[25] *Chron. Bury*, 66 and n. 3; Fox and Shirley-Fox, 'Numismatic History', 97, 130 (app. xii); *CCR 1272–9*, 529; *CPR 1272–81*, 297, 312, 338.
[26] *Chron. Bury*, 66.
[27] Ibid. 66–8.
[28] Fox and Shirley-Fox, 'Numismatic History', 136 (app. xxxii); *CCR 1272–9*, 544.
[29] Harl. 645, fos. 79v, 123v; Fox and Shirley-Fox, 'Numismatic History', 100, 116, 134 (app. xxvi).
[30] For this dispute, see Harl. 645, fos. 79–80, 128r–v, 152: discussed and printed in Fox and Shirley-Fox, 'Numismatic History', 116–17, 138–9 (app. xxxvii).
[31] Powicke, *Thirteenth Century*, 620 and n. 1.
[32] *Chron. Bury*, 57–8. At this time the prior and convent paid the king 100 marks 'for a certain

the town was not part of the abbot's barony but belonged to the convent; the sacrist, on the convent's behalf, was virtually lord of the town.) The abbot and convent, relying on their privilege that no royal 'minister' could exercise power in the town, interpreted Edward's concession to mean that only their officials could hold the view there. This neglected the ancient right of the marshalsea court within the verge. The position was anomalous; conflict between the rival jurisdictions of St. Edmund's and the marshalsea was likely. And in 1285 such conflict broke out.

Edward came to Bury on 20 February, and Ralph de Middlington[33] held the view of weights and measures in the tollhouse. The abbot and convent protested to Ralph that his session was to the prejudice of their Liberty. Since he did not agree, Abbot John, the sacrist William de Hoo, and one of the abbey's most senior councillors, Ralph de Alneto (who acted as spokesman), complained to the king. Edward replied that Ralph de Middlington claimed to have held the view in the town in Henry III's presence. This Ralph de Alneto denied. Edward, therefore, appointed auditors. Ralph de Middlington offered to prove his case by the evidence of the rolls and of a jury. Abbot John, the sacrist, and their councillors produced an estreat showing that when Henry III came to Bury, the bailiffs of the vill exercised the office under the eyes of the king's 'ministers'. They also produced Edward I's charter of liberties, which charter, Ralph de Middlington said, infringed the liberty of the marshalsea. The auditors offered the abbot and convent an inquest, but they refused, fearing to compromise their privileges. To strengthen their case, the two men, William de Walpole and Luke, son of John, who had been bailiffs when Edward came to Bury in 1275, produced 'standard' measures, asserting that they had received them from Ralph de Middlington so that they could seal their own measures, as they were prepared to swear. Nevertheless, the auditors were unwilling to pronounce, and the abbot and convent put themselves on the king's mercy. Edward took counsel and ordained that when he visited Bury, the officials of the marshalsea should exercise their office in the customary way; between whiles, the abbot and convent should view the measures in the same manner once or twice a year, and the profits be used for the shrine of St. Edmund. Evidently Abbot John was still unsatisfied, for on 12 June 1285 Edward conceded, 'out of reverence for St. Edmund', that all revenues from any view held by his own officials should likewise go to St. Edmund's shrine.[34]

When Edward stayed at Bury from 16 to 18 January 1296, he replaced this charter by another (dated 18 January) which specified exactly what the sources of revenue were.[35] The problem of the violation by the king's clerk of the market of the privilege that no royal minister was to exercise power within the *banleuca* was also tackled. Edward's charter of 12 June 1285 contains the clause that sessions of the king's clerk of the market were not to prejudice the liberty of the *banleuca*. During his visit in January 1296 Edward made a more concrete concession. When

confirmation': PRO, E 372/119 [i.e. 29 Sept. 1274–29 Sept. 1275], rots. 17, 34. See also Lobel, *Borough*, 37.
[33] Or 'Middleton' ('Middilton': *CCR 1279–88*, 335). A detailed contemporary account of the dispute is in Harl. 645, f. 49r–v; printed in *Letter-Book of Hoo*, 125–30 (app. 7), and discussed in Lobel, *Borough*, 37–9.
[34] Harl. 743, fos. 65v, 66; PRO, DL 42/5, f. 114v; *CPR 1281–92*, 178, with note that 'vacated because otherwise on roll of 24 Edward I' (see n. 35).
[35] Add. 14847, f. 50r–v; *CPR 1292–1301*, 183, with note that the chancellor instructed William de la Dune, keeper of the hanaper, that he was to receive back the charter of (12 June) 1285 before handing this one over.

his court of the marshalsea sat in the abbot's hall of pleas, Abbot John once again showed his charters of liberties, objecting that the session was contrary to the privilege that no royal minister could exercise power in the *banleuca*. Edward allowed the Liberty, and had it proclaimed that all such pleas should be held outside the boundaries, in the suburbs at Babwell. He granted a charter to this effect. The importance which the monks attached to this charter is indicated by the number of copies (dating from the late thirteenth to the early fifteenth centuries) which survive in the Bury registers.[36] It could be cited as a precedent when there were disputes over the abbey's liberties.[37]

So far we have considered individual cases when Edward's drive for governmental efficiency brought him into conflict with St. Edmund's Liberty, as indeed it often did with other private franchises. In such instances Edward presumably saw liberties as possible hindrances to reform, and their holders as recipients of income which he would have liked. However, the fact remained: the liberties existed. He and his council could dispute claims based on prescriptive right; Abbot John failed to establish his right to a standard and assay for his mint probably because he did not produce written evidence in support of his claim. But Edward could not override a privilege based on a royal charter, although he might well question the charter's purport. As mentioned above, Abbot John appealed to St. Edmund's charter of privilege in his disputes with the king in 1279 and 1285 (in the latter instance he also argued from prescriptive right). Professor Sutherland writes: 'In comparison with the doubtful worth of prescriptive right, a royal charter was a stronghold of defence for the liberty-holder . . .'[38] He wrote this with reference to the *Quo Warranto* campaign, which must now be considered.

In any dealings with a private franchise the king had of necessity to know exactly what its liberties comprised. He could only ascertain this by examining the warrant by which the liberty holder made his claim. In this way he could discover whether a liberty holder was exercising rights and taking income to which he was not entitled. Edward put in motion the first stages of his *Quo Warranto* campaign almost immediately after his return to England in August 1274 (his first appearance since his accession).[39]

The impact of Edward's *Quo Warranto* campaign on Bury is obvious from the Public Records. But even more telling is evidence in the abbey's registers. Clearly, the campaign gave rise to a flurry of research into the origins of St. Edmund's land holdings and liberties, and to assiduous record keeping. Perhaps the list of the abbey's benefactors, versions of which occur in some of the registers, originated at this time in response to Edward's policy. The earliest known copies of the list are late thirteenth century.[40] The list is remarkable because it includes unique copies of

36 Mm. iv. 19, f. 9v; Add. 14847, f. 59; Harl. 645, f. 70; Ff. ii. 29, fos. 5v–6. (This list is probably incomplete.)
37 E.g. it was cited in 1325: Ff. ii. 29, f. 15.
38 D.W. Sutherland, *Quo Warranto Proceedings in the Reign of Edward I 1278–1294* (Oxford, 1963), 111. Although claims of liberty holders that they held by prescriptive right, having held 'from time out of mind', were allowed early in Edward's *Quo Warranto* campaign, such titles began to be challenged in the eyres from 1280 onwards. Sometimes, therefore, claimants might prefer to base their claims on royal charters made before time of memory. See ibid. 82–3; P. Brand, ' "Quo Waranto" Law in the Reign of Edward I: A Hitherto Undiscovered Opinion of Chief Justice Hengham', *The Irish Jurist*, new ser. xiv, pt. 1 (1979), 158–9.
39 Sutherland, *Quo Warranto*, 17.
40 One copy is Harl. 1005, fos. 81r–v, 83. It is in the same hand as the only surviving complete text of the Bury Customary, which is in the same MS (fos. 102–19), which I date to the late 13th c.:

the abbey's Anglo-Saxon charters of donation. The originals of most of them are lost, and the transcripts in the registers the only known texts. Perhaps the monks now focused on them in order to help defend their holdings and rights against the king. The registers also have information directly concerning the *Quo Warranto* campaign, for example, about the inquiry into private franchises which Edward began in October 1274,[41] and about the similar undertaking, Kirkby's Quest, in 1284–5.[42] They also have abundant material about the *Quo Warranto* campaign itself, insofar as it concerned St. Edmund's estate, although for each individual case it tends to be fragmentary.

The Gloucester parliament of 1278 provided that henceforth *Quo Warranto* claims should be heard not in parliament but in sessions of the general eyre and *coram rege* in the counties.[43] David Crook points out that in consequence the pleas became a 'major part' of the work of eyre justices.[44] The Bury registers and the eyre rolls record a number of *Quo Warranto* pleas touching the abbot heard by Solomon of Rochester, mainly in the Suffolk eyre in the winter of 1286–7. At the start of proceedings, on 3 November at Ipswich, Abbot John sought his Liberty. He claimed that pleas in which inhabitants of the Eight and a Half Hundreds were parties, or pleas about his holdings there, should be determined by the king's justices at Cattishall; those concerning inhabitants of, and holdings in, the *banleuca* of Bury itself should be determined by the abbot's own justices, and writs delivered to him. Jurors testified in the same vein that itinerant justices in the county were wont to deliver to the abbot all writs touching holdings within St. Edmund's *banleuca*, to be pleaded in Bury before justices chosen by the abbots.[45] Solomon of Rochester, therefore, held a session at Cattishall, from 14 January to 5 February 1287.[46] On the first day jurors testified in the same way as they had at Ipswich, and Abbot John claimed jurisdiction within the *banleuca*; his claim was allowed.[47]

*The Customary of the Benedictine Abbey of Bury St. Edmunds in Suffolk*, ed. A. Gransden (Henry Bradshaw Soc. xcix, 1973), xxxvi. Another early copy is Ff. ii. 33, fos. 45–50v. These hands resemble those reproduced in A.G. Watson, *Catalogue of Dated and Datable Manuscripts in Oxford Libraries c. 435–1600* (Oxford, 1984), ii, plates 144, 145 (dated 'after 1297'). A later version of the benefactors' list is in *Pinchbeck Reg.* ii. 282–94. Cf. n. 52 below.

41 Harl. 645, f. 257. Cf. *CPR 1272–81*, 59; and Sutherland, *Quo Warranto*, 17–18.

42 A copy of the writ to John de Mettingham and William de Pakenham, dated 6 July 1284, witnessed by John de Kirkby, treasurer, at Westminster, and the text of the articles are in Harl. 645, fos. 213v–215. See *Feudal Aids. Inquisitions and Assessments Relating to Feudal Aids Preserved in the PRO, 1284–1431* (London, 1899–1920), i. pp. viii–xxii, 86–90, Powicke, *Thirteenth Century*, 359 and n. 2; Sutherland, *Quo Warranto*, 167, 171, 172.

43 *Statutes of the Realm (1101–1713)*, ed. A. Luders *et al.* (Rec. Comm. 1810–28), i. 45–6. For a better text of the ordinance, see Sutherland, *Quo Warranto*, 190–3; and cf. ibid. 25, 26, 34, 36, 73, 145.

44 Crook, *Records*, 144.

45 Harl. 645, f. 138.

46 Crook, *Records*, 167.

47 Harl. 645, fos. 81v, 138. Despite this ruling, a judgement was given in 1291 that the abbot did not have the right to appoint his own justices. This judgement was given in the course of the false judgement case brought by Hamo, rector of Attleborough (below, 106–7 and n. 103). It is calendared in *Placitorum in domo Capitulari Westmonasteri asservatorum abbreviatio* (Rec. Comm. 1811), 224. Dr. Paul Brand has contributed the following information from the enrolment on the king's bench plea roll for Mich. term 1290 (PRO, KB 27/125, m. 57), which I quote with his kind permission: 'When the abbot and his two justices appear, the abbot claims that he properly assigned the two justices to hear the case, as when he was created abbot he found his church seised of the franchise of so doing. Hamo claims (on behalf of himself and the king) that the proper

A few examples of *Quo Warranto* pleas heard by Solomon of Rochester will illustrate the kinds of evidence that Abbot John and his attorneys used to support their claims.[48] To defend his right to the Liberty of the *banleuca*, Abbot John cited the precedent of the concession (noted above) made in Martin de Pattishall's eyre of 1228.[49] Jurors presented that he held the vill of Beccles by gift of King Stephen and claimed in it view of frankpledge, amercements from the assize of bread and ale, gallows, a weekly market and two fairs a year, but they did not know by what warrant.[50] Abbot John said that he and his predecessors had held the manor and its privileges from the time of King Eadwig.[51] (Eadwig, who ruled from 955 to 959, appears as the donor of Beccles in a version of the late thirteenth-, early fourteenth-century benefactors' list, with the note 'sine carta'.)[52] To prove that they had held them under Edward the Confessor, he called Domesday Book to warrant.[53] Jurors

practice when the abbot claims pleas for hearing in the *banleuca* court is for such pleas to be heard in the tollhouse by the alderman and burgesses, and puts himself on the record of the Bench justices that, when this case was remitted to Bury, it was for hearing in this way and not before two justices. The case is then adjourned and not resumed till Michaelmas term 1291. Hamo now claims that the abbot is not in seisin of the franchise of appointing his own justices to hear pleas within the *banleuca*. The abbot had claimed this right in the last eyre but it had not been allowed, and it had been the king who had appointed Henry of Guildford and Richard Weyland to determine pleas within the *banleuca* (and this was, he said, the practice also in previous eyres). The abbot apparently cannot deny that this was the case, and since he could not prove that the king had subsequently granted him the right to appoint his own justices, his attempt to do this was now characterized as being a *recens occupacio* against the Crown rather than possession of the *auctoritas judicandi*. The court suggests that even if the abbot is entitled to claim cases for the hearing of his court, the presumption must be that judgement in them should then be made by the suitors of his court rather than by justices he appoints. Hamo is advised that the whole proceedings are therefore null and void, and that he is entitled to bring an assize of novel disseisin to reverse the effect of the purported judgement (as being made before a court not competent to act because it was wrongly constituted).'

48 The cases mentioned below do not exhaust the number of claims by writ of *Quo Warranto* which Abbot John had to answer. On 2 Nov. 1286 he was summoned before Solomon at Ipswich to answer by what warrant he claimed warren in Wetherden, and other liberties: *Placita de Quo Warranto, Edward I–Edward III*, ed. W. Illingworth (Rec. Comm. 1818), 733. In 1287 he was summoned before Solomon during his session at Dunwich, 9–13 Feb., to answer for his right in 'Soke Louel': PRO, JUST. 1/826, rot. 47; cf. PRO, KB 27/104, rot. 10 d; and KB 27/107, rots. 2, 30. He was summoned before Solomon on 16 May 1287, at Hertford, to answer for various liberties he claimed in Sawbridgeworth (Herts.): *Placita de Quo Warranto*, 290.
49 Harl. 645, f. 81v.
50 Stephen granted the abbey everything he had in the manor, except pleas of the Crown: D.C. Douglas, *Feudal Documents from the Abbey of Bury St. Edmunds* (London, 1932), 83.
51 Harl. 230, f. 119. For claimants' preference for a royal charter made before time of memory to prescriptive right based on tenure 'from time out of memory', see n. 38 above.
52 Ff. ii. 33, f. 50v. In the list in Harl. 1005, fos. 81r–v, 83 the original hand gives Stephen as the donor of Beccles but Henry de Kirkstead, subprior of Bury (d. *c.* 1379) adds a note at the foot of f. 81v: '957 Edius rex dedit Sancto Edmundo Becles sed sine carta.' For Kirkstead, see R.H. Rouse, 'Bostonus Buriensis and the author of the *Catalogus Scriptorum Ecclesiae*', *Speculum*, xli (1966), 471–99. For the benefactors' list, see above, 97–8 and n. 40. It does not seem likely that Eadwig gave Beccles to St. Edmunds. Sawyer lists no grant by him in E. Anglia, with the possible exception of one perhaps to Ely: P.H. Sawyer, *Anglo-Saxon Charters* (London, 1968), 219 (no. 646). Eadwig's grants were of lands in the SW., in the W. Midlands and in the Home Counties. By the early years of Edward III's reign Eadwig was considered to be the donor not only of Beccles, but also of 'nearly all the other lands of which, in most people's opinion, the donor is uncertain' ('fere omnes alias terras quarum plerisque incertus est collator'): *Pinchbeck Reg.* ii. 284.
53 Harl. 230, f. 119. Cf. Domesday Book, fos. 369v–70 (ed. J. Morris, xxxiv, Suffolk, ed. A. Rumble (Phillimore, Chichester, 1986), i. 14, 120). For the importance of Domesday Book as evidence in some *Quo Warranto* cases under Edward I, see E.M. Hallam, *Domesday Book through Nine Centuries* (London, 1986), 49–50.

presented that the abbot claimed view of frankpledge and amercements from the assize of bread and ale from his tenants in Wortham, and these and other liberties, which they specified, in Redgrave, Brockford and Palgrave; but they did not know by what warrant. Abbot John by his attorney said that his predecessors had died seised of these liberties. He was summoned to answer the king by what warrant he held them. He said that St. Edmund's had been seised of these manors and liberties from the time of Edward the Confessor, and that the present king had confirmed its right to them. He showed the charter of Cnut, which stated that St. Edmund's should have cognition of all causes in its vills,[54] Edward the Confessor's confirmation (in English) of this privilege,[55] and Edward I's own confirmation 'enrolled in the rolls of the Essex eyre'.[56] Finally, he asserted that he and his predecessors had remained in seisin until the present day, and jurors testified to this.

Because of the large size and high privileges of St. Edmund's Liberty and the abbey's many other holdings, Abbot John must have been much harassed by seemingly endless *Quo Warranto* cases. But one particular aspect of the campaign especially concerned him, the right to amercements and various other profits of justice. This was a matter to which the abbots had long turned their attention. For example, from 1242–3 until at least 1275–6, they were in dispute at the exchequer over their claim to amercements from inhabitants of the Liberty of Eight and a Half Hundreds, even if those inhabitants were not of St. Edmund's fee. Time and again the case was put in respect for further consultation. The abbots appealed to their charters, but these were not precise enough to answer the question.[57] The abbots apparently had some success in simply taking certain profits of justice, without obtaining formal recognition of their right. A mid-fourteenth-century historical narrative of the abbots' battle for the profits of justice states that in 52 Henry III (1267–8) Simon de Luton 'occupied' the chattels of felons in the Eight and a Half Hundreds, and the convent did the same in its manors.[58]

Abbot John's anxiety to obtain the profits of justice must have been particularly acute because of the abbey's financial plight in the later thirteenth century.[59] He petitioned the king (in French) in the Easter (or just possibly in the Hilary) parliament of 1290 that his liberties should be allowed in the exchequer.[60] To support his case he referred to Edward the Confessor's charter of privilege,[61] and to Henry I's

---

54 For the case, see Harl. 230, f. 119; *Placita de Quo Warranto*, 733. Cnut's charter is printed in e.g. J.M. Kemble, *Codex Diplomaticus Aevi Saxonici* (London, 1839–48), iv. 16 (no. 735). At least in its present form, Cnut's charter is of doubtful authenticity: Sawyer, *Charters*, 293–4 (no. 980); Harmer, *Writs*,141, 433–4.
55 Printed in e.g. Kemble, *Codex*, iv. 231 (no.895). Edward the Confessor's charter of confirmation is almost certainly spurious: see Sawyer, *Charters*, 311–12 (no.1045); Harmer, *Writs*, 141 and n. 2.
56 See above, 94 and n. 20.
57 See the extracts from the memoranda rolls in Harl. 743, fos. 92v–94v. Cf. Sutherland, *Quo Warranto*, 21 and n. 1.
58 For this narrative of the occupation by, and allowance to, the abbots from Edmund de Walpole (1248–56) to Richard de Draughton (1312–35) of profits of justice accruing from St. Edmund's liberties, see Ff. ii. 29, fos. 1v–3. Cf. below, 102 and n. 76.
59 See V.H. Galbraith's contribution to the introduction in *Chron. Bury*, xxxi–ii.
60 A copy of the petition is Add. 14847, fos. 54v–5. It is headed 'Forma peticionis Domini I[ohannis] abbatis Sancti Edmundi porrecte domino E[dwardo] regi pro allocacione cartarum libertatis Sancti Edmundi in parleamento sui. Anno eiusdem Regis xviij'. For the importance of the Hilary and Easter parliaments of 1290 in the *Quo Warranto* campaign, see Sutherland, *Quo Warranto*, 91–8, 120–1.
61 Presumably the very dubious charter referred to above, and n. 55.

and Henry II's confirmations.[62] Various of the abbey's charters of privilege were read out in parliament: Cnut's charter, Edward the Confessor's charter of privilege, and also his grant of the Eight and a Half Hundreds,[63] Henry I's and Henry II's confirmations, and Edward I's own confirmation.[64] The record of this occasion notes that 'there was no need to show any other charters because these were the best', and comments that the seal of Edward the Confessor's grant of the Eight and a Half Hundreds was in an embroidered silk pouch.[65]

Particularly remarkable is an entry on the parliament rolls, which shows that Abbot John was one of the leaders of the franchise holders struggling to obtain the judicial profits of their liberties. It reads:

> The abbot of Fécamp [William de Putot], the abbot of St. Edmunds, and various prelates and other magnates of the realm petitioned the king in the parliament after Easter in the eighteenth year of his reign. The king, therefore, by special grace conceded that all liberties and charters allowed in the eighteenth year of Henry, his father [1234], and all charters allowed before that, should henceforth be allowed.[66]

The passage continues that Edward ordered charters of later date to be shown at the exchequer, and only what they specifically granted to be allowed. At least three of the Bury registers have a copy of the writ of 27 May 1290 to the barons of the exchequer implementing this important decision.[67] It must have been Abbot John's part in the Easter parliament, when he acted not only on his own behalf, but also on behalf of other franchise holders, which gave rise to the story told above, at the beginning. St. Edmund had indeed 'raised his banner for them all'.

The decision was important because it restored a useful exchequer practice which had been forbidden in 1234. By it, the exchequer would challenge a liberty holder's claim to amercements and the like; the liberty holder would thereupon show his warrant; if satisfied, the barons of the exchequer would 'allow' the liberty. This established a precedent henceforth to be observed. (After the abolition of this procedure in 1234, pleas initiated by writs of *Quo Warranto* in the counties had multiplied.)[68] Although the old procedure was restored in 1290, franchise holders complained that the exchequer did not implement the king's mandate properly. The matter was raised again in the Epiphany parliament of 1292, and the instructions to the barons of the exchequer were repeated.[69]

In response to the restoration of the old practice, Abbot John had all memoranda

62 Douglas, *Feudal Documents*, 62–3 (no. 21), 93–4 (no. 80) respectively.
63 Probably Sawyer, *Charters*, 319 (no. 1069), but possibly ibid. 323 (no. 1084); Harmer, *Writs*, 154–5 (no. 9), 164–7 (no. 24) respectively.
64 See above, 94 and n. 20.
65 Add. 14847, f. 55.
66 *Rot. Parl.* i. 35; cited Sutherland, *Quo Warranto*, 205. For the procedure established in 1234, see *The Roll and Writ File of the Berkshire Eyre of 1248*, ed. M.T. Clanchy (Selden Soc. xc, 1972–3), xxxvii and n. 6.
67 Add. 14847, f. 55v; Harl. 645, fos. 68, 164; Ff. ii. 29, fos. 18v–19.
68 Sutherland, *Quo Warranto*, 6, 121; T.F.T. Plucknett, *Legislation of Edward I* (Oxford, 1949), 37 n. 9.
69 *Rot. Parl.* i. 79–80; Sutherland, *Quo Warranto*, 120–1, 206–9.

and rolls of the exchequer scrutinized,[70] but no record of any allowance of profits of justice to St. Edmund was found, only that Abbot Simon had 'occupied' the chattels of felons. However, by virtue of this 'occupation' and of St. Edmund's charters, Abbot John's claim was accepted by the barons of the exchequer in 1291.[71] He was allowed amercements worth £655 7s. 4d. in Suffolk and £34 17s. 11d. in Norfolk, on the account of William de Redham, sheriff of Norfolk and Suffolk (1290–4). It is noteworthy that the pipe roll for 19 Edward I (1290–1) has two entries of this allowance. The first was cancelled and a note added: 'cancellatus quia melius in Resid' Norff' et Suff' '.[72] A fuller version of the same entry duly appears in 'Residuum Norff' et Suff' '.[73] It is not until 1292 that the Bury chronicler records Abbot John's success at the exchequer. He writes: 'On the quindene of Easter, on the account of William of Redham, sheriff of Norfolk and Suffolk, our charters of liberties were allowed at the exchequer, and the liberties specified in them, hitherto undifferentiated, adjudged to our church for ever.'[74] He continues, giving examples of the categories of profits, such as common amercements, murder fines, and a year and a day. A much fuller list, dated 20 Edward I (1291–2), is in the 'Lakenheath' register.[75] The chronicler concludes his account of St. Edmund's triumph with the notice that £640 was immediately credited to the abbot. The reason why the chronicler put this entry under 1292 instead of 1291, unless he simply mistook the date, could be that the monks were dissatisfied with the original allowance because it was not precise enough. They needed to have specified the exact categories of profits of justice to which St. Edmund's was entitled. Therefore, the entry in the pipe roll was cancelled and the fuller one substituted.

The attention the chronicler gives to the exchequer allowance, and the number of copies of it in the Bury register, shows the importance that the monks attached to the matter. But the struggle did not end in 1292. Some categories of profits had still not been allowed. Following the example of Abbot Simon, John tried to obtain the allowance of fines by first 'occupying' them in the Liberty of the Eight and a Half Hundreds, and the convent did the same on its manors; they were unsuccessful. It remained for their successors to add fines and other categories of profits to the list won by Abbot John.[76]

So far we have considered cases of confrontation between Edward and Abbot John. This could give a false impression. As Helen Cam pointed out long ago, the object of Edward's inquiries into private franchises, and of the *Quo Warranto* proceedings, was not to abolish or even curtail such liberties as long as they were justly held by royal authority and properly administered. Primarily, the purpose was

---

[70] This is recorded in the historical narrative mentioned above, 100 and n. 58; Ff. ii. 29, f. 2r–v.
[71] A copy of Edward's writ to the treasurer and barons of the exchequer (*CCR 1288–96*, 256–7) headed 'Allocaciones Cartarum Sancti Edmundi facte ad Scaccarium', 19 Edward I, is Harl. 645, f. 164.
[72] PRO, E 372/136, m. 40.
[73] Ibid. m. 34 d. Copies are: Add. 14847, f. 55r–v; Harl. 645, fos. 68r–v, 164r–v.
[74] *Chron. Bury*, 114.
[75] The list is headed: 'Anno xx^{mo} Edwardi Regis filii Henrici Regis coram Baronibus de Scaccario allocata sunt omnia amerciamenta hec que sequitur coram quibuscumque justiciariis domino Johanni abbati de Sancto Edmundo super compotum domini W. de Redham vice comitis Norf': Harl. 743, f. 114v.
[76] See the historical narrative mentioned above, 100 and n. 58; Ff. ii. 29, fos. 2v–3. It does not specify the kind or kinds of fines in question. The list referred to above, and n. 75, has, at the end, categories of profits of justice allowed after 1291–2 up until 1343–4: Harl. 743, f. 114v.

clarification and definition, to make local government more efficient.[77] When the king granted a franchise, he parted with responsibilities as well as rights. As Cam wrote:

> By virtue of [such a] grant the lord of the liberty does certain things which elsewhere are done by the king or his officials, and keeps for himself profits of various kinds which elsewhere go to the king's exchequer. But in so far as these rights and duties are governmental, not proprietary, public, not private, the franchise-holder is the viceroy or agent of the king — responsible to the king, and liable to forfeiture, like any other government official, for maladministration . . .[78]

Writing in particular about the franchises of the greater East Anglian abbots, Cam described them as mere 'cogs in that magnificent machine built up by the practical genius of our Norman and Angevin kings'.[79]

There are plenty of examples of the close supervision that Edward exercised over the administration of St. Edmund's Liberty when it affected the peace and well-being of his subjects. In the last resort the king would take the Liberty into his hands. This Henry III did in 1266, because of the abbot's failure to keep order during the Barons' War.[80] Edward did likewise for a short time in 1285, because of abuse of the assize of weights and measures. When Ralph de Middlington held the view, the assize found that some of the measures were falsely sealed as if by him, and some by the sacrist. He had them all destroyed, and the Liberty was taken briefly into the king's hands *ad cautelam* because of the sacrist's complicity.[81] But these were exceptional cases. Usually, royal power was exerted in a routine way, by means of written instructions to the abbot or his deputies and through personal supervision by royal officials and justices.

For instance, Ralph de Middlington, at the end of the 1285 dispute over the view of weights and measures, took steps to improve its future administration. According to the Bury chronicle (which was, however, written from the sacrist's standpoint)[82] much blame for past lapses was placed on the burgesses. They had, it alleges, argued that the view should only be held in the king's presence, and had prevented the sacrist from holding it. Now it was ordained, on pain of the king again taking over the Liberty, that the sacrist could compel them to act as jurors when he held the view. Any who refused were to be amerced and the obdurate imprisoned at the king's pleasure.[83] The burgesses were fined 50 marks for past breaches of the assize.[84]

---

77 H.M. Cam, 'The Quo Warranto Proceedings under Edward I', repr. from *History*, xi (1926), in id. *Liberties and Communities in Medieval England* (Cambridge, 1944), 180–1. Cf. Sutherland, *Quo Warranto*, 16–17, 184–5.
78 H.M. Cam, 'The King's Government, as administered by the Greater Abbots of East Anglia', repr. from *Communications of the Cambridge Antiquarian Soc.* xxix (1928), in id. *Liberties and Communities*, 184.
79 Cam, 'King's Government', 204.
80 *CPR 1258–66*, 604; *CR 1264–8*, 298; *CPR 1266–72*, 45; PRO, C. 60/64, m. 6.
81 *Letter-Book of Hoo*, 129.
82 A. Gransden, *Historical Writing in England, c. 550–c. 1307* (London, 1974), 396–9.
83 *Chron. Bury*, 83–4; Lobel, *Borough*, 37–8.
84 *Letter-Book of Hoo*, 129.

At the same time Ralph decreed that the sacrist's bailiffs should hold the view once or twice a year, and made penalties for breaches of the assize more severe. Jurors said that by custom brewsters who broke the assize were only amerced and never stood in the tumbrel; Ralph ordained that in future they should do so for the third offence. Similarly, bakers should be put in the pillory for the third offence. The jurors had also said that the assize for Franciscus and puff bread was never held; it was ordained that henceforth it should be held, and the appropriate weights were fixed. Regraters of fish and meat and forestallers were not to buy or sell before the third hour; contraveners were to be punished according to the gravity of the offence, and two burgesses appointed annually to report contraventions to the sacrist's bailiffs.[85]

Ralph took these steps on Edward's (and the sacrist's) advice.[86] Clearly, one of the king's motives was the good of his subjects. The severity of penalties was increased 'pro communi utilitate populi' and 'pro communi plebis profectu'.[87] Ralph instructed the sacrist to seal the measures of the men of the town without demanding or extorting anything, unless otherwise ordered.[88] There are many examples of Edward's responding to appeals from the abbey's tenants for alleged oppression in its courts. For example, in 1287 some complained of unreasonable summons to the abbot's eyre in Lent, of unsuitable jurors from his own household, who maliciously indicted people and whom the accused were forced to use as jurors when tried or to pay intolerable fines (*redemptiones*). They also complained of arbitrary distraint and excessive amercements, and 'various excesses' in the abbot's ecclesiastical court. All this was in contempt of accepted laws and liberties. Edward, therefore, ordered Abbot John to stop all such oppression, and to see that his officials stopped it, without delay. Otherwise, he would have 'to impose the hand of correction'.[89] Also, in 1287, the sacrist, in obedience to a royal mandate, ordered anyone complaining of extortion in the ecclesiastical court to appear before the abbot and hand him any complaint in writing.[90]

The 'Kempe' register, as Richardson and Sayles spotted, has copies, some apparently unique, of documents produced in the course of the dispute between Edward and the clergy over the limits of the jurisdiction of ecclesiastical courts. They are the king's replies to the three sets of *gravamina* presented to Edward in the Easter parliament of 1285.[91] It is interesting to speculate how the documents reached Bury. Perhaps Abbot John brought them back from the Easter Parliament, which presumably he attended. But possibly he acquired them from William de Middleton, bishop of Norwich, a leading figure in the dispute. The dispute had been simmering for many years but finally broke out in 1285, when Edward issued

---

85 Ibid.
86 *Chron. Bury*, 84.
87 *Letter-Book of Hoo*, 129.
88 Ibid. 136.
89 Ibid. 34–5.
90 Ibid. 33.
91 Harl. 645, fos. 224v–5. Discussed and printed by H.G. Richardson and G.O. Sayles, 'The Clergy in the Easter Parliament, 1285', *EHR* lii (1937), 220–34 *passim*; also printed in *Councils and Synods, II: A.D. 1205–1313*, ed. F.M. Powicke and C.R. Cheney (Oxford, 1964), ii. 962–4, 965–7, 972. For another crucial document in the dispute copied into the 'Kempe' register, see below and n. 92. For the dispute in general, see D.L. Douie, *Archbishop Pecham* (Oxford, 1952), ch. 8. No writ summoning Abbot John to the Easter parliament 1285, is in *Parliamentary Writs and Writs of Military Summons, Edw. I–Edw. II*, ed. F. Palgrave (Rec. Comm. 1827–34).

an edict limiting the jurisdiction of ecclesiastical courts strictly to matrimonial and testamentary cases. The edict is not known to survive but its contents appear in a royal writ of 1 July 1285 addressed to the clergy of the diocese of Norwich,[92] where the laity's complaints against the ecclesiastical courts had been particularly loud. It insisted that ecclesiastical judges could force laymen to take oaths as jurors only in matrimonial and testamentary cases. Edward also appointed commissioners to hear pleas arising from breaches of the edict, both past and present. Bishop William, supported by the other bishops, protested, and further *gravamina* were drawn up, until in June or July 1286 Edward issued the famous writ *circumspecte agatis*, addressed to the itinerant justices in the diocese of Norwich. It ordered them to be circumspect in their treatment of the clergy, and listed the pleas which could legitimately be heard in an ecclesiastical court, including a number which were not matrimonial or testamentary at all. It does not, therefore, seem unlikely that Abbot John obtained copies of documents relating to this dispute from Bishop William.

A royal writ of 20 May 1290, addressed to the sacrist of Bury and his commissary, refers to Edward's limitation of spiritual jurisdiction. It orders them to stop compelling laymen to appear before an ecclesiastical judge and to serve as jurors in cases other than testamentary and matrimonial ones 'since we had formerly forbidden [this]'. It also forbids them to force townsmen to appear before them as often as three times a week, and to extort oaths and money at pleasure.[93]

One of the best examples of royal supervision is the trial of the murderers of William, rector of Odell ('Wahill', 'Wadhille'), a *cause célèbre*.[94] On 23 November 1283 William, a man of the knightly class, went to visit his sister, Eleanor de Gowiz, in Bury St. Edmunds. In an alley by the church of St. Mary he was set upon by a gang. One of them, Geoffrey de Redgrave, plunged a knife into William's side.[95] William dropped dead. Eleanor, who was in a house close by, raised the hue and cry. The town erupted in uproar. The alderman, Geoffrey Spot, being old and decrepit and negligent in his duty, did nothing and even refused to hold an inquest. One was, therefore, held by the bailiffs, Nicholas de Fuke and Robert de Melton. The inquest implicated Geoffrey de Redgrave, John de Perers and eleven others, most of whom were captured and imprisoned. Eleanor, intent, we are told, on avenging her brother's death, appealed them of murder in the court of the Liberty. But then she obtained a royal writ, dated 21 December 1283,[96] suspending further proceedings until the king had taken counsel as to how to deal with so grave a scandal to the church (presumably because the murdered man and two main culprits were all clerks) and so shameful a contempt of himself. Meanwhile, the bailiffs were to keep those attached in safe custody and to attach others. Eleanor again appealed to the king, who appointed Reginald de Grey and Roger Loveday to

---

92  *Councils and Synods, II*, ii. 967–9: discussed, and copies noted, by E.B. Graves, '*Circumspecte Agatis*', *EHR* xliii (1928), 2 and n. 3, 3. For a copy not mentioned by Graves, see Harl. 645, f. 205.
93  *Letter-Book of Hoo*, 137.
94  For a vivid contemporary narrative of the murder and the ensuing events, with copies of relevant documents, see *Letter-Book of Hoo*, 130–6. This account is supplemented below from other entries in the Bury registers and from the calendars of public records.
95  Harl. 645, f. 217. William's presentation to the church of Odell is recorded in *Rotuli Ricardi Gravesend, Diocesis Lincolniensis, 1258–79*, ed. F.N. Davis, C.W. Foster and A.H. Thompson (Canterbury and York Soc. 1925; and Lincoln Rec. Soc. xx, 1925), 211. I owe this reference to Dr. Paul Brand.
96  *Letter-Book of Hoo*, 131–2. A commission of oyer and terminer was issued on 26 Dec. 1283: *CPR 1281–92*, 139.

hold an inquest to discover, try and punish the culprits. At this point Abbot John claimed his Liberty. It was allowed, but nevertheless, at the request of the abbot and convent, Edward (in a writ of 6 February 1284) instructed the same justices, and also John de Vaux, to oversee the trial at Bury.[97] Abbot John appointed John de Lovetot, a justice of the (common) bench, and two of his own justices, Richard de Boyland and William de Pakenham, as his bailiffs to try the case, and associated with them William de Saham, like de Lovetot a royal justice.

In view of royal involvement in the trial, the outcome, which is of some interest, must be attributed at least in part to the influence of the king's justices. A number of the accused were convicted and hanged. Two, Geoffrey de Redgrave and John de Perers, pleaded privilege of clergy, but they were not claimed by their ordinary, the abbot. Instead, they were put in prison, condemned to suffer the 'penalty of the statute'.[98] There they languished for nearly ten years. They were not finally admitted to compurgation until 24 July 1293.[99] (Redgrave, indeed, almost lost his immunity because he had broken gaol during this long imprisonment; he only avoided that fate by pleading a bout of insanity, a tendency to which he had inherited from his parents.)[100] In effect, these two criminous clerks suffered what would amount in modern times to 'life sentences'. It does not seem improbable that the royal justices insisted that they should be adequately punished.

There is, of course, the question: how effective was royal supervision? In the Odell case it would seem to have ensured trial in strict accordance with the laws and customs of the realm, and the proper punishment of those convicted. But there is evidence suggesting that in some cases any good results were only temporary. Ralph de Middlington's ordinance of 1285, regulating the view of weights and measures, was not carried out to the letter. When he again held the view there in 1292, the jurors returned that brewsters were always amerced for breaches of the assize (ignoring Ralph's ruling that for the third offence they should stand in the tumbrel), and bakers for the third offence stood in the tumbrel (not the pillory, as Ralph had stipulated).[101]

There is no evidence that in this instance objection was raised to the disregard of a royal ordinance. But sometimes there were protests. For example, the royal writ issued in 1287, ordering the inquiry into oppression in the abbot's ecclesiastical court, accuses Abbot John of scorning 'to emend the excesses' as the king had

---

[97] *CPR 1281–92*, 112.
[98] The Statute of Westminster I (1275), c. 12: notorious felons who refused trial by jury were to suffer 'prison forte et dure'. Cf. H. Summerson, 'The Early Development of the Peine Forte et Dure', in *Law, Litigants and the Legal Profession*, ed. E.W. Ives and A.H. Manchester (London, 1983), 116–25.
[99] Abbot John wrote on 20 June 1293 to the sacrist, William de Hoo, ordering him to have announced on every Sunday and feast day in every parish church and chapel that anyone wishing to accuse Geoffrey de Redgrave and John de Perers should appear before the abbot or his agent in the conventual church on 23 July: Harl. 645, f. 31v; *Letter-Book of Hoo*, 76–7. On the same day he wrote to the prior and precentor ordering them to admit de Redgrave and de Perers to compurgation: *Letter-Book of Hoo*, 149. Sir John de Odell, brother of the victim, William de Odell, objected to the culprits being admitted to compurgation but a jury overruled his objection: Harl. 645, f. 32. Letters of indemnity were issued on the day of the compurgation to Sir John, Eleanor de Gowiz and others in respect of any injury to them by de Redgrave and de Perers respectively: *Letter-Book of Hoo*, 149–50.
[100] This is mentioned in the contemporary record of the compurgation: *Letter-Book of Hoo*, 152.
[101] Harl. 645, f. 249v; cf. Lobel, *Borough*, 103. For a list of those amerced and their amercements at the view in 1292, see Harl. 645, fos. 247–8.

commanded.[102] Persistence was certainly needed to secure justice in the case between Agnes, widow of Walter de Boyton, and Hamo, rector of Attleborough. Agnes sued Hamo sometime before Michaelmas 1289 before Thomas de Weyland (chief justice of common pleas, Michaelmas 1278-Trinity 1289) and his fellows at Westminster over a messuage in the suburbs of Bury.[103] Abbot John successfully claimed his court since the messuage was within the *banleuca*. But Hamo asserted false judgement in St. Edmund's court, and sought a writ of false judgement before Gilbert de Thornton and his fellows, justices of the court of king's bench. Again Abbot John successfully claimed his court. A royal writ instructed the sheriff to attend the abbot's court and record the proceedings. He was to take with him four 'discreet and legal' men of the county (the record wrongly calls them knights), and he and they were to authenticate the record with their seals. The sheriff was to have the record before the king three weeks after Easter 1290. He was also to summon Agnes to appear, and the steward of St. Edmund's Liberty, who was to answer why he had not executed the king's mandate, previously issued, to make a record. Unfortunately, the four men of the county refused to seal the record because they were not suitors of St. Edmund's court, where judgement was given. Abbot John asked for, and was sent, a copy of the writ of false judgement and of the sheriff's record of the plea so that he could emend any error. The sheriff was told to make the suitors of the abbot's court appear and to distrain them if they failed to do so, but the burgesses and the abbot's council pointed out that there were no suitors because the abbot appointed justices, who gave judgement. The sheriff was thereupon told to produce Abbot John and the two justices, Daniel de Beccles and John le Orfever, whom the abbot had appointed to try the case. They were to appear before the king's justices at Michaelmas; and so the dispute dragged on.[104] On 26 September 1292 Edward accused Abbot John of still not having done justice, to Hamo's grave injury. He ordered him to summon the parties, inspect the record, emend any error, and do full and speedy justice 'so that no more complaints reach us'.[105]

It was only occasionally that the central government had to be insistent and peremptory in the supervision of the public functions of the Liberty's administration. Usually it was a matter of co-operation, not confrontation. Often the abbot sought royal help. The writ of false judgement, and the record and process of Hamo's plea, were sent to Abbot John at John's own request. Similarly, Abbot John and the convent asked the king to assign justices to monitor the trial of those accused of murdering William of Odell. No doubt in both cases Abbot John wanted by co-operating with royal authority to avoid a mistrial. In the case of William, parson of Odell he may also have hoped to reduce any blame which might fall on him for the commotion in the town caused by the murder. Either a mistrial or unruliness in the *banleuca* could have resulted in the loss, albeit temporary, of the

---

102 *Letter-Book of Hoo*, 35.
103 The following account of the case is based on the writ of 26 Sept. 1292 and the explanation therein (below, and n. 105) and in the entry on the Coram Rege Roll, no. 124 (Trinity 1290), m. 18, printed in *Select Cases in the Court of King's Bench under Edward I*, ed. G.O. Sayles (Selden Soc. lv, lvii, 1936–8), ii. 3–5 (no. 2).
104 See above, 98–9 n. 47.
105 Mm. iv. 19, fos. 6v–7; Harl. 645, fos. 107v–8 (wrongly dated 26 Dec.); Ff. iv. 35, f. 7; *Pinchbeck Reg.* i. 443–4.

Liberty. But more positively, and above all, the abbot needed royal support, especially in his relations with the town of Bury St. Edmunds.

During the Barons' War, and thereafter, the town was sporadically a source of trouble to the abbey, and sometimes the abbot needed the king to restore order. In 1264 some disaffected townsmen, emboldened by the example of the Londoners and encouraged by the baronial opposition, organized themselves in the Guild of Youth, and seized control of the town's government. The abbot, Simon de Luton, appealed to Henry III, who on 29 October appointed two justices, Gilbert de Preston and William de Bovill, to hear the abbot's and convent's complaints.[106] The civil war also caused trouble in the Liberty at large, with the result that it was taken into the king's hands. On 21 February 1267 Henry appointed Stephen de Edworth and John le Bretun to hold an inquest, in the abbot's presence, touching persons charged with, and indicted of, robberies and other trespasses within and without the town.[107] On 9 March Henry, having restored the Liberty to Abbot Simon, appointed, at the abbot's request, John le Bretun and others deputed by the abbot to inquire touching trespasses against the king in the Liberty. They were to do justice as provided by the king's and the abbot's councils respectively, so that the appointment of le Bretun would not be to the prejudice of the Liberty.[108]

Abbot John was dogged by trouble with the town, notably in the later 1280s and early and late 1290s. The townsmen's complaints to the king against the abbot's administration in 1287–8 have already been mentioned. At least in the 1290s, the ringleaders were burgesses of importance, for example, Stephen, son of Benedict (bailiff 1284–5). In 1290 they organized an attack on the cellarer's new dam in the Teyfan, a marsh just north-east of Bury. The violence caused Abbot John to appeal to Edward, who on 2 February 1292 appointed justices, John de Mettingham, William de Gisleham and Hugh de Cressingham, to hold an inquest at Bury.[109] They sat on 19 September. The proceedings of the inquest were continued in 1293. On 27 February Edward appointed John le Bretun and William de Redham to replace de Mettingham, who was busy, and de Gisleham, who had died; but on 4 March he reappointed de Mettingham.[110] Abbot John rehearsed his grievances against the townsmen, but how they would have replied is unknown because a compromise was reached.

In the late 1290s the townsmen's opposition was non-violent and carefully planned. In 1281 Edward, as mentioned above, had confirmed the confirmations of the abbey's privileges by Henry I and John.[111] This included liberties enjoyed by the town, notably the freedom of the burgesses from toll throughout England.[112] Sometime shortly before, or early in, 1297 two influential townsmen, Peter of Ellingham (alderman 1295–7) and Stephen, son of Benedict, one of the leaders of the opposi-

---

[106] *CPR 1258–66*, 375; Lobel, *Borough*, 126–8, 130. (A copy of the writ is in Ff. ii. 33, f. 32.)

[107] *CPR 1266–72*, 131; Lobel, *Borough*, 130.

[108] *CPR 1266–72*, 45.

[109] Late 13th-, early 14th-c. copies of a record of the inquest, citing the royal writs appointing justices, and of the agreement reached, are in a number of the Bury registers, but not all are complete: Harl. 645, fos. 28–31v (complete); *Pinchbeck Reg.* i. 58–66 (complete); Mm. iv. 19, fos. 25–6v (incomplete); Add. 14847, fos. 59v–62 (incomplete); Harl. 638, fos. 217–18 (incomplete); Ff. ii. 33 (agreement only). Cf. Lobel, *Borough*, 132–3.

[110] *CPR 1292–1301*, 45, not cited in the account mentioned in n. 109 above.

[111] Above, 94 and n. 20.

[112] *CChR 1257–1300*, 258. John's confirmation is printed in *Rotuli Chartarum in Turri Londinensi asservati, 1199–1216*, ed. T.D. Hardy (Rec. Comm. 1837), 38.

tion in the early 1290s, obtained duplicates of these charters and had them read publicly in the tollhouse, all without the abbot's and convent's knowledge. Abbot John and the convent appealed to the king against this piece of presumption — the abbot contended that the town had no privileges except by his grace.[113] On 8 December 1297 Edward issued a writ to the town bailiffs to have the two ring-leaders before Prince Edward on 20 January 1298.[114] They did so, and Peter and Stephen duly surrendered the charters. And on 4 February the most important burgesses appeared before Abbot John, the prior and their counsellors, bound themselves for the transgression, and bought the abbot's good will for 320 marks. However, John remitted 100 marks and put another 100 marks *in respectum*; that is, they undertook to pay it if in future they rose against, or unjustly sued, the abbot and convent.

In general, Edward's relations with St. Edmunds were excellent. It is noticeable that serious conflicts date from 1290 and before. No doubt the settling of franchise holders' and land holders' claims by *Quo Warranto* proceedings and at the exchequer reduced areas of possible dispute. Perhaps another factor contributed to create harmony between Abbot John and the king. John had aged. According to the story related above, after his stand against Edward on behalf of all franchise holders in the Easter parliament of 1290, he went home 'broken by age and exhausted by his labours'.[116] A letter of procuration, in which he excuses himself on grounds of ill-health from attendance at a general chapter of Benedictines, survives. It is undated, but may well refer to the general chapter held at Oxford in September 1300. Alternatively, the reference could be to one of the two or three general chapters held in the late 1290s.[117] The Bury chronicler gives many details about the dispute between Edward and the clergy in 1296 and 1297 over clerical taxation by the king. Especially full is his account of the November parliament at Bury in 1296, when, he alleges, Pope Boniface VIII's bull *Clericis laicos* was read out; his sympathies were, as one would expect, with the clergy.[118] Neither his evidence, nor any other known evidence, suggests that Abbot John played any part in the quarrel.

The good relations between abbot and king certainly owed something to Edward's growing preoccupation with Scotland during the 1290s, first the trial of the competitors for the Scottish throne, and then his campaigns. The Scottish war entailed ever-worsening financial problems. Worry about affairs in Scotland and shortage of money deflected Edward from concern with private franchises. One direct result of his Scottish involvement was more personal contact with Bury. What part, if any, Abbot John and/or any of his monks took in the proceedings at

113 A copy of the abbot's and convent's petition is in *Pinchbeck Reg.* i. l. Cf. Lobel, *Borough*, 136.
114 Harl. 638, fos. 52, 164v–5. Cf. Lobel, *Borough*, 136.
115 Harl. 638, fos. 164v–5.
116 Above, 91–2.
117 The letter is printed, from Harl. 230, f. 73, in *Documents Illustrating the Activities of the General and Provincial Chapters of the English Black Monks 1215–1540*, ed. W.A. Pantin (Camden Soc., 3rd ser. xlv, xlvii, liv, 1931–7), i. 140. The relevant passage suggests that John was suffering from, or approaching, his last illness. He died on 29 Oct. 1301. He had attended the general chapter of the province of Canterbury held at Abingdon in July 1290: ibid. i. 130.
118 *Chron. Bury*, 134–5. For this parliament, including refs. to the Bury chronicle, see *Councils and Synods, II*, ii. 1148–50. See also *Chron. Bury*, 137–41 *passim; Councils and Synods, II*, ii. 1150–62.

Norham in the summer of 1291 it is impossible to say, but Lionel Stones pointed out that the Bury chronicler was exceptionally well informed about the Great Cause and interested in Anglo-Scottish relations.[119] Like a number of other chroniclers, he transcribed, at Edward's command, the letters of submission to his judgement of the competitors for the Scottish throne,[120] and has besides much other information.[121] It is surprising that Bury was not, apparently, one of the monasteries from which Edward obtained chronicle evidence of his right to overlordship; no return has survived from the abbey. However, if indeed no return was made (and it has not simply been lost), the reason is perhaps that a Bury monk or monks gave evidence personally at the trial at Norham.[122] The only piece of possible evidence for this seems to be a pardon issued on 7 May 1292 to a monk called John de Shottesham for taking venison in the king's forest in Essex and in the park at Langham: it was 'in consideration of his service in Scotland'.[123] (Later, sometime before 1 December 1294, de Shottesham became the abbey's precentor, suggesting that he was a learned man and, accordingly, would have been of some use to Edward at Norham.)[124]

Certainly Edward's Scottish policy increased the number of his visits to Bury, because he could conveniently stay there on his way to and from the North. He did so (28 April–2 May) on his way there in 1292, though he spent some of his time on the abbot's manor of Culford,[125] and also in 1296 (16–20 January),[126] and from 8 to 11 May 1300.[127] He also stayed in Bury from 9 to 29 November 1296, on his way back, but on that occasion, during which he held a parliament, he lodged with a burgess, not in the abbey.[128] Overall, the number of his visits when king almost tripled after 1290. In the eighteen years before that date he was there four times, in the subsequent seventeen years, eleven times. His visits to the abbey were nearly always accompanied by some formal recognition of its liberties, and sometimes by other grants. During his visit in May 1300 he granted the abbot and convent fines or amercements from those who traded in the *banleuca* with debased French coins (*kokedones*) contrary to the royal edict.[129] Edward issued the pardon to John de Shottesham on 7 May 1292, just five days after the end of his visit to Bury in that year.

Edward's relations with the abbey were especially cordial during the period of his Scottish involvement, partly because he regarded St. Edmund as a warrior saint.

---

119 E.L.G. Stones and G.G. Simpson, *Edward I and the Throne of Scotland 1290–1296. An Edition of the Record Sources for the Great Cause* (Oxford, 1978), i. 147–8, 207; ii. 127.
120 *Chron. Bury*, 100–3.
121 Ibid. 98–100, 114–15, 130–3 *passim*, 141, 147, 149–50.
122 This is suggested in Stones and Simpson, *Great Cause*, i. 147 and n. 5.
123 *CPR 1281–92*, 488. This writ is not mentioned in Stones and Simpson, *Great Cause*.
124 See the letter from Prior William de Rockland, and John de Shottesham, precentor, announcing the successful purgation of a clerk, William le Eyre, who had been charged with robbery, dated 1 Dec. 1294: Harl. 645, f. 33v. Cf. *Letter-Book of Hoo*, 105–6.
125 *Chron. Bury*, 113; H. Gough, *Itinerary of Edward I, 1272–1307* (Paisley, 1900), ii. 92–3.
126 *Chron. Bury*, 130.
127 Ibid. 156–7.
128 Ibid. 134.
129 Ibid. 156. Edward I's writ to all the sheriffs of England, and to others, forbidding trade with 'pollards and crockards' (base coins), in accordance with an ordinance in council, is dated 23 Aug. 1299. The import of 'bad monies' such as pollards and crockards was forbidden in a writ of 28 May 1299: *Statutes of the Realm*, i. 134–5. Cf. *Munimenta Gildhalles Londoniensis*, ed. H.T. Riley (RS, 1859–62), ii, pt. i, 187, 189–90. Cf. R.E. Latham, *Dictionary of Medieval Latin from British Sources* (Oxford, 1981), 519, *sub* 'crocardus'.

In this way he resembled Henry II and Richard I. Henry fought the battle of Fornham (near Bury) in 1173 under the banner of St. Edmund, defeating the earl of Leicester 'with God's and St. Edmund's help'.[130] In 1190 Richard I's crusading fleet was thought to be under St. Edmund's protection, as well as that of St. Thomas Becket and St. Nicholas;[131] and in the next year Richard sent the imperial banner ('all woven in gold') of Isaac Comnenus, the defeated prince of Cyprus, 'at once to the blessed Edmund, king and glorious martyr'.[132] On his return to England in 1194, Richard delayed at Westminster for hardly a day before he left on pilgrimage to Bury.[133] When Edward I, for his part, first visited St. Edmund's abbey after his return from crusade in 1275, it was also as a pilgrimage and 'in accordance with a vow made in the Holy Land'.[134] Similarly, his visit in February 1285, when he was accompanied by the queen and three of their daughters, was to fulfil a vow he had made to God and St. Edmund during the Welsh campaign.[135] In 1296, at the very hour when he was attending high mass in the abbey church on the feast of St. Edmund (20 November), Rhys ap Rhys surrendered to his forces in Wales; Edward, therefore, according to the chronicler, made suitable offerings to the saint 'with humble devotion'.[136]

Edward's association of St. Edmund with victory in war is most vividly shown by his veneration during the period of the Scottish campaigns. When he visited Bury in May 1300, the chronicler states that Edward issued the following injunction to one of his justices: 'I order you to take care not to harm the written privileges of St. Edmund, for I have no doubt that he will be in Scotland to protect me and mine, and conquer the enemy; he will come brandishing his weapons, ready for battle — much readier than you.'[137] Before leaving the abbey, 'he particularly commended himself to the convent's prayers. When he was mounted on his palfrey ready to leave by the court-yard gate, he twice looked back and bowed most devoutly, bending his head low, to the blessed martyr and his saints.'[138] And shortly after leaving, Edward sent his standard back, with the urgent request to the prior and convent to have 'a mass for St. Edmund celebrated over it, and that it should be touched with all the relics'.[139]

The monks responded with enthusiasm to the challenge of the Scottish war, if the chronicler is to be believed. Instead of the chronicler's usual objection to taxation, he regarded the clerical tenth of 1298 as lawful because it would enable Edward to fight for the safety of the kingdom and the protection of everyone's property: 'to guard one's own possessions is quite a different matter from coveting other people's'.[140] The chronicler was, in fact, echoing the views of the clergy in

130 *Gesta Regis Henrici Secundi Benedicti Abbatis*, ed. W. Stubbs (RS, 1867), i. 61. Henry II went on pilgrimage to Bury and Ely after Easter 1177: ibid. i. 159.
131 Ibid. ii. 116.
132 Ibid. ii. 164.
133 *Radulphi de Coggeshall Chronicon Anglicanum*, ed. J. Stevenson (RS, 1875), 63. Richard's veneration for St. Edmund is also shown by his grant in free alms in 1189 of 10 *l.* in Aylsham (Norf.) to provide four candles to burn forever around St. Edmund's shrine: Harl. 1005, f. 81; Harl. 645, f. 206v.
134 *Chron. Bury*, 57.
135 Ibid. 83.
136 Ibid. 135–6.
137 Ibid. 156.
138 Ibid. 157.
139 Ibid. 157.
140 Ibid. 147.

general. The ecclesiastical council held in the New Temple, London, in June 1298 granted Edward the tenth 'to drive the Scots and other enemies from England, in defence of Church and kingdom', and the clergy promised to pray for victory.[141]

The monks of Bury were clearly affected by the widespread patriotism, fanned by royal propaganda, which burgeoned after the Scots rebelled and invaded the northern counties in 1296.[142] Since Edward's longest stay at Bury was on his return from the campaign which followed the Scottish incursions,[143] the monks would have had immediate, first-hand news of events, and exposure to the full brunt of royal propaganda. Having described in detail the fall of Edinburgh castle to Edward in that year, the Bury chronicler bursts forth in a paean on Edward's conquests:

> Thus the king reduced the whole kingdom of Scotland. In this way he obtained absolute power over England, Scotland and Wales, which together had formed the ancient kingdom of Britain but were for long torn and divided. Such a victory, by a royal person, achieved so quickly, in such a short time and in such an emergency, could hardly be recalled.[144]

These national factors, Edward's preoccupation with Scotland and his subjects' patriotic response to the Scottish war, undoubtedly helped to make harmonious Abbot John's relations with the king during the last ten years or so of his abbatiate.

---

[141] *Councils and Synods, II*, ii. 1191, 1197. For other refs. to the Scottish threat, see ibid. ii. 1183 (arts. 5, 6), 1185.
[142] For Edward I's use of propaganda to support his wars, see M. Prestwich, *War, Politics and Finance under Edward I* (London, 1972), 240–2; D. Burton, 'Requests for Prayers and Royal Propaganda under Edward I': above, 25–35.
[143] Above, 100.
[144] *Chron. Bury*, 133.

# Gothic Architecture in Southern England and the French Connection in the Early Thirteenth Century*

## Lindy Grant

In the summer of 1204 were abruptly severed the close political and administrative links that had bound England and Normandy into, in some sense, a single unit for the previous 140 years. Among the legacies of that 140 years one would expect common artistic traditions and cultural affinities. This paper considers that most expensive of cultural manifestations, ecclesiastical architecture, in the two provinces in the late twelfth and early thirteenth centuries. Given that gothic architecture is by definition French, and given that the upper echelons of both lay and ecclesiastical society (potential achitectural patrons) in the period immediately before 1204 were often equally at home in kingdom and duchy, one might expect English gothic architecture to show strong Norman influence, and that gothic in both areas would have much in common even after 1204.[1]

It would be foolish to pretend that there are no resemblances between the architecture of England and Normandy in the early thirteenth century. Norman rib and arch mouldings have a multiplicity closer to English practice than to the chaste profiles of the Ile de France. The foliate oculi which litter Norman wall surfaces are reminiscent of West Country work, such as the nave at Wells. They appear in abundance in the cloister of Mont Saint Michel, along with moulded capitals, rare in the duchy but standard in England, and dark marble shafts, so rare in the duchy

* I would like to thank Professor Peter Kidson, Professor Peter Fergusson and, among historians, Dr. David Bates, Dr. Paul Brand, Dr. David Crouch and Mr. John Gillingham for their help in discussing various aspects of this paper. I would also like to thank my colleagues in the Conway Library for their help with photographs. Research for this paper was partially financed by a grant from the Central Research Fund, Univ. of London.

1 Most historians have stressed the extent to which, from the political and administrative point of view, the Anglo-Norman, if not the Angevin, realm was a distinct reality: see e.g. C.H. Haskins, *Norman Institutions* (Cambridge, Mass. 1918), 189–93; F.M. Powicke, *The Loss of Normandy* (1st edn. London, 1913), 9–102; J. Le Patourel, 'The Plantagenet Dominions', *History*, 1 (1965), 289–308. J. Gillingham, *The Angevin Empire* (London, 1984), 61–4 stresses the potential political cohesion of the entire 'empire' and the accidental nature of its collapse. W. Stevenson, 'England and Normandy 1204–59' (Leeds Univ. Ph.D. thesis, 1974) explores the continuation of links between England and Normandy after 1204. J.C. Holt, 'The End of the Anglo-Norman Realm', *Proc. British Academy*, lxi (1975), 223–65; and L. Musset, 'Quelques problèmes posés par l'annexion de la Normandie au domaine royal français', in *La France de Philippe Auguste. Le Temps des Mutations*, ed. R-H. Bautier (Paris, 1982), 291–309 both see disintegration between England and Normandy in the last years of the 12th c. Most recently, however, D. Bates, 'Normandy and England after 1066', *EHR* civ (1989), 851–80; and J. Green, 'Unity and Disunity in the Anglo-Norman State', *Historical Research*, lxiii (1989), 115–34, have emphasized the separate identities of England and Normandy from the early 12th c.

that modern writers have assumed them to be of imported English Purbeck marble.[2] (pl. 1) Normanisms in England include the quatrefoil friezes that decorate a series of Kentish buildings in the 1220s, notably Canterbury cathedral cloister,[3] Minster in Thanet and Hythe (pl. 3). The same feature appears at New Shoreham, though this, surely, is a building of the late twelfth century rather than the thirteenth.[4] Both Norman and English architects had a penchant for Y tracery, where all arcs are sprung with the same radius, and its corollary, the sharp subsidiary lancet, as at Bayeux choir (pl. 2) and St. Albans, both of *c*. 1230.[5] Dying mouldings appear almost simultaneously at Salisbury and Rouen choirs.[6] Salisbury shares with its other Norman contemporary, Coutances, the device of a small rib vault roofing window embrasures. In neither case is the direction of influence clear.

Features like these are striking and easy to point to, but the resemblance may be more superficial than real. Often they reflect a common eleventh-century Anglo-Norman architectural heritage rather than direct influence. Both England and Normandy remained committed to thick wall structure (where the wall is thick enough for a clerestory passage to run within it) and some common features are there to disguise the prodigious wall mass that results.[7] This includes the vaulted window embrasure, the multiple mouldings, and the dying moulding, which brings the overrich multiple mouldings safely to rest on their arcade piers. The joint popularity of Y tracery is surely because both areas shared the same lively romanesque tradition of interlaced arcading, from which, as the west front of Peterborough shows, Y tracery is a natural development.

It is not always certain that the source for apparent Normanisms in England is Normandy. The quatrefoil friezes of the Kent group, while undoubtedly a Norman speciality, can also be found in north-east France (in the choir of St. Quentin, for instance underlining the triforium); and there is a mid-twelfth-century example of punched quatrefoils in wall arcade spandrels at Guarbeque in the Pas de Calais. North-east France is probably the source for the fussy elaborations, the gouges and fillets, which distinguish English from Norman arch mouldings.[8] This area of

---

2   See e.g. C.M. Girdlestone, 'Thirteenth Century Gothic in England and Normandy', *Archaeological Journ.* cii (1945), 123; and J. Chazelas, 'La vie monastique au Mont Saint Michel au XIIIe siècle', in *Millénaire Monastique du Mont Saint Michel, I*, ed. J. Laporte (Paris, 1966), 144 n. 111.
3   For the date of Canterbury cloister, see F. Woodman, *The Architectural History of Canterbury Cathedral* (London, 1981), 138–9.
4   See, most recently, S. Woodcock, 'St. Mary de Haura, New Shoreham' (London Univ. unpubl. MA report, 1988).
5   For the dating of Bayeux choir, see L.M. Grant, 'Gothic Architecture in Normandy, c.1150–1250' (London Univ. Ph.D. thesis, 1987), 237–8; for St Albans, see N. Pevsner and B. Cherry, *Hertfordshire*, Buildings of England (London, 1953), 295–6.
6   V. Jansen, 'Dying Mouldings, Unarticulated Springer Blocks and Hollow Chamfers in Thirteenth Century Architecture', *Journ. British Archaeological Assoc.* cxxxvi (1982), 35–54.
7   The classic study of thick wall architecture is J. Bony, 'La technique normande du mur épais à l'époque romane', *Bulletin Monumental*, xcviii (1939), 153–88.
8   Channels, fillets, broad fillets, and gouged rolls are scattered across NE. France, in the Somme, the Aisne area and the Upper Oise in the second half of the 12th c. There is no concentration of types, and there is no trace of the use of these variations further north in the Boullonnais, Artois or French Flanders, though these are the areas where destruction of 12th- and 13th-c. churches has been heaviest. Channels appear at St. Taurin and Fieffes (Somme), Cuise la Motte and Monchy St. Eloi (Oise), and Soissons cathedral, S. transept, and St. Martin, Laon (Aisne); fillets at Airaines (Somme) and Soissons, S. transept, and Bruyères St. Fère (Aisne); broad fillets at Beaufort en Santerre, and the porch of St. Quentin in the Vermandois; and gouged angle rolls at Soissons, S. transept.

France, Ponthieu, the Boullonnais, Artois, eastern Picardy, and French Flanders is a difficult area for the architectural historian to deal with. It is a large area, much less coherent and more complex in terms of communications, economic interests, or political connections, and, I suspect, architectural developments, than is often implied, or than I will have time to deal with in this article. Moreover, almost all the major early gothic buildings in the area, apart from those in the south-east corner (the Laonnois/Soissonnais) have been either rebuilt or destroyed in eight centuries of wealth and warfare, and we have to build our image of them from drawings, fragments, and a few survivals.[9]

In spite of the shared eleventh-century heritage, English and Norman architecture grew increasingly apart in the second half of the twelfth century. The full-scale vaulted tribune, revived in Normandy at Fécamp,[10] was ignored in England in favour of a squat, unvaulted gallery, as, for instance, at Malmesbury. Canterbury established this as the predominant type in late twelfth-century and early thirteenth-century England, as at Lincoln or Salisbury. Triforia in the French manner are rare. Where they do occur, as at Southwark, their height relates them not to Normandy or to the Ile de France, but to eastern French and Flemish designs, such as at St. Omer[11] (pl. 4). Thirteenth-century Norman architects usually retained the full tribune scale, even if all that lay behind it was a triforium, as at Lisieux or Bayeux (pl. 2). The Normans flirted briefly with the sexpartite vault, but then opted wholeheartedly for the rectangular quadripartite, with a very regular, ordered articulation to support it, which chopped the interior into vertical slices, one bay per slice, like slabs of cake.[12] Perhaps because twelfth-century English churches were often unvaulted, their articulation was less decisive, with slender shafting that often only started half way up the elevation. English elevations have a strong horizontal emphasis, with the decorative middle level running the length of the building, like jam spread between two layers of sponge.

Although vaulting was widely adopted in the South by 1200, English articulation remained the antithesis of its Norman contemporaries. Wall shafts in southeast England are usually tight triangular clusters, with no dosseret, *en delit* and often of the dark Purbeck marble, which so unfortunately resembles a drainpipe. It looks as if it is drawn against the wall — the linear quality is often emphasized with fillets or keeling — and seems far too fragile to support the vault above.[13] Its

---

9  For Picardy in general, see R. Fossier, *La Terre et Les Hommes en Picardie* (Paris, Louvain, 1968), 144–9 (for communications), 472–83, 543–4 (for patterns of alliance and affinity among the magnates). For the buildings, see C. Enlart, *Monuments religieux de l'architecture romane et de transition dans la région picarde* (Amiens, 1895); L. Serbat, 'Quelques églises anciennement détruites du nord de la France', *Bulletin Monumental*, lxxxviii (1929), 365–435; P. Heliot, *Les églises du Moyen Age dans le Pas de Calais* (Arras, 1951).
10  For Fécamp, see Grant, 'Gothic Architecture', 61–3.
11  J. Bony, 'The Resistance to Chartres in Early Thirteenth Century Architecture', *Journ. British Archaeological Assoc.* 3rd ser. xx–xxi (1957–8), 50–1 n. 8. The main elevation of Southwark, with its basically octagonal piers, heavy lidded moulded capitals, its triforium passage, edged with small sharp dogtooth, and pendulous arch mouldings often with broad fillets, seems to be the source for the reprise of St. Albans nave in the 1230s.
12  Grant, 'Gothic Architecture', 51–69.
13  Fillets occur on the ribs of the E. crypt at Canterbury, so they are part of the Kentish repertoire, e.g. Hythe and Minster in Thanet, and Southwark and Lambeth, London. They also appear in Sussex and Hants., at Winchester retrochoir, Boxgrove, and St. John, Portsmouth, perhaps emanating from Canterbury. Keeling is not a Kentish feature. Tight triplet shaft groups with keeling are found in Sussex and Hants., e.g. Chichester retrochoir, Winchester retrochoir, Romsey, St. Thomas, Portsmouth, Boxgrove choir, from the 1180s. A very similar configuration, though it is

connections with the wall behind it are tenuous, depending solely on base, capital, and occasional ring moulding extending back into the masonry of the wall. At Winchester retrochoir, subsidence has made the independence of wall and shaft system perilously clear (pl. 7). Pier forms are variations on columnar cores with attached shafting, and often the columnar core is dropped, leaving a see-through cluster of freestanding shafts.[14] Southern English buildings have containing walls, within which pier and respond forms float loosely in a sort of spatial limbo.

Norman buildings, such as Bayeux choir, could not be more completely different. Their multiple mouldings have a rhythmic quality, constructed usually from simple triplet groups of evenly-sized rolls and hollows. This is quite different from the nervous complications of the English moulding, with its extra fillets and gouges. The relentles axes and clear bay divisions of the earliest Norman gothic buildings were softened, slurred and slightly dissolved by the introduction, in the 1180s at St. Etienne, Caen (pl. 5), of a new subtlety in handling the massive pier and respond forms — rounding abaci and bases, using single abaci and bases to support or surmount multiple shafts, above all suppressing angled dosserets into convexities or concavities, or miniature extra shafts.[15] But beneath these elegant devices, vault responds remain massive, set on substantial, if disguised, dosserets and coursed into the wall; and the distinctive corporeality of Norman gothic architecture is still, in the early thirteenth century, underlined by the retention of the cruciform composite pier (pl. 2).

Normandy is more or less alone in northern France at this period in retaining the composite pier. Elsewhere, pier design revolved around columns or multiple columns. Where it does depart from this rather old-fashioned form of Gothic design, it looks to Paris and Parisian design, such as Bourges, for alternative inspiration. This is already the basic architectural alignment of Normandy in the second half of the twelfth century (at Fécamp, Mortemer, Caen and Lisieux) and continues to be so at Rouen, Eu, Hambye and Coutances into the thirteenth.[16]

The principal catalyst for English gothic developments was the choir of Canterbury cathedral. Coloured shafting, complex, occasionally coreless columnar pier and shaft groups, vaulting, elaborate mouldings, rounded and moulded capitals and bases can all be found there.[17] Of the two architects responsible for the choir,

---

always of coursed stone, appears in the W. Country, at Worcester W. end, *c.* 1175, and then becomes standard in the W. It is unclear to me whether, and how, these two groups should be interrelated. I assume that what lies behind both types is the 'Somme Valley' pier type — fat, keeled clusters of shafts, as at Boxgrove crossing piers — slimmed almost beyond recognition.

14 See-through clusters are used at e.g. Hythe, Portsmouth and Boxgrove, Chichester and Salisbury. The immediate source is presumably the coreless clusters in the gallery arcade and the distinctly separated twin columns in the E. crypt, Canterbury.

15 L.M. Grant, 'The Choir of St. Etienne at Caen', in *Medieval Architecture and its Intellectual Context: Essays for Peter Kidson*, ed. P. Crossley and E. Fernie (London, 1990), 113–25.

16 The choir design of Mortemer derives from St. Denis; portal and capital sculpture at Lisieux are by masons from Mantes; Fécamp choir has double aisles, and was originally to have had a double ambulatory; the ultimate dependence of Coutances, and thus Hambye, on Bourges is self-evident. For a full discussion of the question, see Grant, 'Gothic Architecture', *passim* and esp. 340–50. For Parisian elements at St. Etienne, Caen see id., 'St Etienne at Caen'; and for the relationship between Rouen nave (and Eu nave) and Notre Dame and Bourges, see id., 'Rouen Cathedral, 1200–c.1240', in *British Archaeological Assoc. Conference Trans.* for the 1989 Rouen conference (forthcoming).

17 J. Bony, 'French Influences on the Origins of English Gothic Architecture', *Journ. Warburg and Courtauld Institutes*, xii (1949), 1–11. Bony's work on this problem is seminal.

*Plate 1*   Mont Saint Michel: cloister

*Plate 2*   Bayeux Cathedral: choir

*Plate 3*   Hythe: choir piers

*Plate 4*   St. Omer Cathedral: choir (courtesy of Christopher Wilson)

*Plate 5*   Caen: St. Etienne: choir

*Opposite, top.*   *Plate 6*   Boxgrove Priory: choir

*Opposite, bottom.*   *Plate 7*   Winchester Cathedral: retrochoir

*Plate 8* Portsmouth:
St. Thomas: choir

*Plate 9* Graville
Ste. Honorine: choir

*Plate 10* Hambye Abbey: choir

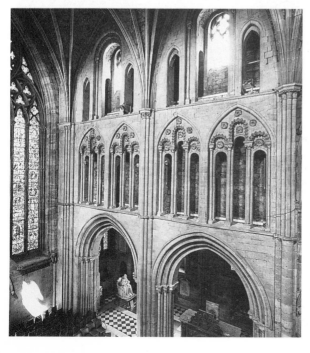

*Plate 11* Worcester Cathedral: nave: west bays

*Plate 12*   Wells Cathedral: west front: central portal: tympanum

*Plate 13*   Mont Saint Michel:
cloister arcade spandrel

*Plate 14*   Coutances Cathedral: nave:
north porch: tympanum

William of Sens knew Parisian as well as north-eastern French building.[18] With William the Englishman, Parisian elements are lost, and there is a new emphasis on quirky mannerisms from Artois and the Boullonais, as well as eastern Picardy.[19] But Canterbury was not the first English building to import Gothic precepts from north-east France and Flanders. The idea of dark marbling came from the Tournaisis and was popularized by Stephen and Henry of Blois, who had strong links with this part of France.[20] Later in the twelfth century, in the vital and formative years *c.* 1165–85, some of the earliest English gothic experiments were fired by the keeled fasciculated pier bunches and waterleaf capitals of the Somme Valley and Ponthieu — certainly in the North, at Ripon and Byland, but also in the South, at the church of the knights of St. John and at the Temple, in London, or at Boxgrove crossing or St. Thomas, Portsmouth.[21] Nevertheless, the influence of Somme Valley designs is limited at Canterbury, apart from the rounding of bases and abaci, and waned thereafter. This may be because the Somme itself seems to have peaked early, architecturally speaking, between *c.* 1150 and *c.* 1170, with little further development until the rebuilding of Amiens cathedral in the 1220s. It is, however, an area which suffered badly in the Hundred Years War, and it may simply be due to accidents of survival that there is little indication of building here between 1170 and 1220, so that we cannot know whether English building continued to draw on it in this period or not.[22] At all events, from Canterbury onwards, English architectural connections seem to shift north and east to eastern Picardy, Artois and the Boullonnais. Post-Canterbury architecture in England is notoriously insular, and to a large

18  Parisian elements in William of Sens' work at Canterbury include his original design for the N. gallery, with oculi and transverse barrel vaults, as at Notre Dame, Paris and Mantes; and responds in the E. transepts with shafts flush with the wall, separated by projecting 'à bec' dosserets as in the aisle responds at Notre Dame.
19  English William seems to have been strongly drawn to the whimsical speculations with screens of shafts, which were obsessing the architects of the Laonnois (shafts sufficiently detached from the wall to create passages behind them: see Bony, 'Resistance to Chartres', 48–9) and Champagne (shafts in front of windows, as at St. Rémi, Reims). His very slender twin marble shafts at the entrance to the E. crypt are reminiscent of the attenuated choir piers at Arras; and his interest in filleted ribs, rounded abaci and bases suggest he was more attuned to building in the Somme and Boullonais than William of Sens had been. There is a comparable shift in sources for the choir capitals. Influences from the Laonnois and N. Champagne are consistently present: up to the E. crossing piers, Parisian influence is also strong, but from the presbytery eastwards it is displaced by influence from Arras: R. Mair, 'The Choir Capitals of Canterbury Cathedral, 1174–84', *British Archaeological Assoc. Conference Trans. Canterbury* (1982), 56–66.
20  Stephen was, of course, count of Boulogne by marriage. For their role in popularizing the use of dark polished marbles, see G. Zarnecki, 'Romanesque Sculpture — Introduction', in *English Romanesque Art, 1066–1200* (Arts Council, London, 1984), 148.
21  For Somme Valley influence at Ripon, Byland and the Temple Church, see C. Wilson, 'The Cistercians as "Missionaries of Gothic" in Northern England', in *Cistercian Art and Architecture in the British Isles*, ed. C. Norton and D. Park (Cambridge, 1986), esp. 91–9, 101–5; for Ripon and Byland, see P. Fergusson, *Architecture of Solitude: Cistercian Abbeys in Twelfth-Century England* (Princeton, 1984), 81–2.
22  Pier fragments (perhaps *c.* 1230) from the largely destroyed church of Longpré les Corps Saints (Somme) are double columns with small extra shafts at their interstices, reminiscent, although the whole group is coursed, of piers in the presbytery at Canterbury. Doullens (of equally indeterminate early 13th-c. date, has slender monolithic double column piers, dying mouldings, and is 'thick wall' with an exterior clerestory passage. The parish church of Maintenay, like Doullens, on the Authie, and also probably early 13th-c., has affinities with English building rather than contemporary Ile de France design, with its rounded abaci, sharply keeled rib profiles and *en delit* vault shafts. All three buildings suggest that this area and S. England were still to an extent architecturally in line in the early 13th c.

extent early thirteenth-century English architects contented themselves with refinements of ideas received at Canterbury and elsewhere in the late twelfth century. But insofar as English architects looked outside England, the north-eastern French/Flemish alignment continued. The flying buttresses at Chichester, Shoreham and Boxgrove (pl. 6) may represent fresh French influence, and certainly the distinctive stepped flyers at the latter reveal their eastern Picard pedigree, pale reflections of the stepped flyers of Soissons, Laon, or Braine. The sacristy vaults at Chichester have rib profiles (a hollow flanked by twin rolls) which are not present at Canterbury. These are most un-English (and, for that matter, most un-Norman) but they are standard in the Laonnois and Soissonnais. The main elevation of St. Omer suggests that the striking austerity of so much early thirteenth-century English building may have been in line with north-eastern French taste, though the austere mode is already present in all its essentials in the eastern crypt at Canterbury.[23] In short, England and Normandy are not even drawing architectural inspiration from the same gothic sources.

English architectural traditions, unlike those of Germany or Italy, were sufficiently lively, and sufficiently sympathetic to French gothic developments, to give as well as take. In the twelfth century this was of major importance, especially for superimposed wall passages.[24] What was practical access at Peterborough transept became in north-eastern France (at Noyon transept, for instance) a very clever game indeed. The thirteenth-century English contribution was more peripheral, but offered novel alternatives to east and west ends. The distinctive English retrochoir, usually rectangular, often with double transepts, and the perfect receptacle for the shrines of important local saints, gradually emerged — at Canterbury, though this was not rectangular, Chichester (begun in 1187), Winchester (begun by 1202), and later Salisbury, Worcester and Lincoln. The Normans showed no interest whatsoever, even before 1204, when the English and Norman clergy was effectively the same personnel, and ought to have had similar liturgical demands and expectations. It is true that the English retrochoir was developed to house a new sort of contemporary saint, and that the Norman bishops, Walter of Coutances or Arnulf of Lisieux, were just not the stuff of sanctity in the manner of Becket or Hugh of Lincoln. But when Normandy did acquire a modern, British saint in Laurence O'Toole at Eu, the choir begun to house him in 1186 had no connection with the emerging English retrochoir, but was a thoroughly French, radiating chapel chevet.[25] Admittedly, no one in north-eastern France fell for the full complexities of the English retrochoir, but some consciousness of English experiments may lie behind the immense, rectangular choir extension at Laon and the doubled transept at St. Quentin.[26] It is the same story with the English western transepts and screen

23 Recently, Jansen has linked this austere style, epitomised at Salisbury, to the circle of Stephen Langton: V. Jansen, 'Lambeth Palace Chapel, the Temple Choir, and Southern English Gothic Architecture of c.1215–1240', in *England in the Thirteenth Century: Proc. 1984 Harlaxton Symposium*, ed. W.M. Ormrod (Woodbridge, 1985), 95–9.
24 J. Bony, *French Gothic Architecture of the Twelfth and Thirteenth Centuries* (Berkeley, 1983), 24–6.
25 For Eu, see Grant, 'Gothic Architecture', 63–4; and *Gallia Christiana*, ed. P. Piolin *et al.* (Paris, 1715–1865), xi. cols. 294–5.
26 Laon choir was begun after 1205: see W.W. Clark and R. King, *Laon Cathedral: Architecture I* (London, 1983), 24. J. Bony, *French Gothic Architecture*, 281–2 compares the massing of St. Quentin with that of Lincoln. St. Quentin was begun before 1220: P. Heliot, *La Basilique de Saint Quentin* (Paris, 1967), 23–41.

facades, like Ely, Peterborough and Wells. The Normans clung to the twin-towered facade, which they had pioneered in the eleventh century, and which had been given a new lease of gothic life at St. Denis, in spite of the dark, cramped western bay which this entailed. It was left to the architects of north-eastern France, notably at Noyon, to exploit the possibilities of the western transept, and to toy with the concept of a screen facade.[27]

So an eternal architectural triangle develops in the late twelfth century, and continues into the thirteenth. Normandy looks consistently to Paris and the Parisis, largely ignoring the lands which flank it to the north-east, in spite of the fact that this is the very area of France with which England pursues a continual, if slightly one-sided, architectural dialogue. I do not want in any way to destroy this picture, but I do want to introduce some shading.

One suspects that the loss of Normandy was not enormously regretted in England, nor, initially, was the loss of England in Normandy. But there was a slow realization in Normandy, especially after the death of Philip Augustus, who had had the wit to leave it largely to its own devices, that conquest had reduced the duchy to a province, and that Parisian orientation was becoming a Parisian stranglehold. There is evidence in the 1220s and 1230s of a growing resistance. The bishops of Coutances, Avranches and Lisieux refused to join Louis VIII's expeditions against Henry III in 1224.[28] Archbishops Theobald and Maurice of Rouen clashed with the French Crown over Norman rights and customs.[29] In 1237 St. Louis went to some lengths to ensure that the next archbishop was a Frenchman, and that the consecration was attended by an abnormally heavy contingent of French bishops; the chapter had voted for an Englishman.[30] A few years earlier, in 1230, Fulk Paynel, lord of Hambye in the Cotentin, begged Henry III to reconquer Normandy, or at least to give Fulk 200 knights, so that he and his companions could drive 'omne genus Francorum de Normannia'.[31] This seems to have been mirrored by a sort of architectural *recherche de l'Angleterre perdue*. The more overt and picturesque Anglicisms, such as emphatic Y tracery and sharp lancets, which appear in Normandy in the 1220s, may not be entirely fortuitous. They occur in just those areas or institutions where links with England had always been strongest, and where there must have been the strongest sense of loss and potential gain, mainly in Lower Normandy, to the west of the Dives, and to an extent in the coastal harbour towns.[32] The divided arcade of the choir at Graville Ste. Honorine

27 For Noyon, see C. Seymour, *La Cathédrale Notre Dame de Noyon au XIIe siècle* (rev. French edn. Geneva, Paris, 1975), 44, 92–8. At Soissons, a broad lateral space is opened at tribune level. An architect working within the distinctive traditions of the Laonnois/Soissonnais built an expansive W. space at tribune level, in conjunction with a very odd screen arrangement between the towers, at Mantes *c*. 1220. Kurmann has recently suggested that the original design for the W. end of Reims cathedral would have been a related type: P. Kurmann, *La Façade de la Cathédrale de Reims* (Lausanne, Paris, 1987), 132. It has to be admitted that one thorough-going W. transept was built on the very border of Normandy, though on the French side, at St. Germer de Fly: P. Heliot, 'Rémarques sur l'abbatiale de Saint-Germer et sur les blocs de façade du XIIe siècle', *Bulletin Monumental*, cxiv (1958), 81–114.
28 'Scripta de Feodis ad Regem Spectantibus', in *Recueil des Historiens des Gaules et de France*, ed. M. Bouquet *et al.* (Paris, 1869–1904), xxiii. 637; and see J. Baldwin, 'Philip Augustus and the Norman Church', *French Historical Studies*, vi (1969), 10.
29 'Chronicon Rotomagensis', in *Recueil des Historiens . . . de France*, xxiii. 332–6.
30 *Gallia Christiana*, xi. 64; and 'Chronicon Rotomagensis', 336–7.
31 Roger of Wendover, *Flores Historiarum*, ed. R. Hewlett (RS, 1889), iii. 5.
32 Powicke, *Henry III*, i. 180.

at Le Havre (pl. 9) is unique in Normandy, indeed France, but it is clearly a copy of the unusual arrangement of St. Thomas, Portsmouth, begun *c*. 1185,[33] (pl. 8) or early thirteenth-century Boxgrove. Contrapuntal arcading, developed in the choir wall arcade at Lincoln (pl. 27), and then used at Chichester retrochoir, Ely porch and Worcester, enjoyed a sudden vogue in Normandy, firstly in the cloister of Mont Saint Michel (finished in 1228) (pl. 1), then at St. Pierre sur Dives, and on several portals, notably at Sées.[34] Graville Ste. Honorine is a special case of pure plagiarism, but it must be said that all the other, decorative 'Anglicisms' existed in Normandy in embryonic form in the 1180s, in the choir of St. Etienne, Caen (pl. 5), though they are certainly used with a new insistence in the 1220s.[35] And inspite of the pugnacious Fulk Paynel's anti-French feelings, the family abbey of Hambye (pl. 10), dependent as it is on Coutances, is as high gothic and French as it was possible for such a modest building to be.[36]

The cloister at Mont Saint Michel must represent some English input into thirteenth-century Normandy, but less, I think, than is often supposed. Most of the cloister arcade capitals are not sculpted but moulded, as was so often the case in England. But moulded capitals were standard in south-west Normandy, where the local building stones are unyielding granites and schists. The cloister shafts are of dark polished stone, very unusual in the duchy, and indeed in France, but ubiquitous in early gothic England. In 1911 G.H. West suggested that they were imported Purbeck marble.[37] This suggestion proved so appealing that it rapidly acquired the status of fact. However, Edouard Corroyer's account of his restoration of Mont Saint Michel in 1877 is quite specific about the cloister columns. They are not Purbeck at all, but a local Norman equivalent, which Corroyer calls granitelle. He reopened the quarries during the restoration, so that replaced columns could be in exactly the same stone as the rest.[38] In fact, dark, polished, *en delit* shafts had already been used at Mont Saint Michel, in the monastic buildings of Robert of Torigni in the late twelfth century. Dark, polished stone was used in the cloister, not necessarily to be as English as possible, but because dark polishable stone, imitating the action of marble, was available in this corner of Normandy.

---

33  N. Pevsner, *Hampshire*, Buildings of England (London, 1967), 393.
34  For the date of the Mont Saint Michel cloister we have the evidence of an inscription, now lost, recorded by Dom Huynes in the 17th c.: 'S.Franciscus canonisatus fuit anno Domini . . . MCCXXVIII quo claustrum istud perfectum'. See J. Huynes, *Histoire générale de l'abbaye de Mont-Saint-Michel*, ed. C. de Beaurepaire (Rouen, 1872), i. 180. Corroborative evidence for the effective completion of the Merveille under the abbacy of Raoul des Iles (retired, 1228) is contained in his petition, dated 1230, to Pope Gregory IX, detailing his achievements as abbot: 'Aedificia tam in capite quam in exterioribus locis . . . refecit et reparavit, et etiam nova construxit, ita quod bene posuit in aedificiis viginti millia librarum Turonensis monetae, . . . et fecit . . ut non in camerulis divisum ut solebant, sed simul in refectorio . . . comederunt.' See E. Martène and U. Durand, *Thesaurus novus Anecdotorum* (Paris, 1717), i. 956–7. From this it is absolutely clear that Raoul built the refectory which opens off the E. wall of the cloister. The destroyed contrapuntal cloister of St. Pierre s.Dives is shown in *Monasticon Gallicanum*, ed. M. Germain (Paris, 1882), ii. pl.131.
35  E.g. visual counterpoint is already present in the shafts set right in front of windows in the clerestory; and the tribune arcade is of Y tracery type.
36  Fulk made a substantial donation to the abbey in 1248: A. du Monstier, *Neustria Pia* (Rouen, 1663), 822. His cousin John, archdeacon of Coutances, made a grant to the abbey in 1232: Stevenson, 'England and Normandy', 112.
37  G.H. West, *Gothic Architecture in England and France* (2nd edn. London, 1927), 242. The first edn. was published in 1911.
38  E. Corroyer, *Guide descriptif du Mont Saint Michel* (2nd edn. Paris, 1886), 111–12.

The fine limestone of the cloister spandrels had to be imported, though from Caen rather than England. For the richness of this sculpture we must look to England, for instance, the south porch of Wells, though there is no use of the ubiquitous English stiff leaf foliage. The fine figure of Christ (pl. 13) has English parallels (King John at Worcester, for instance) but no surviving Norman ones.[39] Part of the cloister team built the portals of the nearby cathedral of Coutances in the late 1220s.[40] The English background of the sculptor of the north porch tympanum is clear (pl. 14). It has close affinities with the early work on Wells west front (pl. 12) — iconographically, in the unusual motif of the Virgin with a foot raised to support the baby on one knee; stylistically, in the soft drapery and typically English sketchy sense of what goes on underneath it; but also technically, in that the figures are freestanding against the tympanum field. The French technique, used in the inferior south porch tympanum — if this is representative of Norman sculptural achievement, one can see why they might turn to an Englishman — is to carve the figures out of the constituent blocks of the tympanum.

Norman influence can, I think, be traced in two areas of England. In the hinterland of the ports serving Normandy it surfaces in decorative details, many of which seem to derive from the choir of St. Etienne, Caen, as, for instance, the small corbels emerging from capitals like worms from an apple in the triforium at Shoreham, just as in the south transept chapel at St. Etienne, or the shafts set right in front of lancets in the axial chapel at Winchester (pl. 7), just as in the clerestory at St. Etienne (pl. 5). Perhaps it is Norman influence that leads Shoreham, Chichester and Romsey to adopt real bay dividing shafts running the full height of the elevation in a most un-English manner.

The other area is the western counties. Sculpture in western Normandy, as we have seen, related to work at Wells and Worcester. Worcester west end (pl. 11), begun after 1175, is the only English building which really does seem to incorporate architectural as opposed to decorative Norman precepts, including bays divided by substantial shaft groups, composite piers, and a tribune-scaled triforium.[41] In the 1180s, Glastonbury and Wells continued to resemble contemporary Norman work in their use of coursed shafting and composite cruciform piers, and in their rejection of colouristic, drainpipe effects. But already the bay divisions have been dropped; and right from the start, the tight triangular keeled shaft bunches of the western counties are quite different from the flat splayed shafts that articulate the piers of their Norman contemporaries.

Norman gothic influence on the Sussex and Hampshire coast is not surprising, though one wonders exactly what it represents and how it worked. Are patrons, such as the de Braose family at Shoreham, or Richard de Lucy at Winchester, deliberately importing masons to build them a church which reminds them of the buildings that they have admired in Normandy? Or are ideas and motifs exchanged

39 King John's effigy is slightly later than Mont Saint Michel cloister, since it was ready in 1232: see the Tewkesbury annals in *Ann. Mon.* i. 84. It may be necessary to look to England for sculptural parallels because no comparable Norman cloister survives, and cloisters are the obvious location for rich spandrel decoration. An indication that there was an indigenous Norman tradition of rich carved spandrel decoration is preserved in the triforium in the W. bay of Evreux nave, c. 1180.
40 Grant, 'Gothic Architecture', 314.
41 For the date of Worcester W. bays, see C. Wilson, 'The Sources of the Late Twelfth-Century Work at Worcester Cathedral', *British Archaeological Assoc. Conference Trans., Worcester* (1978), 80–1.

between English masons and their Norman counterparts, who have come to England in connection with the Caen stone trade, which may have been affected, but was certainly not destroyed, by the *débâcle* of 1204? The fact that so many of the Norman features that permeate these south-coast buildings seem to have a Caennois, never an Upper Norman, origin, suggests that the Caen stone trade played an important role in the transmission of ideas, both before and after 1204. But Caen stone did not penetrate the western counties. Here, the active force must be the patron rather than the artist. This is not impossible. The English possessions of the Norman abbeys are concentrated in two areas, the easily accessible south-coast counties, of course, but also in the western counties.[42] Two ecclesiastical dynasties straddled western England and Normandy: the fitzSamsons dominated the chapters and bishoprics of Worcester and Bayeux; and in the late twelfth and early thirteenth centuries the Bohun family of the Cotentin dominated the chapters and bishoprics of Wells and Coutances.[43] Again the links are with Lower, not Upper, Normandy.

This is speculation, of course. The buildings suggest that architectural influence exists, but the mechanism of transmission is unclear. There is, however, one documented case of a Norman architect working in England in the thirteenth century. Although the building is Beaulieu, situated on Southampton Water, it is clear in this case that the Norman elements in the building are not owing to pervasive Norman influence, but to the deliberate choice of the patron. Because of this, the architectural debt is to Upper, not Lower, Norman building. The Cistercian abbey of Beaulieu was founded by King John in 1204, and was originally intended as his mausoleum (fig. 1). The monks entered the new choir in 1227, and the whole church was dedicated in 1246.[44] The internal stonework was Caen.[45] One of the architects was definitely Norman, since in 1224 a safe-conduct was issued to allow Durandus, 'cementarius', through the port at Southampton on his way to work at Beaulieu.[46] He is often identified with the mason Durandus, mentioned in a charter of Rouen cathedral in 1234, and responsible for finishing the nave vault there.[47]

This is his only documented visit to Beaulieu, but it may have been only one of many. In 1224 he probably came to direct the vaulting of the choir. The remains of Beaulieu are fragmentary, but there is no trace of a Rouennais or even a Norman stylistic idiom. Arch mouldings, the use of moulded capitals and Purbeck shafting

---

[42] I have used Stevenson, 'England and Normandy', app. 1, 336–49: A Provisional List of English Possessions (by counties) of Norman Sees and Abbeys in 1204. Out of a total of 257 possessions listed, 69 (i.e. nearly one-quarter) are in Wilts., Dorset, Devon, Gloucs., Somerset and Worcs. Surprisingly, only 6 holdings in Kent belong to Norman ecclesiastical establishments.

[43] D. Spear, 'The Norman Empire and the Secular Clergy 1066–1204', *Journ. British Studies*, xxi (1982), 4–5.

[44] For the foundation and John's frequent and generous gifts for building, see *VCH Hampshire*, ii. 140; the Waverley annals, in *Ann. Mon.* ii. 254, 256, 304 (for the entry into the choir in 1227). The foundation charter, and charter given by Henry III at the dedication in 1247, are in *The Beaulieu Cartulary*, ed. S.F. Hockey (Southampton Rec. ser. xvii, 1974), 3–5, 7–8.

[45] W.H.St. John Hope and H. Brakspear, 'The Cistercian Abbey of Beaulieu', *Archaeological Journ.* lxiii (1906), 179–80.

[46] *RLC* i. 650.

[47] E.g. by St. John Hope and Brakspear, 'The Cistercian Abbey', 136–7. It is clear that Durandus of Rouen finished the easternmost bays of the nave, since he signed the easternmost vault boss, now in the Musée des Antiquités, Rouen: 'Durandus me fecit.' For documentary evidence for Durandus of Rouen, see A. Deville, *Revue des architects de la cathédrale de Rouen* (Rouen, 1848), 9–15; C. de Beaurepaire, 'Notes sur les architects de Rouen', *Les Amis des Monuments Rouennais* (1901), 78–9.

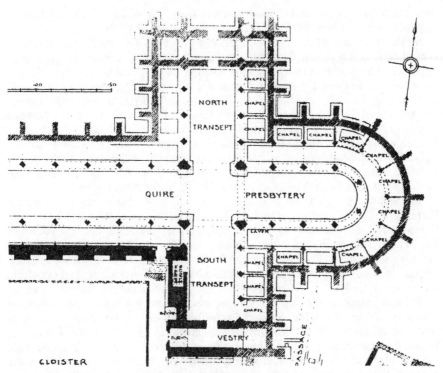

Fig. 1  Beaulieu Abbey: ground plan (after Brakspear)

align it with Winchester retrochoir, or Salisbury. The actual building work and the on-site direction must have been by local masons. Nevertheless, the church at Beaulieu was distinctly and peculiarly Norman in conception. Beaulieu was a daughter house of Cîteaux, colonized directly from the mother house, but the design of its east end was not only completely new in England, but was based not, as might have been expected, on the rectangular east end of Cîteaux, but on the Norman Cistercian plan of Bonport, and ultimately Mortemer. Bonport, with its trapezoidal chapels contained within a continuous outer wall, is clearly the immediate plan source (fig. 2). Henry II had been principal patron of Mortemer, and Richard I founder of Bonport.[48] This type of east end, the radiating chapel chevet, is rare in Cistercian houses, but in Normandy it had clearly become linked to Cistercian abbeys with strong royal connections. Beaulieu preserved these connotations in thirteenth-century England, since the radiating chapel chevet is scarcely

---

[48]  For Mortemer, see 'Le récit de la fondation de Mortemer', ed. J. Bouvet, *Collectanea ordinis Cisterciana reformatorum*, xxii (1960), 159, 162. For Bonport, see *Cartulaire de l'abbaye royale de Notre-Dame de Bonport*, ed. J. Andrieux (Évreux, 1862), 1–3; E. Hallam, 'Aspects of the Monastic patronage of the English and French Royal Houses, c.1130–1270', (London Univ. Ph.D. thesis, 1976), 135–7. For a discussion of both buildings, see Grant, 'Gothic Architecture', 83–90, 196–200, 202–9.

used again, save at Richard of Cornwall's Hailes, Edward I's Vale Royal, and, of course, Henry III's Westminster.[49] It is very much a family affair.

So the Norman architectural impact on England resolves itself into peripheral coastal penetration around Shoreham and Southampton, and what seems to be an important, but quickly transmuted, impetus to gothic in the West Country. Most of the effects of English influence in Normandy are cosmetic rather than structural. Just because they are cosmetic, they should not be underrated. The advantage of the superficial is that it is obvious; the English tone of some Lower Norman buildings of the 1230s was doubtless obvious to contemporaries too. With Beaulieu, Coutances, and Mont Saint Michel, we are in the realm not of pervasive influence, but of the accidental, dealing with foreign craftsmen or architects working within alien contexts. And King John emerges by default as the only patron who demonstrably wanted an English building to look like its Norman equivalent.

The architectural affinities, or lack of them, in England, Normandy and northern France give the impression that life in the early thirteenth century still flows with the great rivers. Normandy is drawn irresistibly by the Seine into the vortex of Paris and the Ile de France. Most English rivers drain to the east, and the natural and easy sea routes to France lead to the Boullonais and Flanders. Neither tides nor prevailing winds are propitious for sailing to Normandy, and all the harbours from the Vimeu to Le Havre are fiendishly difficult without an outboard motor. Inversely, the scarp slope of the Somme, and the inhospitable uplands of the Vimeu, on which Gerald of Wales has some characteristically caustic comments,[50] seem to have formed a remarkably effective barrier to the north-east of Normandy. It cannot be just a matter of trade routes. Surely, only in the specific case of the stone trade did architectural influences travel with the merchant rather than the bishop or the baron, though trade routes have been invoked in the past to explain the dissemination of gothic styles. Behind trade routes lie geophysical factors, which dictate natural patterns of communication and of common interest. Once it develops, a nexus of dynastic, economic and ecclesiastical links is mutually reinforcing. The Flemish abbey of St. Peter, Ghent held lands in Kent before the Norman Conquest.[51] When the monks of Canterbury fled the wrath of King John in 1207, they spent six years at St. Bertin at St. Omer.[52] Successive archbishops of Canterbury who found it expedient to leave the country sought asylum in the northern Burgundian Cistercian house of Pontigny. Successive counts of Flanders, Boulogne, Guines and St-Pol had consistent, often substantial, interests in southeast England.[53] Even that quintessential Anglo-Norman, William Marshal, held

---

49 Westminster is not, of course, a Cistercian house, though it was a royal mausoleum, and its chapels belong to the central tradition of the French gothic cathedral church, rather than to the austere Cistercian variant.

50 *The Autobiography of Giraldus Cambrensis*, ed. and trans. H.E. Butler (London, 1937), 113.

51 D. Matthew, *The Norman Monasteries and Their English Possessions* (Oxford, 1962), 19.

52 Gervase of Canterbury, 'Gesta Regum', in *The Historical Works of Gervase of Canterbury*, ed. W. Stubbs (RS, 1880), ii. 100.

53 See Fossier, *La Terre et les Hommes*, 482–3; P. Feuchère, 'Les origines du comté de Saint-Pol', *Revue du Nord*, xxxv (1953), 136–8 shows the counts of St-Pol oscillating between Capetians and Plantagenets in order to stay independent of Flanders. The ambivalent position of the county of Boulogne goes some way to explaining the unstable career of Renaud de Dammartin, as summed up by a very cross Philip Augustus after Bouvines: see Guillaume le Breton, 'De Gestis Philippi Augusti', in *Recueil des Historiens . . . de France*, xvii. 100.

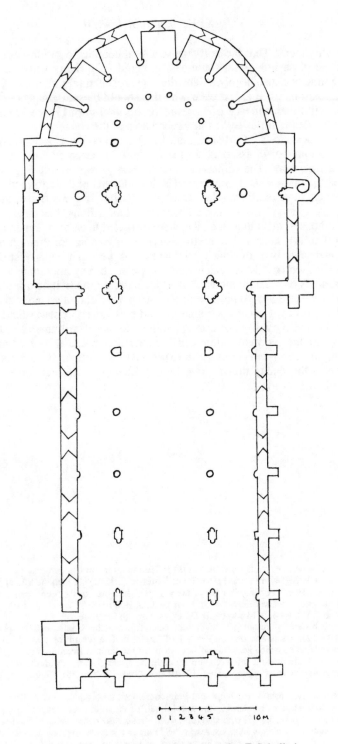

Fig. 2  Bonport Abbey: ground plan (after F. Schaller)

lands in St. Omer.[54] That the northern seaboard counties of north-eastern France should have close links with south-east England is in many ways obvious. But English gothic was also deeply indebted to the architectural traditions of the Laonnois and Soissonnais. It is less clear why this should be so. Perhaps our picture of the architectural dependence of England on north-eastern France is heavily coloured by the fact that this is the one French area in the equation from which many gothic buildings survive. Certainly, both St. Quentin on the Upper Somme and St. Omer show Laonnois/Soissonnais influence, and the seaboard counties may have acted as a filter here. The cathedral of Laon itself, however, had English connections from the mid-eleventh century.[55] The introduction of the reformed orders into England must have reinforced the eastern orientation. In the early twelfth century, houses were founded from Norman Savignac foundations, but the later English Cistercian houses, including Beaulieu, were affiliated to eastern French or Burgundian, not Norman, houses. The north-eastern French orders of Premonstratensians and Arrouaisians, both of which originated and were particularly strong in the Laonnois/Soissonnais, were much more popular in England than the western Fontevraudines or Grandmontines.[56] And for those eternally itinerant bishops and abbots, all roads lead to Rome — but the eastern ones lead there more quickly than others. This nexus of economic, dynastic and particularly ecclesiastical links was strong enough to provide a consistent, parallel, not necessarily mutually exclusive, alternative to the Norman cultural affiliations that political and administrative history might have predisposed us to expect. As for Normandy, architectural evidence shows the duchy drawn, long before 1204, into the cultural orbit of the Parisian Ile de France.

---

[54] Before 1204 William exchanged this land for Trumpington, an English estate of the count of Guines: PRO, KB 26/146, m.9. Earl Hamelin of Warenne (d.1202) claimed the title of advocate of St. Bertin of St. Omer, probably in right of his wife who had previously been married to William, count of Boulogne. See *Les Chartes de St. Bertin*, ed. D. Haignéré (St. Omer, 1886–90), i. 144 (no. 325), 160 (no. 365). I would like to thank Dr. David Crouch for these refs.

[55] Helinand, bishop of Laon (1052–98) had been Edward the Confessor's chaplain; Bishop Gaudri (1106–12) was chancellor of Henry I of England. The wealth of these English bishops seems to have been conspicuous, and probably inspired the famous expedition to England to raise money for the building-fund after Gaudri's death: *Self and Society in Medieval France: The Memoirs of Abbot Guibert of Nogent*, ed. J.F. Benton (2nd edn. Toronto, 1984), 146, 151, 156–7, 194–7.

[56] The preponderant role of Rievaulx and Fountains, with their direct links to Clairvaux, in the Cistercian colonization of England in the second half of the 12th c. is brought out in Fergusson, *Architecture of Solitude*, 32–53, who also (pp. 67–8) stresses the connections of English Cistercian and Premonstratensian abbots with houses in the Laonnois/Soissonnais. See also R. de Foreville, 'Tradition et renouvellement du monachisme dans l'espace Plantagenet au XIIe siècle', *Cahiers de Civilisation Médiévale*, xxix (1986), 72.

# Edward I and Adolf of Nassau

## Michael Prestwich

The Anglo-French war of 1294–8 cannot be counted among Edward I's triumphs. In military terms it witnessed the defeat of English troops at Bellegarde in Gascony, while in Flanders such fighting as took place was among the English themselves, and against their own allies, rather than the French. Diplomacy was no more successful than military action. The king of Germany, Adolf of Nassau, was regarded by the English as a very important ally, yet he failed to provide any assistance, defaulting on his treaty obligations. The question of whether or not this was the result of skilful and devious diplomatic manoeuvres by the French has been the object of bitter controversy among German historians, but the question has been treated fully in English only once, fifty years ago by Barraclough.[1]

Edward I's war against Philip IV was not of the English king's choosing. It had its immediate origins in a private conflict between the men of the Cinque Ports and Norman mariners. The involvement of some of Edward I's Gascon subjects provided the French with an opportunity to put into practice their claims to sovereign jurisdiction over the duchy of Gascony. In the diplomatic preliminaries, the king's brother, Edmund of Lancaster, was duped by the French into handing over towns and fortresses in Gascony without a struggle. English troops were sent to Gascony, with a small expedition in 1294 and a larger one in 1296 under Edmund of Lancaster. They were able to do little more than maintain a foothold. Bayonne and some other towns remained loyal to the English, but Bordeaux sided with the French. It was costly and difficult to send armies to Gascony, and from the outset the main thrust of Edward's strategy was directed elsewhere.[2]

The plan was to combat Philip IV by constructing a massive alliance, encircling France, and by mounting a campaign in Flanders. This was not a new strategy: at the beginning of the thirteenth century King John had adopted a very similar scheme. He had paid out immense sums of money to win the allegiance of the princes of the Low Countries, among whom the count of Flanders was the most important. In addition, he had relied on the support of the German emperor, his

---

1   G. Barraclough, 'Edward I and Adolf of Nassau', *Cambridge Historical Journ.* vi (1940), 225–62. For the controversy in German, see esp. F. Kern, 'Analekten zur Geschichte des 13. und 14. Jahrhunderts, ii, Die Bestechung König Adolfs von Nassau', *Mitteilungen des Instituts für Österreichische Geschichtsforschung*, xxx (1909), 423–43; V. Samanek, 'Der angebliche Verrat Adolfs von Nassau', *Historisches Vierteljahrschrift*, xxix (1935), 302–41; F. Bock, 'Musciatto dei Francesi', *Deutsches Archiv*, vi (1943), 537–42. Esp. valuable is the discussion by F. Trautz, *Die Könige von England und das Reich, 1272–1337* (Heidelberg, 1961), 151–75, to which my debt is obvious. For a brief general account of the Anglo-French war, see M.C. Prestwich, *Edward I* (London, 1988), 376–400.
2   Prestwich, *Edward I*, 376–86.

nephew Otto IV. The plan failed on the battlefield of Bouvines in 1214, but John had at least shown that it was possible to swing such a coalition into action.[3]

Although there is no evidence of research into the precedent, Edward I's coalition was very similar to that built up by his grandfather John. Its most prominent members were the count of Flanders, the duke of Brabant, the count of Holland, the king of Germany, and the count of Bar. Just as under John, massive English subsidies underpinned the somewhat rickety structure.

In some ways Edward I faced greater difficulties than John had done. In 1294–5 his attention was diverted from the French war by revolt in Wales, and in 1296 he had to mount a campaign in Scotland, which had allied itself with France. Eventually, on 22 August 1297, Edward sailed with a relatively small army for Flanders. Fighting between the men of Yarmouth and those of the Cinque Ports marred his landing two days later. By that time, few of his allies were prepared to offer active support. Some had suffered defeat at Veurne on 20 August; others, notably the duke of Brabant, adopted an understandably cautious attitude. The campaign petered out with a truce agreed on 9 October 1297, before the English had engaged in any real fighting. One piece in the complicated diplomatic jigsaw has proved difficult for historians to fit into place. The king of Germany, Adolf of Nassau, was regarded as a very important ally by the English, yet he failed to provide Edward with any assistance, defaulting on his treaty obligations. Was this because he had secretly accepted bribes from the French, or is there some other explanation?

The evidence for the suggestion that Adolf was bribed by the French to abandon his English ally, Edward, is largely provided by a tantalizing memorandum in French, now in the Archives Nationales, on the conduct of the war. This analyses the diplomatic moves and discusses the financial expedients adopted by Philip IV to pay for the conflict.[4] The origins of the war are briefly described, as are the naval preparations and the first two French armies sent to Gascony. The document explains that in 1295 Edward I exported large sums of money to buy allies, the most important of whom were the king of Germany and his brother, the duke of Brabant, the count of Juliers, the count of Bar, the count of Savoy, and Jean de Chalon-Arlay, a Burgundian noble. The French response was to build up a counter-alliance. In the Low Countries they obtained the support of the counts of Luxembourg, Hainault, and Holland, and of Godfrey, brother of the duke of Brabant. A number of Burgundian allies are also listed, while further afield the French looked to John Balliol in Scotland, the king of Norway, and the rulers of Navarre, Majorca and Aragon. The document then turns to the question of Germany. The account suggests that Philip sent the bishop of Bethlehem and the prior of the Dominicans of Paris to the German king, but that they achieved nothing. They were followed by the Italian banker Musciatto dei Francesi, who was better supplied with funds. As a result of his negotiations, Adolf sent his brother secretly to Lille, where a treaty was agreed. Musciatto then returned to Germany and concluded the negotiations which were intended to ensure that Adolf would not move against Philip IV. Subsequently, he took steps to ensure the neutrality of the duke of Brabant, which was to be

---

[3] A.L. Poole, *From Domesday Book to Magna Carta 1087–1216* (2nd edn. Oxford, 1955), 463–4; *Foedera*, I. i. 104–10.
[4] *Constitutiones et Acta Publica, III*, ed. J. Schwalm (Monumenta Germaniae Historica, 1906), 632–5; F. Funck-Brentano, 'Document pour servir à l'histoire des relations de la France avec l'Angleterre et l'Allemagne sous le règne de Philippe le Bel', *Revue Historique*, xxxix (1889), 328–34.

maintained even in the event of the latter's son marrying an English princess. So successful was French diplomacy that only the count of Bar and Jean de Chalon-Arlay were prepared to make war on Philip. The document does not set out clearly the subsidies paid out by the French, but arabic numerals are written over the names of some of those mentioned, and it seems probable that these refer to the sums that were handed over. The figures thirty, twenty, and again thirty occur in the context of Musciatto's dealings with the German ruler, implying a subsidy of 80,000 *livres tournois.*

The chronology of the document is not as clear as might be hoped. The next section moves to 1297. Edward is described as making further efforts to build up his alliance system by means of subsidies and marriages. He was successful in winning over the count of Flanders, but as the count's daughter was in the French court it was not possible to marry her to Edward's son. The king's discomfiture after his landing in August 1297 is then briefly described. Others, the section concludes, should draw the moral from this. The last part of the document is very different in character from this narrative. It provides a sketch of the various financial expedients adopted in 1294–5 by Philip IV to raise money to pay for the war.

The reliability of the memorandum is rendered suspect by various errors. The dauphin of Vienne is called Robert, *recte* Humbert. Godfrey of Brabant is described as the brother of the duke, *recte* his uncle. The author was unaware that John of Brabant had married Edward I's daughter, Margaret, as early as 1290; he considered that the wedding had not taken place by the mid-1290s. It may be that the author confused the duke of Brabant with John, count of Holland who married the English king's daughter, Elizabeth, in 1296. The date of Edward I's arrival in Flanders in 1297 is put in June, not late August. The arabic figures do not all fit with the known subsidies paid by the French. For example, Florence, count of Holland was promised 4000 *livres tournois* for life, and a lump sum of 25,000 *livres tournois*, of which 12,500 *livres tournois* was definitely paid over. Yet the figure written above the count's name is '9', seemingly indicating a sum of 9000 *livres tournois.*[5] A highly implausible claim is made — that the duke of Brabant was retained by Musciatto dei Francesi, and in receipt of robes from him.

There are surprising omissions in the account. There is no mention of the kidnap and murder of Florence, count of Holland in 1296, and the fact that his son, John, was a supporter of Edward I is ignored. The English king's attempt to win over the count of Flanders in the early stages of the war is not included; the account mentions only the alliance formed in January 1297. The battle of Veurne, in which some of Edward's allies were defeated shortly before the English king landed in Flanders, is not included in the narrative. The final section of the document, which deals with financial matters, covers the years 1294 and 1295 only, and does not take the story up to 1297.

Knowledge of the date of composition, and of the authorship, of this remarkable memorandum would greatly assist an assessment of its value. There are some clues which suggest that it was not contemporary. A reference to Philip's advancing on Flanders 'with the first army of Lille' suggests that it was written after a second French army had besieged Lille, which it did in 1304.[6] The financial section of the text states that it appears 'from the documents of the treasury' that there was about

5 *Acta Imperii Angliae et Franciae, 1267–1313*, ed. F. Kern (Tübingen, 1911), 279–80.
6 Trautz, *Könige von England*, 156.

200,000 *livres tournois* in the Louvre, a phrase which might imply that it was written quite some time after the events it describes. There is insufficient evidence to indicate authorship. Bock's suggestion that the memorandum was the work of Musciatto dei Francesi himself is tempting, in view of the prominence given to the Italian.[7] However, the author was unable to give a precise figure to the loans made by Musciatto and his brother Albizzo (known as Biche), and refers again to treasury records, which makes Italian authorship seem unlikely; Musciatto would surely have had his own private financial records. It seems very possible that the document was written by some French government official as late as the early stages of the Hundred Years War, as a *mémoire* on the diplomacy and financial arrangements of an earlier and similar struggle. If so, such a date would give added relevance to the moral drawn by the author, for in the late 1330s the French were facing problems very similar to those of the 1290s. A late date of composition would also help to explain how an obviously well-informed author could make the mistakes he did.

Other French sources provide little corroboration for the account of the dealings of Philip IV and his agent Musciatto with Adolf of Nassau. A papal document, however, has been seen as suggestive. Pope Boniface VIII confirmed, on 13 June 1297, a grant by Adolf of Nassau to Musciatto dei Francesi of Poggibonsi and Fucechio in Tuscany. This was made in return for Musciatto's services, past and future, in acquiring and recovering imperial rights.[8] The date seems very early for a grant made to reward Musciatto for his diplomatic activities, for Edward I had not yet launched his invasion of Flanders, and it cannot have been clear that Adolf would succeed in staying clear of the conflict. The grant is perhaps better explained in terms of Musciatto's activities as a receiver of papal taxes; it does not provide proof of secret diplomacy conducted by the Italian on Philip IV's behalf. It should also be noted that the Italian also received a grant from Adolf's successor, Albrecht.

Some negotiations between the French and the German king did take place, for on 30 July 1297 Philip IV authorized a commission to treat for peace and to investigate disputed claims. The count of St-Pol and Godfrey of Brabant were to be the French representatives, and the count of Juliers with the provost of Cologne the German ones. It made excellent sense for Adolf to agree to such talks, and to attempt to play off Philip against Edward. There was no secrecy about the matter: when Adolf wrote to the count of Flanders on 31 August, the possibility of his reaching agreement with the French was mentioned. It is clear, however, that at that stage negotiations had not been concluded. There is no mention in these letters of any part played by Musciatto.[9]

The English sources provide a much fuller account than the French of relations between Edward I and Adolf, and of the German king's place in the complex diplomatic manoeuvres. Adolf was seen as important from the very start of the war. One chronicle account suggests that, in a stirring speech to the royal council, the bishop of Durham, Anthony Bek, stressed the importance of buying foreign assistance if Philip IV was to be dealt with easily. As a result, Bek was sent with other envoys in June 1294 to make alliances with the German king, Adolf of Nassau, the

---

7   Bock, 'Musciatto dei Francesi', 541.
8   Bock, 'Musciatto dei Francesi', 543–4; Barraclough, 'Edward I and Adolf of Nassau', 257 argues that this papal letter shows that Boniface VIII was fully aware of the basis of Franco-German negotiations, but the text hardly bears this interpretation.
9   *Constitutiones et Acta Publica, III,* 539–40.

archbishop of Cologne, and a number of Rhineland nobles.[10] A treaty was drawn up on 10 August between the English and German envoys, which was ratified by Adolf on 21 August, and by Edward on 22 October. Edward was to assist Adolf against Philip IV; there was to be a joint campaign against France; neither party was to negotiate a peace or truce separately. No mention was made of subsidies, but an English paymaster's account reveals that two instalments of £20,000 were paid by Christmas 1294.[11] There was also, it seems, agreement that a further £20,000 should be paid once Edward landed on the continent, ready for the joint campaign.[12] Diplomatic relations were maintained between Edward and Adolf during 1295 and 1296, with few evident signs of strain. In 1295 Edward had to postpone his planned meeting with Adolf: in that year, the problems of the Welsh revolt prevented any campaign on the continent. He employed, as envoys to Adolf, two German brothers, Eustace and Gerlac Baumgarten. Both men were retained as members of the English king's household; they must have been in a good position to assess the situation in both Edward's court and Adolf's.[13]

In 1296 the diplomatic offensive was entrusted to a powerful mission headed by the unscrupulous and clever treasurer, Walter Langton. It included in its number Count Amadeus of Savoy, Otto de Grandson and a clerk, John of Berwick. Accounts for this embassy survive from 23 July 1296 until August 1297.[14] In the early stages attempts were directed towards negotiating a peace with papal assistance, but the emphasis soon changed. Early in 1297 the English achieved a vital diplomatic success, when they succeeded in detaching the count of Flanders from the French alliance. This was essential if Edward was to campaign effectively on the continent, as the Flemish ports were the most suitable for disembarking troops. A range of letters issued on 6 February gave the English ambassadors authority to negotiate virtually as they chose.[15]

Contacts with Adolf were reasonably frequent. On 15 December 1296 one of the German king's knights, Robin von Kobern, was given £10 to cover the cost of his return journey to Germany. In the same month Itier d'Angoulême was twice sent to negotiate in Germany, and on 27 March 1297 another Gascon, Arnold de Rama, was sent on the same mission. He repeated his journey in May. A German friar, brother Gilbert, spent March in the Low Countries negotiating with the English, the count of Hainault and others.[16] The English negotiators in the Low Countries appear to have acted with due efficiency in all this, but the same cannot be said where the administration in England was concerned.

One problem was a lack of proper information. Edward I himself evidently considered that he was kept in the dark. On 17 April he complained that, although various rumours had reached him, he had no firm news from the Low Countries

10 *The Chronicle of Pierre de Langtoft*, ed. T. Wright (RS, 1868), ii. 200–4; *Treaty Rolls, I (1234–1325)*, ed. P. Chaplais (London, 1955), 89–90.
11 *Constitutiones et Acta Publica, III*, 489–98; *Foedera*, I. ii. 812; P. Chaplais, *English Medieval Diplomatic Practice, I* (London, 1982), ii. 483–7; J. de Sturler, 'Deux comptes enrôlés de Robert de Segre, receveur et agent payeur d'Edouard I^er, roi d'Angleterre, aux Pays-Bas (1294–1296)', *Bulletin de la commission royale d'histoire*, cxxv (1959), 578–9, 597.
12 *Documents Illustrating the Crisis of 1297–8 in England*, ed. M.C. Prestwich (Camden Soc. 4th ser. xxiv, 1980), 113.
13 Chaplais, *English Med. Dipl. Practice, I*, i. 352, 354.
14 G.P. Cuttino, *English Diplomatic Administration 1259–1339* (2nd edn. Oxford, 1971), 224–50.
15 *Treaty Rolls, I*, 126–31.
16 Cuttino, *English Dipl. Admin.* 229, 230–1, 244, 246.

about his allies, or the English embassy. On 7 May he wrote in some concern to the exchequer, saying that he could not find the treaties that had been made with the German king, or with the archbishop of Cologne; nor could anyone in his entourage give him any advice about the matter. A week later he wrote to John Botetourt, who had helped to negotiate the agreements, asking him to send to the exchequer as soon as possible the text of the treaty with the archbishop of Cologne. The impression is one of confusion and uncertainty. It is quite extraordinary that such important documents could not be located swiftly.[17] On 17 May Hugelino de Vikio left the court at Waltham and set out for Germany; it was perhaps in preparation for this mission that the treaty had been needed. At the beginning of June Edward received a letter from Adolf. He requested a meeting in Holland, and suggested a marriage alliance involving Edward's heir. The English king's response was a negative and unhelpful one, hardly best calculated to preserve an alliance which was beginning to falter. Further communication with Adolf took place in July, though the contents of the letters are not known.[18]

At some point during these exchanges it is likely that Adolf reminded Edward of his financial obligations. In late July the English king wrote to inform the exchequer that, as soon as he crossed the Channel, he was due to pay 30,000 marks to Adolf of Nassau. In addition, 25,500 marks was due to the duke of Brabant. Edward was clearly alarmed that he might not be able to pay the sums due. A prise of wool was ordered in an attempt to raise the necessary funds.[19] There were evidently no suspicions as far as the English were concerned about Adolf of Nassau's reliability. Nor were doubts raised once Edward had crossed to Flanders in late August. In mid-September Adolf sent an envoy to Edward, and the news must have been encouraging, for Edward wrote to the exchequer on 18 September, to inform them that he gathered that Adolf was on his way to assist him, and that it was vital that he should be able to pay out the promised subsidy.[20] The money, however, was not forthcoming, and Adolf stayed in Germany. Edward had been forced by rumours of a pro-French rising to move from Bruges to Ghent. His position was becoming increasingly difficult, and it is easy to see why he agreed to a truce with Philip IV on 10 October 1297. Edward was, of course, going against the terms of his original treaty with Adolf. The English took care, however, to ensure that a clause was included in the agreement with Philip's envoys, which permitted Adolf to break the truce provided he gave fifteen days' notice. That this clause was not merely inserted for form's sake is suggested by the fact that Edward mentioned it specifically when he wrote to Walter Langton, in England, to inform him of what had happened.[21] The king still had real hopes that Adolf would come to his aid. When Edward wrote to the exchequer on 16 October, after the truce had been agreed, he gave as his prime financial obligation the need to pay the German king and the duke of Brabant: 'Know that it would be most disadvantageous, and dishonourable to us and our people, if the king of Germany does not come by reason of a default in the agreement, or that if, when he does come, the promises

---

17  *Docs. Illustr. Crisis of 1297–8*, 69, 80, 86; Chaplais, *English Med. Dipl. Practice, I*, ii. 738–41.
18  *Constitutiones et Acta Publica, III*, 537–8; *Foedera*, I.ii. 866–7; BL, Add. MS 7965, fos. 24, 34v.
19  *Docs. Illustr. Crisis of 1297–8*, 113.
20  Ibid. 148–9.
21  Ibid. 162; *Foedera*, I.ii. 878–9; *Constitutiones et Acta Publica, III*, 541.

made to him are not kept.'[22] There was no hint in the letter that Adolf might renege on his treaty obligations; the clear implication was that Edward himself had failed to meet Adolf's terms, by failing to pay the promised subsidy.

Diplomatic exchanges between Edward and Adolf continued after the truce was agreed. John of Cuyck, a subject of the duke of Brabant much employed by Edward at this time in diplomatic matters, was sent to see Adolf. He wrote to Edward on 15 October from Sinzig on the Rhine, and reported that he had met the German king, who was optimistic that he would soon be able to set out, once various men had joined with him. A letter from John, written on 21 October after his return from Germany, gave no good news, however, but merely promised a verbal report. According to the chronicler Pierre Langtoft, Adolf wrote to Edward, excusing himself from joining him because he was overtaken by war at home.[23] It must have become clear to Edward that there was little chance that Adolf would renew the war under the terms permitted by the truce agreement.

Money was at long last sent from England in November. Twenty-three barrels containing coin, probably totalling about £11,500, were sent on the orders of the treasurer, Walter Langton. Such was Edward's need that when the shipment arrived at Ghent, it was hastily unloaded on arrival, at night.[24] This money, however, does not appear to have been sent to Adolf. Edward had more urgent needs: his troops had to be paid, and his household supplied. Hope of renewing the war was abandoned. In late November he wrote to his son and the council in England to inform them that the truce had been extended, and that 'we have good hope that by God's grace the matter can be settled in this way so that a good peace will follow to the profit, peace and tranquillity of Christendom'. No mention was made now of any treaty obligations to Adolf of Nassau, and although reinforcements were sought, this was only in order to be able to put up a show of strength for negotiating purposes. The only allies to whom Edward continued to consider he had an obligation were the Burgundians; on 5 February 1298 he sent two officials home from Flanders to try to raise the funds needed.[25] The funds were eventually provided by Italian merchants, and Edward was able to return to England, having abandoned those of his allies who had not already deserted him.

The story revealed by the English records does not fit well with the account provided by the French memorandum. The French were, as events prior to the outbreak of the war had shown, certainly very capable of highly duplicitous diplomacy. It is hard, however, to see why Philip should have chosen to keep secret an agreement with Adolf right through the summer and autumn of 1297, to the length of permitting Edward to list Adolf as an English ally in the Truce of Vyve-Saint-Bavon. Adolf was perfectly open about his dealings with the French at the end of July, and there was little point for him to pretend to be an ally of Edward's while secretly supporting Philip. A more plausible explanation of his failure to support Edward is twofold. First, Edward had not kept his part of the bargain. He had been

---

22 *Docs. Illustr. Crisis of 1297–8*, 162.

23 Ibid. 161–2, 166–7; *Chron. Langtoft*, ii. 294. German chroniclers confirm this explanation of Adolf's inactivity: see V. Samanek, 'Studien zur Geschichte König Adolfs', *Sitzungsberichte der Akademie der Wissenschaft in Wien, Phil.-Hist. Klasse*, ccvii (1930), 219.

24 BL, Add. MS 7965, f. 24v. An earlier shipment (detailed on f. 22v) shows that one barrel contained £500.

25 *Docs. Illustr. Crisis of 1297–8*, 174–5, 184.

unhelpful when Adolf had requested a meeting, and had not provided the money that Adolf needed if he were to recruit an effective army. Second, Adolf faced a conspiracy in Germany, which was formed on the occasion of the king of Bohemia's coronation at Prague in June 1297. Albrecht of Habsburg was a leading participant in this; it would eventually lead to Adolf's deposition in 1298.[26] In such circumstances Adolf's refusal to march to Flanders is hardly surprising.

If this interpretation is correct, then what is the explanation for the story given in the French memorandum? Samanek put forward an alternative hypothesis to the view that Adolf of Nassau was, in effect, bribed by the French to remain neutral.[27] He suggested that the author of the memorandum confused Adolf with his successor on the German throne, Albrecht of Habsburg. The German king is not actually named in the text, and while there is no evidence to corroborate the account of the visit of the bishop of Bethlehem and the prior of the Dominicans of Paris to Adolf, they certainly did go on an embassy to Albrecht in 1295. One chronicler reported Albrecht as saying: 'If my lord the king of the Romans has become a stipendiary of the English, then there will be less shame in my being a stipendiary of the French.'[28] It would have been easy for a researcher in the French archives in the late 1330s to be confused between the two German monarchs. A letter about a proposed marriage alliance between Albrecht's son and Philip IV's daughter, Blanche, written in 1295 when Adolf was king, was endorsed as being from the king of Germany.[29] It is certainly very curious that the memorandum nowhere mentions Albrecht, who was an ally of Philip IV; and this omission gives further weight to the theory that the author confused or conflated the figures of Adolf and Albrecht.

The main difficulty in accepting this tempting theory is that much is made of the role of the king of Germany's brother in the negotiations. Albrecht of Habsburg, unlike Adolf of Nassau, had no brother. Various possibilities have been suggested to explain this away. It could be that, as in the case of Brabant, the memorandum has confused a brother with an uncle, and that Albrecht's uncle, Otto of Ochsenstein, who was an envoy to France in 1295, was intended. Alternatively, there may have been confusion between Boemund, archbishop of Trier, who took part in negotiations in 1297, and Adolf's brother, Diether, who succeeded him in 1300. It could even be that the 'Frater Gilbertus', a friar, who was negotiating in the Low Countries in March 1297, was later wrongly thought to have been a brother of the German king.[30] Certainly, if the memorandum was written more or less at the time of the events it describes, confusion between Adolf and Albrecht is most unlikely.

---

[26] Trautz, *Könige von England*, 144. No mention was made of Adolf's accepting subsidies in the deposition proceedings, but it is worth noting that the Hirsau annals accused him of serving under Edward I, and did mention his failure to support the English king, or any dealings with Philip IV: W. Stubbs, *Constitutional History of England* (4th edn. Oxford, 1906), ii. 384.

[27] Samanek, 'Der angebliche Verrat'; see also the works referred to by Trautz, *Könige von England*, 154 n. 265.

[28] Cited in Trautz, *Könige von England*, 163 n. 328.

[29] *Constitutiones et Acta Publica, III*, 626. The endorsement reads 'Littera regis Alemanie super matrimonio contrahendo'. Edward I's anger at Blanche's marriage is suggested by the celebrated letter that he wrote to his second queen, Margaret, Blanche's sister, when he received news of the latter's death, and said that she should not grieve, as Blanche had been as good as dead since her marriage. See P. Chaplais, 'Some Private Letters of Edward I', *EHR* lxxvii (1962), 82–5.

[30] Trautz, *Könige von England*, 165. There is a possibility of an additional confusion between an uncle and a brother in the document. In listing Edward's allies at the start of the war, it names the

If, however, the suggestion that it may have been composed at the start of the Hundred Years War is accepted, then this hypothesis becomes very plausible.

The evidence of the French memorandum, with all its obscurities and errors, is not sufficient to prove that Adolf was bribed by the French. The story it tells of Musciatto's secret deal with the German king should not be given credence in the absence of corroboration. Conspiracy theories are always tempting, but these events in the 1290s are better explained in terms of muddle and confusion. Barraclough, while he accepted the evidence of the French memorandum, centred his interpretation not on the alleged bribery, but on the imprudent and mistaken, if understandable, policy adopted by Adolf of Nassau — a weak figure in the face of the greater armed might and unscrupulous diplomatic skill of the kings of England and France.[31] In fact, Edward I displayed little skill and very limited armed might, and it is hardly surprising that he failed to obtain Adolf's support. It was misguided of Edward and his advisers at the start of the war in 1294 to expect much of the German ruler; they were clearly unaware of the very limited resources that Adolf could muster. Campaign plans were then frustrated as a result of the Welsh rebellion of 1294–5, and the Scottish campaign of 1296. By 1297, Edward lacked the financial resources needed to carry out his ambitious plans for a combined assault on Philip IV. It was difficult to co-ordinate the diplomatic offensive, and the failure to find the Anglo-German treaty was symptomatic of the confused situation. It proved to be impossible to pay Adolf the subsidy that he had been promised, and the German king cannot have been pleased when his approaches to Edward suggesting a marriage alliance were rebuffed. Adolf's position was made more difficult by Albrecht of Habsburg's manoeuvres against him. Just as John of Cuyck informed Edward of the inadequacy of Adolf's military strength, so Adolf must have become aware, soon after the English landing in Flanders in August 1297, that Edward did not have sufficient forces for an effective campaign. The English had failed in their treaty obligations towards Adolf, and his decision not to assist Edward was thoroughly understandable. It is unlikely that he took money from the French. It would, indeed, have been a waste of money for them to bribe a man who was very unlikely to provide Edward with the support he so desperately needed.

The French memorandum on the war had suggested that there was a moral to be drawn from the failure of Edward I's plans. It was one which the English under Edward III were slow to see. It is extraordinary that after the plan for a grand coalition against France had failed, both in 1214 and again in 1297, that a very similar strategy should have been adopted in 1337. Once again, an elaborate network of alliances was created, including many princes in the Low Countries and the German ruler, Ludwig IV. As before, the cost was immense. The difficulties of co-ordinating action between the allies proved no less in the late 1330s than they had been in the 1290s. Even Edward III's remarkable naval victory at Sluys in 1340 did not galvanize the coalition, which broke apart at the siege of Tournai. The English were compelled to accept the Truce of Esplechin much as they had been forced to accept that of Vyve-Saint-Bavon in 1297. In all the three cases where

king of Germany and his brother. It could be that here Adolf's uncle, Eberhard, count of Katzenellenbogen, is intended, since he was included in the treaty arrangements: *Treaty Rolls, I*, 104. For 'Frater Gilbertus', see Cuttino, *English Dipl. Admin.* 244.
31  Barraclough, 'Edward I and Adolf of Nassau', 255.

grand coalitions were constructed against the French, under John, Edward I, and Edward III, the story was not so much one of plots and diplomatic coups, of secret diplomacy and underhand betrayals, but rather of incompetence and inadequacy in trying to put over-ambitious plans into practice.

# Crusades, Crusaders, and the Baronial *Gravamina* of 1263–1264*

The compromise pronounced by King Louis IX at Amiens in January 1264 between King Henry III and his baronial opponents led by Simon de Montfort may well be the most famous failure in the history of medieval arbitrations. By annulling the entire reform programme which had been enacted since 1258, Louis's 'compromise' in fact cut away whatever middle ground still remained between the two sides, thereby radicalizing both parties and accelerating the drift toward civil war. Although aspects of the Mise remain obscure, its importance has long been recognized, and analysis of it integrated into the standard narrative histories of the period.

The statements of grievances which Henry III and his opponents submitted to Louis in the course of this arbitration are not so well known. Treharne published and analysed the king's statement in 1948, but it was not until the 1950s that the corresponding baronial party documents were published by Walne, too late to find a meaningful place in the works of either Treharne or Powicke.[1] Although all of these documents have since been reprinted in Treharne and Sanders's *Documents of the Baronial Movement of Reform and Rebellion, 1258–1267* [*DBM*], no analysis of the baronial party's arguments has yet appeared. Before examining the Montfortians' case, however, it is necessary to clear up one or two points concerning the documents themselves.

The baronial grievances against the king survive today as two separate documents preserved in the same *carton* in the Archives Nationales in Paris.[2] J 654/12 is a document of three membranes, two of which are sewn together, chancery style, to form a single squared sheet of parchment 6.75″ wide and 18.25″ long. A third membrane, 7.25″ wide and 5″ long with an additional 1″ tail, is sewn to the right

* Portions of this argument were presented in 1981–2 to research seminars at the Universities of London and Oxford. I am grateful to participants there, and at the Newcastle Conference, 1989 for their comments and suggestions, and particularly to Simon Lloyd, whose searching criticisms of an earlier draft have considerably improved this one. I must also acknowledge the financial support of the University of Washington, Dept. of History, and particularly the Howard and Frances Keller Fund, which helped make possible my participation at the Newcastle Conference.
1 R.F. Treharne, 'The Mise of Amiens, 23 January 1264', in *Studies in Medieval History Presented to F.M. Powicke*, ed. R.W. Hunt, W.A. Pantin, and R.W. Southern (Oxford, 1948), 223–39; P. Walne, 'The Barons' Argument at Amiens, January, 1264', *EHR* lxix (1954), 418–25; *EHR* lxxiii (1958), 453–9. F.M. Powicke merely took note of Walne's first publication in his *The Thirteenth Century* (2nd edn. Oxford, 1962), 183 n. 2. He did, however, suggest that the king's statement, printed by Treharne, be redated to Sept. 1263 (ibid. 179 n. 2): see n. 18 below.
2 I wish to thank the staff of the Archives Nationales, esp. Mon. J. Guerout, for kindly making the originals of these documents available to me.

hand side of m.2. This document was the first to be discovered and published by Walne, and has been reprinted as document 37B in Treharne and Sanders.[3] J 654/17 is a single membrane of parchment, 9″ wide and 20.75″ long, and appears in Treharne and Sanders as document 37C.[4] That there is some connection between these documents is universally agreed, but there has been confusion concerning their proper order. Walne saw immediately that doc. 37C was a kind of historical introduction to the reform measures undertaken in 1258 and after, which were described in doc. 37B. Indeed, he was able to surmise the main argument of doc. 37C from the contents of doc. 37B, even before learning of the survival of doc. 37C itself.[5] Treharne and Sanders, however, although they adopted most of Walne's interpretation of the texts, rejected his ordering of the documents, and printed the texts in reverse order in their collection: first doc. 37B, then doc. 37C.[6]

There is no question, however, that Walne was correct about the proper ordering of these documents, and that Treharne and Sanders were wrong. The form of the documents themselves is sufficient to establish this fact, even aside from an analysis of their contents. Doc. 37C has a centred heading, 'Gravamina quibus terra Anglie opprimebatur et super quibus necesse fuit statum eiusdem reformare', which links the two now separate documents together in their proper order: first, the grievances by which England was oppressed (doc. 37C), then the reforms which followed (doc. 37B). Doc. 37B has no heading, and begins at the very top of the page with the conjunctive phrase 'Post hec vero, cum dominus rex attenderet statum regni sui . . .'. Doc. 37B thus presumes the historical account of events prior to 1258 which doc. 37C provides, and even echoes, in its first line, the language of the heading on doc. 37C, which is obviously intended to apply to the entire document. Both documents were written by the same hand, and appear to have been rolled together in the archives before being separated, most likely during the nineteenth-century reorganization of the Archives. That they were rolled together I cannot prove incontrovertibly, but my own experiments have satisfied me that the only order in which these two documents *can* physically have been rolled together is with doc. 37C on top and doc. 37B beneath. That they *were* rolled together in this order originally is strongly suggested, moreover, by the position of the thirteenth-century endorsements which each document carries. When the two documents are rolled in the order I suggest (doc. 37C on top of doc. 37B) both endorsements are clearly legible: 'Remedia super statu Regni anglie tempore henrici Regis' (on doc. 37B) immediately followed by 'In quodam rotulo quedam scripta super statu regni Anglie' (on doc. 37C). The nineteenth-century endorsements, however, are both covered, and were therefore probably added after the two rolls were separated. When rolled in the order suggested by Treharne and Sanders, a feat which can be achieved only very unsatisfactorily, all of the endorsements disappear from view.

The clearest proof of the correct ordering of these documents is, however, the coherence and subtlety of the argument which emerges when the documents are read in their proper sequence. As all its editors have remarked, doc. 37C does indeed present 'the more general and enduring causes of the breach between the King and his subjects'.[7] More precisely, however, the baronial grievances begin

3   *DBM* 256–67.
4   *DBM* 268–79. The king's grievances are doc. 37A.
5   Walne, 'Barons' Argument' (1954), 418.
6   *DBM* 44–5.
7   Walne, 'Barons' Argument' (1958), 455; *DBM* 45.

with a sustained historical argument accusing Henry of having violated Magna Carta, whose liberties his subjects had purchased with the fifteenth of 1225, the aid of 1235 to marry his sister, Isabella, to Emperor Frederick II, and the thirtieth of 1237. In eight clearly demarcated paragraphs the barons accuse the king of having violated, first, Magna Carta, cap. 1 (which guaranteed the liberty of the church) by his spoiling of ecclesiastical vacancies and by impeding free elections; second, of violating Magna Carta, caps. 4–6, by wasting the wardships and escheats which fell in to him, and disparaging the heirs by 'marrying such noble persons to obscure and unknown persons ... against the terms of the charter'; third, of selling, denying and delaying justice contrary to the terms of Magna Carta, cap. 40, which is cited explicitly; fourth, of raising new suits of court, seen here, I would suggest, as a violation of Magna Carta, cap. 16, which forbade the holders of free tenements from being compelled to perform more service than was due from them; fifth, of violating Magna Carta, cap. 41, again cited explicitly, which protected merchants from unjust exactions, such as Henry's excessive prises; and sixth, of having impoverished the realm by raising new and unsupportable increments on the shire farms, and of having appointed outsiders as sheriffs, who were unknown in the shires and ignorant of them. Although the Charter is not specifically mentioned in this sixth paragraph, references to 'the customs of past times' which were thus being violated leave the strong impression that the barons were here alleging violations of Magna Carta, cap. 25, which guaranteed that 'all shires, hundreds, wapentakes and ridings shall be at the ancient farm without any increment', and cap. 45, which promised that no sheriff, justice or constable would be appointed who did not know the law of the land and intend to observe it.[8] If this is indeed the implication of the charges in paragraph six, then the barons would appear to have been staking a claim to revive at least two of the provisions of Magna Carta (1215) which had been dropped from all subsequent reissues of the Charter.[9]

Two additional paragraphs follow, which detail further grievances of the baronial party but make no reference to the Great Charter. Paragraph seven complains that leagues of courtiers and aliens had banded together to monopolize grants of escheats and wardships, and to secure large money-fees from the exchequer, the combination of which had exhausted the king's treasury and forced him to abuse his rights of purveyance in order to support his household. Although not specifically tied to Magna Carta, this complaint obviously bears a close relationship to the grievances which precede it, all of which portray injustices and abuses which had arisen as a result of the king's poverty. Paragraph eight, however, is of a completely different type. It portrays Henry as having betrayed the cause of the Holy Land by the commutation of his crusader vow to Sicily.[10] This is a striking charge, to which I shall return. For the moment, however, let us follow through the baronial argument to its conclusion.

Doc. 37C ends with these allegations about the betrayal of the crusade, bringing

---

8    Unless otherwise indicated, all translations from the 1264 *gravamina* are from *DBM*. Translations of Magna Carta are from J.C. Holt, *Magna Carta* (Cambridge, 1965), app. iv.
9    For discussion of the numerous variant versions in which Magna Carta circulated during the 13th c., see S. Reynolds, 'Magna Carta 1297 and the Legal Use of Literacy', *Historical Research*, lxii (1989), 233–44.
10   A.J. Forey, 'The Crusading Vows of the English King Henry III', *Durham University Journ.* lxv (1973), 229–47 proves that the pope did not commute the king's own vow from the Holy Land to Sicily, but nevertheless this was certainly a widely-held perception in England of the pope's actions.

us to the eve of 1258. Doc. 37B continues the historical narration begun in doc. 37C:

> Eventually, however, when the lord king realized that the state of his realm required manifold reforms, for the reasons already given and for an infinity of other causes which it would take too long to detail here, it pleased him to grant to the leading men and the magnates of the kingdom that twelve should be chosen by himself and twelve others on behalf of the magnates, and that these chosen men should set in order, rectify, and reform the state of the realm accordingly as they should see most fitting to the honour of God, the faith of the king, and the advantage of the realm.[11]

Although its modern editors have divided the first section of doc. 37B into six numbered paragraphs, in fact the entire account of the appointment of the council of twenty-four is contained in a single long paragraph (*DBM* para. 1–3). The king's assent to the creation of this council is emphasized, the council's appointment of new castellans is justified on the now familiar grounds that 'the lord king had received many subsidies from the community and had tricked them every time, promising to observe the charter of the liberties of England and then speedily and specifically breaking his oath', and the narrative then concludes with the making of 'certain provisions or ordinances' for the reform of the realm.[12] Henry's public declarations of 16 July and 20 December 1263, stating that he wished to observe these provisions, are then recalled, and Louis is asked to enjoin the king and establish guarantees 'that in future he [Henry] will observe them in good faith, and cause them to be firmly observed by his subjects'.[13]

This long paragraph finally concludes with three sentences (*DBM* para. 4–6) stating the terms of the arbitration as the barons understood them. The arbitration was to 'cover every issue fully, so that all disputes and disagreements hitherto occuring shall be included, and so that full peace and agreement can be obtained on all points, every scruple of doubt being taken away'.[14] Second, although the official letters of submission had charged Louis to rule on all disputes prior to 1 November 1263, the date of the truce by which both sides agreed to arbitration,[15] the barons now asked that Louis first restore to them the encroachments which the royalists had made against the truce after 1 November.[16] These violations are detailed on m.3 of this document, attached as a schedule to the right side of m.2 (*DBM* para. 14–19), and they allow us to fix the composition of these grievances at some date after 24 December 1263.[17] Finally, the barons indicate that although only certain

---

11 *DBM* 257.
12 *DBM* 259.
13 *DBM* 259; *CPR 1258–66*, 269–70, 357. Henry made a similar declaration on 17 Oct. 1263: *CPR 1258–66*, 290.
14 *DBM* 261.
15 R.F. Treharne, *The Baronial Plan of Reform, 1258–63* (Manchester, 1932), 322–9; id., 'Mise of Amiens', 227.
16 Not since 16 July 1263, as *DBM* 45 suggests. Violations prior to 1 Nov. were already included in the terms of Louis's arbitration: *DBM* 280, 284. The barons were asking simply that the situation be restored to what it had been when the truce was agreed.
17 *CPR 1258–66*, 357–8 (24 Dec. 1263) records many of the appointments complained of here.

names appear on their documents of submission, all their followers wish to be included in the terms of the arbitration.

This concludes m.1 of doc. 37B, and also marks the end of the historical section of the baronial case. Doc. 37B, m.2 presents, instead, a point by point reply to the grievances which the king had presented to Louis; the baronial author obviously had a copy of this document.[18] Each of the king's complaints is answered, in order, in a separate paragraph. The lack of justice made a justiciar essential; Henry's excessive fees and gifts made a treasurer necessary to supervise his finances; the partiality of justice required the appointment of a chancellor to supervise the issuance of judicial writs and to prevent the sealing of unreasonable grants; and local men were appointed as sheriffs on an annual basis so that 'they would know plainly that at the end of the year they would lay down their offices to give an account of their stewardship', a requirement interestingly reminiscent of Louis IX's own reforms in his *Grand Ordonnance* of 1254–6.[19] At this point a paragraph was inserted, out of order, justifying the appointment of a continuing council to advise the king, and laying down strict requirements to prevent bribery of the councillors by the king or anyone else. The latter was another provision reminiscent of the *Grand Ordonnance*. The baronial argument then concludes at the bottom of m.2 with the ringing assertion:

> that this provision or ordinance is sanctified and honest, and that it is made for the honour of the lord king and for the common advantage of the kingdom, the king being bound to give justice to every one. As human malice grows this purpose could be achieved by no other way; but those who strive to overthrow this provision or ordinance and to draw the lord king by the snares of deception into the opposing party, are seeking to pull him into confusion, which heaven forbid, and his kingdom into ruin.[20]

Two aspects of this argument are particularly important to note. First, the Provisions of Oxford (a general term comprehending the entire body of reform legislation since 1258)[21] are presented here as simply a restatement and guarantee of the liberties already secured to the realm by Magna Carta. In their own eyes, de Montfort's supporters were asking for nothing more than the rights which they had

---

The baronial statement gets some of the details wrong (e.g. Alan la Zouche was appointed sheriff of Somerset and Dorset, not Henry of Almain: cf. Walne, 'Barons' Argument' (1954), 425 n. 1), probably because these appointments had just been made, and the barons' information was incomplete when this statement was drafted.

18  *DBM* 252–7 (doc. 37A), 278 n. 7. Powicke, *Thirteenth Century*, 179 n. 2 suggested that this statement by the king was actually submitted to Louis at Boulogne in Sept. 1263, citing the description of conditions in Wales and the Marches as proof: *DBM* 254–5. This description, however, is an historical complaint which almost certainly refers to the Montfortians' harrying of the Marches in spring and summer 1263, and esp. to their attacks on the property of the bishop of Hereford. It does not help us to date the document either to Sept. or to Dec. 1263. The question must remain open, but it is at least clear that the baronial statement was drafted after the king's statement, and with a copy of the king's complaints in front of the baronial author.

19  *DBM* 263; *Ordonnances des Rois de la troisième race*, ed. E-J. de Laurière (Paris, 1723), i. 67–75.

20  *DBM* 265.

21  Walne, 'Barons' Argument' (1954), 421 and refs.

already bought and paid for in 1225, 1235 and 1237. The limitations that they had imposed on the king's powers in 1258, to modern eyes unprecedented, were simply the minimum measures necessary to secure Magna Carta from the king's attempts 'gradually to whittle away those liberties'.[22] The meaning and significance of the Charters to the baronial reformers in 1258 continues to be controversial,[23] but by 1264 the Montfortians, at least, were portraying the entire baronial movement since 1258 as a straightforward battle for the Charters. Their passionate commitment to the Provisions of Oxford may in part be explicable on this score.

In the second place, the baronial argument at Amiens leaves no doubt that the continuance of the Provisions of Oxford was *the* essential issue on which Louis was being asked to arbitrate. As has been frequently noted, the terms of the actual letters of submission to Louis are vague. Although these letters charge Louis to rule on 'all the provisions, ordinances, statutes and obligations of Oxford, and on all contentions and discords which we have and have had up to the feast of All Saints just past',[24] it remains possible to argue that de Montfort expected the arbitration to extend only to modifications of the Provisions, while dealing mainly with the contentious and difficult land disputes which had resulted from the baronial harrying of the countryside in the spring of 1263.[25] These were the terms of the victorious de Montfort's order to the royalists in July 1263; but both the royal and the baronial statements at Amiens make it clear that these were *not* the terms on which the eventual submission to Louis's arbitration was accepted on 1 November. Henry's grievances presented to Louis flatly request that 'the provisions, upon which his adversaries rest their case, and all ordinances, statutes, and obligations and everything else which has resulted from them or on account of them, shall be quashed and invalidated, and declared null and void'.[26] The barons had seen the king's submission already, and their response tackles Henry's arguments directly, defending the Provisions collectively as a restatement of Magna Carta, and individually as necessary to rectify specific grievances which had arisen as a result of the king's violations of the Charter. Moreover, unless additional documents were submitted to Louis (of which there is no hint in either the royal or baronial statements) the Capetian had as yet received no information which would have enabled him to arbitrate on the land disputes which both sides had agreed to submit to him.[27] Presumably, the two sides intended to submit details of these disputes only if Louis upheld the main body of the Provisions as binding. Treharne and Powicke disputed this, arguing that it was unreasonable to suppose that de Montfort would have agreed to any arbitration which called into question the fundamental validity of the

---

[22] *DBM* 269.

[23] J.R. Maddicott, 'Magna Carta and the Local Community, 1215–59', *Past and Present*, cii (1984), 25–65 is the most stimulating recent contribution.

[24] *DBM* 280, 284.

[25] Powicke, *Henry III*, ii. 450–3; Treharne, *Baronial Plan*, 306–8; id., 'Mise of Amiens', 224–5, 235–7.

[26] *DBM* 255.

[27] Treharne, *Baronial Plan*, 322 n. 4 was uncertain whether Louis had been asked to arbitrate on these land disputes, but the evidence seems to me clear. The Dover chronicle, in *Historical Works of Gervase of Canterbury*, ed. W. Stubbs (RS, 1880), ii. 225–6; and *De duobus bellis apud Lewes et Evesham commissis*, ed. J.O. Halliwell (Camden Soc., old ser. xv, 1840), 16 both state that these disputes were included in the commission to Louis. The letters appointing the baronial proctors to Amiens imply the same thing (*De duobus bellis*, 122–3), as does para. 4 of doc. 37B (*DBM* 260–1).

Provisions of Oxford;[28] but this may seriously underestimate the precariousness of de Montfort's position by November and December 1263. With the earl's support dwindling daily, Louis's arbitration must have appeared to him as the only chance he had to preserve some aspects of the reform programme through negotiations, and to resolve the land disputes which had undermined his support between July and October. On 1 November, de Montfort accepted the best terms he could then get from the resurgent royalists.

The great skill of the author of the Montfortian party's grievances is evident in the way in which he systematically responds to the king's complaints, while simultaneously presenting the reforms of 1258 as logical and necessary solutions to the abuses detailed already in his historical narration. As an exercise in scholastic disputation, the argument is a minor *tour de force*, the quality of which must reinforce the case for Thomas Cantilupe, recently retired chancellor of Oxford University and the baronial proctor at Amiens, as being the probable author of the statement he presented there.[29] 'His prestige and training as a scholar, and his familiarity with Louis IX, whom he had met whilst studying in Paris, made him an ideal choice to promote the cause of the Provisions at Amiens.'[30] And if indeed Cantilupe was the author of these *gravamina*, his role at Amiens further underscores the wisdom of Maddicott's recent observations about the Mise of Lewes: 'If anything had become more evident during the negotiations, it was the close connection between the practical world of politics and the academic world of the schools, a linkage often noted but rarely so well substantiated.'[31] It would appear now that this linkage dates back at least to the latter months of 1263 and, if so, that we should take seriously the role that such academic influences may have played in shaping the principles of the Montfortian opposition in the six months which separated the preparations for Amiens from the battle at Lewes. And it is in this context, perhaps, that we should consider the role of the crusade in the baronial party's grievances against the king.

It is important to remember, of course, that the baronial statement at Amiens portrays all of these pre-1258 grievances from the perspective of the Montfortians in late 1263 and early 1264. This is not, in other words, a transparent historical record of the grievances which moved the reformers in 1258. For a number of reasons the crusade was on the Montfortians' minds by the end of 1263, and this charge may therefore reflect current rather than historically accurate preoccupations. It is also possible that the allegation that Henry betrayed the Holy Land was inserted because of the peculiar importance of the Holy Land to King Louis. The charge may be simply special pleading of a particularly obvious kind.

Both these objections must be acknowledged. But there is some reason, nevertheless, to take the crusade seriously as an issue in the opposition to King Henry expressed in 1258, more seriously, at least, than has yet been done. The stated purpose of the initial reforms of the king's council in May 1258 was, after all, to clear the way for the Sicilian project to go ahead.[32] This was in keeping with

---

28 Treharne, 'Mise of Amiens', 235–7; Powicke, *Thirteenth Century*, 181; id. *Henry III*, ii. 450–3.
29 Treharne, 'Mise of Amiens', 234; M.T. Clanchy, *England and its Rulers, 1066–1272* (London, 1983), 277; D.A. Carpenter, 'St. Thomas Cantilupe: His Political Career', in *St. Thomas Cantilupe, Bishop of Hereford: Essays in his Honour*, ed. M. Jancey (Hereford, 1982), 63–9.
30 Carpenter, 'St. Thomas Cantilupe', 63.
31 J.R. Maddicott, 'The Mise of Lewes, 1264', *EHR* xcviii (1983), 591.
32 *DBM* 72–3; *Ann. Mon.* i. 170–4.

standard crusade theory, which required that pressing grievances at home be remedied before embarking upon a crusade abroad, and although his new baronial
councillors may not have taken this justification for the reforms seriously, there is
reason to think that Henry did. His enthusiasm for reform flagged noticeably after
October 1258, when the pope withdrew the Sicilian offer. Recriminations continued until at least 1261, when Henry claimed damages of 200,000 marks against
the baronial council for his losses from the abortive Sicilian venture, and the king
was still talking about mounting a Sicilian expedition in 1263.[33] The 200,000 marks
in punitive damages which Henry sought at Amiens were probably also connected
with the Sicilian affair.[34] This was certainly how the barons interpreted Henry's
demand, and they responded to it here by portraying the entire Sicilian negotiation
as a betrayal of Henry's true crusader obligations to Jerusalem.

Henry's continuing commitment to Sicily conflicted flatly with his subjects'
presumptions about crusades. As Tyerman has shown, popular opinion in thirteenth-century England was remarkably consistent in regarding expeditions to the
Holy Land as the only true crusades, irrespective of papal declarations to the
contrary.[35] In 1239 Richard of Cornwall's crusaders swore an oath not to allow the
pope to direct their crusade elsewhere than to the Holy Land.[36] In 1247 Pope
Innocent IV formally conceded that no English crusader, if fit to fight, should be
forced either to commute his vow for money, or to fight on any other crusade than
one to the Holy Land.[37] Popular resistance to the papal nuncio Rostand's efforts to
commute crusader vows to Sicily was intense during the 1250s; and after 1265 the
papacy seems largely to have given up trying to preach crusades in England
elsewhere than to the Holy Land. In decrying the conversion of the king's vow of
1250 'from a crusade against the Saracens who are the foes of Christ's cross into an
attack on fellow-subjects of the same Christian religion', the Montfortians in
1263–4 were giving voice to sentiments already widespread in England by 1258.[38]

The circumstances of Henry's crusader vow of 1250 give further point to the
charge that the king betrayed the Holy Land by his conduct. Although he had
previously exhibited at least a conventional dedication to the cause of the Holy
Land, Henry was conspicuously cold toward Louis IX's crusade preparations,
throwing obstacles where he could in Louis's path towards Jerusalem. When the
truce between the French and the English expired in 1248, Henry refused Louis's
requests for a lengthy extension. Although previous such truces had been for three
to five years each, Henry now refused to agree to anything longer than a six-month
truce, giving rise to suspicions that he intended to use Louis's absence abroad as an
opportunity to recapture the Angevin territories in France.[39] Henry also attempted

[33] *DBM* 212–13, 230–7; C. Tyerman, *England and the Crusades, 1095–1588* (Chicago, 1988),
120.
[34] *DBM* 254–5, 278–9.
[35] See Tyerman, *England and the Crusades*, 89–95; id., 'Some Evidence of English Attitudes to
the Crusade in the Thirteenth Century', in *Thirteenth Century England I: Procs. Newcastle upon
Tyne Conference 1985*, ed. P.R. Coss and S.D. Lloyd (Woodbridge, 1986), 168–74; and id., 'The
Holy Land and the Crusades of the Thirteenth and Fourteenth Centuries', in *Crusade and Settlement*, ed. P.W. Edbury (Cardiff, 1985), 105–12.
[36] Paris, *CM* iii. 620.
[37] *Les Registres d'Innocent IV*, ed. E. Berger (Bibliothèque des Écoles françaises d'Athènes et de
Rome, 1884–1921), i. no. 2960.
[38] *DBM* 279.
[39] S.D. Lloyd, *English Society and the Crusade, 1216–1307* (Oxford, 1988), 214; W.C. Jordan,

to frustrate English participation in Louis IX's crusade, discouraging the bishop of Beirut from preaching the crusade in England, securing a papal order in 1247 that prevented English crusaders from departing until a year after the French, and appointing his unpopular half-brother, Guy de Lusignan, to head the English contingent if and when it did depart.[40] By the spring of 1250, however, it had become clear that Henry could no longer restrict the flow of English crusaders to the Holy Land by such means. William Longsword, Robert de Vere and a company of about 200 English knights had already departed on crusade in 1249, and by the spring of 1250 the bishops of Worcester and of Hereford, the earls of Leicester, Hereford and Winchester, and a host of English barons, including Geoffrey de Lucy and Roger de Montalt, were preparing to follow at midsummer, with a force that Matthew Paris reckoned at 500 knights, not counting dependants.[41]

Henry took the Cross in March 1250, in my judgement because he could not prevent the departure of this force by any other means, a motive more widely recognized at the time than it has been subsequently.[42] The English crusader army immediately saw the king's intent and swore to depart anyway, notwithstanding the king's desire that they now wait to accompany him in six years' time. It took a direct papal mandate to prevent their departure; this mandate was one of the first crusade-related measures that Henry took after making his vow.[43] The Tewkesbury chronicler blamed the resulting delay directly on Henry;[44] and within a month Alphonse of Poitiers's chaplain reported to his master the widespread belief that Henry had taken the Cross specifically to prevent these English crusaders from departing to aid Louis IX.[45] News of the disaster at Mansourah, of Longsword's death, and of the capture of Louis IX reached England in August, five months after the king had blocked the departure of the English crusaders. These disasters must have made the consequences of the king's delay provocatively clear.[46]

Whether Henry was sincere in his intention to go on crusade to the Holy Land matters little to my purpose here; I am persuaded by Tyerman's and Lloyd's arguments that, in his own way, he probably was.[47] But it remains true that Henry

---

*Louis IX and the Challenge of the Crusade* (Princeton, 1979), 25–6; Paris, *CM* iv. 488–9; v. 131, 134–5, 280–1.

40 Tyerman, *England and the Crusades*, 108–15; Lloyd, *English Society and the Crusade*, 237, 241.

41 Paris, *CM* v. 98–102. The numbers are doubtless exaggerated, but the impression of a considerable force is probably not mistaken.

42 Forey, 'Crusading Vows', 231–2 disputed this interpretation, but the evidence seems to me convincing. Tyerman comes to the same conclusion I had reached: *England and the Crusades*, 114–15; for a different view, see Lloyd, *English Society and the Crusade*, 210–29. Lloyd is undoubtedly correct to emphasize that Henry's motive in blocking English participation in this crusade was his rivalry with Louis IX, and not any opposition to the crusade *per se*; but this rivalry does not seem to me to explain the timing of Henry's sudden vow in 1250, after years of refusing to have anything to do with this particular crusade.

43 Paris, *CM* v. 102–3, 135; vi. nos. 97–8; Lloyd, *English Society and the Crusade*, 91 and refs. cited there.

44 *Ann. Mon.* i. 141.

45 T. Saint-Bris, 'Lettre adressée en Égypte à Alphonse, comte de Poitiers, frère de Saint Louis', *Bibliothèque de l'École des Chartes*, i (1839–40), 400–1; cited in Forey, 'Crusading Vows', 231–2; and Lloyd, *English Society and the Crusade*, 217 n. 90.

46 Paris, *CM* v. 103.

47 Tyerman, *England and the Crusades*, 111–23; Lloyd, *English Society and the Crusade*, 207–32, esp. 212–15.

did little in the eyes of his countrymen at large to persuade them of his enthusiasm. He failed particularly to enact the kinds of domestic reforms of his administration which were expected of a crusader king, and for which Louis IX was an obvious exemplar, or to pronounce the moral and sumptuary legislation that had also become traditional.[48] The earliest example of such legislation I have found comes from 1188, when Roger of Howden records Henry II's pronouncing of decrees against swearing, dice-playing, prostitution and extravagant dress, but the tradition may well be older.[49] Distantly, such prohibitions had roots in Roman Law, especially in the connection they presumed between blasphemy and gambling.[50] But more directly, such vices were the commonest causes alleged for the failure of crusading armies from the Second Crusade onwards. Crusades failed because people sinned. If Christ's armies were to triumph, Christ's people must be virtuous. Kings who were crusaders bore a responsibility to make them so, a lesson reinforced in England by Louis IX's efforts at moral reform in the wake of his own failed crusade. By 1254, when Louis's *Grand Ordonnance* forbade gambling, blasphemy, dice-playing, prostitution, and chess, the list of vices a crusader king was obliged to correct was virtually standardized.

Henry III, however, did nothing to respond to such expectations, except to pronounce against blasphemers in a speech in the exchequer in 1250.[51] The English bishops, by contrast, did rather more, or at least tried to. In the late 1240s several bishops, including Robert Grosseteste, attempted to mount full-scale investigations into vices such as gambling, blasphemy and oath-taking by summoning laymen to answer before them on oath concerning their lives.[52] The king prohibited such procedures, but in 1253 the bishops were at it again, inquiring into a list of sins notably similar to those prohibited in Louis's *Grand Ordonnance* a year later.[53] Whether or not the bishops saw their inquests as directly related to the crusade (the sources are silent either way, although the timing seems to me suggestive), such activities epitomized the kind of moral and spiritual preparation for his crusade which King Henry never undertook.

Henry did no better in fulfilling his crusader obligations to amend the injuries that he and his bailiffs had committed. Louis IX's *enquêteurs* of 1247–8 are the classic example of this royal obligation realized. Groups of Franciscans and Dominicans toured the French countryside, hearing the grievances of the poor and oppressed, ordering immediate recompense where the sums were not large, and reporting the most serious cases directly to the king himself for correction. The *Grand Ordonnance* of 1254 was based on the reports of these *enquêteurs*, and attempted to restrict the powers of the bailiffs to oppress in future. Oaths of good conduct were enforced upon all royal officials, bribery and extortion strictly prohibited, and limits placed even on their acceptance of food and drink. Thereafter, the *enquêteurs* became a permanent feature of French royal administration; and although their composition changed somewhat after 1254, under Louis IX approxi-

---

48  A fact noted also by Tyerman, *England and the Crusades*, 116.
49  *Chronica Magistri Rogeri de Hovedene*, ed. W. Stubbs (RS, 1868–71), ii. 336–7.
50  Justinian noticed that when gamblers lost, they frequently swore, and in *Codex* iii.43 had therefore prohibited both.
51  M.T. Clanchy, 'Did Henry III Have a Policy?', *History*, liii (1968), 215–16.
52  Paris, *CM* iv. 579–80.
53  *Ann. Mon.* i. 307–10.

mately one-half of them remained friars, and they retained an important corrective role.[54]

By 1258, Henry III had done none of this either, despite the rising chorus of complaints in the countryside against oppression by the royal bailiffs and household officials: prises not paid for, arbitrary tallages raised, poor men's resources wasted to feed the sheriffs and their agents. The king's own financial demands increased the pressure on the countryside, and increased the abuses as well. Henry's difficulties were explicable, but still inexcusable. Such abuses were precisely those which a crusader king was most clearly obliged to correct.

The other area in which Henry noticeably failed to live up to his crusader obligations was with respect to the Jews. From the point of view of the crusade, Jews and Jewish money-lending were regarded as a sort of standing injury to the realm.[55] Canon law spelled out the right of crusaders to be free from usury while they bore the Cross, and kings were expected to enforce this. In October 1250 Henry did so, granting that for a period of five years no usury would run against crusaders.[56] But he did nothing more. There were no general relaxations of interest payments on Jewish debts, nor general prohibitions of Jewish money-lending, such as Louis IX had declared in 1230 and vigorously enforced from 1247 on.[57] In 1253 Henry did issue a new and more restrictive Statute of Jewry, but this was a highly inadequate response to the problems which his own excessive Jewish tallages had created at court and in the countryside.[58] It did not begin to meet the real grievances of his subjects with respect to Jewish lending and its consequences.

The reforms undertaken by the baronial council in 1258–9 were precisely those which Henry, as a crusader king, ought to have enacted himself during the 1250s. The commission to four knights of every shire to inquire into all abuses by the royal officials, and to report them to the new justiciar on special eyre, may well have been designed with Louis IX's inquests in mind.[59] The Ordinance of the Sheriffs is another piece of early reform legislation in imitation of Louis's example; its provisions bear striking similarities to the *Grand Ordonnance*.[60] The reforms promised at the Jewish exchequer also fit comfortably into this model.[61] Some of the barons in 1258 may even have seen these measures as essential preliminaries to launching the crusade to Jerusalem which they had sworn a decade before to undertake. The need to establish peace and justice at home before crusading abroad was a standard part of crusade ideology by this date; this was, in effect, what Simon de Montfort himself had done when he postponed his 1247 crusader vow in order to go to Gascony on the king's business instead.[62] By 1258, there were many such unful-

---

54  Jordan, *Louis IX*, 61–3.
55  In France, legislation restricting Jewish lending can be traced in connection with the crusade from at least 1188: *Recueil des Actes de Philippe Auguste*, ed. H-F. Delaborde (Paris, 1916), i. no. 228 (1188); iv (ed. M. Nortier, Paris, 1979), no. 1554 (1219); and see the discussion in W.C. Jordan, *The French Monarchy and the Jews* (Philadelphia, 1989), 81–7.
56  *CPR 1247–58*, 75, 164.
57  See now the discussion in Jordan, *French Monarchy*, 129–36, 144–50, 155–62.
58  *CR 1251–3*, 312–13. On the effects of Jewish taxation during these years, see R.C. Stacey, '1240–60: A Watershed in Anglo-Jewish Relations?', *Historical Research*, lxi (1988), 135–50.
59  On these 1258 inquiries, see Treharne, *Baronial Plan*, 108–17; *DBM* 112–15.
60  *DBM* 118–23.
61  *DBM* 86–7, 108–9.
62  Although nowhere does Simon's friend Adam Marsh state this rationale explicitly for Simon's decision to postpone his crusade, Adam does go to elaborate lengths to emphasize to Simon the holy nature of his mission in Gascony: cf. *Monumenta Franciscana*, ed. J.S. Brewer (RS, 1858–

filled vows on baronial consciences, and the king's own actions were largely responsible for the fact that these vows remained unperformed.

In 1258 the crusade was an implicit issue in the opposition to Henry's government, acting to lessen popular respect for the king, and perhaps serving as a kind of organizing principle for some of the early baronial reform measures. By 1263, however, the crusade had emerged explicitly as an issue between the king and his opponents.[63] De Montfort himself may have been speaking the language of holy war as early as April 1263,[64] but the first unequivocal evidence of the direction in which the Montfortians' thoughts were moving comes from December 1263, when Simon's troops, surrounded outside the walls of Southwark in violation of the truce of 1 November, put on crusader Crosses in preparation for battle with the encircling royalist forces.[65] The baronial *gravamina* at Amiens were composed only a few weeks later; and the crusade issue would emerge again at Lewes, when de Montfort's troops took on the formal status of a crusader army, probably at the hands of Walter Cantilupe, bishop of Worcester, chief preacher of the crusade between 1247 and 1254, and uncle of the probable author of the baronial *gravamina* at Amiens.[66] Cantilupe's commission to preach the crusade to the Holy Land had been renewed by Pope Urban IV less than a year before the battle of Lewes in connection with the new crusade that the pope began to promote during 1263.[67] There is thus little doubt that the Montfortian spokesmen understood what they were doing in justifying their opposition to the king by reference to the crusade. The difficulty lies in interpreting this appeal. Were they simply shoring up the morale of an outnumbered and beleaguered force? Or were they making a much more precise ideological statement about the nature of their opposition to the king?

The Montfortians certainly needed the encouragement that a holy cause could provide — and for the rank and file of Simon's supporters in 1264 this may have been as far as the crusade issue went. But for men like the Cantilupes, and indeed for de Montfort himself, I do not think that the crusade issue can be dismissed quite so quickly. The situation in the Holy Land had deteriorated rapidly since 1260;[68] the pope had begun organizing a new crusade in 1263, reminding both King Henry and his opponents to fulfill their vows by July 1264;[69] and the presence of John de

---

82), i. nos. 135–9. Given Adam's interest in the crusade (e.g. his letter to Simon after the defeat at Mansourah: ibid. i. no. 145), it seems reasonable to infer some connection in both Adam's and Simon's minds between Simon's divinely inspired efforts in Gascony and the crusade.

63 S.D. Lloyd, ' "Political Crusades" in England, c.1215–17 and c.1263–5', in *Crusade and Settlement*, 113–20; Tyerman, *England and the Crusades*, 133–51; and see also *De antiquis legibus liber*, ed. T. Stapleton (Camden Soc., old ser. xxxiv, 1846), 57, which alleges the crusade to have been the principal subject discussed at Boulogne, in Sept. 1263.

64 Tyerman, *England and the Crusades*, 146, citing the chronicle of St. Benet Holme.

65 *Ann. Mon.* iii. 226; *Gervase of Canterbury*, ii. 231.

66 Cantilupe's role is attested only by *De duobus bellis*, which dates from the 14th c. and whose account is based on that in *Flores Historiarum*, ed. H.R. Luard (RS, 1890), ii. 495. The author of *De duobus bellis* appears, however, to have had some additional, contemporary source for his account of the Barons' wars. Several such accounts were apparently circulating in the early 14th c.: cf. C.H. Lawrence, 'The University of Oxford and the Chronicle of the Barons' Wars', *EHR* xcv (1980), 99–113; and now D.C. Cox, 'The Battle of Evesham in the Evesham Chronicle', *Historical Research*, lxii (1989), 337–45.

67 Tyerman, *England and the Crusades*, 145–6.

68 P. Jackson, 'The Crisis in the Holy Land in 1260', *EHR* xcv (1980), 481–513.

69 William, archdeacon of Paris was in England on the pope's behalf in Dec. 1263, 'to demand that Henry and his barons should fulfil their crusading obligations by preparing to start for Palestine on July 8th, 1264': Treharne, *Baronial Plan*, 338. Treharne thought that these demands

Valenciennes, lord of Haifa, as the most persistent mediator between King Henry and de Montfort in the months leading up to Lewes was a continuing reminder of a larger world and of higher obligations.[70] Even King Henry felt the pull; on the night before the battle of Lewes he gave John 2000 marks to assist the Holy Land.[71] The Holy Land was on men's minds during these months, and in view of the criticism which the Montfortians at Amiens had levelled at the king for his own betrayal of the crusade during the 1250s, I am reluctant to conclude that they were simply manipulating the symbolism of the crusade in 1263–4 by turning it into a party badge utterly divorced from its intrinsic associations with Jerusalem. However we interpret the crusader Crosses at Lewes, the Holy Land has to be part of the story.

What did the Montfortians mean, then, by taking the Cross against Henry? At least three possibilities are worth considering. They may have meant to justify their opposition to the king as necessary to restore domestic peace and justice to the realm prior to mounting a crusade to Jerusalem. This would be particularly telling in light of the argument that they had advanced at Amiens — that Henry had been the principal obstacle standing in the way of mounting just such a crusade. Second, the Montfortians may have been declaring Henry a tyrant. Crusades against a tyrannical monarch were a commonplace of crusade ideology by the 1260s, and a plausible case could be made by 1264 that Henry was indeed a tyrant by the standard scholastic definitions of that term. Robert Grosseteste had written about tyranny in 1250, in a pamphlet that de Montfort is known to have had in his possession,[72] and Thomas Cantilupe would have known well the Aristotelian arguments on which all such discussions of tyranny were based. A tyrant, said Grosseteste following Aristotle, prefers his private ends to the common good. What else had Henry done in preferring the cause of Sicily to the Holy Land, and in overthrowing the reform measures of 1258? A tyrant, said Grosseteste, rules by his will rather than by reason and the law. Henry's attempts to overthrow Magna Carta, detailed at Amiens, are obviously to the point here; so too, of course, is the *Song of Lewes*, which makes this its principal charge against the king. And a tyrant, finally, oppresses the Church; and here we may note not only the first of the grievances at Amiens, but also the complaints levelled by the English church against King Henry at Merton in 1258, and even, perhaps, the similar grounds put forward by the pope for the deposition of Frederick II in 1239, as these were recorded by Matthew Paris.[73] The difficulty with claiming that Lewes was a crusade against a tyrant,

---

passed 'almost unnoticed': ibid. 338. But the continuator of Gervase of Canterbury heard about them: *Gervase of Canterbury*, ii. 231–2; and the fact that this visit occurred only a few week prior to the drafting of the *gravamina* presented at Amiens makes it possible that the Montfortian author might even have had the pope's message in mind when drafting these grievances. William's message was, after all, directed at the Montfortians also.

70  Powicke, *Thirteenth Century*, 186; B. Beebe, 'The English Baronage and the Crusade of 1270', *BIHR* xlviii (1975), 129. Lloyd, *English Society and the Crusade*, 127 n. 51 corrects Beebe in some particulars of John's visit, but may be overly skeptical in denying any connection between this visit and the crusade.

71  *CPR 1258–66*, 317.

72  For discussion of this pamphlet, and an English paraphrase of its arguments, see W.A. Pantin, 'Grosseteste's Relations with the Papacy and the Crown', in *Robert Grosseteste*, ed. D.A. Callus (Oxford, 1955), 178–215, esp. 212–13. The pamphlet itself is ed. S. Gieben, 'Robert Grosseteste at the Papal Curia, Lyons 1250: Edition of the Documents', *Collectanea Franciscana*, xli (1971), 340–93.

73  Paris, *CM* iii. 533–6; *Councils and Synods with other Documents relating to the English Church: II*, ed. F.M. Powicke and C.R. Cheney (Oxford, 1964), i. 568–85.

however, is that after the rebels won at Lewes, they did not depose the king. But this fact does raise a third and final possibility.

On 24 July 1245 Pope Innocent IV issued the decretal *Grandi*, by which he deprived King Sancho II of Portugal of the rule over that kingdom.[74] Sancho was to remain king, but his brother Afonso was declared custodian of the realm, with Sancho placed in what amounted to perpetual wardship. Sancho resisted this decree, but Afonso arrived in the kingdom with a crusader army, and eventually drove Sancho out. Afonso did not, however, become king himself until 1248, when Sancho died and he ascended the throne by hereditary right. By the terms of *Grandi*, Sancho remained king until his death, but only in name. As a *rex inutilis*, he had forfeited his right to rule. The proof of his uselessness, and the reason offered by *Grandi* for his deprivation, was his failure to prosecute the crusade against the Saracens. This case was incorporated in Pope Innocent IV's *Decretals*,[75] and it was probably known in England, even outside the academic circles of the universities and the canon lawyers, through the personal connections which bound several of the participants to England. Sancho fought the decision in alliance with Alfonso of Castile, brother of the Lord Edward's wife, Eleanor; and the bishop of Toledo, who had sheltered Sancho in his exile, resided in England during 1255.[76] If de Montfort and his fellow rebels had an academic model for their actions between 1263 and 1265, this may well have been it — a somewhat equivocal conclusion, perhaps, but the best that the evidence at present can support.

We are still a long way from understanding the world of ideas in which royalists and rebels moved between 1263 and 1265. What I have tried to offer here is encouragement to speculate about the meanings and motives which some of de Montfort's supporters were prepared to find in their party's actions in the months leading up to the battle of Lewes. By their nature, such speculations are probably incapable of any incontrovertible proof, and I would not pretend to have offered such proof here. In all such speculations, however, it seems to me that the baronial *gravamina* presented at Amiens deserve to occupy a central place. But they need to be read aright, and in their proper order. And I hope at least that I have done that.

---

[74] E. Peters, *The Shadow King: Rex Inutilis in Medieval Law and Literature, 751–1327* (New Haven, 1970), 135–69; and id., 'Rex Inutilis: Sancho II of Portugal and Thirteenth Century Deposition Theory', *Studia Gratiana*, xiv, Collectanea Stephan Kuttner, iv (1968), 253–305.
[75] *Corpus Iuris Canonici*, ed. E.J. Friedberg (Leipzig, 1879–81), ii. cols. 971–4.
[76] Paris, *CM* v. 509–10.

# The First Convocation, 1257?

R.L. Storey

In the later fourteenth century, the name convocation was commonly used to refer to occasional institutions peculiar to the church of England. Archbishops of Canterbury then referred to their 'consilium sive convocacio provincialis', and in 1402 Thomas Arundel to his 'consilium provinciale vulgariter nuncupatum convocacio'. Although the terms provincial council and convocation were by this time being used interchangeably, these assemblies were not restricted in their membership to the archbishop and his suffragans, as were the provincial councils prescribed throughout Catholic Europe by canon law. Notices of that smaller gathering are rare in England from after the mid-fourteenth century, and from then the usual kind of assembly convoked by archbishops had a few hundred members, including elected representatives, and for these the name convocation is a useful term to distinguish them from the traditional councils of bishops. Like parliament, convocations had a pre-history dating from the thirteenth century. Assemblies which could be called 'model convocations' were held in 1283. In that year Archbishop Pecham called the bishops, abbots and priors of his province, deans of cathedral and collegiate churches, archdeacons, a proctor for every chapter and two proctors chosen by the clergy of every diocese. The archbishop of York held an assembly of the same composition, save that the parochial clergy were represented by two proctors from each archdeaconry. Such was to be the pattern of membership of the two provincial assemblies whenever they were subsequently convoked in order to receive and satisfy royal requests for clerical subsidies.[1] Given that this was their purpose, it is not remarkable that archbishops generally called their convocations at the behest of royal government. In 1344 the king's council decided that the archbishop of Canterbury should hold 'une convocation' of his prelates and clergy to assist Edward III's military operations in France.[2] Far less often, convocations were summoned on the initiative of their provincial rulers to deliberate on entirely ecclesiastical business; perhaps the earliest example in the northern province is a 'convocacio generalis' held by the chapter of York during the vacancy of the see in

---

1   E.W. Kemp, 'The Origins of the Canterbury Convocation', *Journ. Ecclesiastical History*, iii (1952), 142–3; J.A. Robinson, 'Convocation of Canterbury: its Early History', *Church Quarterly Review*, lxxxi (1916), 131–5; E.W. Kemp, *Counsel and Consent* (London, 1961), 76–7, 80–1, 86, 91, 101–12, 119; D.B. Weske, *Convocation of the Clergy* (London, 1937), 119–24, 240–69, 273–95; R.M. Haines, *Archbishop John Stratford* (Toronto, 1986), 70–8, 447–51; M.V. Clarke, *Medieval Representation and Consent* (London, 1936), 126–50.
2   *Rot. Parl.* ii. 146.

1340, for the purpose of defending provincial jurisdiction against rebellious clerical subjects.[3]

There was certainly no royal encouragement for the holding of the first assembly of ecclesiastics known to have been described by the royal chancery as a convocation. The earliest example cited by the *Dictionary of Medieval Latin* (from *Councils and Synods*) of 'convocatio' meaning an assembly of clergy is a notice in an Abingdon chronicle of a meeting of bishops and abbots at Reading in 1251; but this chronicle extends to 1304.[4] We have no reason to doubt the precise date of the usage of the word 'convocatio' in 1257, because it occurs in a writ on the close roll dated 19 July. Indeed, the word appears seven times in the enrolment, if we count its marginal heading 'De convocatione revocanda'.[5] King Henry had heard that Archbishop Boniface of Savoy had summoned his bishops to meet in London on 22 August. The king required their presence in his campaign against the Welsh. Perhaps Henry had first given this order verbally, but did not trust Boniface to obey and revoke the citations to the meeting. Copies of this writ were directed to all bishops of Canterbury province, and to the officials of those who were abroad. The king threatened all who dared attend this convocation with forfeiture of their lands. The manner in which the word 'convocatio' is repeated emphasizes the king's disapproval of this meeting. The archbishop's clerks, however, promptly adopted the word as a description for the assembly and its immediate precursor.[6] The meeting was held despite the king's ban. The cause of the prelates' defiance, as of the royal prohibition, was their sense of oppression by papal demands to finance the king's Sicilian adventure, and by simultaneous alleged threats to their liberties from his judges and officials. There had been a series of church councils since January 1253, a total of six before the meeting of August 1257.[7] Such frequency was unusual.

As Archbishop Wake was to observe, the canon of the Fourth Lateran Council (1215) requiring annual assemblies of provincial councils 'was not accounted of any force among us'.[8] Seven years passed between Lateran IV and Stephen Langton's first known council of his suffragans at Oxford in 1222. The earliest period when English church councils were quite frequent was during the legation of Cardinal Otto: he held eight between 1237 and 1241, the later ones to arrange a papal subsidy.[9] This earlier series of meetings may usefully be compared with those

---

[3]   *Registrum Palatinum Dunelmense*, ed. T.D. Hardy (RS, 1873–8), iii. 484–5; Cumbria Record Office, Carlisle, Diocesan Registers, 1, p. 422 (now being edited for the Canterbury and York Soc.). Kemp, *Counsel and Consent*, 104–12 dates the 'fusion' of provincial councils and convocations as somewhat later in Canterbury province; Archbishop Stratford clearly distinguished between the two kinds of assembly in 1342.

[4]   *Dictionary of Medieval Latin from British Sources*, ed. R.E. Latham (London, 1975–  ), fasc. ii. 483–4; *Councils and Synods with other Documents relating to the English Church: II*, ed. F.M. Powicke and C.R. Cheney (Oxford, 1964), 449.

[5]   *CR 1256–9*, 142; *Councils and Synods II*, 532. See n. 57, below for possible confirmation that *convocacio* could mean an assembly of dubious legality.

[6]   An agenda for the Aug. meeting describes the previous assembly of prelates and clergy (in May 1257) as a 'convocatio'. This agenda was written after the prohibition to which it refers as an order to prelates 'ne venirent ad hujusmodi convocationem': *Councils and Synods II*, 532–3.

[7]   *Handbook of British Chronology*, ed. E.B. Fryde *et al.* (3rd edn. London, 1986), 592, citing notices in *Councils and Synods II*.

[8]   W. Wake, *The State of the Church and Clergy of England* (London, 1703), 91; quoted in M. Gibbs and J. Lang, *Bishops and Reform 1215–1272* (Oxford, 1934), 143–4.

[9]   D.M. Williamson, 'Some Aspects of the Legation of Cardinal Otto in England, 1237–41', *EHR*

of the 1250s, because then also prelates used the opportunities for regular discussion and definition of common grievances. The initiative for this exercise may have come from Bishop Robert Grosseteste of Lincoln. He first expressed to his archbishop outrage that the abbot of Ramsey had been appointed a royal justice itinerant. In a later letter he documented other examples of bishops and clergy being subjected to the jurisdiction of courts of common law: bishops were summoned to answer; they were ordered to enforce judgments by taking revenues from benefices, and prevented from instituting clerks when the patronage of benefices was the subject of litigation in the king's courts; church courts were prevented from acting by writs of prohibition from the royal chancery. It is possible that Grosseteste prepared this document for one of the legatine councils, and so started the process of discussion among his brethren.[10] The bishops were reported to have presented the legate with a list of grievances in either 1238 or 1239.[11] There were twenty-nine articles, including five of Grosseteste's original complaints. They reflect a wide range of experience, and refer to objectionable practices from places as far apart as the city of London and the diocese of Carlisle.[12] The principal burden of these articles was the subjection of clergy and canonical jurisdiction to the common law of the realm. This was an affront to the ideal of ecclesiastical liberty, to the conditions in which the church could discharge its responsibilites for the cure of souls.

In the preface to these *gravamina* of 1238–9 the legate was reminded that Henry III had granted a general charter of liberties to ecclesiastics as well as to barons and other subjects, a reference to the confirmation of Magna Carta in 1237. The prelates had underwritten this confirmation by announcing the excommunication of all violators of the charter. Grosseteste had therefore argued that the king's own soul was imperilled by his tolerance of violations of the liberties of the English church.[13] The Great Charter, however, was very vague on the nature of ecclesiastical liberties; Stephen Langton had lamented that the reissue of 1225 gave little profit to bishops and abbots.[14] Cap. 1 merely declared that the English church should be free and enjoy undisturbed possession of its rights and liberties. The *gravamina* of 1238–9 may be regarded as an attempt to define and gain recognition of particular church liberties. This they failed to do. Possibly the legate was reluctant to press for them, because in 1238 his master the pope ordered the king to revoke his recent concessions to prelates and magnates.[15] The prelates themselves therefore submitted their articles directly to the king in a great council in January 1240. Here,

lxiv (1949), 145; W.E. Lunt, *Financial Relations of the Papacy with England to 1327* (Cambridge, Mass. 1939), 197–9.

10 *Roberti Grosseteste Epistolae*, ed. H.R. Luard (RS, 1861), 105–13, 205–34; *Robert Grosseteste*, ed. D.A. Callus (Oxford, 1955), 165–7, 200–1; F.M. Powicke, *The Thirteenth Century* (2nd edn. Oxford, 1962), 453.

11 1239 is preferred in *Councils and Synods II*, 280–4. They were dated 1237 when printed in *Ann. Mon.* i. 254–7. It is, however, arguable from that text (Burton annals) that the articles were presented at a legatine council on 17 May 1238, and that other complaints, about financial burdens, were made to the legate in 1239. See *Councils and Synods II*, 260–1, 279–80.

12 *Councils and Synods II*, 280–4; W.R. Jones, 'Bishops, Politics, and the Two Laws: the *Gravamina* of the English Clergy, 1237–1399', *Speculum*, xli (1966), 209–12.

13 Grosseteste, *Epistolae*, 212, 230–1; *Councils and Synods II*, 206–7.

14 *Councils and Synods II*, 162.

15 *Foedera*, I. i. 234; *Les Registres de Grégoire IX*, ed. L. Auvray (Bibliothèque des Écoles françaises d'Athènes et de Rome, Paris, 1890–1955), ii. nos. 4091–3; *Calendar of Entries in the Papal Registers Relating to Great Britain and Ireland: Papal Letters I (1198–1304)*, ed. W.H. Bliss

Henry's 'evil councillors' were blamed for violations of ecclesiastical liberty despite the confirmation of Magna Carta in 1237. Henry was reported to have agreed that advisers who thus endangered his soul should suffer excommunication, but there is no notice of any substantive redress of any of the issues of complaint.[16] Perhaps the lay members of the great council again declared: 'Nolumus leges Anglie mutare.'

The next period when prelates had opportunities for regular discussions opened in January 1253. Grievances were drawn up in a Canterbury council which had seemingly met for another purpose.[17] It is not known if these complaints were pressed any further in that year, but they were revived in the series of national councils of the church which followed the arrival of the papal nuncio Rostand to preach a crusade against the Hohenstaufen. In October 1255 the barons in parliament refused to make an immediate grant to support the king's Sicilian enterprise, and the bishops rejected an appeal from the nuncio for advance payments of the crusading tenth.[18] This was not a tax which they could refuse to pay, because it had been ordered by the pope after Henry took the Cross in 1250. There was no crusade to the east, of course, but in 1254 Henry had undertaken to conquer Sicily, and the original mandatory tax from the English clergy was extended to five years. The nuncio needed to convoke prelates and other clergy to make arrangements for assessment and collection, and to secure payments in advance, as the pope had ordered. These national assemblies vainly tried to convince the nuncio of their inability to pay.[19] Simultaneously, however, they compiled and refined a list of grievances against the king's government for its alleged violations of ecclesiastical liberties. As in the period of legatine councils which produced the first *gravamina*, the bishops were mindful of Magna Carta. In 1253 they had pronounced another sentence of excommunication to reinforce Henry's latest confirmation.[20] Moreover, they had then sought and obtained the pope's ratification of this sentence, and had it distributed throughout the network of the English church, down to the rural deaneries.[21] In the later middle ages it became more usual for the church to lend these offices to spread the king's propaganda.[22] On this occasion it could appear that the clerical establishment sympathized with lay subjects oppressed by maladministration.

The pope's confirmation of the bishops' sentence might seem to be a significant reversal of policy. As recently as 1249 Innocent IV had announced royal grants of liberties to be void.[23] In 1254 he was apparently persuaded that the charters protected ecclesiastical liberty. This was the avowed reason why the prelates had sued

---

(London, 1893), 167. See also J.W. Gray, 'Archbishop Pecham and the Decrees of Boniface', in *Studies in Church History II*, ed. G.J. Cuming (London, 1965), 215–16.
16 *Councils and Synods II*, 284–5.
17 Ibid. 467–72.
18 Ibid. 501–2; Paris, *CM* v. 520–1, 524–7; Lunt, *Financial Relations*, 259–60, 269.
19 Lunt, *Financial Relations*, 254–6, 262–6, 269–72.
20 *Councils and Synods II*, 477–8.
21 *Les Registres d'Innocent IV*, ed. E. Berger (Bibliothèque des Écoles françaises d'Athènes et de Rome, Paris, 1884–1921), iii. no. 8070; *Cal. Papal Letters*, i. 306; *Ann. Mon.* i. 318–22; *Councils and Synods II*, 474.
22 W.R. Jones, 'The English Church and Royal Propaganda during the Hundred Years War', *Journ. British Studies*, xix (1980), 18–30; see also 25–35, above.
23 *Reg. Innocent IV*, ii. no. 4393; *Cal. Papal Letters*, i. 251–2.

for his approval of their sentence. They certainly appeared to believe this themselves, and they were perhaps encouraged by the pope's confirmation to put forward their claims for redress of grievances in this context. Indeed, it is quite striking how the clerics appropriated the Great Charter in the elaboration of their *gravamina*, so that it was eventually stated, in a canon of 1261, that the charter was granted to the church by the king and his predecessors (*sic*).[24]

More remarkable was the reference to Magna Carta, c. 1 in the final articles of 1257. Here, the complaints were that prelates were compelled to appear before royal judges to show their titles to liberties, and to produce charters which might be disallowed if there was no 'express mention' of the liberties they held.[25] Bishops and religious houses were most concerned in such cases about the threat to their receipts of amercements of their tenants in the king's courts. In recent years ecclesiastical claimants of this liberty had found that it was no longer given automatic recognition. The general eyre of 1254 appears to have been particularly severe in this respect. Certainly, this complaint did not appear in known *gravamina* of before 1257, although Dr. Carpenter has shown that the courts' policy on claims to amercements dates from a ruling of the king and council in 1233–4.[26] It was a new development, and surely rather far-fetched, to claim that entitlement to amercements of tenants was a liberty of the church. It was, after all, a franchise also enjoyed by some secular magnates, hardly a liberty of a spiritual nature which could be portrayed as essential for the freedom of the church to carry out its pastoral mission. That had been the nature of the *gravamina* of 1238–9.

Many of those earlier complaints were again brought forward in 1257, and there were additions of the same general kind: new sorts of writ were interfering with the church's jurisdiction; visitations by bishops and archdeacons were being impeded because they were not allowed to have sworn juries; sheriffs were not executing writs to imprison excommunicates; clergy convicted in lay courts were still being hanged or, if delivered to their ordinaries, not being restored their possessions; there had been violations of sanctuary.[27] In 1238–9 there was a very brief, general request that the last wills of 'bishops and others' should not be impeded.[28] There were three articles about testamentary matters in 1257.[29] Modern commentators appear usually to have stressed continuity from the *gravamina* of 1238–9 to those of 1257, and to have overlooked the addition of grievances about material assets and franchises.[30] In 1257 first place was given to the waste of temporalities by royal custodians of vacant bishoprics and abbeys. There were complaints, too, about purveyance, forced hospitality and exactions of public tolls.[31] It is hardly surprising

---

[24] *Councils and Synods II*, 680 (no. 18); see also 483 (for 1254), 543, no. 24 (for 1257).
[25] Ibid. 547–8.
[26] D.A. Carpenter, 'King, Magnates and Society: the Personal Rule of Henry III', *Speculum*, lx (1985), 49–50.
[27] *Councils and Synods II*, 547 (no. 44), 541 (nos. 9–13), 542 (nos. 15, 18), 543 (no. 22).
[28] Ibid. 281 (no. 4).
[29] Ibid. 534 (no. 9), 543 (nos. 24–5).
[30] C.R. Cheney, 'The Legislation of the Medieval English Church', *EHR* l (1950), 402, repr. in id. *The English Church and its Laws* (London, 1952); Powicke, *Thirteenth Century*, 454; Jones, 'Bishops, Politics', 215; Gray, 'Archbishop Pecham', 215–16; W.R. Jones, 'Relations of the Two Jurisdictions: Conflict and Co-operation in England during the Thirteenth and Fourteenth Centuries', *Studies in Medieval and Renaissance History*, vii (1970), 91–3.
[31] *Councils and Synods II*, 539–40, 546–7 (nos. 36, 41–3); see also 158, below.

that clerics were anxious about their sources of revenue when these were threatened by the demands of king and pope, by what Matthew Paris called 'the alliance of shepherd and wolf'.[32]

In these straits, prelates and clergy had a hitherto improbable champion in Archbishop Boniface, the king's Savoyard uncle who had antagonized his suffragans during earlier, occasional stays in England. But, in Mandell Creighton's words, 'in 1256 Boniface returned and again behaved as though the air of England inspired him with a fictitious patriotism'.[33] On his last visit he had participated in the excommunication of violators of Magna Carta. Also, in 1254, Boniface and his bishops had offered the king a clerical tenth on certain conditions, including the reform of grievances.[34] The same tactic was adopted in a church council held by the papal nuncio in May 1257. The king was offered £52,000 as an alternative to the papal impositions, and subject to grievances being remedied. As the crusading tenths had already been imposed by papal mandate, it is not surprising that Henry seemingly ignored the offer.[35] Because he had not replied by mid-July, Boniface summoned a council for 22 August, the meeting which the king prohibited. This was not a provincial council of bishops only, as the writ suggests. Deans of cathedrals and heads of monastic houses were also called, and they were to have letters of proxy from their chapters. Archdeacons were likewise called with powers to represent their lower clergy.[36] The preparation of these letters of proxy will have given parochial clergy an opportunity to air their grievances, as they had done in 1256. Some of the articles in the *gravamina* came from this ground level in clerical society. There was, for instance, a plaint that clergy were more heavily fined for breaches of forest law than convicted laymen; this was one of the 'articuli pro communitate' of Coventry and Lichfield diocese.[37]

The archbishop's agenda for this convocation shows his commitment to the cause of reforming the condition of the English church. One of his points assumed that the king would not remedy the clergy's grievances. He asked the council what provision might be made to defend the liberties of the church against its oppression by secular judges.[38] Convocation replied that bishops should resist by excommunicating violators of church property and by putting their lands under interdict; and it was proposed that measures should be devised for responding to other attacks on the liberty of the church.[39] It is apparent that a substantial programme of drafting was put in hand. The most comprehensive and articulated list of fifty *gravamina* may have been completed after this assembly.[40] Ten months later, a set of ordered proposals was ready for publication. They were dated at Westminster on 8 June 1258 as letters patent of Archbishop Boniface and his suffragans, who were said to have made the ordinances with the consent of inferior prelates, cathedral and conventual chapters, and the 'universitas' of English clergy; and in testimony the representatives of this 'universitas', as well as the senior prelates (none of them

---

32  Paris, *CM* v. 532.
33  *DNB* ii. 813.
34  *Councils and Synods II*, 475–9, 482–3.
35  Ibid. 529–30; Lunt, *Financial Relations*, 276–8.
36  *Councils and Synods II*, 531–2.
37  Ibid. 506–9, 542 (nos. 19, 20).
38  Ibid. 532–3.
39  Ibid. 537–9.
40  Ibid. 539–48.

named), attached their seals. The occasion was described as a solemn 'conventio' of the prelates and clergy of the English church.[41]

The provisions may be described as a programme for direct action by the bishops, a code prescribing the measures to be taken in response to particular acts deemed to violate liberties of the church of England ('ecclesia Anglie').[42] Caps. 1–4 concerned royal writs citing prelates to secular courts to answer for their exercise of spiritual authority in, for instance, the admission of clergy to benefices, the excommunication, or prosecution, of their subjects for sins like perjury, sacrilege or breaches of liberties of the church. Bishops were not to obey such writs, but to ask the king to revoke them. If he scorned their exhortations and attempted to enforce appearance in his court by distraint, the royal officials responsible were to be excommunicated and their lands put under interdict, while any clergy involved, whether as plaintiffs or for writing the writs, were to lose their benefices. Should these measures fail to persuade the king, his castles, towns and estates in the diocese of the bishop being summoned were to be laid under interdict, and the other archbishops and bishops would extend this interdict throughout the kingdom after twenty days. Any bishop who failed to take part would be punished by his metropolitan, and his diocese interdicted. Similar means of canonical coercion were to be adopted when secular officials arrested clergy accused of crime (c. 7), prevented ecclesiastical inquests into the behaviour of lay subjects (c. 12), failed to arrest excommunicates (c. 6), or seized the goods of intestates or impeded the execution of testaments (c. 22). Bishops were not to be required to compel clergy to pay amercements ordered by secular courts; they were to respond to their own consequent distraint by censures (c. 8). Similar penalties were to be incurred by laymen who sued writs of prohibition in cases of perjury, while clerical or religious plaintiffs would be punished canonically (c. 10). The secular franchises of ecclesiastics were likewise to be protected against the king's justices, who would incur excommunication and interdict for pronouncing charters worthless as warranty of liberties not expressly mentioned (c. 19), or for defrauding ecclesiastics of amercements, in violation of Magna Carta (c. 21).

After the provisions of the council of 1258 were reshaped as the canons of the Council of Lambeth in 1261, Pope Urban IV observed that its measures seemed proper and just.[43] The pope's opinion indicates that the programme conformed to the framework of the 'common law' of the church: the archbishop and his colleagues could not make 'new' law. Boniface's canons were to be incorporated in Lyndwood's *Provinciale* 170 years later, though he noted that they had rarely been applied, and that must be an exaggeration.[44] Despite his approbation, Urban IV did not confirm the canons through deference to King Henry. As Dr. Gray has written, 'By promulgating canonical legislation which affected the rights of the Crown, Boniface broke a rule of English custom, and also threatened to disregard that other customary rule which forbade that the sanctions of interdict and excommunication

41 Ibid. 573, 585. The likelihood that this was a national church council is discussed in ibid. 568–9.

42 Ibid. 573–85.

43 Ibid. 669–86; *Foedera*, I. i. 424; C.R. Cheney, *Medieval Texts and Studies* (Oxford, 1973), 119–20.

44 Cheney, 'Legislation', 202–4, 404. Lyndwood's comment actually refers to the canon *Contingit etiam aliquando* on the arrest of clergy suspected of crime: *Provinciale seu Constituciones Anglie* (Oxford, 1679), 92; cf. *Councils and Synods II*, 677 (c. 9 of 1261, based on c. 7 of 1258: ibid. 577–8).

should be used against the Crown and royal officials *rege inconsulto*.'[45] At the time, however, it would have been understandable if some ecclesiastics believed that these rules had been suspended in respect of breaches of Magna Carta, given that in 1253 the king and magnates had apparently assented to the excommunication of its violators.[46] Immediately after reporting the publicity given to this sentence, Matthew Paris noted that the king was still wasting the temporalities of the archbishopric of York, which was vacant for twelve months from May 1255 because Henry opposed the chapter's candidate.[47] There was a longer vacancy at Ely for the same reason.[48] Eventually, in January 1258, the temporalities were delivered to the monastic chapter's choice, Hugh Balsham. He soon sought the pope's authority to excommunicate the royal custodian, John de Walerand, claiming that John's depredations contravened Magna Carta and thus incurred the sentence pronounced at its confirmation in 1253.[49] Alexander IV seemingly accepted this argument and ordered the dean of Lincoln to excommunicate John and his associates if they persisted in refusing reparations; the papal letters made no reference to any immunity for royal agents.[50] When he petitioned the pope, Bishop Hugh must have known that royal exploitation of vacant temporalities was said to be 'against the king's charter' in the articles of complaint so recently compiled.[51]

When Henry III vainly forbade the convocation of August 1257, he was doubtless advised that the prelates were set on a course against the Crown and its servants. He is not known to have tried to prevent the next ecclesiastical assembly in June 1258. Boniface issued his mandates calling the council on 19 April 1258,[52] when a parliament was furiously discussing the king's plea for financial support, and a week after seven magnates (among them the archbishop's brother, Peter of Savoy) had sworn their compact of mutual aid. The archbishop's stand against the king may not be unconnected with the behaviour of the bishop-elect of Winchester but, as it has already been said, 'there was much more to the revolution of 1258 than the expulsion of the Lusignans'.[53] Unlike the lay magnates, the prelates had already made plans for the reforms they wanted, and after they had sought and received the complaints of their dependants.

The 'first convocation' was a stage in a movement of ecclesiastical protest against the government of Henry III. Because clergy considered themselves to be doubly threatened, by papal taxation as well as by royal judges and officials, they

[45] Gray, 'Archbishop Pecham', 215–16; see also Paris, *CM* v. 109–10.
[46] That such belief would have been mistaken, see J.W. Gray, 'The Church and Magna Carta in the Century after Runnymede', in *Historical Studies: Papers read before the Irish Conference of Historians, VI* (London, 1965), 23–8.
[47] Paris, *CM* v. 500–1, 516; Gibbs and Lang, *Bishops and Reform*, 81; see also *CR 1254–6*, 203.
[48] Paris, *CM* v. 611, 635–6; Gibbs and Lang, *Bishops and Reform*, 77, 84.
[49] The papal letters actually refer to a promise of Henry III to take only 'reasonable issues' from vacant temporalities. This undertaking appeared in Magna Carta (1216), c. 5.
[50] *Les Registres d'Alexandre IV*, ed. C.B. de la Roncière (Bibliothèque des Écoles françaises d'Athènes et de Rome, Paris, 1902–53), ii. no. 2650; *Cal. Papal Letters*, i. 359. John, a canon of Wells, was escheator south of Trent. His brother Robert, the well-known king's knight, was also a guardian of Ely in the vacancy: *CPR 1247–58*, 446, 580, 603, 612.
[51] *Councils and Synods II*, 539–50; see also 155, above.
[52] *Councils and Synods II*, 571–2 (as in 1257, archdeacons were to have letters of proxy from their 'subjects'). This council was called to Merton but soon moved to Westminster.
[53] D.A. Carpenter, 'What Happened in 1258?', in *War and Government in The Middle Ages: Essays in Honour of J.O. Prestwich*, ed. J. Gillingham and J.C. Holt (Woodbridge, 1984), 119; see also 113–14.

might have persisted in their defiance of the king in other circumstances. It is more than likely, however, that the prelates were emboldened by the contemporary baronial hostility to the king. The Provisions of Oxford included a direction to the council of twenty-four to reform 'le estat le seint eglise' when time allowed.[54] The programme of Archbishop Boniface and his council for this reform, sealed three days earlier, seemingly failed to commend itself to influential lay opinion. Only one of the grievances addressed in that programme, the exploitation by royal custodians of the temporalities of vacant bishoprics and abbeys, was repeated in the articles of complaint listed by Henry's baronial opponents as they prepared their case for the arbitration of Louis IX at Amiens in 1264. These articles also protested against the king's denial of free capitular elections and his imposition of unworthy candidates for bishoprics, and against the impoverishment of the church by papal taxation; but there was no mention of any of the other ecclesiastical liberties whose disregard had distressed Boniface and his suffragans.[55] If French nobles conspired to oppose the jurisdiction of their ecclesiastical courts, as Matthew Paris documented (under 1247), it would have been strange if their peers in England would have wished to strengthen church courts in their land.[56] When Henry III, in 1252, ordered Bishop Grosseteste not to assemble laymen to give evidence of sinful behaviour under oath, this prohibition was said to be the result of complaints made to the king by magnates as well as other subjects of Lincoln diocese.[57] As the fully-developed convocations of the fourteenth and fifteenth centuries were to learn, lay members of parliaments were not sympathetic to ecclesiastical liberties, and they had to be defended by grants of clerical subsidies.[58]

54  *DBM* 106–7.
55  *DBM* 268–71, 278–9. Dr. Carpenter kindly drew my attention to these articles.
56  Paris, *CM* iv. 591–3.
57  *CR 1251–3*, 224–5. The writ referred to these juries called by the bishop as 'convocaciones populi'. Such gatherings of parochial representatives became a normal feature in bishops' diocesan visitations.
58  R.L. Storey, 'Simon Islip, Archbishop of Canterbury (1349–66): Church, Crown and Parliament', in *Ecclesia Militans*, ed. W. Brandmüller, H. Immenkötter and E. Iserloh (Paderborn, 1988), i. 139–51; id., 'Episcopal King-Makers in the Fifteenth Century', in *The Church, Politics and Patronage in the Fifteenth Century*, ed. R.B. Dobson (Gloucester, 1984), 88–94.

# The Marriage of Henry of Almain and Constance of Béarn

Robin Studd

Henry of Almain and Constance of Béarn were married at Windsor on 19 May 1269. He was the elder son of Richard of Cornwall, king of the Romans; she was the eldest of the four daughters of Gaston VII, *vicomte* of Béarn. It was a union whose political significance was of sufficient moment to justify comment by contemporaries. To Thomas Wykes, whose knowledge of, and admiration for, Richard of Cornwall and his family has been chronicled by Denholm-Young, the explanation lay in the expectation of the inheritance of the *vicomte*: 'cui prae caeteris Aquitanniae magnatibus . . . in divitiis et potentia nec non terrarum latitudine nullus potuit aequiparari'.[1]

But, as is well known, the marriage was short-lived. Just under twenty-one months later, on 13 March 1271, Henry was murdered in Viterbo. The political success that the marriage represented for Henry III and the Lord Edward and, of course, for Henry of Almain himself, was destroyed. The opportunity had been lost to establish an English dynasty to govern not only in Béarn itself, the most powerful of southern Gascon and trans-Pyreneean territories, but also in those Gascon lordships which had come by inheritance into the hands of the *vicomtes* of Béarn, and stretched in an embracing arm north-eastwards through Marsan, Gabardan and Brulhois to the banks of the Garonne. With our advantages of hindsight we know that, within months of his accession, Edward I faced a serious rebellion by the *vicomte* which disturbed Gascon affairs at least until 1279. What, therefore, had Henry III and the Lord Edward sought to achieve by this marriage? What did Gaston de Béarn see to his advantage? And what did Henry of Almain hope for by this contract with a southern Pyreneean heiress? These are the questions to be addressed here.

## I

Twice before, during the previous century or so, the *vicomté* of Béarn had passed through the female line to a non-Béarnais family. When Centulle VI, direct male descendant of the first-known holder of the title, died in 1134, his inheritance passed to his sister's son, Pierre de Gabarret, *vicomte* of Gabardan and Brulhois,

---

[1] *Ann. Mon.* iv. 222; N. Denholm-Young, 'Thomas de Wykes and his Chronicle', *EHR* lxi (1946), 157–79; repr. in id. *Collected Papers on Medieval Subjects* (new edn. Cardiff, 1969), 245–66.

and vassal of the duke of Aquitaine. Then, on the death in 1173 of Gaston V without direct heirs, the succession went to his sister and her husband Guillaume, lord of Moncada and Castelvieilh, who was a vassal of the king of Aragon.[2] A change of political direction for the dynasty had accompanied each of these transfers of power and is to be explained by the geographical location of Béarn astride the Pyrenees. Besides the dukes of Aquitaine, as conquerors of the duchy of Gascony, the Crowns of Aragon, Castile and Navarre separately entertained claims to the region which, from time to time, they attempted to assert. In 1204, for instance, Alphonso VIII of Castile, styling himself duke of Gascony, invaded and remained in occupation for about a year.[3]

The *vicomtes* of Béarn, nevertheless, retained their Aragonese allegiance during the later years of the twelfth century. As long as the formidable Alphonso II was on the throne they had little choice, and even performed homage for the lands which they held in Gascony of the dukes of Aquitaine. It was only after the battle of Muret (1213), with the consequent withdrawal of Aragonese interests into the Iberian peninsula and the Mediterranean islands, that any loosening of the relationship is to be detected. Tucoo-Chala has argued that for about twenty years, at the beginning of the thirteenth century, a kind of political vacuum existed in Béarn, during which the *vicomtes* chose to reside on their Aragonese lands and rarely crossed to the north of the Pyrenees. However, he asserts, Gaston VII had to transfer his political base back to Béarn because of the debts his father had amassed in the service of the Spanish kingdom.[4]

That may not be the whole story. Their political pre-occupations further north kept the dukes of Aquitaine away from their southern Gascon frontier. Richard I did make a couple of sorties into the region, and in 1187 secured the homage of the *vicomte* of Béarn for his Gascon lordships.[5] But John's wars with Philip Augustus required the Angevins to involve themselves more directly in the affairs of the south. The chief concern of the duke throughout the period from 1202 to the ratification of the Treaty of Paris in 1259 was, first, the military defence of his French territories and, second, their protection from the constant encroachment of the Capetians' courts and officials by the use of peaceable devices such as *paréage* agreements and letters of non-alienation.[6]

The homage that Gaston VII rendered in person at Bordeaux to Henry III in 1242, which, it is often argued, was not only for his other Gascon lordships but also for the *vicomté* of Béarn, needs to be seen in this context. Following the French withdrawal from the duchy in 1228, an effort was made to create a more systematized and centralized administration for Gascony. During the two periods of office of the seneschal Henry de Trubleville (1227–32 and 1234–7), important castle-building works were put in hand throughout the duchy, vassals' castles were

[2] P. Tucoo-Chala, *La Vicomté de Béarn et le Problème de sa Souveraineté* (Bordeaux, 1961), 37–48.
[3] Ibid. 50–1, citing a document transcribed into a Dax cartulary.
[4] Ibid. 52–8.
[5] J. Gillingham, *Richard the Lionheart* (London, 1978), 79, 138–9.
[6] J.R. Studd, 'The "Privilegiati" and the Treaty of Paris, 1259', in *La 'France Anglaise' au Moyen Age. Actes du III° Congrès National des Sociétés Savantes, Poitiers, 1986* (Paris, 1988), 176–80.

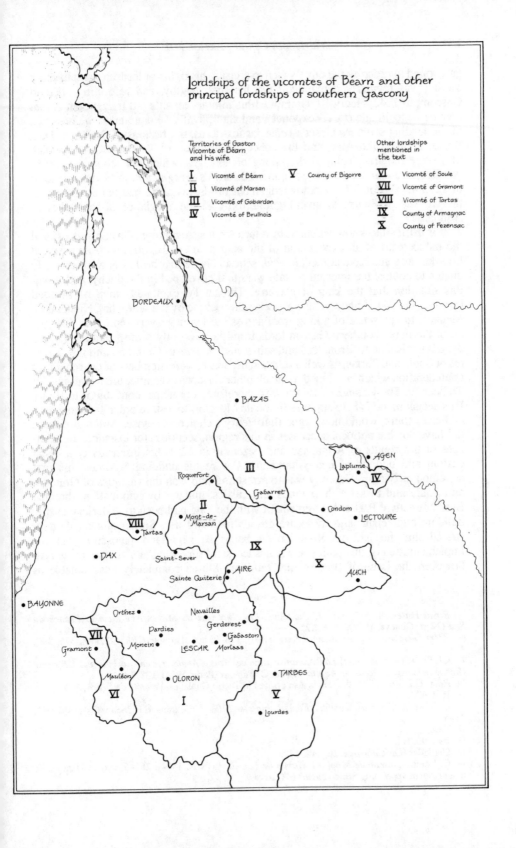

Lordships of the vicomtes of Béarn and other
principal lordships of southern Gascony

Territories of Gaston
Vicomte of Béarn
and his wife

I   Vicomté of Béarn
II   Vicomté of Marsan
III   Vicomté of Gabardan
IV   Vicomté of Brulhois

V   County of Bigorre

Other lordships
mentioned in
the text

VI   Vicomté of Soule
VII   Vicomté of Gramont
VIII   Vicomté of Tartas
IX   County of Armagnac
X   County of Fezensac

BORDEAUX

Garonne

BAZAS

AGEN
Laplume
III
Roquefort
Gabarret
IV
II
Condom
LECTOURE
Mont-de-
Marsan
VIII
Tartas
IX
DAX
Saint-Sever
AIRE
X
AUCH
Sainte Quiterie
BAYONNE
Orthez
Navailles
Gerderest
VII
Pardies
Gabaston
Gramont
Monein
LESCAR
Morlaas
Mauléon
VI
OLORON
I
TARBES
V
Lourdes

garrisoned to order by the duke's men exercising his rights of lordship, and military service was regularly demanded.[7] On his first lengthy, and reforming, visit to Gascony in 1242, Henry III summoned his military tenants 'ad tractandum coram rege de negocio que rex eis exponet', and significantly he demanded the presence of the leading southern Gascon ecclesiastical lords, the bishops of Bayonne, Dax, Bazas, Oloron, and Aire, and the abbot of Saint-Sever.[8] The business for which they were required included the taking of homages, which was done as fully as possible, in a manner which prefigures Edward I's *recogniciones feodorum* inquest of 1273-4.[9] Gaston VII's acknowledgement of his vassalage marked the return of the *vicomté* of Béarn, in unambiguous form, to the allegiance of the dukes of Aquitaine.[10]

It is difficult to know whether, in return for his submission, Gaston was offered the inducement of an expectation of the acquisition of Bigorre, with its castle at Lourdes, as some have argued.[11] Weak seneschals during the 1240s were certainly unable to control the internal private wars that developed in the duchy, and it was this situation that the king of Navarre, Thibaut IV, exploited when he invaded Gascony in 1244. Although he was soon sent packing by the seneschal, Nicholas de Meulles, the presence of a king from across the Pyrenees was enough to dislodge all of the major southern Gascon lords from their recently-professed allegiance to the duke.[12] Raimond-Brun, lord and self-styled *vicomte* of Gramont, and the *vicomtes* of Soule and Tartas, as well as Gaston de Béarn, were members of the rebellious confederation which continued to attack other Gascons even after the withdrawal of Thibaut IV. The *vicomte* of Béarn was, therefore, a principal contributor to Henry III's decision, in 1248, to appoint Simon de Montfort to restore order in the duchy.[13]

Few, I think, would now argue that Henry's choice was wise. Although Simon did have notable political successes in this region, securing, for instance, the homages of the counts of Armagnac and Fezensac in 1251, his insensitivity to local custom and undoubted heavy-handedness were his undoing.[14] Almost his first action on arriving in Gascony was to arrest and imprison the *vicomtes* of Gramont and Soule and to seize their lands and castles, and so, by implication, threaten Béarn directly.[15] Part of his agreement with the king had been to undertake castle-building and repair, and to secure castles for royal use; Simon quickly demonstrated that he had no intention of being so slow and painstaking in his implementation of this policy as his unsuccessful seneschal predecessors.[16] It was, however, the issue of Bigorre that rendered Simon completely unacceptable as

---

[7] *Royal Letters*, i. 317, 320; J. Gardelles, *Les Châteaux du Moyen Age dans la France du Sud-Ouest* (Geneva, 1972), 25–6, 225.

[8] *Rôles Gascons I*, ed. F. Michel (Paris, 1896), 158–9; but also note *CPR 1232–47*, 376, 399, 401.

[9] Cf. *Recueil d'Actes relatifs à l'Administration des Rois d'Angleterre en Guyenne au XIIIᵉ siècle (Recogniciones Feodorum in Aquitania)*, ed. C. Bémont (Paris, 1914), 138, 140.

[10] *Rôles Gascons I*, 721; the text is also printed in Tucoo-Chala, *La Vicomté de Béarn*, 152.

[11] Ibid. 60.

[12] C. Bémont, *Simon de Montfort, Earl of Leicester 1208–1265*, trans. E.F. Jacob (Oxford, 1930), 73–5.

[13] Ibid.

[14] Ibid. 90.

[15] Gardelles, *Les Châteaux*, 26, 142, 172.

[16] C. Bémont, *Simon de Montfort, Comte de Leicester* (Paris, 1884), 264–5: text of Henry III's letters patent appointing Simon *custos* in Gascony.

Henry's lieutenant in the duchy in the eyes of Gaston de Béarn, and this will be considered shortly.

By 1253, Gascony was in tumult. With the *vicomte* of Béarn's assistance, the king of Castile arrived in the duchy to stake his claim. Henry III had to return to Gascony to attend to matters himself and, although it took more than a year, he was successful in restoring order, in negotiating away the claims of Castile, and in arranging the marriage of his son to Eleanor. Gaston came to terms with the Lord Edward in the autumn of 1255, and had to surrender a younger daughter, Mathe, as a surety for his good behaviour.[17] The *vicomtes* of Béarn were too strategically located geographically between France and the Spanish kingdoms, and too powerful and influential politically within Gascony (where their territorial control extended far to the north of the Pyreneean foothills) to be isolated politically by the dukes of Aquitaine. They had to be contained. The assistance that the *vicomtes* had given to each of the Spanish armies that had entered Gascony during the the first fifty or so years of the thirteenth century demonstrated graphically the fragility of their allegiance, and therefore threatened the defence of the duchy as a whole. What Henry III and the Lord Edward therefore sought by the marriage of Henry of Almain and Constance of Béarn was a stability in feudal relationships that had not hitherto existed in the region. As *vicomte*, in right of his wife, as a Plantagenet himself, and as a close and loyal advisor of his cousin, Edward, Henry was likely to prove co-operative with ducal policy in the region.

II

The benefits of the marriage contract for Gaston de Béarn would seem to be less immediately apparent. His kinship with the ducal house would be reinforced, and to that extent he was probably flattered by it. But what he almost certainly sought from it was, in short, to strengthen his prospect of acquisition of the county of Bigorre. This county, lying immediately to the east of Béarn, had long been an objective of the *vicomtes*. They coveted it politically but also sought its lowland pastures around Tarbes and its high valleys beyond Lourdes, which were ideal for the practice of transhumance which was the basis of wealth of the *vicomtes* and their neighbours.[18] When, in 1192, both Béarn and Bigorre were under Aragonese lordship, a marriage was arranged between Gaston VI and Perronelle, countess in her own right of Bigorre, which should have brought about the political union of

---

17 *Rôles Gascons*, I. ii. no. 4610; she was entrusted to the care of Pierre de Bordeaux, who was instructed to restore her to her father in Apr. 1257: *CPR 1247–58*, 548.

18 In Oct. 1254 the Lord Edward issued letters patent of safe-conduct to enable the men of the valleys of the Aspe and Ossau, and others in the *vicomté* of Béarn, to drive their beasts to the lands of the bailliages of St. Sever and Sault de Navailles, to remain there during the winter and to return in the spring: J-P. Trabut-Cussac, 'Un rôle de Lettres Patentes emanées du Prince Édouard pendant son premier séjour en Gascogne (Mai–Octobre 1254)', in *Recueil de travaux offert à M.Clovis Brunel* (Paris, 1955), ii. 610. In the following Oct. similar letters were issued in favour of Gaston's wife, Mathe, to permit the passage of 1000 cows: *Rôles Gascons*, I. ii. no. 4616. For discussion of the practice of transhumance in Béarn and Bigorre, see also C. Dartigue-Peyrou, *La Vicomté de Béarn sous le Regne d'Henri d'Albret 1517–1555* (Paris, 1934), 340–4; C. Higounet, 'Granges et Bastides de l'Abbaye de Bonnefont', in id. *Paysages et Villages Neufs du Moyen Age* (Bordeaux, 1975), 278–81.

## The *vicomtes* of Béarn, the de Montfort family, and the Bigorre succession

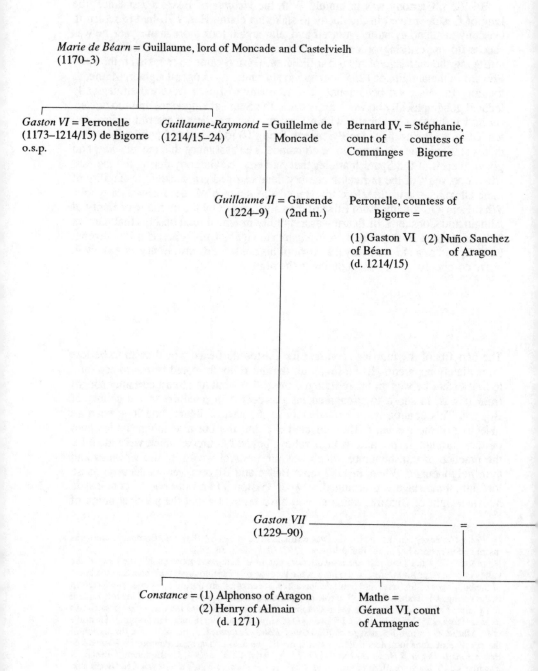

Marie de Béarn = Guillaume, lord of Moncade and Castelvielh
(1170–3)

Gaston VI = Perronelle    *Guillaume-Raymond* = Guillelme de    Bernard IV, = Stéphanie,
(1173–1214/15) de Bigorre    (1214/15–24)    Moncade    count of    countess of
o.s.p.    Comminges    Bigorre

*Guillaume II* = Garsende    Perronelle, countess of
(1224–9)    (2nd m.)    Bigorre =

(1) Gaston VI    (2) Nuño Sanchez
of Béarn    of Aragon
(d. 1214/15)

*Gaston VII* _____ =
(1229–90)

*Constance* = (1) Alphonso of Aragon    Mathe =
(2) Henry of Almain    Géraud VI, count
(d. 1271)    of Armagnac

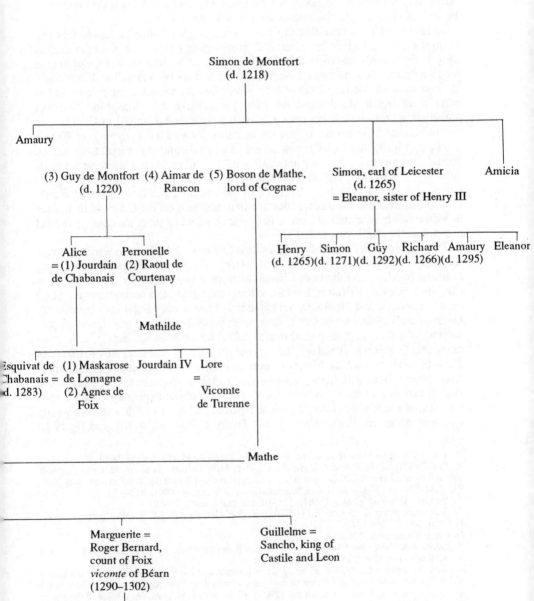

Simon de Montfort
(d. 1218)

Amaury

(3) Guy de Montfort    (4) Aimar de    (5) Boson de Mathe,        Simon, earl of Leicester        Amicia
(d. 1220)        Rancon       lord of Cognac              (d. 1265)
                                                        = Eleanor, sister of Henry III

Alice       Perronelle             Henry    Simon    Guy    Richard   Amaury   Eleanor
= (1) Jourdain   (2) Raoul de         (d. 1265)(d. 1271)(d. 1292)(d. 1266)(d. 1295)
de Chabanais     Courtenay

Mathilde

Esquivat de    (1) Maskarose    Jourdain IV   Lore
Chabanais =   de Lomagne               =
(d. 1283)      (2) Agnes de             Vicomte
            Foix                  de Turenne

Mathe

Marguerite =                 Guillelme =
Roger Bernard,            Sancho, king of
count of Foix               Castile and Leon
*vicomte* of Béarn
(1290–1302)

counts of Foix,
*vicomtes* of Béarn

the two lordships. Nothing came of it, however; Gaston died without heirs in 1214, and Perronelle was swiftly married off to an Aragonese lord. After Peter II's defeat at the battle of Muret, Bigorre passed under the political control of Simon de Montfort, the crusader, who used his position to marry his second son, Guy, to the countess. This third marriage produced two female children, but Guy himself died in 1220. Perronelle married twice more, producing a single child of her fifth marriage to the lord of Cognac. That daughter was Mathe, who was destined to be the wife of Gaston VII.[19] (See genealogical table, pp. 166–7.)

Accounts of the extraordinarily bitter and complex family squabble that developed have been given by others.[20] It is sufficient for present purposes to note Gaston de Béarn's assertion that Guy de Montfort's children were illegitimate because Perronelle's marriage to Nuño Sanchez had not been annulled. If this could be demonstrated, Mathe, Gaston's wife, would be sole heiress to the county and to other lands in La Marche and the Limousin. This is why Simon de Montfort prevailed upon Countess Perronelle, very shortly after his arrival in Gascony, to permit him the guardianship of Bigorre in return for an annual payment of 7000 *s. morlaas* (which, incidentally, was never fully paid) and the stipulation that he should continue to hold it after her death until he had recovered his expenses in its defence.[21] Jointly, they colluded to prevent the *vicomte* of Béarn from securing the inheritance. In her will (dated 1251) Perronelle dictated that the succession should pass to Esquivat and his brother Jourdain first, and only on the failure of their lines to Mathe. Within a matter of months Esquivat acquired seisin of the county, and did homage to Henry III for it in 1253.[22]

Political necessity certainly dictated that Esquivat should acknowledge his vassal status, and he came to terms with Henry III to lease his castles, including Lourdes. In May 1255 the Lord Edward attempted to arbitrate by appointing John fitzGeoffrey, then justiciar of Ireland, to bring the parties to a negotiation at a place between Sendets and Montaner, but apparently to no avail.[23] Subsequent events are not absolutely clear, except that Gaston was openly hostile and threatened dispossession, and that, in response, Esquivat called for de Montfort's help. It is presumed that Esquivat resigned his title in some act which he subsequently revoked. In 1259–60 both he and de Montfort were styling themselves count of Bigorre,[24] while Henry III himself, having bought out the claims of overlordship of the bishop and chapter of Le Puy, which went back to the mid-eleventh century, had accepted the offer of a seven-year lease of the county from de Montfort.[25] It is this ambiguity which is recognized in that clause of the Treaty of Paris which required Henry III

---

[19] Tucoo-Chala, *La Vicomté de Béarn*, 50; Bémont, *Simon de Montfort*, trans. Jacob, 79 and n.
[20] Ibid. 79–81, 126–8; Powicke, *Henry III*, i. 220–6; M.W. Labarge, *Simon de Montfort* (London, 1962), 128–40. The text of Gaston de Béarn's complaint about Simon de Montfort's conduct (from BL, Add. Charter 3303) is printed in Bémont, *Simon de Montfort* (1884), 313–17.
[21] Bémont, *Simon de Monfort* (1884), 315–16; and trans. Jacob, 79–80.
[22] *Gascon Register A (Series of 1318–19)*, ed. G.P. Cuttino and J-P. Trabut-Cussac (London, 1975–6), 640–1; *CPR 1247–58*, 305–6.
[23] *Gascon Register A*, 612–14.
[24] *Layettes du Trésor des Chartes: Inventaire et documents publiés par la Direction des Archives*, ed. A. Teulet *et al.* (Paris, 1863–1909), iii. no. 4476.
[25] *Gascon Register A*, 383, sale of the castle of Lourdes and the county of Bigorre by the bishop of Le Puy for 3200 *livres* of Le Puy money (not, as stated by Powicke, *Henry III*, i. 223, in the money of Pau); ibid. 640, *vidimus* of 1290–1 of letters of William de Valence, William de Cantilupe and Peter de Montfort, dated June 1254, concerning the homage of Esquivat de Chabanais for the county of Bigorre, and noting the new count's undertaking to send an embassy to the

'to perform as is determined concerning the homage of Bigorre'. Consequently, in 1260, Henry appointed his Lusignan half-brothers to hold the castle at Lourdes and the city of Tarbes in his name, while the Lord Edward instructed his seneschal to be prepared to assist them, and to set up another commission to attempt a settlement 'super dissensionibus et guerris inter dominum Simonem comitem Leycestrie ... et dominum Eschivatum comitem Bigorre'.[26] It was presided over by the bishops of Oloron and Lectoure, and it awarded Lourdes and its appurtenances to Simon de Montfort to hold until Christmas 1261; Esquivat was to have the rest. It was clearly an unsatisfactory arrangement.[27]

In 1262 attempts were made in England to come to an arrangement between the parties to the disputed inheritance, but none would concede. After Earl Simon's death in 1265, his son, Simon, and the Countess Eleanor granted away their rights in Bigorre to the king of Navarre.[28] Gaston may have hoped to benefit by the political defeat of de Montfort, and it is perhaps significant that it was precisely at this point that negotiations for a marriage between Henry and Constance began. But, although Gaston's wife remained likely to inherit under the terms of Perronelle's will, since neither Esquivat nor Jourdain had children themselves, Esquivat remained in effective control of the county in this period, and did so until his death in 1283. Neither Henry III nor Edward I was in a position to do so, or even wished to disturb that situation, not least because the succession to Bigorre was referred on appeal to the *parlement* of Paris.[29]

## III

Negotiations for the marriage between Henry of Almain and Constance of Béarn seem to have begun in earnest during 1265. Queen Eleanor of Provence was in Gascony between at least February and July of that year securing funds and political support for the royalist cause.[30] She found Gaston de Béarn already some way towards concluding a contract of marriage for his eldest daughter with Henry, brother of the king of Navarre.[31] Through her father's first marriage to Garsende, whose second marriage was to the *vicomte* Guillaume II (1224-9), Eleanor was a kinswoman of the *vicomte*, and was in a position to exploit her close kinship, to appeal to (and probably to flatter) Gaston as the most consistent and staunchest

church of Le Puy to ascertain the customary dues and services rendered to the church by the counts of Bigorre. See also Powicke, *Henry III*, i. 220–6.
26 *Rôles Gascons*, I.ii. pp. xcii–iii, 20–3.
27 *Recueil d'Actes . . . (Recogniciones Feodorum)*, 152–5; J. Balancie, 'Le Procès de Bigorre' [Part 2], *Revue des Hautes Pyrénées*, iv (1909), 40–9.
28 Bémont, *Simon de Montfort* (1884), 346–7; trans. Jacob, 180–3.
29 Balancie, 'Le Procès de Bigorre' [Part 2], 169–80, 321–32; [Part 3] *Revue des Hautes Pyrénées*, v (1910), 5–15; J-P. Trabut-Cussac, *L'Administration Anglaise en Gascogne sous Henry III et Edouard I de 1254 à 1307* (Paris, Geneva, 1972), 72–7.
30 *Gascon Register A*, 501–4; *Archives Historiques de la Gironde*, v (1863), 4–8; M. Gouron, *Catalogue des Chartes de Franchises de la France, II. Les Chartes de Guienne et Gascogne* (Paris, 1935), 553.
31 Archives Départementales des Pyrénées Atlantiques, E 369; A. Luchaire, *Notice sur les origines de la maison d'Albret, 977–1270* (Pau, 1873), 38; Trabut-Cussac, *L'Administration Anglaise*, 35.

opponent of de Montfort in Gascony. It was a degree of relationship that mattered politically in the thirteenth century, so that in these negotiations the queen was not a shadowy figure, but necessarily involved at every stage. What inducements or blandishments, if any, she put in the *vicomte*'s way are not revealed in the documentation that survives, although references to the county of Bigorre in some instruments may suggest that his expectations were once more raised at this point. Gaston certainly seems to have broken off his negotiations with Navarre at some time before October 1265 — before, that is, the younger Simon and Countess Eleanor conceded their claims to Thibaut IV.[32]

The *Fonds Albret*, in the Archives Départementales des Pyrénées Atlantiques at Pau, preserve a series of acts relating to the marriage, including a roll of transcripts written in a typically angular Gascon hand of the thirteenth century. There are fourteen instruments on the roll representing various stages in the making of the marriage contract.[33] The earliest, preserved in the form of a *vidimus* by the bishop of Oloron, is a draft contract published in London in February 1266, in the presence of the queen and the Lord Edward, and of the five counsellors Roger Mortimer and Thomas de Clare, who were among the most prominent of the Lord Edward's advisors after the battle of Evesham, Jean de Grilly, the Savoyard who had recently been given the Gascon lordship of Benauges and was to become seneschal in the duchy later in the year, Robert Kilwardby, at that time prior provincial of the Dominican order in England, and the archdeacon of Bath, William de Ozarto, whose name suggests that he probably came from Uzerche in the Limousin.

The instrument itself falls into four main sections dealing with issues of enfeoffment, dower, inalienability and security. Gaston's grant to Henry of Almain of the two *vicomtés* of Brulhois and Gabardan is given prominence.[34] Henry was to receive these on the occasion of the marriage with Constance as grants of life-fees. Every eventuality that might befall beyond that seems to be covered in a qualifying section that follows, and is intended to guard, in particular, against the possibility of alienation of any territory conceded from the inheritance of the *vicomtes* of Béarn. The stipulations set out covered, for example, what would happen if Gaston had male offspring of his present wife after his daughter's marriage, what was to happen if he died without heirs male, or if he had a male child by a subsequent marriage, and what was to ensue if that child died without heirs, or if Constance herself had no offspring.

---

[32] *Layettes du Trésor des Chartes*, iv. nos. 5101–2. Henry III complained to the king of Navarre of his interference in Gascon matters. Thibaut promptly invaded Bigorre and the Bayonnais. Lourdes was besieged, Bayonne destabilized and the castle of Gramont in Soule returned to its former Navarrese allegiance: Trabut-Cussac, *L'Administation Anglaise*, 35 and n. A three-year truce ended the row in Aug. 1266: *CPR 1258–66*, 674, 679.

[33] Arch. Dép. des Pyrénées Atlantiques, E 290. For a synopsis of the contents, see the Appendix, 178–9 below. Numbers given in brackets in following references to this MS correspond to this listing.

[34] The *vicomté* of Brulhois was situated on the left (west) bank of the R. Garonne opposite Agen, with its administrative centre at Laplume. It was held by the *vicomte* of Béarn as a fief of the bishop of Agen and, until 1327, comprised one of two archdeaconries of the diocese on this side of the river. In 1327 Pope John XXII created the dioc. of Condom; Brulhois then became one of four *archprêtrés* of the new bishopric: *Dictionnaire d'Histoire et de Géographie Ecclesiatiques*, ed. A. Baudrillart, A. De Meyer and E. Van Cauwenbergh (Paris, 1912–    ), *sub* Agen and Condom. The *vicomté* of Gavardan was the inheritance of the *vicomte*, Pierre III de Gabarret (1134–53), who succeeded to Béarn as the nephew of Centulle VI (1131–4). Its administrative centre was at Gabarret in the Landes: Tucoo-Chala, *La Vicomté de Béarn*, 37.

The issue of dower occupies the next section. Henry of Almain was required to provide 1000 *librates* sterling in land and rents as dower and as an earnest of his intentions to marry. Queen Eleanor and the Lord Edward, or one or other of them as appropriate, were assigned to oversee the allocation. The expectation appears to have been that this would be made from the estates of Henry's father, Richard, king of Almain, but Richard's role is unclear. He was not a party to the contract at any stage in its negotiation, and there is no evidence that he was consulted about the proposed marriage.

For some months after his release from captivity at Kenilworth on 6 September 1265, Richard's whereabouts are not exactly known. Denholm-Young suggests that he was mainly pre-occupied with restoring his plundered estates to good order, but he was certainly at Canterbury to meet with the legate Ottobuono, at the end of October, and appears to have kept his company for a period.[35] Richard is known to have been opposed to the policy of disinheritance agreed at the Winchester parliament of September 1265.[36] Whether under the influence of the legate, or of his own accord, he seems quite genuinely to have set his face against reprisal and to have sought reconciliation. Indeed, it may have been a condition of his release from prison that he should act as an intermediary between his brother, Henry, and his party, and his sister Eleanor, and hers. How else are we to interpret his affirmation that 'nos estre tenuz a ma dame Aleanor, nostre swer, cuntese de Leycestre, a toz ses enfaunz e a tote lor gent, a estre lor leal ami e enterin'?[37] We know that it was directly as a result of this that Richard took upon himself the duty of securing the safe-passage of Eleanor de Montfort and her youngest sons, Richard and Amaury, and the negotiation of an amelioration of the lot of her other sons, Guy and Simon. Even after the separate flights of the latter pair to safety in France, Richard continued to act as their English agent, trying to arrange for the sale of their estates; and he also appears to have fostered the idea of the submission of what he saw as a family dispute to the arbitration of Louis IX.[38]

Richard cannot have been unaware of the contradictions of his own political stance implicit in the proposal for the marriage of his elder son, Henry, to the daughter and heiress of Gaston de Béarn, the chief opponent, and long-term political rival, of the de Montfort interest in south-western France. We cannot be sure that this was why Richard was not a party to his son's arrangements, but it certainly looks as though it may be. Here too, perhaps, we can conclude with Denholm-Young that 'Richard was as good as his word in endeavouring to help Eleanor and her sons'.[39] The terms of the draft contract required no action of Richard of Cornwall during his lifetime, and merely stipulated that, in the event of his death, Henry, if he outlived his father, should assign the dower and other settlements according to English custom.[40]

---

35  N. Denholm-Young, *Richard of Cornwall* (Oxford, 1947), 131–3.
36  Ibid. 133–9; Powicke, *Henry III*, ii. 505–6, 541.
37  Bémont, *Simon de Montfort*, trans. Jacob, 252 n. gives the text of Archives Nationales, J 1024 no.45.
38  Denholm-Young, *Richard of Cornwall*, 133.
39  Ibid.
40  Arch. Dép. des Pyrénées Atlantiques, E 290 (3): 'Et si contingat dominum regem Alamannie patrem suum decedere ipso superstite ipso assignabit dictam dotem seu arras secundum consuetudinem Anglie ad cognicionem dictorum domine A. regine Anglie et Edwardi vel alterius eorum ut dictum est'. For dower in England, see F. Pollock and F.W. Maitland, *The History of English Law*, ed. S.F.C. Milsom (Cambridge, 1968), ii. 420 ff.

In its final section, the draft instrument of February 1266 sought to provide guarantees of the integrity of Gaston de Béarn's territorial holding. His four *vicomtés* (Béarn, Marsan, his wife's inheritance, Gabardan and Brulhois) are declared to be inalienable in any way from the heirs of Constance; and the indivisibility of Béarn and Marsan, in any future settlement upon heirs of the marriage, is proclaimed. Lastly, assurances for compliance with the terms of the agreement are to be secured from the parties to it, and the terms submitted for local consideration. That the instrument is preserved in the form of a *vidimus* (16 June 1267) of the bishop of Oloron, the senior member of the court of Béarn, is an indication that this took place.

Consulting local lords and communities was a patently slow process which had to take place before Henry III as king-duke was likely to give his assent to the marriage. In the meantime, amendments and further elaboration of the contract, which incorporated the results of the consultations in Béarn and certainly expressed the *vicomte*'s new reservations, were contained in undated letters patent of the queen and the Lord Edward, which were also sealed by Henry III, and issued in the presence of the *vicomte* of Béarn. The date and place of issue is unknown, but the date precedes the ratification of the contract in Gascony in November 1268.[41] As neither the king nor the Lord Edward crossed to France in this period, it can be inferred that Gaston de Béarn came to England for this purpose, but when is not clear.[42]

The most likely date seems to be the early summer of 1267. In March of that year Gaston was nominated, with Jean de Grilly, the seneschal of Gascony, as Henry III's proctor to demand of Louis IX 'all lands and fees' in the three dioceses that the French king had granted in the Treaty of Paris, of which Henry had been unable to take possession, and/or compensation for the failure of the *privilegiati* to transfer allegiance.[43] This would have necessitated travel to the French court and would, therefore, have provided an opportunity for travel on to England later in the year, and thus the chance to raise, at first hand, matters that had bearing upon the proposed marriage settlement. It is at this time, during the summer of 1267, that the issue of outstanding fees, which Gaston claimed were payable to him at the exchequer and in Bordeaux, was raised with Henry III. Was the matter taken up in person at this time? It is possible that it was, and that Gaston was seeking to profit as far as he could from his restoration to political favour. Gaston had two claims against the king-duke: the first, for arrears of an annual fee of 2000 *livres tournois* payable from the great custom of Bordeaux, which appears to have been conceded by the Lord Edward, probably as part of the peace settlement of 1255; the second, for arrears of a fee of 50 marks *per annum* payable at the exchequer, claimed in right of his wife, Mathe, as heiress to Boson de Mathe, lord of Cognac, as count of Bigorre.[44] Henry III made several attempts to meet the payments, but not all the claimed arrears; it was in his interest for the marriage of Henry and Constance to proceed. In October 1267 Ottobuono was asked to pay Gaston and Mathe out of the

---

[41] Arch. Dép. des Pyrénées Atlantiques, E 290 (4).
[42] *Handbook of British Chronology*, ed. E.B. Fryde, D.E. Greenaway, S. Porter and I. Roy (3rd edn. London 1986), 38; J.R. Studd, 'A Catalogue of the Acts of the Lord Edward, 1254–72' (Leeds Univ. Ph.D. thesis, 1971), app. ii. 820–6.
[43] *CPR 1266–72*, 45; Studd, 'The "Privilegiati" ', 178–88.
[44] *CPR 1266–72*, 258, 361.

clerical tenth which the pope had granted in 1266 to settle the king's debts.[45] In the following May the treasurer, barons and justices of the Jews were ordered to let Gaston have 200 marks 'in all haste', 'forthwith and without fail' as part of a payment of 500 marks which were to be paid in instalments to Gaston's envoy in England, Géraud Ariller.[46] More promises to pay up were made during 1268, and in November the receivers of monies from Llywelyn ap Gruffydd were instructed to hand over 1000 marks to the Lord Edward for payment to the *vicomte*.[47] There is little reason to doubt that the issue of the outstanding fees became enmeshed in the negotiations for the marriage contract, and that Gaston de Béarn was himself responsible for some of the delay which occurred between the drawing-up of the draft contract and the publication of the agreed terms in November 1268.

The *vicomte* swore, in the presence of the queen and the Lord Edward, to uphold the variations in the draft terms which are set out in the undated letters patent of (?)1267. His wife, Mathe, a party to the original contract, was not present, so Gaston was required to secure from her her ratification of all the amendments agreed. Here is further evidence that 1267 is the likely date of the instrument. The new terms varied the original conditions of Henry of Almain's enfeoffment by setting a monetary limit of 2000 marks on the value of the land to be assigned as dower, and by providing, at the insistence of both parties, for oaths guaranteeing the settlement from Constance's brothers-in-law, the counts of Armagnac and Foix, and from the barons, vassals and knights of the *vicomtés* of Béarn and Marsan. Possible inheritance problems arising after Gaston's death, and the defraying of costs that were likely to fall on Henry in maintaining the settlement, are dealt with. Further security oaths were to be demanded of the men of Marsan, Béarn, Brulhois and Bigorre. Gavardan is not mentioned, and the men of Gaston's Castilian fiefs were specifically exempted.

By 21 November 1268 the contract was ready for ratification and publication. At Mont-de-Marsan, and in the presence of Henry of Almain's proctor, Roger Mortimer and his agents — and before the archbishop of Auch, the four diocesans of southern Gascony, the counts of Armagnac and Bigorre and the *vicomte* of Tartas; before Jean de Grilly whose term as seneschal had ended shortly before; and before lords from Béarn — Gaston confirmed the terms of his contract and indicated that, as required, Constance would leave his lands early in February 1269 in order to marry Henry.[48] The terms and conditions of the settlement were re-hearsed in full. Gaston and Mathe formally renounced their rights in the lands conceded to Henry and Constance. Henry and Constance undertook not to sell, transfer or alienate any of the lands involved. The expectation that Henry would settle dower on his wife after the death of his father, Richard of Cornwall, was re-iterated. Finally, two knights, John de St. Brice and Michael Malconduit, Henry

---

45 Ibid. 119.
46 *CLR 1267–72*, 85–6.
47 *CPR 1266–72*, 258, 299, 302.
48 Arch. Dép. des Pyrénées Atlantiques, E 290 (1). The witnesses to the ratification of the contract at Mont-de-Marsan (21 Nov. 1268) were as follows: Amanieu d'Armagnac, archbishop of Auch (*c.* 1262–1318), Pierre II, bishop of Aire and Sainte Quiterie (1267–84), R..., bishop of Bigorre (*recte* Tarbes), Géraud de Mont-Lezun, bishop of Lectoure, Compain, bishop of Oloron (1260–88), Esquivat de Chabanais, count of Bigorre (1251–83), Géraud V, count of Armagnac (1254–85), Pierre de Dax, *vicomte* of Tartas, John de Grilly, seneschal of Gascony (Oct. 1266 – after May 1268), Thomas of Ippegrave, the current seneschal of Gascony, Garsie-Arnaud de Navailles, and other knights.

of Almain's attorneys, were named to take seisin on his behalf, and it was agreed that, after the wedding, Henry of Almain would visit his Gascon lands. Thomas of Ippegrave, the new seneschal of Gascony, also formally confirmed the contract, proclaimed Constance's emancipation from Gaston's *patria potestas*, and took note of the transfer of the seisin of Brulhois and Gabardan to Constance pending her marriage.[49] The seneschal's role and presence on this occasion are of some significance for, in acting as he did as the representative of his lord, the king, he demonstrated unequivocably the vassal status of Béarn, and confirmed the fact that Gaston's homage of 1242 was for his whole lordship, including his chief holding of Béarn, and not for any restricted part of it.

It was only in March 1269, after the *vicomte* and his party had set out from Béarn, that Henry III confirmed the terms of the contract.[50] In April 1269 Constance and her parents were in Paris and, from here, Gaston and Mathe wrote to Henry confirming their obligations under the arrangements for the marriage.[51] On 19 May the wedding took place at Windsor,[52] but there were still matters to be attended to. Within the week, Eleanor and Edward issued letters patent recording oaths sworn by Henry and Constance to abide by the terms of the settlement.[53] During the summer, Henry returned with his wife to Gascony. There, in August, he came to an arrangement with Gaston de Béarn to receive the 2000 *livres tournois* that Gaston agreed to pay him as part of the contract, out of the annual fee that the *vicomte* received in the great custom of Bordeaux.[54] In the following month Henry did homage to the bishop of Agen for the lands in Brulhois held as an episcopal fief,[55] and in the following March, having returned to London, Henry and Constance nominated Edward's chaplain, John Clarel, as their proctor to take seisin of lands in Gascony on their behalf.[56] In Gascony, Clarel was soon active on Henry's behalf, raising cash for his crusade and,[57] in January 1271, mortgaging Henry's interest in the great custom to a Bordeaux money-lender for a six-year period in return for payment of the 2000 *livres*.[58]

Finally, in a series of instruments which provide important evidence for the sophistication of the administration of Gaston's Béarnais state, the oaths that were required by the agreement (from the *vicomtesse* Mathe and from local lords and communes) were taken by the local bishops and senior clergy in September and

[49] Ibid. (2). Ippegrave appears to have been a professional lawyer. He was a former attorney in the service of Simon de Montfort in Gascony: *CPR 1247–58*, 350. He was one of two knights appointed, with a clerk, by Henry III, in 1259, to defend the Crown's interests in the Gascon courts in the case brought by Renaud de Pons and his wife, Marguerite de Turenne, which subsequently became the subject of the first appeal from Gascony to go to the *parlement* of Paris: *CPR 1258–66*, 73; Trabut-Cussac, *L'Administration Anglaise*, 30–1. He was apparently in the Lord Edward's service by Jan. 1260: PRO, C 61/4, m. 4; and was with him on a visit to France in Nov. 1260: PRO, E 368/94, m. 47.
[50] *CPR 1266–72*, 323.
[51] Arch. Dép. des Pyrénées Atlantiques, E 290 (6).
[52] *Ann. Mon.* ii. 107; iv. 223; see also T.F. Tout, 'Henry of Cornwall', in *DNB* ix. Richard of Cornwall was not present. He was at this time in Germany, and at Kaiserslaubern married Beatrice of Falkenburg (16 Jun.): F.R. Lewis, 'Beatrice of Falkenburg, the Third Wife of Richard of Cornwall', *EHR* lii (1937), 282.
[53] Arch. Dép. des Pyrénées Atlantiques, E 290 (5).
[54] *Gascon Register A*, 608–11.
[55] Ibid. 454–5.
[56] Arch. Dép. des Pyrénées Atlantiques, E 290 (8).
[57] E.g. from the abbot of St-Sever: PRO, SC 1, 11/46.
[58] *Gascon Register A*, 608–11; *Foedera*, I. ii. 480.

October 1270. The mayor and commune of Mont-de-Marsan issued letters patent sealed with the communal seal, recording their oath taken on 14 September 1270, in the presence of the *vicomte* and his wife, to observe the terms of the marriage contract.[59] On 21 September following, the bishop of Aire and Sainte-Quiterie recorded the oaths of several of the communities in Marsan.[60] In mid-October, the bishop of Lectoure reported the receipt of oaths from communities in Bigorre.[61] The nine jurats of the court of Béarn and eighteen knights and *domicelli* of Béarn swore as a group (as members of the *cour des communautés*) to uphold the conditions of the contract on 14 October;[62] and, finally, the archbishop of Auch, acting together with the bishops of Lectoure, Bazas and Oloron, reported that oaths had been taken by the various communities in Béarn.[63] It is, however, not known whether either the count of Armagnac or the count of Foix swore the oath required of him by the terms of the agreement.

## IV

There are postscripts to the events described here which will raise queries, but they may, at least tentatively, point towards answers to the questions posed earlier and focus upon individual participants in this episode. First, we must consider Henry of Almain, who left England on 15 August 1270 to join the crusade, a week after the Lord Edward. He travelled through France to Gascony to visit his new estates as had been agreed on his behalf, but it was a necessarily brief stay, intended for the giving and taking of homages. Within a few days he continued on to Aigues-Mortes to meet up with his cousin, Edward, leaving Constance behind in Gascony. It is likely that he intended to link up with his father-in-law's contingent, for Gaston had also agreed to go with Edward, who had borrowed 25,000 *livres tournois* from King Louis IX specifically to finance the *vicomte*'s expedition.[64]

Henry's short career as a crusader to Tunis and then to Sicily is well known. However, it should be noted that Thomas Wykes, without other corroboration, asserts that it was while wintering on Sicily that Henry was commissioned by

---

59  Arch. Dép. des Pyrénées Atlantiques, E 290 (10).
60  Ibid. (11). The communities were Roquefort-de-Marsan, Villeneuve-de-Marsan, ?Perquie, and the unidentified 'Bascor' and 'Arrenum' (?Arue).
61  Ibid. (12). Seven knights of the court of Rivière-de-Bigorre and five jurats of Maubourguet are named as having sworn.
62  Ibid. (14). The jurats of the court of Béarn are named as Compain, bishop of Oloron, Garsie-Arnaud, lord of Navailles, Arnaud-Guillaume, lord of Andoins, B., lord of Coarraze, R[aimond]-Arnaud, lord of Gerderest, Odet, lord of Miossens, Auger de Onramon, R[aimond]-Arnaud, lord of Dunes, and Arnaud, lord of Gabaston (father of Piers Gavaston). These were the members of the *Cour Majour de Béarn*: P. Tucoo-Chala, 'Les institutions de la Vicomté de Béarn', in *Histoire des Institutions Françaises au Moyen Age, I*, ed. F. Lot and R. Fawtier (Paris, 1957), 326. Eighteen knights are also named in the instrument.
63  Arch. Dép. des Pyrénées Atlantiques, E 290 (13). Five jurats of Morlaas, six from Sauveterre-de-Béarn, seven from Orthez, six from Oloron-Sainte-Marie and thirty inhabitants of the communities at Pardies-de-Béarn, Monein and the unidentified 'Larvallo' and 'Darriba' Gaver' (clearly a settlement on the Gave de Pau) are named.
64  *Foedera*, I. i. 481; *Diplomatic Documents, I (1101–1272)*, ed. P. Chaplais (London, 1964), 293; *DNB* ix, 'Henry of Cornwall'. The best account of the events leading to the murder is F.M. Powicke, 'Guy de Montfort (1265–71)', *TRHS* 4th ser. xviii (1935), 1–23.

Edward to return to deal with affairs in Gascony.[65] But to what extent did Henry require to be persuaded to return? Although he fought at Lewes, and was responsible for taking Robert de Ferrers into custody, his military career hitherto does not suggest that anything other than Christian obligation can account for his taking the Cross. How far, in reality, should Henry's action be characterized as loyal service to the Lord Edward, and how much should his departure from the crusade at this point be seen as serving a personal interest? The opportunity to return to Gascony was certainly convenient to him, and should, perhaps, lead us to conclude that it was as much his own 'affairs' as those of the Lord Edward that needed attention in the duchy. In a similar vein, some chroniclers attributed Henry's presence at Viterbo, on 13 March 1271, to a wish to bring about a reconciliation between Edward and his de Montfort cousins, although there is little evidence for it other than Edward I's claim to the pope two years later that this is why Henry had gone there.[66] Surely, this is nothing more than *post hoc facto* propaganda intended to exaggerate the horror of the murder, and so to extend the political mileage to be made from Henry's vile death.

Gaston de Béarn, whose history during these years has been sketched briefly by Sir Maurice Powicke, must be spoken of next.[67] His expectations were dealt a heavy blow by the murder. After all his careful political manoeuvres, he was left with a thirty-year old widowed heiress on his hands, the prospect of a divided succession, and the possibility of the dismemberment of his fiefs after his death.[68] Although Constance, at Queen Eleanor's request, secured her dower lands in England (the honour of Tickhill, which the Lord Edward had granted to Henry of Almain, and the honour of the Peak, which had also comprised part of the Lord Edward's appanage), her father's disappointment quickly turned to rancour. Does his failure to crusade indicate dissatisfaction with the terms and consequences of the marriage contract, and were worries about his possible behaviour a further reason for Henry of Almain's decision to return to France in the company of the new French king, Philip III? Was there already suspicion of the strength of Gaston's allegiance? The question of the succession to Bigorre remained an issue,[69] and the failure to settle his claims to the outstanding fees certainly rankled. It is also possible, although the evidence is wanting, that Edward made difficulties in assigning the 25,000 *livres tournois* which he agreed to make available to the *vicomte* for his crusade.[70] Although the appointment of Luke de Tany as seneschal of Gascony

65 *Ann. Mon.* iv. 237.
66 Powicke, 'Guy de Montfort', 15–20, discusses the problem of the sources and of identifying the precise date and location of the murder. *Foedera*, I. ii. 501 provides the only evidence for the mission of reconciliation.
67 F.M. Powicke, *The Thirteenth Century* (2nd edn. Oxford, 1963), 284–7.
68 In 1283 Gaston proposed to settle Béarn on Constance and, after her death, on her younger sister, Marguerite, countess of Foix, while the other sisters were to receive the *vicomtés* of Brulhois and Gavardan and the *vicomte*'s Iberian fiefs. These terms were varied in the *Cour Majour* of Béarn in 1286 to permit the succession of Marguerite and her husband on condition that they performed homage at once to the king-duke for their inheritance: Tucoo-Chala, *La Vicomté de Béarn*, 67–70.
69 Esquivat de Chabanais retained the county until his death in 1283, when Gaston invoked the terms of the Countess Perronnelle's will in the name of Constance. In Sept. 1283 she took the homages of the men of Bigorre in spite of orders from the seneschal not to proceed: Trabut-Cussac, *L'Administration Anglaise*, 72–7; Powicke, *The Thirteenth Century*, 287 and n.
70 J-P.Trabut-Cussac, 'Le financement de la croisade anglaise de 1270', *Bibliothèque de l'École des Chartes*, cxix (1961), 113–15, 123–4.

(June 1272) is usually said to be the reason, circumstances arising directly or indirectly from negotiations of the marriage contract already appear to have been present to cause Gaston to rebel once again. His refusal to appear in the court of Gascony to answer complaints made before the seneschal, and his resort to arms at Orthez, merely herald the decade of rebellion that disturbed the politics of the duchy.[71]

Thirdly, and finally, it is necessary to speak of Henry of Almain's cousins, his murderers Guy and Simon de Montfort, for their role poses the question of whether there was a connection between the Béarnais marriage and the events at Viterbo. A central theme of this paper has been concerned with the significance of family interconnections as one of the mainsprings of political action in the thirteenth century; all the main actors in this business were closely related to one another. The bitterness, the bloodshed and the unwillingness to compromise do no more than exemplify the cliché that family squabbles are the most acrimonious.[72] To his de Montfort cousins, Henry of Almain was an interloper in the politics of Gascony, the usurper of their rightful place and the direct political challenger, through his marriage to Constance of Béarn, of their position in the duchy. To Simon and Guy, Henry of Almain was clearly not the accidental object of their revenge, as some have claimed him to be — the wrong man in the wrong place at the wrong time. It was no matter to them that he was not on the field of Evesham, and could not, therefore, have been a party to their father's brutal slaughter. Henry's assault on their Gascon inheritance may have been enough to precipitate their attack on him. Nor is it likely that Henry would have seen himself as the innocent victim either. Giovanni Villani records in direct speech, and in the French vernacular, the words uttered by Guy on leaving the church of the murder: 'J'ai fait ma vangeance.' They are not specific. 'Remember Evesham', he was exhorted by one of his following, recalling the brutal treatment of the elder Simon's corpse, and egging the count on to a comparable revenge. 'Remember Evesham' may well have been the cry of the brothers as they wielded their weapons on Henry. Their victim would equally have understood their hostility had they cried 'Remember Bigorre.'[73]

71 Powicke, *The Thirteenth Century*, 285–7; Tucoo-Chala, *La Vicomté de Béarn*, 62–3; Trabut-Cussac, *L'Administration Anglaise*, 41–77.
72 Cf. K.J. Leyser, *Rule and Conflict in an Early Medieval Society: Ottonian Saxony* (London, 1979), 9–23; J. Larner, *Italy in the Age of Dante and Petrarch 1216–1380* (London, 1980), 83–105.
73 Giovanni Villani, *Cronica*, ed. F.G. Dragomanni (Florence, 1844), 368–70. Villani's account of affairs in England preceding the murder, at Evesham, and of Edward's crusade, is often confused and events conflated. His report, in direct speech and in the French vernacular, of what was said outside the church of Viterbo has a ring of authenticity, suggesting transmission of oral testimony.

# Appendix

## Synopsis of the Contents of
### Archives Départementales des Pyrénées Atlantiques, E 290

1.  Mont-de-Marsan, 21 Nov. 1268

    Agreement in the form of letters patent between Gaston, *vicomte* of Béarn, lord of Moncade and Castelvielh, and his eldest daughter, Constance, and the Lord Edward, and Roger de Mortimer, the attorney of Henry of Almain, concerning a contract of marriage and the arrangement of dower and sureties.

2.  Mont-de-Marsan, 21 Nov. 1268

    Letters patent of Thomas of Ippegrave, seneschal of Gascony, confirming the terms of the contract and undertaking that the Lord Edward and his heirs will ratify the arrangements made.

3.  Sauveterre, 16 July 1267

    *Vidimus* by Compain, bishop of Oloron of a memorandum (dated London, 9 Feb. 1266, in the presence of the queen, the Lord Edward, Roger de Mortimer, Thomas de Clare, Jean de Grilly, Robert Kilwardby, prior provincial of the Dominican order, and W. de Ozarto, archdeacon of Bath) setting out proposals of terms for a settlement and dower relating to the projected marriage of Constance of Béarn to Henry of Almain.

4.  undated (?1267)

    Letters patent of Queen Eleanor and the Lord Edward amending the terms of the contract in the light of consultation.

5.  Windsor, 26 May 1269

    Letters patent of Queen Eleanor and the Lord Edward forbidding alienation from lands comprising the marriage settlement.

6.  Saint-Germain-des-Prés, 14 Apr. 1269

    Notification by Gaston, *vicomte* of Béarn and his wife, Mathe, of their undertaking on oath to abide by the terms of the agreement with Henry of Almain and of any award made by Queen Eleanor and/or the Lord Edward.

7.  'apud Ernoluum' (?Ornon, Gironde), 17 Sept. 1269

    Letters close of Gaston de Béarn to the Lord Edward asking him to issue letters patent in favour of Henry of Almain, recognizing his agreement to transfer his 2000 *livres tournois* annual fee from the great custom of Bordeaux to Henry.

8.  London, 29 Mar. 1270

    Letters patent of Henry of Almain and his wife, Constance, appointing Master John Clarel, chaplain of the Lord Edward, as their proctor to receive dower lands on their behalf.

9.  Mont-de-Marsan, 14 Sept. 1270

    Letters patent of Mathe, wife of Gaston, *vicomte* of Béarn, declaring that, having inspected letters of Queen Eleanor and the Lord Edward, she has sworn an oath to keep their contents in perpetuity.

10. Mont-de-Marsan, 14 Sept. 1270

    Letters patent of Arnaud de Corbin, mayor of Mont-de-Marsan, the jurats and the whole commune, sealed with the seal of the commune, proclaiming that they had sworn an oath that, in the event of Gaston and Mathe dying without male heirs, they would be intendant to Constance and Henry of Almain and their heirs as their lords, and that they would maintain inviolable the agreements made concerning the marriage contract.

11. Villeneuve-de-Marsan, 21 Sept. 1270

    Letters patent of Pierre, bishop of Aire and Sainte-Quiterie, noting that the knights, jurats and communes of Roquefort, Villeneuve, ?Perquie, 'Bescor' and Arue have sworn an oath to be intendant to Henry of Almain and Constance, his wife, as their lords, should Gaston and Mathe die without heirs, and to observe and keep inviolable the terms of the agreements made concerning the marriage contract.

12. Morlaas, 14 Oct. 1270

    Letters patent of Géraud, bishop of Lectoure and Aimeri, abbot of 'Tascen" noting that, in their presence, seven knights (named) of Rivière-de-Bigorre, and five jurats (named) of Maubourguet had read letters of Queen Eleanor and the Lord Edward, and had sworn oaths on behalf of themselves,the court and county of Bigorre to preserve inviolable their contents.

13. Morlaas, 16 Oct. 1270

    Letters patent of Amanieu, archbishop of Auch, Géraud, bishop of Lectoure, Guillaume, bishop of Bazas, and Compain, bishop of Oloron noting that, in their presence, letters were read concerning an agreement between the *vicomte* of Béarn and his wife and Henry of Almain and Constance, his wife, and that the jurats of Morlaas, Sauveterre, Orthez and Oloron (all named) had sworn, together with men of the communities at Pardies, Monein, 'Larvallo' and 'Darriba'Gaver', to preserve inviolable their contents.

14. Morlaas, 14 Oct. 1270

    Letters patent of Compain, bishop of Oloron, Garsie-Arnaud de Navailles, Arnaud-Guillaume, lord of Andoins, B., lord of Coarraze, R.-Arnaud, lord of Gerderest, Odet, lord of Miossens, Auger de Onramon, R.-Arnaud, lord of Dunes, Arnaud, lord of Gabaston, jurats of the court of Béarn, and of eighteen knights of Béarn (named) noting that they had seen, heard and understood letters concerning agreements between the *vicomte* of Béarn and his wife and Henry of Almain and Constance, his wife, as well as letters of Queen Eleanor and the Lord Edward, and had promised and sworn oaths to keep all of them inviolable.

# The Early Thirteenth-Century Architecture of Beverley Minster:
## Cathedral Splendours and Cistercian Austerities*

### Christopher Wilson

In 1541 the antiquary John Leland arrived in Beverley and noted, with his habitual terseness, that the collegiate church of St. John was 'of a fair uniforme making'.[1] This earliest recorded comment on the Minster's architecture has proved to be prophetic both of the brevity and of the emphasis of subsequent writing, for the short articles, and the even shorter discussions in general surveys, which make up the existing literature on the thirteenth-century work are unanimous in laying great stress on the aesthetic merit of the design and on the rare regularity and consistency of its execution.[2]

The failure of the Minster to attract the sustained attention of nineteenth- and twentieth-century architectural historians has no doubt much to do with the geographical isolation of Beverley in post-medieval times, but the main reason must surely be that the uniformity which Leland admired has made this church not very susceptible to the kind of analysis of constructional sequences which has for so long preoccupied students of English medieval architecture. In fact, the two most distinguished exponents of that tradition, Robert Willis and John Bilson, both wrote briefly on the early work at Beverley, and in each case their interest centred on the building history of the eastern parts.[3] Despite the recent publication of an account of some of the northern English analogies for various elements of the design,[4] it is still true to say that the interrelated problems of the origin and

* To John White, on his retirement from the History of Art chair at University College, London. I am very grateful to Stuart Harrison for valuable discussion of the evidence for the reconstruction of Fountains and for permission to reproduce plate 32, and to David Wilson, Head Verger of Beverley Minster, who greatly facilitated my study of the building.

1 *The Itinerary of John Leland*, ed. L.T. Smith (London, 1906–10), i. 46.
2 The main accounts of Beverley Minster's 13th-c. architecture are J.L. Petit, 'Remarks on Beverley Minster', in *Memoirs Illustrative of the History and Antiquities of the County and City of York Communicated to the . . . Archaeological Institute of Great Britain and Ireland . . . 1846* (London, 1848), separately paginated 1–26; J. Bilson, 'On the Discovery of Some Remains of the Chapter House of Beverley Minster', *Archaeologia*, liv, pt. 2 (1895), 425–32; id., 'Beverley Minster', *Architectural Review*, iii (1894–8), 197–204, 250–9; L. Hoey, 'Beverley Minster in its 13th-Century Context', *Journ. of the Soc. of Architectural Historians*, xliii (1984), 209–24 (discussions in general works listed at p. 209 n. 5) The proportional system is treated briefly in C. Wilson, *The Gothic Cathedral. The Architecture of the Great Church 1130–1530* (London, 1990), 172–3. The Royal Institute of British Architects Drawings Collection has Bilson's finished drawings of Beverley (some unpubl.), boxed at X/15, and notes and sketches in small sketchbooks, nos. 1–5.
3 Willis's contribution, contained in a footnote to Petit, 'Remarks', 7, is discussed at n. 55 below. For Bilson's discussion of the E. crossing piers, see n. 59 below.
4 Hoey, 'Beverley Minster'. The tentative suggestion of French (High Gothic) influence on the band triforium and the tall proportioning made in G. Webb, *Architecture in Britain: the Middle*

meanings of Beverley's distinctive architecture remain to be tackled. No doubt the lack of influence from Beverley on the subsequent development of English Gothic has contributed to its relative neglect by specialists, particularly authors of synoptic works concerned to chart a short path through the great mass of material which survives from England's early thirteenth-century church-building boom.[5] In this paper, I shall argue that the aspect of Beverley which gives it a claim to importance in the general history of English medieval art is its unique position relative to the two main traditions of large-scale church architecture current during the early thirteenth century. The title of my paper alludes to this overlapping of an hierarchical distinction sustained both by the Cistercians' concern to safeguard their primitive traditions and by the older foundations' need to uphold their regional pre-eminence in the face of the challenge posed by the burgeoning houses of the reformed orders, including the Cistercians.[6]

The most direct way of establishing the importance of Beverley Minster's thirteenth-century architecture is by reference to the standing of the institutional patron. Not only was the Minster the most prestigious and ancient religious house in its region, the East Riding of Yorkshire, but it ranked among the very richest foundations in the North, coming after only York Minster, Durham Cathedral Priory, St. Mary's Abbey, York and the two Cistercian houses of Fountains and Furness. Its revenues were far greater than those of its two peer institutions within the York diocese, the minsters of Ripon (West Riding) and Southwell (Nottinghamshire).[7] What little we know of the Romanesque church at Beverley suggests architecture commensurate with this dignity and wealth: a nave occupying the same area as the present fourteenth-century nave and resembling the latter in having twin western towers, a crossing (no doubt surmounted by a large tower), transepts with galleries over eastern chapels, and a liturgical choir contained within the eastern arm and standing over a crypt.[8] These bare lineaments, and the few extant

*Ages* (2nd edn. Harmondsworth, 1965), 100–1 is accepted as fact in V. Jansen, 'Superposed Wall Passages and the Triforium Elevation of St. Werburgh's Chester', *Journ. of the Soc. of Architectural Historians,* xxxviii (1979), 235–6; and Hoey, 'Beverley Minster', 217. Hoey also attributes the high vault springing to the influence of early 13th-c. French architecture. Neither discusses the English antecedents of these features.

[5]   For the influence of Beverley, see n. 60 below.

[6]   The only other major instances of Cistercian influence on early 13th-c. northern great church architecture occur in the W. transept of York Minster, where the W. aisles are narrower than the E. aisles, as at Byland, and the timber tunnel vaults (now 15th- to 20th-c. replacements and re-replacements for 13th-c. tunnels vouched for as regards their main lines by stone springers) look like a cross between the timber tunnels at Fountains and Byland and the masonry vaults with steeply-sloping lateral ridges in the Fountains choir (pl. 31). Since the York transept includes so few Cistercian-derived forms, there is no question of its being a hybrid like Beverley.

[7]   D. Knowles and R.N. Hadcock, *Medieval Religious Houses. England and Wales* (2nd edn. London, 1971), 53, 57, 58, 113, 119, 413, 417–19.

[8]   The N. bell tower mentioned in 1310 can hardly be other than a NW. nave tower: *Memorials of Beverley Minster: The Chapter Act Book of the Collegiate Church of S. John of Beverley A.D. 1286–1347,* ed. A.F. Leach (Surtees Soc. xcviii, cviii, 1898–1903), i. 264. The remains of St. Martin's Chapel, completed *c.* 1324 (ibid. ii. 45) on the S. face of the present SW. tower indicate the presence of an earlier tower. A crossing earlier than the crossing piers and tower under construction *c.* 1213–15 is implied in an account of a miracle of St. John of Beverley: *Historians of the Church of York,* ed. J. Raine (RS, 1879–94), i. 337; another miracle in the same collection (ibid. 328–30) mentions a stair turret overlooking the churchyard on the N. side of the church, and a high-level stone roof (no doubt a vault) over the chapel of St. Martin, where the great rood was temporarily placed (presumably on account of the building of the crossing tower) and from where a boy fell after dislodging a stone — all of which fits a N. transept with galleries or false galleries

scraps of early twelfth-century moulded and geometric decoration, hint at a structure at least as ambitious as the church of Selby Abbey, Beverley's nearest Benedictine neighbour.[9]

The one fixed point in the history of the Romanesque church is its burning in 1188.[10] An important stage in the repair work following this disaster was probably marked by the opening in 1197 of the original grave of St. John of Beverley in the second bay of the nave from the east,[11] but the next major event in the Minster's architectural history is reported only in the account of a miracle datable to *c.* 1213–15.[12] A crossing tower described as very high and splendid, and which presumably formed the final phase of the post-1188 repairs, was on the point of completion, lacking only its stone spire,[13] when huge cracks began to open up in its supports because they had been imperfectly grafted onto the adjoining parts of the church. Building work was halted, and around the beginning of October in the

on the E. side. For discussion of a mid 12th-c. or earlier reference to a crypt or undercroft, and proof of the absence of such a feature from the choir after 1188, see R. Morris and E. Cambridge, 'Beverley Minster Before the Early 13th Century', *Medieval Art and Architecture in the East Riding of Yorkshire* (British Archaeological Assoc. Conference Trans. ix, for 1983, 1989), 16. The proposal (ibid. 19) that the Minster as remodelled in the 1050s survived until the late 12th c. is hard to accept, given the lack of parallels at other comparably important institutions and the extensive re-use of Romanesque masonry in the present fabric: see n. 9 below. The nave which preceded the present 14th-c. structure is dated to the 12th c. in Bilson, 'Beverley Minster', 198.

9  The 13th-c. builders were unusually careful to conceal any decoration on the many Romanesque blocks which they re-used, but still visible are an early 12th-c. base set in the jamb of the window lighting the roof space over the W. aisle of the SW. transept, and numerous 12th- and early 13th-c. pieces in the spandrels revealed by the demolition in the restoration (1716–20) of the vault over the W. aisle of the N. transept. The fragments above the E. crossing were almost certainly all placed there during the 1716–20 restoration, as they include the bosses of the high N. transept vault demolished then, and some of the other pieces may come from the ruins of St. Mary's Abbey, York, used in 1717–20 as a quarry for the repairs.

10  Roger of Howden, *Chronica*, ed. W. Stubbs (RS, 1868–71), ii. 354; O. Lehmann-Brockhaus, *Lateinische Schriftquellen zur Kunst in England, Wales und Schottland vom Jahre 901 bis zum Jahre 1307* (Munich, 1955–60), i. no. 331. The date 21–2 Sept. 1188 for the fire was given on a lead plaque found in 1664 in St. John's original tomb (see n. 11 below); *The Visitation of the County of Yorke . . . by William Dugdale*, ed. R. Davies (Surtees Soc. xxxvi, 1892), 22.

11  Ibid. 22. The delay between the 1188 fire and the search for the relics in the tomb surely reflects the minor importance of the latter compared to the relics in the main shrine near the high altar, where they had been since the 1060s. The 1197 opening probably occurred in connection with a reconstruction of the tomb following the completion of the repairs to the nave after the fire, an hypothesis confirmed by the reference to its marble columns in an early 13th-c. account of a miracle: *Historians of the Church of York*, i. 342–3. The final miracle in the same collection implies that the tomb's superstructure was wrecked by the fall of the crossing tower *c.* 1213–15: ibid. 347.

12  The miracle involving the collapse of the central tower is the last in a collection of six, which appear to be arranged in chronological order and which are said, in a prefatory section, to have taken place within the space of five years. Since the fifth miracle contains a reference to the ending of the papal interdict, it is very unlikely that the collapse happened after 1214 or 1215: ibid. 327, 337. It is clear that the sixth miracle was the only source for the tower collapse and subsequent rebuilding available at Beverley in the later Middle Ages: Morris and Cambridge, 'Beverley Minster', 15, 26 no. 116, 30, nn. 59–60.

13  The 'tectum lapidei operis, proportionatae celsitudinis', lacking at the time of the collapse, was surely a spire rather than a vault, as the height of a vault relative to a tower is normally fixed when the tower walls are built, whereas the implication here is that the height of the missing element was not yet fixed: *Historians of the Church of York*, i. 345. This early evidence for a stone spire appears not to have been taken account of in any of the general works on English medieval architecture. The oldest masonry spire on a crossing tower to have survived in England is that of St. Frideswide's, Oxford, usually dated *c.* 1200–20.

same unspecified year, the tower crashed to earth. There was no loss of life among the Minster clergy only because the sacristan had inadvertently summoned them to their night office an hour too early.

How soon after the collapse of *c.* 1213–15 work started on the new church is not known. Collectors for the fabric were active by 1221, and Archbishop Walter de Gray issued an indulgence in 1232, six years after his similar grant in favour of the works of the west transept at York Minster. The timing of the grant of the Beverley indulgence should probably be seen as reflecting the archbishop's acknowledgement that the mother church of the diocese and province had a prior claim on his support, and is certainly not evidence for a start of work at Beverley as late as the early 1230s.[14] No written documents give us any sense of where in the Beverley chapter the impulse to rebuild originated, whether it was a truly collective effort or whether, as so often seems to have been the case in major church-building projects, its impetus derived from an enthusiastic individual or group. To gain any insight into the corporate patron's aims in undertaking the rebuilding, we have no option but to approach the problem by the usual, indirect route of enquiring how the end result of the patronage relates to other northern English churches of the same period.

In common with all major early thirteenth-century churches in northern and central England, Beverley Minster is indebted to Lincoln Cathedral, in every sense the central monument of 'Early English' Gothic. Most of Beverley's borrowings from Lincoln are obvious and have been recognized for a long time.[15] Such are the eastern transepts and the so-called 'syncopated' arcading in the triforium, the latter clearly modelled on the wall-arcading in St. Hugh's Choir, begun in 1192. But comparison of the syncopated arcades at Beverley and Lincoln (pls. 17, 26) only highlights the spiritual gulf separating their designers. Lincoln's spatial richness gives way at Beverley to flatness and linearity, and the disruptive quality of the earlier design relative to the bay divisions has been eliminated by fitting the arches in the front plane between the vault shafts and by breaking up the arcading in the rear plane into runs ending with half-arches which are widely separated and hence unable to offer any challenge to the bay divisions.[16] A comparable reworking of a Lincoln concept can be seen in the clearstorey, where the congested richness of the St. Hugh's Choir clearstorey is transformed into elegantly graduated, five-part arcades, whose slight structure reveals much of the window wall beyond (pls. 17, 27).[17] Despite its lack of spatial interest, the triforium at Beverley attracts and holds

[14] *PR 1216–25*, 318; *PR 1225–32*, 230 (1228); *CPR 1232–47*, 105, 108 (1235); *The Register, or Rolls of Walter Gray, Lord Archbishop of York*, ed. J. Raine (Surtees Soc. lvi, 1872), 55–6. Henry III granted 40 oaks from Sherwood forest in 1252: *CR 1251–3*, 63.
[15] A Lincoln borrowing not discussed in print hitherto is the placing of a pier of exceptional richness and complexity at the point in each arm of the E. transept, where it can best be seen from different angles. At Beverley, sixteen-shaft clustered piers are located in the E. arcade, whereas at Lincoln the equivalent piers are in the W. arcade and, until the building of a treasury in the NE. transept and a vestry in the SE. transept, it was possible to walk all round them. A remarkable anticipation of, though presumably not an influence on, this use of special piers occurs in the chapels between E. arm and transepts at S. Maria im Kapitol, Cologne (*c.* 1040–65).
[16] The motif of wall arcading incorporating arches bisected by vault shafts occurs at Beverley only on either side of the chapter house door in the N. choir aisle, where the aim is clearly to enhance the setting of an important entrance by generating greater richness and by striking a note of greater formality relative to the corbelled-out vault shafts used in the rest of the aisles.
[17] The slimness of the supports of the Beverley clearstorey arcades, and the extreme stilting of the outer halves of its 2nd and 4th arches, are anticipated in the tripartite clearstoreys of the

one's attention more than the clearstorey by virtue of the denseness and intricacy of its patterning, and though unlike Lincoln's gallery in terms of its detailed architectural character, it resembles the latter in the more basic matter of conforming to the long-established English tradition of prominent and richly-treated middle storeys.

Another traditional English usage developed importantly at Lincoln, and adhered to at Beverley, is that of enriching the soffits of the main arcade arches with very complex profiles (pl. 19).[18] At Beverley, the arcade arches are even more prominent than at Lincoln, because they and the piers are virtually as thick as the triforium and clearstorey which they carry (pl. 18), whereas at Lincoln the main arcades are considerably thinner than the upper storeys.[19] Elaborately profiled arcade arches were clearly regarded by the architect as a *sine qua non* of great church architecture, for the rest of his design is notably sparing in its use of expensive trimmings. The omission of marble shafts from the piers, the lack of bosses in the aisle vaults, and the restriction of foliate capitals to the main portals and aisle wall-arcading are all indicative of an appropriately prudent response to the chapter's situation of having lost much of the work done since 1188 and being compelled to bear the unforeseen burden of beginning all over again.[20]

It is possible to pinpoint at least one of the experiences which formed the Beverley master's distinctive architectural vision. Analogies for individual elements of the design have been found by a number of scholars in the eastern parts of Fountains Abbey, begun between 1203 and 1211, but the formal correspondences between Beverley and the earlier phase of the Fountains east end, the presbytery, are in fact so numerous and of so many kinds as to suggest very strongly that both were designed by the same individual.[21] In common with every other important

presbytery extension at Chichester Cathedral (after 1186) and the choir and presbytery at Rochester Cathedral (begun *c.* 1190?). For other connections between Chichester and Beverley, see 189–90 and nn. 36–9 below.

18  The mouldings of the main arcade arches are consistent, except that in the arches which give access from the E. transept aisles to the Lady Chapel, and those at the E. end of the choir aisles, the innermost order is of a slightly simpler pattern, acknowledging their abnormally narrow span (pl. 19); cf. Hoey, 'Beverley Minster', 214 and figs. 11, 12 (captions transposed). The very unusual central element of the basic pattern (pl. 19) is to be seen on the southernmost pier of the S. transept arcade at the Cistercian Abbey of Jervaulx, 10 km. NW. of Ripon, and numerous mouldings lying loose on the site are sufficiently close to the Beverley arch mouldings to suggest a specially close relationship between the two buildings.

19  The French Gothic device of false bearing (i.e. upper storeys oversailing aisle vaults) in use at Ripon some 20–30 years before Lincoln was begun, was rejected by most English architects in favour of the traditional usage of giving the piers and upper walls of main vessels the same thickness throughout. Beverley's restrained use of false bearing (pl. 18) was anticipated at Byland but apparently not in the Fountains choir, where the upper walls seem to have been no thicker than the piers.

20  Only extreme cost-consciousness can explain the single unworked face of each of the concave-sided octagonal Purbeck shafts in the choir clearstorey: illustr. in I. and E. Hall, *Historic Beverley* (York, 1973), 14. These, and all the other Purbeck components, are now painted licorice-colour and create a rather harsh contrast with the warm light brown of the Newbald limestone used for the rest of the fabric. A very different effect is generated by the pale blue-grey of the unpainted Purbeck visible in some abaci on the end walls of the W. transept.

21  The high-springing main vaults at Beverley and Fountains are compared in P. Brieger, *English Art 1216–1307* (Oxford, 1957), 11. The internal elevations of the aisles at Fountains and Beverley, which Bilson, 'Beverley Minster', 200 considered to be so similar 'as to stamp the two as works of the same school', share vault shafts corbelled at the level of the window sill, blind lancets with asymmetrical heads linking the springings of the window heads and the vaults, and trefoil wall arcading in which no uprights correspond to the bay divisions (although Beverley's wall arcade at

early thirteenth-century work of church architecture in the North, the Fountains presbytery drew on Lincoln's cornucopia of novel ideas. Of course, Beverley, not being a Cistercian foundation, could have — and in a very real sense had to have — features too ambitious to be employed at Fountains, but its soberly elegant aesthetic is unmistakably the same and it functions in the same way as a filter to influences from Lincoln's artistically and financially extravagant inventions. Unfortunately, demonstration of the relationship between Beverley and the Fountains presbytery is hampered by the virtual disappearance of the latter's central vessel. The reconstructed elevation (pl. 31) is based chiefly on the small fragments remaining *in situ* and on the analogous parts of the later phase of the east end, the Nine Altars Chapel (pls. 23, 25). The reconstruction view by J.A. Reeve (pl. 24), although not reliable as regards the high vault and the clustered piers, nevertheless gives a good impression of the whole.[22]

Before considering Beverley's indebtedness to the Fountains presbytery, it is appropriate to ask why the chapter should have recruited an architect working for a foundation very different from their own and more than fifty miles distant. The answer to their problem of finding a successor to the architect of the ill-fated crossing tower may have been, almost literally, staring them in the face, for Meaux Abbey, only six kilometres away to the east, had begun an ambitious rebuilding as recently as 1207.[23] Along with Kirkstall, Meaux was the most important northern daughter of Fountains, and its enduring ties with the parent house can hardly be unconnected with the virtually exact conjunction in time between its founding of a complete new church and the inception of the east end at Fountains.[24] There must be a good chance that Fountains, Meaux and Beverley were all under the direction of a single architectural pluralist — a type documented from the mid-thirteenth century — but without excavating the site of Meaux the hypothesis of common authorship cannot be tested. Of course, there are other less obvious ways in which Meaux might have acted as a channel through which influences passed from

least follows a regular rhythm relative to the bays, whereas that at Fountains does not). Elements common to the central vessels of Fountains and Beverley, other than those discussed at 187–90 below, include the extensively used moulding of two rolls separated by an arris (pl. 19), the mouldings of the bases and sub-bases of the piers, and the capitals with polygonal abaci in the clearstorey arcades. Although the Nine Altars Chapel was planned when the presbytery was begun (P. Draper, 'The Nine Altars at Durham and Fountains', *Medieval Art and Architecture at Durham Cathedral* (British Archaeological Assoc. Conference Trans. iii, for 1977, 1980), 79–80), its later date is attested by numerous small changes of detail, e.g. the moulding of the external window heads. The E. responds of the choir arcades belong to the second campaign (W.H. St. J. Hope, 'Fountains Abbey', *Yorkshire Archaeological Journ.* xv (1900), 292), so there must have been a temporary blocking wall to the W. in order to enable the presbytery and choir to be used before the completion of the Nine Altars, some time well into the abbacy of John of Kent (1211–47).

22  A more detailed reconstruction than pl. 31 would have to take account of the many detached fragments from the presbytery which, with others from the Nine Altars, have recently been transferred from the E. guest house to a store elsewhere on the site. The reconstruction view by Reeve errs in showing the wall ribs of the high vaults rising higher than the wall heads, which are attested by existing remains, and the clustered piers uniform with the E. responds, which belong to a second phase of construction: see 187 and n. 27 below.

23  The natural assumption — that the architect of the crossing tower, who had perhaps been in charge of the post-1188 remodelling, was not re-employed after the tower collapsed — is confirmed by the presence of early 13th-c. elements with profiles unlike any in the post-collapse work re-used in the W. aisle of the NW. transept: see n. 9 above.

24  *Chronica Monasterii de Melsa*, ed. E.A. Bond (RS, 1866–8), ii. 325. The main vessels of this church were ceiled in wood rather than stone-vaulted: ibid. iii. 166.

Fountains to Beverley, but a direct link, independent of Meaux, existed in the person of the provost of Beverley from 1201, Morgan (or Morgant), an illegitimate son of King Henry II, whose ecclesiastical career had evidently begun when, in flat contravention of the Cistercian statutes, he was received at Fountains as a child oblate. Morgan's feeling for Fountains remained sufficiently strong to cause him to have himself taken there to die in 1217, so it is more than probable that he was aware of the splendid work under construction at his old monastery when the Beverley chapter found themselves in need of the services of an architect to undertake the complete rebuilding of their church.[25]

The capacity, already mentioned, of the austere aesthetic of Fountains and Beverley to act as a filter to their borrowings from Lincoln is well illustrated by their piers. From St. Hugh's Choir Fountains takes the concept of a purely decorative variation in the form of its supports[26] as well as the octagonal plan of its 'weak' piers, whereas the western transepts at Lincoln, by a second architect, are the source of the 'strong' piers with four coursed shafts of freestone and four edge-bedded marble shafts attached to the core by mid-height rings (pl. 24). Yet this indebtedness is much less comprehensive than it sounds. The 'strong' piers are still essentially of the clustered pattern introduced into the North by the Cistercians about half a century earlier, and thereafter used regularly by them; the octagonal piers are less like the concave-sided polygonal pier-cores of St. Hugh's Choir than the plain octagonal supports used earlier in Cistercian claustral buildings; and the simple alternation of clustered and octagonal piers recalls nothing so much as the clustered and cylindrical piers in the mid-twelfth-century nave at Furness Abbey, the North's most important Cistercian house after Fountains.[27] The Beverley piers also alternate (pl. 17), and though some of the shafts incorporate Lincoln-derived fillet mouldings, and the general level of richness is increased by comparison with Fountains, the piers are all still recognizably of the clustered pattern so favoured by the northern Cistercians.

The clearstoreys at Beverley and Fountains are apparently the earliest thirteenth-century English clearstoreys to omit short transverse tunnel vaults linking the lancets in the window wall to the open arcade occupying the front plane, a feature which Lincoln took over from Canterbury and retained through all its phases (pl. 27). At both Fountains and Beverley, there are just single, wide tunnels set directly behind the wall ribs of the high vault (pls. 23, 17), and at Beverley the front arcades form screens unattached to the window wall except by inconspicuous

---

25 Morgan's oblation to Fountains and death there are mentioned in a letter of Pope Honorius III to Archbishop de Gray (6 Nov. 1217): *Memorials of Fountains*, 165–6. For Morgan's appointment to the Beverley provostship by his half-brother, Archbishop Geoffrey, see Roger of Howden, *Chronica*, iv. 174.
26 As distinct from pier variations with symbolic or iconographic intent, e.g. the E. arm of Canterbury Cathedral, or structural significance, e.g. Durham Cathedral.
27 As the plan of the 'strong' piers of the Fountains presbytery in Hope, 'Fountains Abbey', 292 shows, they differ from the Lincoln W. transept piers in that their 'marble' shafts are not cylinders set in hollows, but keel shaped and placed tangentially in relation to the adjoining shafts. For clustered piers and the Furness nave, see C. Wilson, 'The Cistercians as "Missionaries of Gothic" in Northern England', in *Cistercian Art and Architecture in the British Isles*, ed. C. Norton and D. Park (Cambridge, 1986), 102–4, 110–11. The octagonal piers in the Augustinian churches of Worksop and Brinkburn, which presumably derive at several removes from those in the Canterbury choir, may predate the Fountains presbytery by a few years. There appear to be no earlier Cistercian examples in churches.

iron bars.[28] No doubt the more open structure of the front arcades suggested the singular idea of echoing them in corbelled blind arcades on the window wall.[29] At Fountains, where the front arcades were taken out in the late fifteenth century, both sets of arcades adhered to the usual tripartite scheme rather than the five-part Lincoln-derived scheme used at Beverley.[30] A still more important resemblance than the two-layer clearstorey arcades is the exceptionally high springing level of the vaults over the main vessels — a total contrast to the general English preference for vaults which spring at or below the base of the clearstorey.[31] In order to secure their high springings, the Beverley and Fountains vaults incorporate the most highly developed early thirteenth-century English examples of the *tas-de-charge* technique.[32] At Fountains, the demolition of the vault in the fifteenth century entailed cutting back the component blocks of the *tas-de-charge* (pl. 23), but with the disappearance of the plaster and whitewash which would have covered the spandrels formed above the clearstorey windows, the characteristic large stones and horizontal joints have become far more conspicuous than in the perfectly preserved *tas-de-charge* at Beverley. The role of the latter in stabilizing the high vaults is complemented by flying buttresses equally exceptional in their thickness and in the elevation of their springings (pl. 15).[33]

The high-springing vault at Fountains was not merely a manifestation of the architect's idiosyncratic taste; it was the solution to a unique problem arising from the circumstance that the twelfth-century nave and transept incorporate a feature that was abnormal in English Romanesque terms. Whereas in virtually every other church built in the century following the Norman Conquest the crossing arches rise only as high as the top of the clearstorey, the Fountains crossing arches rose so much higher than the clearstorey that the central vessels could not be covered by flat ceilings of the usual kind (pl. 31). The most likely form of covering is a timber tunnel vault or wagon roof, perhaps echoing the curvature of the great semicircular rear arch in the west wall of the nave.[34] Since there was no question of demolishing

[28] The earliest such screens whose constituent lancets are not each linked to the window wall by transverse tunnels are in the upper storeys of the transepts of Noyon Cathedral (*c.* 1160–70?) and the W. nave wall of St-Remi in Rheims (*c.* 1170). The earliest English examples appear to be those in the aisles of the 'retrochoir' of Winchester Cathedral (after 1202).

[29] The corbelled arcading on the back wall of the passage to the refectory pulpit at Beaulieu Abbey may just possibly reflect a feature of the now almost totally destroyed church of the abbey, which was founded in 1204 by Provost Morgan's half-brother, King John.

[30] The elevation of the front arcades of the Fountains presbytery clearstorey, as preserved in the corbelled arcading on the window wall of the Nine Altars clearstorey (pl. 23), was a cross between the choir clearstorey and westernmost nave bay 'triforium' at Ripon, but it is not clear whether the supports were double, as in the Ripon choir, or single, as in the nave. Precursors of the small polygonal capitals of Fountains and Beverley occur in the openings linking the lower wall passages of the nave to those in the E. wall of the W. towers: M.F. Hearn, 'Ripon Minster. The Beginnings of the Gothic Style in Northern England', *Trans. American Philosophical Soc.* lxxiii, pt. 6 (1983), pls. 35, 39.

[31] The other main English Gothic examples of vaults springing above the base of a clearstorey are at Wells, Chichester and Rochester Cathedrals (choir and presbytery); see also n. 38 below.

[32] The early incidence of the *tas-de-charge* in England has not been studied, but see n. 39 below.

[33] The flying buttresses at Beverley are probably the highest-springing early 13th-c. English examples still surviving. The flyers on the N. side of the presbytery, evidently an experimental design, spring at a still higher level than the rest and from taller pinnacles. For other examples of inconsistent execution of the design, see n. 46 below. The sheer, set-off-less wall buttresses at Beverley are unusual in the early 13th c., but can be paralleled in the W. front at Ripon, a work unfortunately not closely datable.

[34] Tunnel vaults of timber can be bracketted with the pointed main arcade arches, the transverse

the half-century-old nave and transepts, it was decided that the presbytery should follow the two-storey elevations of the old work and adhere to the overall heights of its lateral walls and vaults. Evidently, a timber tunnel vault was deemed insufficiently modern or impressive, yet the masonry vault installed over the presbytery did maintain a measure of continuity with the nave and transept, for in rising high enough to clear the crossing arches, its longitudinal ridges came far above the top of the clearstorey. The resulting steeply inclined lateral ridges are quite outside the norms of English Gothic vault design.[35]

The Beverley master's adoption of the high vault springings of Fountains must indicate that he liked them for themselves, as he was not in the position of having to devise special forms which would relate satisfactorily to a tunnel-vaulted nave and transept. He chose to follow the normal English usage of making the longitudinal and lateral ridges horizontal and setting them at the same level as the apexes of the wall ribs, an arrangement which could only be combined with high springings by making two adjustments to the Fountains design. One of these is to increase the overall height of the wall ribs, and the other is to use compound curvatures for the transverse and diagonal ribs — four-centred for the former, and three-centred for the latter. It is, in fact, highly likely that the idea of employing such unusual arch forms derived from the remodelling of Chichester Cathedral (*c.* 1187–99),[36] a work known to the architect of St. Hugh's Choir, and very possibly accessible to other northern architects, including the designer of the Fountains presbytery, *via* drawings kept in the Lincoln lodge (pl. 29).[37] The Chichester vaults resemble the Beverley vaults not only in the conspicuously compound curvature of their transverse and diagonal ribs, but also in the way the lower parts of their webs form inverted half-hexagonal pyramidoids (pls. 28, 17). These vaults obstruct clearstorey windows far less than any other extant quadripartite rib vaults of the late twelfth and early thirteenth centuries, although at Chichester this trait was probably a by-product of fitting a vault onto the Romanesque clearstorey, virtually the only one in England other than those of the nave and transepts at Fountains, which extended below the springing level of the crossing arches.[38] Like the Beverley and

tunnels over the aisles, the pointed tunnels over the transept chapels and the low N. and S. crossing arches as reflections of the scheme used at Fontenay and many other Cistercian houses both in Burgundy and beyond. The 12th-c. presbytery was probably covered by a large version of the transept chapel vaults, and it is suggestive that at Kirkstall, which follows Fountains in so much, the presbytery has extremely thick walls and very low-set lateral windows in the E. bay, features which would be more appropriate accompaniments to a tunnel vault than to the rib vault still in place. Wooden tunnel vaults over the transepts and nave at Fountains are likely to have influenced those formerly at Byland: cf. P. Fergusson, 'The South Transept Elevation of Byland Abbey', *Journ. British Archaeological Assoc.* 3rd ser. xxxviii (1975), 167.

35 The Fountains presbytery vault was of a kind extensively used over the central vessels of 12th-c. French Gothic churches, but the only such vault designed by an architect active in N. England is in the chapter house of Trondheim Cathedral, Norway, to all appearances by the same architect as York Minster choir and Furness Abbey nave: Wilson, 'Cistercians', 89 n. 7.

36 The history of compound curvatures in late 12th- and 13th-c. English and French Gothic architecture has yet to be written. The arch opening from the E. presbytery wall into the rectangular ambulatory at Chichester exemplifies their use in situations where height was limited.

37 As has long been recognized, the Chichester presbytery represents an important stylistic advance on the Canterbury choir, and although not so important an influence on Lincoln as Canterbury, its E. triforium seems to have been the source of the syncopated arcading in the aisles of St. Hugh's Choir (pl. 26). For other, previously unnoticed, debts of Lincoln's to Chichester, see nn. 38, 39 below.

38 Apparently the only other English Romanesque example of a clearstorey extending well below the crossing arch springings was in the originally unvaulted 12th-c. nave of Hereford Cathedral,

Fountains vaults, that at Chichester combines exceptionally high springings with an exceptionally deep *tas-de-charge*. The Minster's closer similarity to Chichester than to Fountains in the matter of vaults probably indicates a conscious decision on the part of its designer to revert to forms sanctioned by use in a church of comparable ambition.[39]

The Beverley master was clearly aware that the three- and four-centred ribs of the high vault would appear odd if they were the only obtusely pitched arches in the interior, for he gave similar proportions to the other most important arches, those of the main arcades. Some encouragement to notice this correlation between the two series of arches is given by making the height-to-width ratio of the arcade arches very similar to that used in the main vessels themselves.[40] Another, even more important, instance of this concern to promote overall formal consistency is likewise dependent on the use of a high springing level for the main vaults. Already at Fountains, a uniquely close correlation between the elevations of the central vessel and the side aisles had been achieved by abolishing the traditional disparity between the springing levels of central vessel and aisle vaults, and by linking both sets of windows and vault springings with asymmetrical intermediary arches (pl. 31, 25). At Beverley, the concept is developed to the point where the upper storeys of the central vessel can be read as elaborations of the wall arcades and windows of the aisles, in which there are roughly twice as many arches and in two layers of arches instead of one (pls. 17, 18).[41] It was surely the desire to generate this unique relationship which determined the selection of the 'band' type of triforium, a type rarely found in the North, but used in conjunction with a wall passage in the eastern arm of Canterbury Cathedral, the main architectural influence on Lincoln and *ipso facto* a work known to northern architects if only 'on paper'.[42]

---

remodelled after 1806. The Chichester clearstorey differs from those at Fountains and Beverley in that only the floor of its wall passage, and not the sills of the windows, descends below the springings of the vault. The arrangement of openings in the Chichester clearstorey allowed the relatively gently ascending wall ribs essential to the generation of pyramidoidal vault webs. The high vault in the presbytery at Rochester appears to be heavily influenced by Chichester, but because of the shape of the clearstorey openings it has French-style 'ploughshared' lateral webs, totally different from Chichester's. The vault of the N. transept of Hereford Cathedral (*c.* 1260–70) is the only other 13th-c. high vault of the Beverley-Chichester type, though the fact that similar pyramidoids are present in the peripheral parts of the vaults of all the surviving 13th-c. chapter houses of centralized plan suggests that this feature had occurred in the Beverley chapter house and some or all of the late 12th-c. centralized chapter houses which have been destroyed. The strange high vault springings in St. Hugh's Choir (pl. 27) may be an attempt to retain Chichester-type pyramidoids in a vault of much greater overall height.

[39] The high vaults in St. Hugh's Choir (pl. 27) make relatively restrained use of the technique, perhaps on account of their low springing level. Chichester is the likeliest source of the Lincoln *tas-de-charge* as there appear to be no examples in the E. arm at Canterbury. A further instance of the Beverley master's preference for cathedral forms to the Cistercian simplicity and conservatism of Fountains is the abandonment of overhanging eaves in favour of parapets, replaced in the 14th c. but attested by traces on the buttresses at the meetings of the W. transept aisles with the nave aisles.

[40] The height-to-width ratio of the main vessels is 2.5:1, and the mean of the height-to-width ratio of an arcade arch overall and of an aperture bounded by an arcade arch is 2.45:1.

[41] The relationship adumbrates that between the upper and lower elevations in the naves of St. Denis and other major Rayonnant Gothic churches.

[42] Late 12th-c. examples of band triforia by architects active in N. England are in the naves of St. John, Chester and Kelso Abbey, and the transept of Trondheim Cathedral. All these incorporate wall passages, as does the band triforium (*c.* 1200–10) in the choir of Cartmel Priory. The early 13th-c. blind-arcaded triforium in the nave of Holy Trinity Priory, York probably follows in its

The extraordinarily confident handling of concepts proper to cathedral and great church architecture which can be seen in the early thirteenth-century work at Fountains is only one episode in the northern English Cistercians' long history of involvement with architectural ideas which ought, in theory, to have been beyond their reach. As far back as *c*. 1150 the designer of the nave at Fountains had adopted the high drum piers which were almost the hallmark of the Romanesque great church in northern England; by the late 1150s the Cistercians had introduced into the region a version of Gothic architecture more evolved than any used at that time in French Cistercian churches; and by *c*. 1160 the architects of northern Cistercian churches had become designers of cathedrals. In the 1170s Byland Abbey embarked on building an enlarged and enriched version of one of the region's great churches, Ripon Minster, and though Byland rapidly became the preferred model for the most ambitious churches put up in the North during the last quarter of the twelfth century, it was never to be equalled by any of its imitators.[43] With hindsight, this efflorescence looks almost inevitable, for the wide, open spaces settled by the northern Cistercians brought them not the isolation they sought, but rather the status of great ecclesiastical lords, proprietors of vast and increasingly valuable estates. The exceptional nature of the architectural activity of the northern English abbeys has been obscured by the ruination that has overtaken its products, but to appreciate its abnormality within the Cistercian order as a whole, one need only turn to the French heartlands of Gothic architecture. The blunt simplicity and massiveness of one of north-east France's largest Cistercian churches, that begun in 1154 at Ourscamp (Oise), stands at an opposite pole from the intricately articulated play of forms in the contemporary cathedral of Noyon, only six kilometres away, and thus illustrates how scrupulously the French Cistercians steered clear of any entanglement with the more ambitious genres of church architecture.[44] Admittedly, the early thirteenth century saw the building of a few north French Cistercian churches which considerably narrowed this gulf, but none of these parallels the influence exerted by the Fountains presbytery on the development of great church design.

Once one recognizes the extent and the long duration of the northern Cistercians' implication in great church architecture, it ceases to be surprising either that the Beverley chapter should have recruited a designer who seems previously to have been employed only by the white monks, or that his work was influenced by Byland, the *locus classicus* of Cistercian architectural revisionism. Debts to Byland include the transept with western as well as eastern aisles, the large rose window formerly in the east wall of the choir, the tall proportioning of the main arcades and of the central vessels, and, perhaps most strikingly of all, the combination of high main arcades with upper storeys which are primarily horizontal bands, despite the presence of slender shafts demarcating conventional bay divisions (pl. 32).[45]

general disposition that in the destroyed late 12th-c. choir, although it differs from Beverley in including much plain walling between the arcades and the wall shafts.

43  For these developments, see R. Halsey, 'The Earliest Architecture of the Cistercians in England', in *Cistercian Art and Architecture*, 65–85; Wilson, 'Cistercians'.

44  C.A. Bruzelius, 'The Twelfth-Century Church at Ourscamp', *Speculum*, lvi (1981), 28–40.

45  By far the fullest and most detailed study of Byland is S.A. Harrison, 'The Architecture of Byland Abbey' (York Univ. MA dissertation, 1988). All trace of the Beverley E. rose was removed when the present E. window was inserted *c*. 1416, but its former existence is suggested by the roughly semicircular profile of the E. wall rib of the high vault (pl. 22) (cf. the pointed wall ribs above the transept end wall lancets, although cf. also the semicircular E. wall rib in the Chichester

Byland's clearstoreys carried timber tunnel vaults, whose horizontally continuous form reinforced the role of the upper storeys in stressing the longitudinal integrity of each main vessel; and though Beverley adheres to the convention of great church architecture in having stone rib vaults, the exceptionally high level of their springings ensures that they interfere only minimally with the band aspect of the lateral walls.

This dialectic between the vertical and the longitudinal is inherent in all English great church interiors of the late twelfth and thirteenth centuries. Even in fully vaulted churches, the sense of upward movement generated by the systematic use of pointed arches is offset by their context — long central vessels bounded by walls so thick as to obviate the need for the kind of substantial vault shafts which in French Gothic churches, reinforce not only the walls but also the verticality inherent in the largest arches, the ribs of the high vault. The completeness of the vertical-longitudinal synthesis attained at Beverley can be appreciated by contrast with the nave of Wells Cathedral (pl. 30), where both lower storeys are richly linear bands untrammelled by any bay-defining articulation, and the clearstorey is a quite un-band-like series of tall, widely spaced and plainly treated units. At Beverley, all the most important arches in the lateral elevations — the main arcades, the central clearstorey openings, the front layer of the triforium arcading — are not only of similar upright proportions, but are serried into horizontal bands. The use of comparable proportions for the central vessels creates receding vistas consisting of tall transverse arches, and thereby matches the spatial character of the interior to its surface treatment more completely than in any other early thirteenth-century English church. At Wells, the powerful sense of verticality generated by the steeply pitched high vault appears disproportionate to the diminutive shafts under its ribs, whereas at Beverley the equivalent shafts are extended down as far as possible without impinging on the main arcades — a highly effective device for keeping both the vertical and the longitudinal in play throughout the design.

The absolute chronology of the construction of Beverley Minster in the thirteenth century is a virtual blank,[46] so one can only guess the date at which work came to a halt in the first and second bays of the nave (pl. 20). Perhaps *c.* 1240 would not be too wide of the mark.[47] The most westerly thirteenth-century supports are the freestanding piers nearest the crossing, whose construction was necessitated

presbytery, which surmounts lancets) and by the disposition of quatrefoils on the external spandrels (cf. those above the E. transept lancets). The height-to-width ratio of the main vessels at Byland (including the tunnel vault in the total height) and Beverley are 2.53:1 and 2.52:1 respectively, and the height-to-length ratio of the bay elevations is roughly 4:1 at both places (excluding the tunnel vault at Byland).

[46] The relative dating is established by minor changes of detailing, all of which indicate that building followed the usual E.-W. pattern, but with work consistently farther advanced on the S. side. The most significant modifications to the original design (none of which is the result of outside influences such as would provide indications of absolute date) are the succession in the W. bays of the choir clearstorey of shafts of concave-sided octagonal section by simple cylindrical shafts, the lowering of the buttress pinnacles and springing level of the flyers (see n. 33 above), the omission of dogtooth ornament between the vault shafts and clearstorey arcades (cf. pls. 21, 22), and the elimination from the NE. transept front of the awkward overhanging of corner buttresses by pinnacles which occurs on the SE. transept front. See also Hoey, 'Beverley Minster', 213.

[47] The surviving 13th-c. stained glass is located in the E. chapels of the W. transept and dated to the 1230s in D. O'Connor, 'The Medieval Stained Glass of Beverley Minster', *Medieval Art and Architecture in the East Riding of Yorkshire* (British Archaeological Assoc. Conference Trans. ix, for 1983, 1989), 68.

by the inclusion of western aisles in the main transept.[48] Exactly what the stoppage at the east end of the nave signifies is not clear, but the pauses in construction which often occur around this point in major medieval churches seem usually to be due to the institution's need to recoup after the completion of the liturgically and symbolically more important parts of the church. At Beverley, the 'pause' lasted at least until the second decade of the fourteenth century. We know that the Romanesque nave as repaired after the 1188 fire was sufficiently unscathed to serve as a temporary choir after the collapse of the crossing tower *c.* 1213–15,[49] and no doubt it was still serviceable enough for its replacement not to seem urgent when the transepts had been finished. In any event, our mental picture of the thirteenth-century work in its first seventy or so years of existence has to encompass the old nave to which it was joined. The progressive diminution towards the west of the amount of thirteenth-century fabric in the eastern nave bays is what generally occurs when a total rebuilding has been interrupted; and if the thirteenth-century eastern parts had been intended to be joined permanently to the Romanesque nave, one would expect to see all three levels of the eastern bays complete. Nevertheless, it remains possible that the decision not to proceed immediately with the replacement of the Romanesque nave (and so risk that it would never be replaced) was influenced by York Minster, where the huge west transept, a self-contained project not designed to be continued further west, must have made a bizarre contrast with the aisleless late eleventh-century nave.[50] The juxtaposition of modern and spacious eastern parts with older and simpler western parts was common in late twelfth- and early thirteenth-century England, although the division between new and old usually coincided with the screen shutting off the choir, and thereby reinforced the sense of clerical exclusiveness.[51] At Beverley and York, the meaning is unlikely to have been radically different, but it is striking that in both churches the original burial site of a major local saint was at the east end of the nave, where it functioned as a secondary 'working' shrine, continuously accessible to suppliants.[52] At Beverley, St. John's main relics were in the conventional place behind the high altar, and though St. William's relics were only transferred to the equivalent position in York Minster in 1284, there can be little doubt that this move had been intended as soon as he was canonized in 1227.[53] It is possible that the transepts at Beverley and York were meant to be perceived as a kind of backdrop to the secondary shrines; certainly, the concept of expressing allegiance to York through architecture is paralleled at Ripon Minster and at the archiepiscopal foun-

48 The same pattern recurs at the E. end of the nave (liturgical choir) of Westminster Abbey. At Beverley, the arches W. of the easternmost pier on each side are 13th-c. in their masonry (pl. 20), but the only parts *in situ* are those immediately above the piers, whose curvature indicates the intention to build at least a second bay as long as the existing 13th-c. bays (the 14th-c. piers are much closer together, perhaps reflecting the Romanesque plan).
49 *Historians of the Church of York*, i. 347.
50 As can be seen in the Undercroft Museum, the bays of the W. aisles next to the aisleless Romanesque nave had solid W. walls which had to be pierced when the aisled nave was built in the late 13th c.
51 As e.g. at Canterbury, Rochester, York (before the building of the 13th-c. transepts), Southwell and Carlisle.
52 There is a distinct possibility that the placing of the burial of St. William near the E. end of York was, like some of his miracles, a borrowing from the cultus of St. John.
53 The lateness of the translation of St. William's relics into a shrine behind the high altar, the arrangement which was *de rigueur* by this date in most of W. Europe, may have been partly due to reluctance to disturb what appears to have been the site of a successful cultus.

dation of Kirkham Priory (East Riding), both of whose ground plans are recognizably reproductions of York's anomalous configuration of aisleless nave, projecting western towers, and spacious eastern parts.[54]

St. John's main shrine was intended to be accorded architectural honours which have no counterpart elsewhere. Above the vault of the eastern crossing are remains of a lantern tower which, had it ever been completed, would have bathed the shrine and high altar in a flood of light whose symbolism would have been obvious to all.[55] Externally, the effect of a crossing tower of oblong plan would have been odd in itself, and odder still in relation to the square-plan tower intended to rise over the main crossing;[56] and it was perhaps recognition of these demerits which led, apparently within a few years, to its being abandoned and concealed from below by a vault.[57] The only other component of the Minster's design which can be represented as having been determined by functional considerations was the provision for the nine subordinate altars which, most unusually, gave their names to prebends.[58] Six altars stood in the eastern aisles of the main transept, and one each in the Lady Chapel and the eastern aisles of the lesser transepts (pl. 16).

A more regrettable departure from original intentions than the abandoning of the eastern lantern tower is the present appearance of the eastern crossing piers (pl. 22). At an unknown time fairly soon after their completion, the lower parts of the piers were cut back and encased in overhanging tiers of arcading and stumpy shafts. The aim may have been to augment the floor area of the sanctuary, but another possible explanation is that the original crossing piers, which were without any Purbeck marble shafts, had been found too plain for their position next to the high altar and shrine.[59] If this really was the thinking behind the change, it would

---

54  Hearn, 'Ripon Minster', 87; plan of Kirkham in C.R. Peers, *Kirkham Priory* (London, 1972).
55  Willis (in Petit, 'Remarks', 7) thought that the surviving W. spandrels of the lantern belonged to an E. front destroyed soon after its construction when the E. transept, crossing and Lady Chapel were added. In support of this theory, he adduced the break in the coursing at the E. end of the N. choir aisle (shown in the interior elevation drawing of the aisle in Bilson, 'Beverley Minster', 203). However, this break must represent rather a pause in the building of the outer wall in an E.-W. sequence, for the intention to build an E. tower is proved by the presence of stairs rising up from the clearstorey passages at all four corners of the crossing. The lighting of the comparable ensemble of high altar and shrines under the E. crossing at Worcester Cathedral was achieved not by a lantern tower but by aisleless transepts whose walls are entirely given over to windows.
56  One can only speculate as to whether the Beverley architect was aware of Cluny, where there were two crossing towers, both oblong in plan. Cluny was one of the sources of Ernulf's Choir, Canterbury, and its 12th-c. remodelling will have been known to many northern architects *via* Lincoln. The evidence of the intention to build a tower over the W. crossing consists of the spandrels of its lantern and the stairs rising from the clearstorey passages at three of the corners.
57  It is tempting to associate the lack of any sign of the N., E., and S. sides of the lantern with the marked settlement of the E. piers of the crossing relative to the W. piers. However, the N. and S. arches of the crossing are undistorted and take account of the different levels of the piers that carry them, so either they and the E. crossing arch are an early rebuild, or the walls adjoining the E. piers of the crossing were left to settle before the crossing arches were built.
58  Another of the rare instances of this usage was at St. Mary's, Warwick.
59  Bilson, 'Beverley Minster', 202 thought it likely that the E. crossing had been planned at first to have piers like those of the main crossing, but he accepted the existing piers as primary work and explained their overhang as a way of freeing floor space, and also as a structural device for adding weight to the piers to enable them to resist thrusts from the main arcades. This is endorsed by Hoey, 'Beverley Minster', 212 who notes, incorrectly, that the piers course through with the adjoining main vessel walls. Brieger, *English Art*, 50–1 suggests that the primary work is the topmost parts of the piers, which resemble closely the main crossing piers, and that the arcade and shafting below were afterthoughts. That this is correct is evident from the many glaring discrepancies between the arcaded parts of the piers, whose existence is doubly remarkable in the context of

tend to confirm the obvious construction to be placed on Beverley's almost total lack of influence on the course of English architecture,[60] which is that by *c.* 1240 the tide was beginning to turn decisively in favour of the ornamental profuseness pioneered in the nave of Lincoln and the presbytery extension at Ely. Few, if any, later thirteenth-century English churches were to equal the formal integration and intellectual elegance of the early work at Beverley, and it is notable that around 1330, when ornamental profuseness was near its apogee, the inability of contemporary architects to better the eastern parts of the Minster was tacitly acknowledged in the decision to build a nave whose main vessel reproduces, in all but small details, the noble design established over 100 years earlier.[61]

the very high standard of workmanship prevailing at Beverley. Certainly, there is no comparison between the E. crossing piers and those of the W. crossing, which course immaculately with the adjoining parts of the main vessels. The anomalies in the E. crossing piers are too many to enumerate, but the most important are the disparities in level between the arcading on the E. and W. piers, and between that on the N. and S. piers (pl. 22), and the awkward gap between the abacus of the lower arcades on the E. side of the SW. pier and the abacus of the adjoining main arcade respond. The detailing of the secondary work is stylistically indistinguishable from that of the primary work.

60  Influence from Beverley can be detected at Hedon church, 18 km. SE., most notably in the curious rounded and undercut fillet on the choir piers (cf. the piers of Beverley E. transepts arcades). The flat-faced piers between the Fountains presbytery and Nine Altars (pl. 24), part of the second phase of work, read like 'rationalized' versions of the Beverley E. crossing piers. Between these piers and behind the high altar ran a platform on arcades, which may derive from a 13th-c. predecessor of the present arcaded shrine platform at Beverley. It is difficult to imagine how such a feature could have been justified in a Cistercian church.

61  Other possible influences on the decision to adhere to the old design are the fact that the nave had been partly built in the 13th c. (cf. the even more archaizing, late 14th-c. continuation of Westminster Abbey) and the similarity between the heights of its storeys and those of the nave of York Minster, a building mainly influential in Yorks. in matters of detail, but whose overall design influenced Guisborough Priory, the most important new church begun from scratch in the North at the end of the 13th c.

*Plate 15*    Beverley Minster, exterior from the south-east (as in 1984)

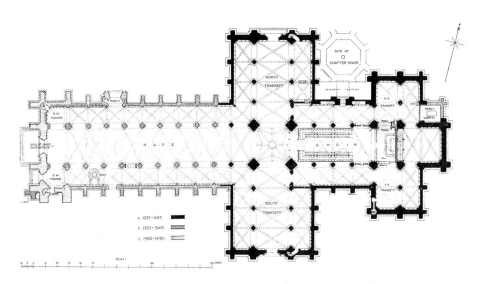

*Plate 16*    Beverley Minster, plan by J. Bilson (*Architectural Review*, iii, 1894–8)

*Plate 17*   Beverley Minster, south transept looking east

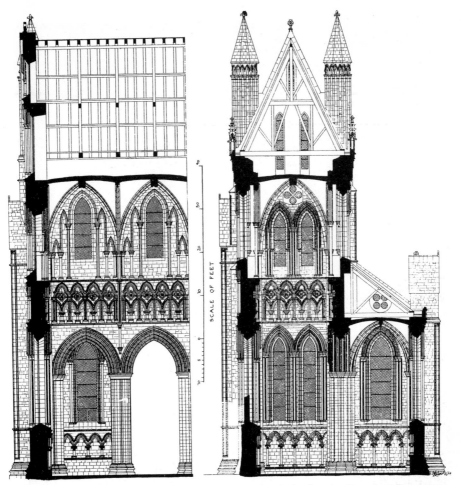

*Plate 18*   Beverley Minster, north-east transept, elevations of east and north walls
by H. Downes (*Building News*, 18 July 1884)

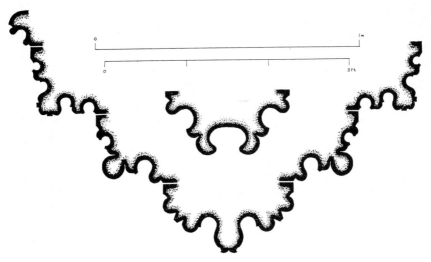

*Plate 19*   Beverley Minster, profiles of regular main arcade arches: above, inner order
of narrower than regular arches

*Plate 20* Beverley Minster, north wall of nave, easternmost bays

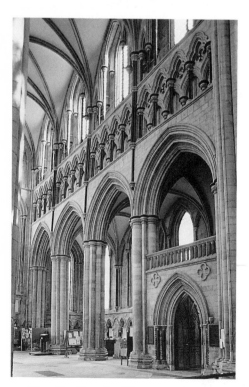

*Plate 21* Beverley Minster, north transept looking north-east

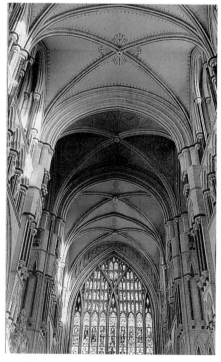

*Plate 22* Beverley Minster, choir looking east showing discrepant treatment of east crossing piers

*Plate 23*   Fountains Abbey, east clearstorey of north arm of Nine Altars Chapel

*Plate 24*   Fountains Abbey, reconstruction of presbytery looking north-east, by J. A. Reeve (*Builder*, 8 January 1887)

*Plate 25*   Fountains Abbey, presbytery and Nine Altars Chapel looking north-east

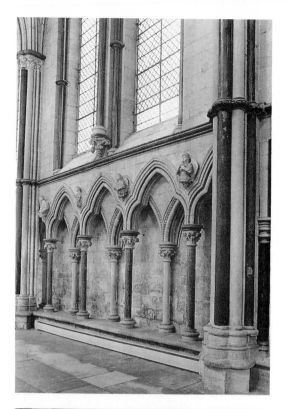

*Plate 26* Lincoln Cathedral, wall arcade in north aisle of St. Hugh's Choir

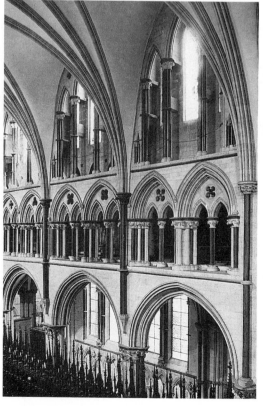

*Plate 27* Lincoln Cathedral, north wall of St. Hugh's Choir looking north-west

*Plate 28*   Chichester Cathedral, high vault of choir looking north

*Plate 29*   Chichester Cathedral,
high vaults looking east

*Plate 30*   Wells Cathedral, nave looking west

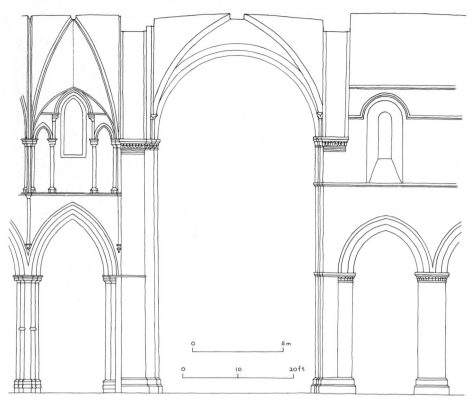

*Above.* *Plate 31* Fountains Abbey, reconstruction of westernmost presbytery bay, south crossing arch and easternmost nave bay

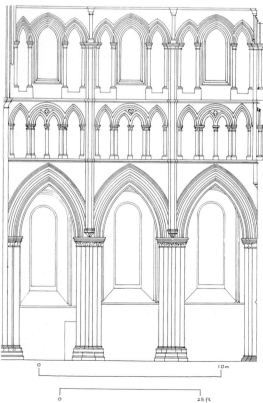

*Plate 32* Byland Abbey, reconstruction of east wall of south transept